D1562604

LANGUAGE PROTOTYPING

AN ALGEBRAIC SPECIFICATION APPROACH

AMAST SERIES IN COMPUTING

AMAST Series in Computing: Vol. 5

LANGUAGE PROTOTYPING

AN ALGEBRAIC SPECIFICATION APPROACH

Editors

Arie van Deursen
CWI, Amsterdam

Jan Heering
CWI, Amsterdam

Paul Klint
CWI and University of Amsterdam

 **World Scientific**
Singapore•New Jersey•London•Hong

Published by

World Scientific Publishing Co. Pte. Ltd.

P O Box 128, Farrer Road, Singapore 912805

USA office: Suite 1B, 1060 Main Street, River Edge, NJ 07661

UK office: 57 Shelton Street, Covent Garden, London WC2H 9HE

British Library Cataloguing-in-Publication Data
A catalogue record for this book is available from the British Library.

LANGUAGE PROTOTYPING: AN ALGEBRAIC SPECIFICATION APPROACH

ISBN 981-02-2732-9

This book is printed on acid-free paper.

Printed in Singapore by Uto-Print

Preface

In all branches of information technology, languages play a crucial role. Most prominent among them are general purpose programming languages, but in practice languages tailored toward specific application areas are no less important. Virtually unlimited in number, they address such diverse applications as user interface definition, module interconnection, knowledge representation, and financial product specification. Depending on the character of the language involved, the corresponding programs may be specifications, definitions, scripts, or true programs. Their construction requires language specific tools such as compilers, typecheckers, debuggers, and program understanding facilities.

In view of the increasing number of application areas and the demand for higher expressive power, new languages are being developed continually. All of them have to be designed and implemented. By incorporating the knowledge and experience collected by many practitioners over the years into computerized tools, language development can at least partly be automated.

Automated language development is what this book is all about. Its point of departure is the ASF+SDF *language prototyping system*, an interactive development environment for both programming and application languages, covering syntax analysis, typechecking, translation, and execution of programs.

The ASF+SDF Meta-Language Any language development system needs a meta-language in which to specify the syntax and semantics of the language under construction. Syntax is usually specified in a BNF-like formalism. Typechecking and translation are often defined by attribute grammars. The meta-language used in this book is ASF+SDF, a combination of the Syntax Definition Formalism SDF and the Algebraic Specification Formalism ASF. SDF is an extension of BNF covering concrete and abstract syntax. ASF has sufficient expressive power for describing typechecking, translation and program execution. It includes attribute grammars as the subclass of algebraic specifications using definition by primitive recursion.

Thanks to the user-definable syntax provided by SDF, ASF+SDF specifications are easy to read. Not only does SDF allow the most appropriate notation to be defined, it also permits concrete syntax to be retained in the specification of the language's semantics. Moreover, ASF+SDF specifications are easy to understand, based as they are on *term rewriting*, the simplification of algebraic expressions everybody is familiar with. Model-theoretic or other logical properties of algebraic specifications are not

v

used directly in this book and the reader need not be familiar with them. The interested reader should consult the references given in Chapter 1.

The ASF+SDF Meta-Environment The ASF+SDF system is both an interactive development environment for ASF+SDF specifications and a generator producing interactive development environments for languages whose ASF+SDF specifications are entered. It extends the principles of generator technology, well-established in the areas of parser generators and compilers, to the full range of program development tools. The facilities it offers the user for developing ASF+SDF specifications of languages are very similar to those of the environments it generates. For this reason it is usually called the ASF+SDF *Meta-Environment.*

From the viewpoint of the ASF+SDF Meta-Environment, language specifications are executable. Using the Meta-Environment's editing, parsing and term rewriting facilities, they can be modified, tested and debugged just like other programs. Hence, the formal specification of a language in ASF+SDF is not only an aid to get a better understanding of certain of its features, it is also the input specification from which program development tools are generated.

Although an interesting subject in itself, the implementation of the ASF+SDF Meta-Environment is beyond the scope of this book. The reader interested in the techniques used for parser generation, efficient term rewriting, and user-interfacing should consult the references given in Chapter 1.

Topics Covered This book emphasizes the *use* of ASF+SDF as a meta-language for the specification of syntax and semantics. After introducing ASF+SDF, a number of language specification case studies are presented and various styles for writing language specifications are illustrated. The problems encountered in writing such specifications and in generating tools from them suggest new ways in which to enhance the expressive power of language definition formalisms as well as new techniques for deriving language implementations.

Since the use of ASF+SDF is a very broad subject, we decided to narrow it by focusing on typechecking (static semantics) rather than program execution (dynamic semantics). Actually, the specification of typechecking in ASF+SDF is the main subject of the book. This limitation is not as serious as it may appear. Typechecking deals with context-sensitive language requirements, and it is well-known that for many languages, such as strongly typed object-oriented or functional ones requiring type inference, typechecking is more complicated than dynamic semantics. Furthermore, making a sharp distinction between specifications of static and dynamic semantics would be artificial and counterproductive. In ASF+SDF the same meta-language is used for both. As a consequence, many of the techniques developed for typechecking can be used immediately for dynamic semantics, translation, and program transformation. Several chapters take advantage of this by explicitly formulating the correspondence between static and dynamic semantics as expressed in ASF+SDF.

The case studies presented span a wide range of language features and type systems. Among the cases treated are the typechecking of Pascal, the derivation of the static semantics specification of an object-oriented language from its dynamic semantics specification, and the modelling of advanced type systems by multi-level specifications. Existing methods of abstract interpretation and attribute grammars are transferred to the algebraic specification domain, leading, for example, to incremental term rewriting. Moreover, novel techniques are developed, e.g., for automatic error message generation based on origin tracking and the modular specification of error handling.

The case studies discussed in the first five chapters are examples of *literate* specifications. With the exception of Chapter 2, they include the complete specifications. The ASF+SDF Meta-Environment provides a facility to typeset ASF+SDF specifications and associated documentation by translating source modules to LaTeX. Readers who would like to extend, modify, or reuse specifications discussed in this book can obtain the ASF+SDF sources at URL

$$\texttt{http://www.cwi.nl/\~{}gipe/}$$

They can be run using the ASF+SDF Meta-Environment, which is available at the same URL.

Finally, we hope readers will share our enthusiasm for using ASF+SDF for language prototyping purposes, and that they will be incited to contribute to the advancement of language prototyping technology.

Overview of Chapters

Although written by different authors, the chapters are fully integrated. We give a summary of each chapter.

Chapter 1 (An Overview of ASF+SDF) introduces the main features of the algebraic specification formalism ASF+SDF and its supporting environment and tool generator, the ASF+SDF Meta-Environment. A specification of the λ-calculus serves as running example. The Meta-Environment turns it into an interactive λ-calculus environment, which can be used for teaching and experimentation. This chapter also provides bibliographic notes, an overview of related work, and a summary of current and future developments. The notions introduced here are used throughout the remainder of the book.

Chapter 2 (The Static Semantics of Pascal) gives a specification of the complete static semantics of ISO Pascal. The emphasis is on an extensible, readable, specification style staying as close as possible to the original ISO definition by taking advantage of the syntactic freedom offered by ASF+SDF. The chapter illustrates the need for several extensions discussed in later chapters, such as incrementality, origin tracking, systematic ways of dealing with error handling, and higher-order specifications.

Chapter 3 (A Kernel Object-Oriented Language) presents the dynamic semantics of a simple object-oriented language and shows how the static semantics can be derived from it systematically. The derived static semantics is then extended to a full typechecker. The chapter shows how several object-oriented concepts, such as inheritance, redefinitions, self-objects, and state changes, can be dealt with in an algebraic specification framework.

Chapter 4 (Typechecking with Modular Error Handling) describes how a specification of static semantics can be extended in a systematic way to a complete typechecker. The resulting specification addresses pragmatic issues such as showing the location in a source program where a violation of the static semantics occurred as well as explaining the cause of the violation. It stresses that a specification of static semantics should be designed in such a manner that error processing can be added as a modular extension. This chapter uses the origin tracking technique more fully explained in Chapter 7.

Chapter 5 (Multi-Level Specifications) shows how ASF+SDF can be used as a vehicle to design new, sophisticated, specification formalisms. It gives a full account of multi-level specifications in which the algebra of types is definable. As a result, user-definable type constructors, polymorphism, type classes, and many other concepts occurring in various type systems can be easily expressed. It introduces the syntax, semantics, type assignment, and typechecking of the MLS language in various stages, providing numerous MLS examples. It is a strong illustration of the literate specification philosophy that specifications can be executable by machines, without sacrificing their real purpose, which is to be readable by people. The chapter gives many pointers to the literature on types and type systems.

Chapter 6 (Incremental Typechecking) addresses the problem how algebraically specified typecheckers can be executed efficiently in an interactive editing environment in which programs are subject to frequent modification. Rather than repeatedly typechecking the modified program in its entirety, results of previous typechecks are reused as much as possible. This is achieved by identifying a subclass of algebraic specifications (primitive recursive schemes) permitting incremental evaluation in a fashion resembling incremental evaluation in attribute grammars. Since algebraic specifications offer a uniform way of describing syntax trees and data types (such as, e.g., a symbol table) an evaluation technique for layered primitive recursive schemes is developed solving the well-known "aggregate update problem" in attribute grammars.

Chapter 7 (Origin Tracking and its Applications) extends the basic approach advocated in this book: (a) specify a particular aspect of a language, for instance, typechecking; (b) construct an initial term by applying the typecheck function to the abstract syntax tree of the source program; (c) use term rewriting to simplify the initial term to a result representing the error messages (if any). Origin tracking extends this scheme by automatically establishing a relation between subterms of the result (the error messages) and their so-called origins, which are subterms of the initial term (i.e., locations in the original program). Several variants of origin tracking are discussed. So-called syntax-directed origin tracking is suited for error pinpointing and source-level debugging purposes. It is based on the primitive recursive schemes introduced in Chapter 6. Another variant, dynamic dependence tracking, is tailored toward program slicing applications.

Chapter 8 (Second-Order Term Rewriting Specification of Static Semantics: An Exercise) observes that most first-order static semantics specifications need unnecessary dependencies to express, for instance, the relation between declaration and use of a program variable. Higher-order rewrite rules are used to give a less deterministic specification of static semantics that does not need a type environment. Error recovery as well as the early detection of errors in incomplete programs are discussed.

Chapter 9 (Origin Tracking for Higher-Order Term Rewriting Systems) extends the notion of origin tracking to higher-order term rewriting and illustrates its suitability using the second-order typechecker presented in the previous chapter.

Relation with ASF+SDF Meta-Environment Chapters 1, 2, 3, 4, and 5 are case studies that can be executed directly using the standard version of the ASF+SDF Meta-Environment. An experimental implementation of origin tracking exists. It is usable, although not yet smoothly integrated in the Meta-Environment. This facility is needed for Chapters 4 and 7. An experimental implementation of incremental rewriting as described in Chapter 6 exists as well. Second-order rewriting and higher-order origin tracking as described in Chapters 8 and 9 are not yet supported by an implementation.

Intended Audience

The material in this book is presented at a level aiming at graduate students, researchers and professionals in Computer Science. It is suitable for use in courses on software engineering, language design and implementation, compiler construction, and semantics of programming languages. We assume the reader to have some background in programming language syntax and semantics (both at the level of introductory courses only), as well as in data structures and abstract data types. Our viewpoint throughout is an operational one based on term rewriting. Hence, the book does not require a background in algebraic specification or mathematical logic. Also, we do not assume readers to be familiar with the earlier book (Bergstra *et al.*, 1989), which emphasized the design of the ASF+SDF formalism. For readers familiar with it we note that the parameterization, parameter binding, and renaming constructs discussed in the earlier book are not available in the current version of the Meta-Environment.

Acknowledgements

The work described here was carried out at the Department of Software Technology of the Centrum voor Wiskunde en Informatica (CWI) in Amsterdam, the Programming Research Group of the University of Amsterdam, and for a small part at the Computing Science Department (Formal Methods Group) of Eindhoven University of Technology.

It was supported in part by the European Communities under ESPRIT project 348 (Generation of Interactive Programming Environments — GIPE), ESPRIT project 2177 (Generation of Interactive Programming Environments II — GIPE II), and ESPRIT project 5399 (Compiler Generation for Parallel Machines — COMPARE); by the Netherlands Organization for Scientific Research (NWO) and its subsidiary, the Netherlands Computer Science Research Foundation (SION), under NWO project 612-317-420 (Incremental Parser Generation and Context-Dependent Disambiguation: A Multidisciplinary Perspective), NWO project 612-17-418 (Generic Tools for Program Analysis and Optimization), NWO project 612-16-433 (Higher-Order and Object-Oriented Processes), and an NWO Special Computer Science Program project (Incremental Program Generators); and in the final editing phase by bank ABN Amro, software company DPFinance, and the Dutch Ministry of Economic Affairs under Senter project ITU95017 (SOS Resolver).

Springer-Verlag kindly permitted us to reprint (parts of) the following papers. An earlier version of Chapter 4 appeared in D. J. Andrews, J. F. Groote, and C. A. Middelburg (eds.), *Semantics of Specification Languages (SoSL '93)*, pages 216–231, Workshops in Computing Series, Springer-Verlag, 1993. Chapter 9 is an updated version of a paper by the same authors and with the same title that appeared in J. Heering, K. Meinke, B. Möller, and T. Nipkow (eds.), *Higher-Order Algebra, Logic, and Term Rewriting (HOA '93)*, volume 816 of *Lecture Notes in Computer Science*, pages 76–95, Springer-Verlag, 1994.

It was a pleasure to cooperate with Dinesh, Emma van der Meulen, Frank Tip, and Eelco Visser on the preparation of this book. Their enthusiasm and persistence made all the difference.

For their contributions to individual chapters in the form of discussions, suggestions or comments, we are indebted to Jan Bergstra, Yves Bertot, John Field, Art

Fleck, Pieter Hartel, Karl Meinke, Bernhard Möller, Leon Moonen, Peter Mosses, Jon Mountjoy, Femke van Raamsdonk, Teo Rus, Alex Sellink, Susan Üsküdarlı, and Machteld Vonk.

For their contributions to the design and implementation of ASF+SDF and the ASF+SDF Meta-Environment, we would like to thank Jan Bergstra, Huub Bakker, Wiet Bouma, Mark van den Brand, Niek van Diepen, Casper Dik, Hans van Dijk, Dinesh, Steven Eker, John Field, Job Ganzevoort, Paul Hendriks, Jasper Kamperman, Wilco Koorn, Monique Logger, Emma van der Meulen, Leon Moonen, Pieter Olivier, Jan Rekers, Frank Tip, Susan Üsküdarlı, Ard Verhoog, Eelco Visser, Bas van Vlijmen, Paul Vriend, Pum Walters, Arjen van Waveren, and Freek Wiedijk. Their suggestions, ideas, and hard work are greatly appreciated.

The users of ASF+SDF often manage to surprise us by the unexpected character of the languages they want to develop and the applications they have in mind. We can only thank them for using the system. Their feedback is a constant challenge to extend its capabilities.

Finally, we thank the editors of the *AMAST Series in Computing* for their invitation to contribute this volume to their series.

Amsterdam, May 1996

Arie van Deursen
Jan Heering
Paul Klint

Addresses of Authors

Arie van Deursen
Centrum voor Wiskunde en Informatica
Department of Software Technology
P.O. Box 94079
1090 GB Amsterdam
The Netherlands
Email: arie@cwi.nl

Jan Heering
Centrum voor Wiskunde en Informatica
Department of Software Technology
P.O. Box 94079
1090 GB Amsterdam
The Netherlands
Email: jan@cwi.nl

Paul Klint
Centrum voor Wiskunde en Informatica
Department of Software Technology
P.O. Box 94079
1090 GB Amsterdam
The Netherlands
Email: paulk@cwi.nl

and

Programming Research Group
University of Amsterdam
Kruislaan 403
1098 SJ Amsterdam
The Netherlands

T. B. Dinesh
Centrum voor Wiskunde en Informatica
Department of Software Technology
P.O. Box 94079
1090 GB Amsterdam
The Netherlands
Email: dinesh@cwi.nl

Emma van der Meulen
MeesPierson
Rokin 55
Amsterdam
The Netherlands
Email: emma@fwi.uva.nl

Frank Tip
IBM T.J. Watson Research Center
P.O. Box 704
Yorktown Heights, NY 10598
USA
Email: tip@watson.ibm.com

Eelco Visser
Programming Research Group
University of Amsterdam
Kruislaan 403
1098 SJ Amsterdam
The Netherlands
Email: visser@fwi.uva.nl

Contents

1

An Overview of ASF+SDF

Arie van Deursen

Abstract The main features of the algebraic specification formalism ASF+SDF are introduced, covering context-free and lexical syntax, signatures, associative lists, and conditional equations. Moreover, the supporting environment and tool generator, the so-called ASF+SDF Meta-Environment, is discussed. The formalism is illustrated using a small example, a specification of the λ-calculus with valid substitutions, α, β, and η-conversion, and left-most reductions. The tools generated automatically from this specification, which together constitute a small λ-calculus environment, are presented.

1.1 Introduction

Some familiarity with ASF+SDF will help the reader to understand the case studies in the chapters to come. Rather than just listing the features of ASF+SDF, we illustrate its use by discussing a small example. Our example is the λ-calculus, which is (i) concise enough to be presented completely, (ii) sufficiently well-known to be understood easily, (iii) nevertheless non-trivial, and (iv) useful in practice (indeed, the generated environment has been used to teach the λ-calculus).

The idea to use a specification of the λ-calculus came to mind while reading Gordon's (1988) book *Programming Language Theory and Implementation*. Gordon devotes one chapter to an informal description of the λ-calculus. He needs a second chapter to cover an implementation (in Lisp) of a λ-calculus environment, consisting of tools to experiment with conversions, left-most reductions, let-constructs, and so on. In this chapter, we replace Gordon's informal description by a formal specification in ASF+SDF. On the basis of this specification, the required tools are then generated *automatically* by the ASF+SDF Meta-Environment. Combining these tools yields an integrated λ-calculus environment consisting of syntax-directed editors for

1

λ-expressions and let-constructs, extended with a graphical user-interface to initiate α, β, and η-conversions, let-expansions, and left-most reductions.

This chapter is organized as follows. After briefly mentioning some important concepts underlying algebraic specifications and the ASF+SDF formalism, we will present all eleven ASF+SDF modules of the λ-calculus specification. Next, we will discuss the generated λ-calculus environment. Finally, we will illustrate how the ASF+SDF Meta-Environment has contributed to the development of the specification.

The single motivation for this chapter is to illustrate the use of ASF+SDF. The reader is referred to Bergstra *et al.* (1989); Heering *et al.* (1989); Klint (1993, 1995a) for all details of ASF+SDF, to Barendregt (1984) for a treatise on the λ-calculus, and to Abadi *et al.* (1990); Hardin (1993) for more specifications of the λ-calculus.

1.2   Algebraic Specifications in ASF+SDF

In addition to discussing various important concepts underlying algebraic specifications, such as constructors, sufficient-completeness, and conditional equations, the main features of ASF+SDF are illustrated by examples.

1.2.1   Algebras, Terms, and Equalities

The ASF+SDF formalism is an *algebraic specification formalism*. Algebraic specifications are advocated because of their universality, simplicity, and abstractness (Goguen *et al.*, 1978; Wirsing, 1990; Meinke and Tucker, 1992). An algebraic specification is used to define *algebras*. An algebra consists of a set of *values* and a number of *functions* operating on these values. The relationships between the values and the operations can be expressed as *equalities*. A well-known example of an algebra is the ring of integers with values $\ldots, -2, -1, 0, 1, 2, \ldots$, and operations such as $+$ for addition or $*$ for multiplication. Equalities that we expect to hold true are, for instance, $3 = 3 * 1$ or $3 + 0 = 4 + -1$.

An algebraic specification aims at characterizing a particular algebra.[1] To that end, algebraic specifications identify a collection of *terms*, as well as a series of *equations* over these terms. Terms are built from *function symbols*, also called *constants* if they have no arguments.

An example of a simple algebraic specification is ASF+SDF Module Booleans (1.1). The first five lines after the keyword **context-free syntax** introduce two constants 'true' and 'false', and three function symbols, _ ∧ _, _ ∨ _, and ¬_. This set of five symbols is called the *signature* of the specification. It can be used to build *ground* terms (without variables), such as 'true', 'false', 'true ∨ false', 'true ∧ false', '¬ (true ∧ false)', ..., as well as *open* terms (possibly with variables), such as 'true ∨ P', 'P ∧ Q', ...

---

[1]More precisely, an isomorphism class of algebras.

---

module Booleans

imports Layout[1.3]
exports
  sorts BOOL
  context-free syntax
    true   → BOOL {**constructor**}
    false   → BOOL {**constructor**}
    BOOL "∧" BOOL → BOOL {**left**}
    BOOL "∨" BOOL → BOOL {**left**}
    "¬" BOOL   → BOOL
    "(" BOOL ")"   → BOOL {**bracket**}
  priorities
    "¬" > "∧" > "∨"
  variables
    P → BOOL
equations

[1]	true ∨ P = true	[3]	true ∧ P = P	[5]	¬ true = false
[2]	false ∨ P = P	[4]	false ∧ P = false	[6]	¬ false = true

Module 1.1: Booleans. The Boolean data type in the ASF+SDF formalism.

An equation (listed after the **equations** keyword) expresses a relation between two open terms. Equations can be used to deduce equalities over terms. For instance, the equations given are sufficient to deduce

$$\text{true} \wedge (\neg\text{false}) \overset{[6]}{=} \text{true} \wedge \text{true} \overset{[3]}{=} \text{true}$$

In fact, the six equations suffice to deduce that any term over the Boolean signature is either equal to 'true' or equal to 'false'. For this reason 'true' and 'false' are called the *constructors* of the Booleans, as opposed to _∧_, _∨_, and ¬_, which are *defined functions*. It is possible to indicate which symbols are intended as constructors by attributing them with the keyword **constructor**.

A more operational point of view may provide some further intuition. The equations can be regarded as asserting, in addition to the symmetrical equality relation, a one-way *rewrite* possibility. When oriented from left to right, the equations of Module Booleans (1.1) have a "simplifying" effect, i.e., they can be used to rewrite complex terms to simpler ones. For instance, in the previous paragraph the term 'true $\land$ ($\neg$ false)' was reduced to just 'true' using equations [6] and [3] as *rewrite rules*.

The result of repeatedly applying rewrite rules can be a term to which no rule can be applied anymore. Such a term is said to be in *normal form*. We typically expect our normal forms to consist of constructors only. In other words, the defined functions should be eliminated by the rewrite rules, which has the effect of "executing" the defined functions (computing their values). For example, equations [1] and [2] can be used to compute result values for $\lor$ functions; equations [3] and [4] for $\land$, and [5] and [6] for $\neg$. A specification where all terms can be reduced to terms built from constructors only is said to be *sufficiently-complete* (Guttag and Horning, 1978).

1.2.2   Models

For this book, it is sufficient to consider ASF+SDF from the term rewriting point of view only. Nonetheless, it is useful to have some understanding of what the models of a specification are. One algebraic specification S characterizes various *algebras*, and these are the *models* of S. Let $\langle \Sigma, E \rangle$ be a specification consisting of signature Σ and equations E. An algebra $\langle A, O \rangle$ consisting of a set A of values and a collection O of operations mapping values from A to A is a model of S if:

- Every function in the specification has a counterpart in the model, i.e., there exists a function α mapping every operation f in Σ to a function $\alpha(f)$ in O.

- The model satisfies the equations in the specification.

  For this, we define X as the set of all variables used in S. A *valuation* v is a mapping from variables in X to values from A. It is extended to an *interpretation* $v^*(t)$ of a term t in A (w.r.t. v) as follows:

  1. $v^*(x) \stackrel{\text{def}}{=} v(x)$, if x is a variable from X;

  2. $v^*(f(t_1, \ldots, t_n)) \stackrel{\text{def}}{=} \alpha(f)(v^*(t_1), \ldots, v^*(t_n))$ for f a function from Σ and $t_1, \ldots, t_n$ terms built from Σ and X ($n \geq 0$).

  An algebra satisfies an equation $t_1 = t_2$ if for every valuation v the value $v^*(t_1)$ is the same as $v^*(t_2)$.

It may well be possible to find several models for one specification. When trying to deduce equalities that are valid in all these models, the rules of *equational logic* can be used, which formalize how to replace equals by equals.

When using ASF+SDF, we are mostly interested in one particular model, which is the *initial model*. This model is characterized by (1) the only values in the algebra are those for which there is a term representation (the *no junk* property); and (2) the only identities between these values are those that are derivable from the specified equations (there is *no confusion*). For the specification of Module Booleans (1.1), a model with junk could include a third value for representing "unknown"; a model with confusion would be a one-point model in which true and false are the same.

The initial model is attractive since it is very close to the intuitive term rewriting understanding of a specification: the set of values is spanned by the ground constructor terms, and the operations are the defined functions of the specification. To prove open equalities (such as $P \lor Q = Q \lor P$) in such a model, induction on the structure of the terms can be used.

In the literature, numerous articles exist dealing with models, model construction, and relations between models. For our purposes, the informal description given above should suffice. The interested reader is refered to Meseguer and Goguen (1985); Wirsing (1990), who cover all details of algebras, homomorphisms between algebras, and initial elements in categories of algebras.

1.2.3 Signatures and Grammars

In our specifications we will encounter several *sorts* of values, such as BOOL, NAT, LIST, etc., which are listed after the keyword **sorts**. The sorts of the arguments and result of each function are declared in the signature, as in "¬" BOOL → BOOL.

A closer look at sort and function declarations in algebraic specifications reveals that together they form a *context-free grammar*. Regarding sorts as nonterminals, and function declarations as grammar productions, we can read the ¬ declaration also from right to left: ⟨BOOL⟩ ::= "¬" ⟨BOOL⟩. This provides a way to check whether a sentence denotes a term over a given signature: It must be possible to parse the sentence according to the derived grammar.

It would be ideal if such a parse attempt would yield one term corresponding to that sentence. Unfortunately context-free grammars are known to be possibly ambiguous: One sentence can sometimes be built in two (or more) different ways from the same grammar. To help overcome this problem, ASF+SDF supports disambiguation using *priority declarations* and *function attributes*. In Module Booleans (1.1), e.g., we have given ∧ a higher **priority** than ∨, thus forcing 'true ∧ false ∨ true' to be parsed as '(true ∧ false) ∨ true' rather than 'true ∧ (false ∨ true)'. Likewise, we indicated that 'true ∧ false ∧ true' is to be read as '(true ∧ false) ∧ true' rather than 'true ∧ (false ∧ true)' by declaring ∧ to be **left** associative. The symbols '(' and ')' declared as **bracket** can be used to override these priorities. Related attributes that can be given between { and } braces include **right**, **assoc** (a synonym for **left**) and **non-assoc** (forbids associative constructions). The details of priority and bracket declarations are discussed in (Heering *et al.*, 1989, Chapter 6).

Now we are finally in a position to explain the name "ASF+SDF" a bit further. Initially, the Algebraic Specification Formalism called ASF (Bergstra *et al.*, 1989) was developed, featuring conditional equations and modularization constructs based on on textual expansion of imported modules, such as hidden and exported signatures, extended with parameterization and renaming. It only allowed unambiguous prefix notation for writing down terms. The Syntax Definition Formalism named SDF

module Identifiers

imports Layout[1.3]
exports
  sorts ID
  lexical syntax
    [a-z][a-z0-9\\−]*[′]* → ID
  context-free syntax
    prime(ID) → ID
  variables
    "ξ" → CHAR+
equations

[1] $\qquad\qquad\qquad\qquad$ prime(id(ξ)) = id(ξ "′")

Module 1.2: Identifiers. Function prime(ID) adds a prime character to an identifier.

(Bergstra *et al.*, 1989; Heering *et al.*, 1989) was designed later, aiming at providing one formalism to define lexical, concrete, and abstract syntax (which determine the basic words, actual sentences, and abstract signature, respectively) The combination of the ASF and SDF formalisms was based on the fixed mapping between signatures and context-free grammars. The result of the merge[2] was baptized "ASF+SDF". It is an algebraic specification formalism which can be used to define context-free syntax for arbitrary languages, and which supports complete notational freedom for function names introduced in signatures.

1.2.4 Lexical Syntax

A **lexical syntax** section can be used to define basic lexical words like numbers (consisting of a series of digits) or identifiers (built from letters and digits). Module Identifiers (1.2) defines the lexical shape of identifiers using *character classes*. The class '[a-z]' denotes one of the letters in the range between 'a' and 'z'. The class '[a-z0-9\\-]' denotes a choice between a lowercase letter, a digit, or the '-' sign; the latter is escaped with a \\ in order to distinguish it from the range indicator. This second class is iterated by the '*' which indicates zero or more occurrences of mem-

---

[2]During this merge, the parameterization and renaming constructs of ASF disappeared.

---

module Layout

exports
  lexical syntax
    [\t\n]   → LAYOUT
    "%%"~[\n]* → LAYOUT

Module 1.3: Layout. Definition of white space and comment.

---

bers of that class. The lexical definition ends with again an iteration, this time of the singleton class containing the prime character.

Module Layout (1.3) contains more lexical definitions: it uses a character class built from spaces (written as a space), the special characters '\t' and '\n' to denote a tab and a newline. Moreover, it exploits the ~ operator for obtaining the complement of a class, to get any character but a newline symbol, which iterated gives the rest of a line. In short, these lexical classes define the special sort LAYOUT to consist of white space (spaces, tabs and newlines), and comment, which starts by two percent signs, and runs until the end of the line. In every ASF+SDF specification, a definition of the sort LAYOUT is needed.

Besides defining the identifiers, the signature of Module Identifiers (1.2) introduces a function 'prime'. This function will be used in the λ-calculus specification, Module Variables (1.6), to produce new identifiers prime(v), prime(prime(v)), ..., given an identifier 'v'. The equation of module Identifiers simply states that the result of applying the 'prime' function to an identifier built from character list ξ (using special sort CHAR[3]) is the same as concatenating a prime character to ξ.

Finally, a rather surprising use of lexical syntax is found in the declaration of variables. Arbitrary regular expressions can be given to define the names of variables. Thus, a declaration like **variables** P [*0-9*]* → BOOL defines all variables P, P_1, P_2, P_{01}, ..., to be of sort BOOL. Observe that we can use arbitrary characters in variable names; we will particularly encounter P "*" → BOOL, which in the equations will be written as P^*.

All remaining details concerning lexical definitions can be found in (Heering *et al.*, 1989, Chapter 4).

1.2.5 Built-in Associative Lists

ASF+SDF supports associative list functions and variables (Hendriks, 1991). List functions have a varying number of arguments, and list variables may range over

---

[3]In more detail: every sort LEX-SORT occurring in a lexical syntax section generates an implicit function "lex-sort(CHAR+) → LEX-SORT", i.e., a function with the sort name written in lowercase only, mapping a sequence of CHAR to the sort LEX-SORT itself. This function can be used to (1) access individual characters in lexical tokens, and (2) to compose new tokens from such characters.

module Id-Lists

imports Identifiers[1.2] Booleans[1.1]
exports
  sorts ID-LIST
  context-free syntax
    "[" {ID ","}* "]"   → ID-LIST {**constructor**}
    ID-LIST "−" ID   → ID-LIST
    ID-LIST "++" ID-LIST → ID-LIST {**left**}
    ID "∈" ID-LIST   → BOOL
  variables
    Id $[12]$ "*" → {ID ","}*
    $[XY]$ → ID
    $Id\text{-}List$ → ID-LIST
equations

[1] $\qquad\qquad\qquad\qquad [Id_1^*] \mathbin{+\!\!+} [Id_2^*] = [Id_1^*, Id_2^*]$

[2] $\qquad Id\text{-}List - X \quad = Id\text{-}List$ **when** $X \in Id\text{-}List =$ false
[3] $\qquad [Id_1^*, X, Id_2^*] - X = [Id_1^*, Id_2^*] - X$

[4] $\qquad X \in [] \qquad\qquad =$ false
[5] $\qquad X \in [Id_1^*, X, Id_2^*] =$ true
[6] $\qquad X \in [Id_1^*, Y, Id_2^*] = X \in [Id_1^*, Id_2^*]$ **when** $X \neq Y$

Module 1.4: Id-Lists. Lists of Identifiers.

any number of arguments of a list function. As an example, Module Id-Lists (1.4) introduces lists of identifiers, with operations for membership test, concatenation, and element removal. The line "[" {ID ","}* "]" → ID-LIST defines terms like [ ], [v1], [v1, v2], ..., to be lists of $0, 1, 2, ...$, elements. The asterisk * indicates zero or more elements, while the comma is the concrete representation for the separators (note that by definition they are separators and not terminators). The [and] symbols serve as list delimiters. The list notation is an abbreviation for the declaration of infinitely many functions [...] each with a different number of arguments. When necessary, instead of an asterisk indicating "zero or more", the plus character can be used to indicate "one or more". Lists without separators can be defined by omitting the curly braces and the separator (e.g., ID+).

List variables are needed to define equations over list functions. Module Id-Lists defines the variables Id_1^* and Id_2^* as ranging over zero or more elements separated by commas. Equation [1] concatenates two lists; equations [2] and [3] remove all occurrences of one particular element from a list. Equations [4] to [6] define the membership function on lists.

One thing should be clear about list variables: there is a difference between a variable over sort ID-LIST (which ranges over the term including the [...] delimiters), and a variable over sort { ID "," }*, which ranges over zero or more identifiers separated by commas (and does not include the [...] delimiters). The difference is illustrated by the tree representation for these variables given in Figure 1.1. It should be emphasized that this distinction is still there if the constructor function [...] happens to be "invisible", as in the declaration:

sorts IDS
context-free syntax
    {ID ","}* → IDS
variables
    Ids [12]   → IDS
    Id [12]"*" → {ID ","}*

For new users of ASF+SDF, the distinction between variable Ids_1 and Id_1^* is often one of the most difficult features to understand. The typical error is to write "Ids_1 , Ids_2" in an equation, rather than the intended "Id_1^* , Id_2^*". If such a list concatenation is required at the IDS level, an explicit function — like the ++ function of Module Id-Lists (1.4) — needs to be defined. Finally, observe that the syntax for the empty list is invisible if no delimiters are used. For example, if IDS would be used instead of ID-LISTS, then equation [4] of Module Id-Lists (1.4) would read '[4] $X \in$ = false'.

More information on lists, list variables, and their effect on the grammar and signature specified can be found in (Heering *et al.*, 1989, Chapter 5).

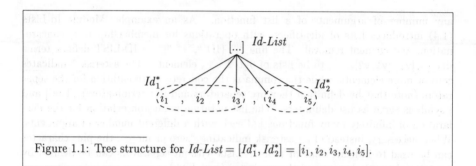

Figure 1.1: Tree structure for $Id\text{-}List = [Id_1^*, Id_2^*] = [i_1, i_2, i_3, i_4, i_5]$.

1.2.6 Conditional Equations

To obtain more flexibility in algebraic specifications, *conditional equations* can be used. In Module Id-Lists (1.4) we have seen examples of the use of a *positive* condition [3], and a *negative* condition [6]. The idea of conditions is that the consequence (at the left of **when**) only holds if the sides of the conditions (at the right of **when**) can be proved equal or unequal. Alternatively, we may use a horizontal line to write conditional equations, as done, e.g., in Module Substitute (1.7).

Readers familiar with the theory of algebraic specifications will be aware of the fact that the use of negative conditions causes certain model-theoretic problems (Kaplan, 1988; Bergstra *et al.*, 1989, Chapter 9). The use of negative conditions, however, typically reduces the size of the specifications significantly, which makes them indispensable when writing very large specifications. Moreover, a disciplined use is harmless. For instance, an inequality test over a sufficiently-complete sort with respect to a set of free constructors is equivalent to a positive equality test between the Boolean value 'false' and a Boolean equality predicate over that sort. Mohan and Srivas (1988, 1989) provide a further analysis of these issues.

To facilitate the description of equations having an if-then-else like character, ASF+SDF supports the **otherwise**[4] construct. It can be used to cover "the remaining cases" in one equation. For instance, using **otherwise**, the ∈-function, which was defined using three equations one of which had a negative condition, can be defined by the following two equations:

[5'] $X \in [Id_1^*, X, Id_2^*]$ = true
[4'6'] $X \in Id\text{-}List$ = false   **otherwise**

---

[4]The **otherwise** construct was proposed by Klint. The original name is "default-equation", which is still in use in the implementation. To mark an equation as a default equation, a tag starting with `default-` should be used. For example, the equations above are entered as '[default-4'6'] $X \in Id\text{-}List$ = false'.

---

module Lambda-Syntax

imports Identifiers[1.2]
exports
  sorts L-EXP
  context-free syntax
    ID   → L-EXP {**constructor**}
    "λ" ID+ "." L-EXP → L-EXP {**constructor**}
    L-EXP L-EXP   → L-EXP {**constructor, left**}
    "(" L-EXP ")"   → L-EXP {**bracket**}
  priorities
    {L-EXP L-EXP → L-EXP} > "λ" "."
  variables
    E [0-9]∗   → L-EXP
    V [0-9]∗   → ID
    V [0-9]∗"+" → ID+
  equations

[1] $\lambda\ V_1^+\ V_2^+\ .\ E = \lambda\ V_1^+\ .\ \lambda\ V_2^+\ .\ E$

Module 1.5: Lambda-Syntax. Syntax of λ-expressions.

---

otherwise equations are, by definition, equivalent to a series of equations using positive conditions only. The so-called *complement set* of a term built of constructors only (Thiel, 1984) can be used to construct this set of alternative positive conditional equations, as will be illustrated in Section 1.3.3. The **otherwise** construct is related to the ordering given to clauses in Prolog, or the priority rewrite systems discussed by Baeten *et al.* (1989) and Mohan (1989).Operationally, during rewriting, one may think of it as if otherwise equations are only applied if no other rule applies anymore.

1.3   Example Specification: The λ-Calculus

We will now illustrate the use of the features and concepts just introduced by discussing a small example. The modules to come define the syntax of the λ-calculus, as well as a series of useful operations on λ-terms.

    The λ-calculus originated in the 1930s from the work of Church as a theory of functions. Ever since, it has inspired many other important developments, such as

Lisp, denotational semantics, and functional programming languages. By now, λ-calculus has grown into a major topic in programming language theory. It is used to study computation, design and semantics of programming languages, as well as specialized computer architectures (Gordon, 1988).

1.3.1 Syntax of the λ-Calculus

The consecutive lines of the context-free syntax section of Module Lambda-Syntax (1.5) define λ-expressions to consist of:

1. variables (identifiers) $x, y, \ldots$;

2. *abstractions* of the form $\lambda\, V_1 \cdots V_n$. E, where $n \geq 1$. We sometimes refer to $V_1 \cdots V_n$ as the *formal parameters*, and to E as the *body* of the abstraction. The ID+ indicates that we allow a list of one or more variables immediately after the λ.

3. Function *applications*: if E_1 and E_2 are λ-expressions, then so is $E_1\ E_2$. It denotes the result of applying function E_1 to an argument E_2.

The **left** declaration indicates that function application is left-associative, i.e., $E_1 E_2 E_3$ means $((E_1 E_2)E_3)$. The **priorities** declaration indicates that $\lambda V.E_1 E_2$ is to be read as $\lambda V.(E_1 E_2)$ rather than as $((\lambda V.E_1)E_2)$ (i.e., the scope of the variable V extends as far to the right as possible). The **brackets** (and) can be used to override these conventions. In the variables section we have defined $V_1, V_2, E_1, E_2, \ldots$ which we will use for arbitrary variables and λ-expressions respectively in the modules still to come.

The single equation of the module states that $\lambda V_1 \cdots V_n.E$ is just an abbreviation for $\lambda V_1.(\cdots.(\lambda V_n.E) \cdots)$. Because of this equation we only need to deal with abstractions binding exactly one variable in the modules still to come. Note the use of list-variables V_1^+ and V_2^+ to match sequences of one or more identifiers (as indicated by ID+).

1.3.2 Substitutions

In Section 1.3.3 we will see how a function abstraction $\lambda V.E_1$ can be "called" with actual value E_2 by replacing all occurrences of the formal parameter V in body expression E_1 by the actual value E_2. Before doing so, we have to define substitutions themselves, which is done in Module Substitute (1.7). A substitution of expression E in expression E_1 for all free occurrences of variable V is denoted by $E_1[V := E]$. A variable is *free* in an expression, if it is not bound by a λ abstraction. This notion of free variables is made precise by the first three equations of Module Variables (1.6). When defining substitutions $E_1[V := E]$ one has to take care that variables free in E do not become bound in $E_1[V := E]$. The specification does so, and defines so-called

module Variables

Free variables are defined as in (Barendregt, 1984, Definition 2.1.7).
imports Id-Lists[1.4] Lambda-Syntax[1.5]
exports
  context-free syntax
    "FV"(L-EXP)   → ID-LIST
    get-fresh(ID, ID-LIST) → ID
equations

[1] $\text{FV}(V)$ $= [V]$
[2] $\text{FV}(E_1\ E_2)$ $= \text{FV}(E_1) + \!\!+ \text{FV}(E_2)$
[3] $\text{FV}(\lambda\ V\ .\ E) = \text{FV}(E) - V$

[4]
$$\frac{V \in \textit{Id-List}\ =\ \text{true}}{\text{get-fresh}(V, \textit{Id-List})\ =\ \text{get-fresh}(\text{prime}(V), \textit{Id-List})}$$

[5]
$$\frac{V \in \textit{Id-List}\ =\ \text{false}}{\text{get-fresh}(V, \textit{Id-List})\ =\ V}$$

Module 1.6: Variables. Fresh and free variables.

valid substitutions as defined[5] in (Barendregt, 1984, Definition C.1). As a result, the
λ-expression $(\lambda y.y\ x)[x := y]$ equals $\lambda y'.y'\ y$.

It is perhaps instructive to make some observations concerning the style used to
define the substitution operation. It is defined by distinguishing the three constructor
possibilities for its first L-EXP argument. The variable case is covered by equations [1]
and [2], application is covered by [3], and abstraction by [4],[5], and [6]. The variable
and abstraction cases need further distinction, according to the variable argument of
the substitution (the ID at the second argument position). This distinction is made
using conditional equations. It is important to realize that the various conditions
identify *disjoint* cases: the variables are either equal or not, and the complex Boolean
expression in equations [5] and [6] is either true or false.

Also note that the last condition of equation [6] acts like a let expression assigning

---

[5]Originally we used the definition of (Gordon, 1988, p.73), but this definition allows the result of
$(\lambda f.f)[f' := f]$ to be $\lambda f'.f$, which is wrong. The forgotten case seems to be that the fresh variable
generated should not be equal to the variable that is being substituted. Barendregt's definition
recognizes that no fresh variable needs to be generated in this case.

---

module Substitute

imports Variables[1.6]
exports
  context-free syntax
    L-EXP "[" ID ":=" L-EXP "]" → L-EXP
  priorities
    "[" ":=" "]" > {L-EXP L-EXP → L-EXP}

equations

[1]
$$V[V := E] = E$$

[2]
$$\frac{V_1 \neq V_2}{V_1[V_2 := E] = V_1}$$

[3]
$$(E_1 \, E_2)[V := E_0] = E_1[V := E_0] \, E_2[V := E_0]$$

[4]
$$(\lambda \, V . E_1)[V := E_0] = \lambda \, V . E_1$$

Simple case where the $\lambda V_1.E_1$ does not require a renaming of bound variable V_1

[5]
$$\frac{V_1 \neq V_0, \; V_0 \in FV(E_1) \wedge V_1 \in FV(E_0) = \text{false}}{(\lambda \, V_1 . E_1)[V_0 := E_0] = \lambda \, V_1 . E_1[V_0 := E_0]}$$

Find a suitable renaming for V_1, i.e., a variable not yet occurring in E_0 or E_1

[6]
$$\frac{V_1 \neq V_0, \; V_0 \in FV(E_1) \wedge V_1 \in FV(E_0) = \text{true}, \quad V_2 = \text{get-fresh}(V_1, FV(E_0) \mathbin{+\!\!+} FV(E_1))}{(\lambda \, V_1 . E_1)[V_0 := E_0] = \lambda \, V_2 . E_1[V_1 := V_2][V_0 := E_0]}$$

Module 1.7: Substitute. Valid substitutions, following the variable convention.

a value to V_2, rather than a condition imposing a real restriction. In fact, the condition side containing a new variable like V_2 need not be one variable occurrence; it can be a pattern including several variables.

For these reasons, the _ [_ :=_] operation can always be eliminated: It is easy to see that a substitution term operating on λ-expressions built of L-EXP-constructors only is always equal to a term also built of constructors only. In other words, the equations defining the _ [_ :=_] operation are *sufficiently-complete*.

1.3.3 Conversions

Conversion rules are ways to transform one λ-expression into another. Module Convert (1.8) defines the so-called α, β, and η-conversions. The most important one is β-conversion, which simulates evaluating a function: $(\lambda V.E_1)E_2$ is by β-conversion equal to $E_1[V := E_2]$, i.e., by replacing the formal parameter V by an actual value E_2. (equation [1]). Functions that have the same form apart from the names of the bound variables denote the same function by α-conversion. Thus, $\lambda V.E$ can be replaced by $\lambda W.(E[V := W])$ provided W does not occur freely in E (equation [2]) (Barendregt, 1984, p. 26). By η-conversion, it is allowed to eliminate formal parameters from an abstraction if those parameters do not occur in the body. Thus, $\lambda V.EV$ is the same as just E, provided V does not occur in E.

If a λ-expression E is not α, β, or η-convertible, (i.e., equations [1], [2], and [3] do not apply) then the **otherwise** equations [4], [5], and [6] guarantee that functions α, β, and η are equal to the unchanged expression E (**otherwise** equations were discussed on page 10). As this is a relatively simple case, let us see how the **otherwise** construct can be eliminated for equation [5]. Instead of equation [5], we can also write the following four equations:

[b1]	$\beta(V)$	$= V$
[b2]	$\beta(\lambda\,V\,.\,E)$	$= \lambda\,V\,.\,E$
[b3]	$\beta(V\,E)$	$= V\,E$
[b4]	$\beta(E_1\,E_2\,E_3)$	$= E_1\,E_2\,E_3$

These four cases correspond to the four *complement terms* of the term $(\lambda V.E_1)E_2$, occurring in the left-hand side of equation [1]. Equations [b1] and [b2] deal with the alternative constructors for the top application node. Equations [b3] and [b4] have an application as top symbol, but the first argument is different from an abstraction, i.e., it is a variable [b3] or an application [b4]. These four equations cover all possible cases that are not dealt with by equation [1]; i.e., they enumerate all possible "otherwise" situations. Thiel (1984) describes an algorithm to compute such a *complement set* of constructor terms.

---

module Convert

imports Substitute[1.7]
exports
  context-free syntax
    α(L-EXP) $\rightarrow$ L-EXP
    β(L-EXP) $\rightarrow$ L-EXP
    η(L-EXP) $\rightarrow$ L-EXP
equations

[1] $$\beta((\lambda\ V\ .\ E_1)\ E_2) = E_1[V := E_2]$$

[2] $$\frac{V_1 = \text{get-fresh}(V_0, \text{FV}(E))}{\alpha(\lambda\ V_0\ .\ E) = \lambda\ V_1\ .\ E[V_0 := V_1]}$$

[3] $$\frac{V \in \text{FV}(E) = \text{false}}{\eta(\lambda\ V\ .\ E\ V) = E}$$

[4] $\alpha(E) = E$ **otherwise**
[5] $\beta(E) = E$ **otherwise**
[6] $\eta(E) = E$ **otherwise**

Module 1.8: Convert. α, β, and η conversions.

1.3.4 Leftmost Reductions

If a λ-expression E is in such a form that the term $\beta(E)$ can be rewritten using equation [1] of Module Convert (1.8), then E is called a β-redex. In general, a λ-expression may contain several β-redexes. Repeatedly applying β-conversion may produce a λ-expression in which no β-redex is present, a *normal form*. Whether a normal form is found may depend on the order in which β-reduction is applied to the redexes. A strategy that always leads to a normal form (if it exists at all) is leftmost reduction, which repeatedly reduces the leftmost redex (Gordon, 1988, p.121). Module Reduce (1.9) defines leftmost reductions on λ-expressions. The function 'lm-step' yields the result of exactly one leftmost step. It uses the auxiliary function 'has-β-redex?' to find the leftmost redex. The function 'lm-red' repeats leftmost steps until the λ-expression no longer changes. If a λ-expression E has a normal form, then lm-red(E) is equal

---

module Reduce

imports Convert[1.8]
exports
  context-free syntax
    lm-step(L-EXP)   → L-EXP
    lm-red(L-EXP)   → L-EXP
    "has-β-rx?"(L-EXP) → BOOL
    "is-β-rx?"(L-EXP)   → BOOL
equations

[h0]   is-β-rx?$((\lambda\ V\ .\ E_1)\ E_2)$ = true
[h1]   is-β-rx?(E) = false   **otherwise**

[h2]   has-β-rx?(V) = false
[h3]   has-β-rx?$(\lambda\ V\ .\ E)$ = has-β-rx?(E)
[h4]   has-β-rx?$(E_1\ E_2)$ = is-β-rx?$(E_1\ E_2)$ ∨ has-β-rx?(E_1) ∨ has-β-rx?(E_2)

[m1]   lm-step$(\lambda\ V\ .\ E)$ = $\lambda\ V\ .$ lm-step(E)
[m2]   lm-step(V) = V

[m3]
$$\frac{\text{is-}\beta\text{-rx?}(E_1\ E_2)\ =\ \text{true}}{\text{lm-step}(E_1\ E_2)\ =\ \beta(E_1\ E_2)}$$

[m4]
$$\frac{\text{is-}\beta\text{-rx?}(E_1\ E_2)\ =\ \text{false, has-}\beta\text{-rx?}(E_1)\ =\ \text{true}}{\text{lm-step}(E_1\ E_2)\ =\ \text{lm-step}(E_1)\ E_2}$$

[m5]
$$\frac{\text{is-}\beta\text{-rx?}(E_1\ E_2)\ =\ \text{false, has-}\beta\text{-rx?}(E_1)\ =\ \text{false}}{\text{lm-step}(E_1\ E_2)\ =\ E_1\ \text{lm-step}(E_2)}$$

[m6]
$$\frac{\text{has-}\beta\text{-rx?}(E)\ =\ \text{true}}{\text{lm-red}(E)\ =\ \text{lm-red}(\text{lm-step}(E))}$$

[m7]
$$\frac{\text{has-}\beta\text{-rx?}(E)\ =\ \text{false}}{\text{lm-red}(E)\ =\ E}$$

Module 1.9: Reduce. Leftmost reduction.

to that normal form. Module Reduce only defines leftmost β-reduction. It can easily be extended to cover η-reduction as well, but we omitted this to keep our example simple.

Note that in this module the sufficient-completeness is lost: the function 'lm-red' operating on a "looping" λ-expression like '$(\lambda x . x x) (\lambda x . x x)$' cannot be eliminated. In other words, the term 'lm-red$((\lambda x . x x) (\lambda x . x x))$' cannot be reduced to a term built from the three L-EXP constructors only (variable, application or abstraction).

1.3.5 λ-Definitions

Besides being a language for reasoning about functions, the λ-calculus is used to represent all kinds of objects. Similar to the way in which in set theory natural numbers can be represented by the sets $\emptyset, \{\emptyset\}, \{\emptyset, \{\emptyset\}\}, ...,$ all kinds of objects can be represented by λ-expressions. Module Let (1.10) introduces notation for such λ-definitions. For example, in the classical method of Church, a number N is represented by the normal form $\lambda f x . f^N x$ A way to obtain this is by defining:

$$
\begin{aligned}
&(\text{let } (\text{zero} : \lambda\, f\, x\, .\, x) \\
&\quad\ \ (\text{succ} : \lambda\, n\, f\, x\, .\, n\, f\, (f\, x)))
\end{aligned}
$$

According to these definitions, (succ (succ zero)) can be β-reduced to λf x.f(f x). In order to use such definitions in λ-expressions, the names must be replaced by their definitions. This is specified by the 'expand' function. It is possible to extend the Module Let (1.10) to cover 'letrec' structures for recursive functions as well (which can be rewritten to a 'let' containing a fixed point operator, and an application of this operator to the function defined in the 'letrec'). We omitted this to keep the specification as small as possible.

1.4 Generating Environments

Now we move from the ASF+SDF specification formalism to the ASF+SDF tool generator. We discuss various basic tools that can be derived automatically, and consider the composition of integrated interactive environments from basic tools. We illustrate the various ideas using the generated λ-calculus-environment.

1.4.1 Syntactic Tools

In Section 1.2.3 we encountered *parsing* as the technique to check whether a string is built according to a given signature. *Parsers* can be generated automatically from the sorts, lexical and context-free syntax, and priorities sections of an ASF+SDF module. The parser generation facility of ASF+SDF does not impose any restrictions

---

module Let

imports Lambda-Syntax[1.5] Substitute[1.7]
exports
    sorts DEF LET
    context-free syntax
        expand(L-EXP, LET) $\rightarrow$ L-EXP
        "(" ID ":" L-EXP ")" $\rightarrow$ DEF   {**constructor**}
        "(" "let" DEF+ ")" $\rightarrow$ LET   {**constructor**}
    variables
        $D~[0\text{-}9']*$"+" $\rightarrow$ DEF+
        $D~[0\text{-}9']*$ $\rightarrow$ DEF
equations

[e1]   expand(E, (let ($V : E_1$))) = $E[V := E_1]$
[e2]   expand(E, (let $D^+ D$))   = expand(expand(E, (let D)), (let D^+))

Module 1.10: Let. Abbreviations.

(such as being LR, LL, LALR, ... (Wilhelm and Maurer, 1995)) on the input context-free grammar. The parsing technique used is generalized LR parsing (Lang, 1974; Tomita, 1985; Rekers, 1992). The trees constructed are *abstract* syntax trees, rather than parse trees: in other words, the parser builds *terms*.

An editor which knows about the intended syntax of the texts entered is called a *syntax-directed editor*. In addition to the text, such an editor maintains an abstract syntax tree of the text. Typical tasks of the editor are to perform checks on the syntactic correctness, to inform the user about the syntactic structure, and to allow *structural editing* involving the replacement of non-terminal symbols (place holders, meta-variables) by grammar productions (context-free functions). The editor developed for ASF+SDF is called GSE (Generic Syntax-Directed Editor). The most important concept in GSE's editing model is the so-called *focus* which designates a subtree of the full abstract syntax tree. Ordinary text editing is allowed within the focus (Koorn, 1994).

A last syntactic tool that is needed is a *prettyprinter*, i.e., a tool mapping a term to a sentence (string). In the ASF+SDF Meta-Environment, there is no need to define prettyprinters for the specified grammars: they are derived automatically. However, when using ASF+SDF to define languages in which layout is semantically relevant (e.g., COBOL, or Tcl/Tk), the prettyprinting rules that need to be adjusted can be overwritten by adding rules manually (van den Brand and Visser, 1996).

1.4.2 Term Rewriting Tools

Term Rewriting Systems (TRSs) can be used to execute ASF+SDF specifications. In Section 1.2.1 we have seen a small example of a rewrite according to the equations of Module Booleans (1.1) reducing 'true $\wedge \neg$ false' to 'true'. The assumption made in ASF+SDF is that all equations can simply be oriented from left to right.[6]

Repeated application of rewrite rules can result in normal-forms, i.e., terms to which no rewrite rule is applicable anymore. When using term rewriting to execute algebraic specifications, it is desirable that the rules are *strongly normalizing* (or *terminating*) and *confluent* (the order in which rewrite rules are applied is immaterial). These two properties together guarantee that every term in the rewrite system has a *unique* normal form (Klop, 1992). The ASF+SDF experience here is in accordance with the OBJ observation that "we have found that experienced programmers usually write rules that satisfy these properties" (Futatsugi *et al.*, 1985, p.54). Notice, however, that sets of rewrite rules describing an operational semantics (an interpreter) of some language usually *cannot* be terminating. For instance, the 'lm-red' function of Module Reduce (1.9) does not terminate when applied to a looping λ-expression.

Conditional equations are executed by first trying to normalize the various condition sides. Only if the two sides of each condition yield the same normal form, the conclusion is applied as a rewrite rule. In the terminology of (Bergstra and Klop, 1986), conditional rewrite rules are executed as *join* systems. Finally, as seen in the last condition of equation [6] in Module Substitute (1.7), the ASF+SDF system can deal with conditions where at most one side introduces variables not yet occurring in the left-hand side of the conclusion. This typically is used as a "let"-like construct, giving new variables a temporary value. The new variables obtain a value by matching with the normalized non-introducing condition side.

The built-in lists of ASF+SDF are *associative*, and to rewrite specifications exploiting lists associative matching is used. Associative matching is not unitary, which is illustrated in Figure 1.1 (which we encountered before on page 10). The match shown gives $Id_1^* = i_1, i_2, i_3$ and $Id_2^* = i_4, i_5$. Clearly other matches are valid as well, such as $Id_1^* = i_1$ and $Id_2^* = i_2, i_3, i_4, i_5$. When reducing terms, the ASF+SDF Meta-Environment non-deterministically selects one of the possible list matches. If a list pattern occurs in a condition, and the selected match causes the condition to fail, the implementation will *backtrack* and try whether one of the other list matches can cause the condition to hold.

---

[6]The best known examples of equations for which this assumption leads to termination problems deal with commutativity, $x + y = y + x$. In fact, the reason we have been using *lists* rather than *sets* in Module Id-Lists (1.4) is to avoid the equation

$$[Ids_1, X, Ids_2, Y, Ids_3] = [Ids_1, Y, Ids_2, X, Ids_3]$$

which expresses that the order of elements in sets is irrelevant. One possible solution is rewriting based on *commutative matching* as used in, e.g., OBJ (Goguen *et al.*, 1996). We will not concern ourselves with commutative matching in this book.

Term rewriting issues are discussed in Klop's (1992) as well as in Dershowitz and Jouannaud's (1990) survey. Several interesting details concerning the ASF+SDF rewrite implementation, such as list matching, rewrite strategies, and conditional rewriting, are discussed by Walters (1991).

1.4.3 The Generated λ-Calculus Environment

Instances of the various tools mentioned can be generated from the λ-calculus specification and combined into an integrated λ-calculus environment. An editing session in such an environment is shown in Figure 1.2. It displays four windows, each containing a syntax-directed editor. These editors are extended with buttons to apply specified functionality to the subterm in the focus. The large window is the *Definitions* editor containing the user's favorite λ-definitions. In the three smaller editors λ-expressions can be manipulated. The subexpression in the focus can be changed by the various buttons attached to each λ-editor. There are buttons to α, β, or η-convert the focus, to perform one leftmost reduction step, or to reduce the expression in the focus by leftmost reduction to its λ normal form. The expand button replaces (within the focus) all occurrences of λ-defined identifiers by their corresponding definition given in the let-construct of the big *Definitions* editor.

As an example of the practical use of such a generated environment, let us consider λ-definitions of numerals. Wadsworth (1980) gives several alternative λ-definitions for numbers, and proves various propositions for them. To develop some intuition concerning his definitions, one could edit the λ-definitions in a *Definitions*-editor, and add Wadsworth's numbers:

$$(\text{let } (\mathbf{k} : \lambda\, \mathbf{x}\, \mathbf{y}\,.\, \mathbf{x})$$
$$(\mathbf{i} : \lambda\, \mathbf{x}\,.\, \mathbf{x})$$
$$(\mathbf{wzero} : \mathbf{k}\, \mathbf{i})$$
$$(\mathbf{wsucc} : \mathbf{k}))$$

Now a term like (wsucc (wsucc wzero)) can be entered in some λ-editor. In this editor it is possible to experiment with the Wadsworth numeral representations by clicking the various buttons with the focus at different positions, thus performing α, β, η-conversion, or leftmost reduction (steps) on any desired subexpression. The intuition thus gained may help in conjecturing, proving, or refuting statements about Wadsworth's λ-definitions for numbers.

1.4.4 From Tools to Environment

One question still open is how the generated λ-calculus environment should know that the button "Beta" corresponds to function β as defined in Module Convert (1.8), that "LMStep" corresponds to 'lm-step', and, more miraculously, how button "Expand"

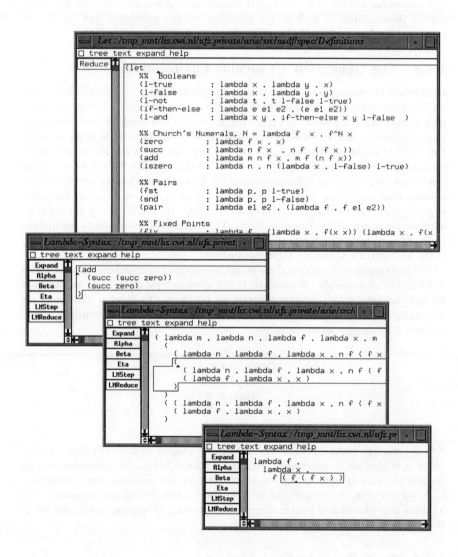

Figure 1.2: Example of the generated λ-calculus environment.

Configuration for language Lambda-Syntax **is**

button Expand
    when focus is L-EXP
    enable FocusVar := **focus** ;
        LetDefs := "Definitions" . **focus root**;
        focus := Let : expand(FocusVar, LetDefs)
    doc : "Expand names in an expression using file 'Definitions'"
button Beta
    when focus is L-EXP
    enable FocusVar := **focus** ;
        focus := Convert : beta(FocusVar)
    doc : "Beta-reduce the focus-expression"

Figure 1.3: Definition in SEAL of some of the λ-calculus environment buttons.

---

knows that its second input argument comes from the Definitions editor and its first from the editor in which it was invoked. In ASF+SDF, this final connection between specified functionality and user-interface events is made using the script language SEAL[7] (Koorn, 1994). SEAL is an abbreviation for Semantics-Directed Environment Adaptation Language. It has various primitives to describe focus movements and replacements, application of functions to terms occurring in editors, etc.

The SEAL description of the λ-calculus environment consists of six button definitions for Expand, Alpha, Beta, Eta, LMStep, and LMRed. Two of these button descriptions are shown in Figure 1.3. The second one is for Beta and is the simplest: It states that if we are on any λ-expression (i.e., when the focus is of sort L-EXP), we can replace the focus by the result of applying function β as defined in Module Convert (1.8) to the old focus. The first button definition deals with expand. The focus of a file called "Definitions" is retrieved and set to the root position (i.e., covering the entire text in the editor). The term in this focus is passed as argument to the 'expand' function as defined in Module Let (1.10).

The full details of the SEAL language and its implementation are described by Koorn (1994). He also gives a much more elaborate SEAL script for the λ-calculus environment, dealing for instance with an undo facility as well as enabling and disabling the Alpha, Beta, Eta, LMStep, LMRed buttons, depending on whether or not the focus is an α, β, or η redex, or contains a β-redex.

---

[7]SEAL is not needed when one is content the "environment" that is generated by default, which consists of a syntax-directed editor with one button "Reduce" to normalize the term in the editor.

1.5   The ASF+SDF Meta-Environment

The ASF+SDF system acts as an environment itself in that it gives support during the development of the specifications used to generate other environments. For this reason, it is called the ASF+SDF Meta-Environment. We conclude with a brief description of the Meta-Environment's main features.

1.5.1   Specification Development Support

The Meta-Environment supports syntax-directed editing of both signature parts and equations of ASF+SDF specifications. The syntax-directed editors for the equations depend on the context-free syntax introduced in the signature part. In addition to syntactic checks on ASF+SDF specifications, context-sensitive analysis is performed in order to detect such errors as priority declarations referring to undefined functions or the use of undeclared sorts. The equations are inspected for their executability as rewrite rules. For instance, a warning is given if the right-hand side of an equation uses a variable which does not occur in the left-hand side.

An example editing session of the λ-calculus specification is shown in Figure 1.4. The two large windows contain the syntax and equation editors for modules Lambda-Syntax and Variables respectively. The smaller window, called "ASF+SDF Meta-Environment", is the main window, and is used to open new modules, start editing terms, start reducing in debugging mode, etc. It is also used to deal with error handling. All errors appear in this window, and for each error a click on more information can be obtained by clicking on it. In the figure, a user has just clicked on the error message displayed. As a result, module Variables is raised, and the relevant text part, in this case the right-hand side of the first equation, is high-lighted.

In addition to these analysis features of the Meta-Environment, specifications can be executed and tested. A tricky term like $(\lambda\,y\,.y\,x)[x := y]$ can be entered and reduced to normal form in order to see whether the defined substitution function behaves as intended. Attempts can be made to verify or refute the conjecture that the specification indeed models the behavior one had in mind.

The analysis and testing of specifications is supported by the Meta-Environment's most distinctive feature, namely its high level of incrementality. Syntactic analysis of the equations is possible because a parser is generated from the function declarations. In the ASF+SDF Meta-Environment, changing the function declarations, like adding or removing a function, does not lead to a regeneration from scratch of the parsers involved. Instead, they are informed about the change and updated accordingly. In other words, parser generation proceeds incrementally. Not only parsers, but also lexical analyzers and term rewriting systems are updated incrementally (Hendriks, 1991; Heering et al., 1990, 1992, 1994).

A last important feature of the ASF+SDF Meta-Environment is the support for literate specifications (Visser, 1995a), in the sense of the literate programming approach advocated by Knuth (1992). For instance, the text as entered interactively

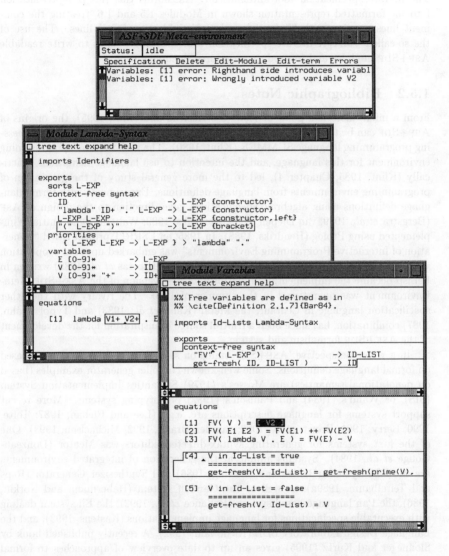

Figure 1.4: Meta-Environment while working on the λ-calculus specification.

for modules Lambda-Syntax and Variables is visible in the windows of Figure 1.4. The literate specification tool automatically transforms this ASCII representation into the formatted representation shown in Modules 1.5 and 1.6, treating the comment lines starting with %% (as in module Variables) as LaTeX lines. The use of the so-called ToLaTeX literate specification tool encourages users to write readable ASF+SDF modules and to produce structured documentation.

1.5.2   Bibliographic Notes

From a micro-historical point of view (see Heering and Klint, 1995), the origins of ASF+SDF can be traced back to the design and implementation of the string processing programming language SUMMER (Klint, 1980). The wish to have a programming environment for this language, and the intention to use language definitions practically (Klint, 1985, Chapter 4), led to the more general study of the generation of programming environments from language definitions. Experiments with formal language definitions using algebraic specifications gave direction to the design of ASF (Bergstra *et al.*, 1989; van Diepen, 1989; Hendriks, 1989; Walters, 1989), initially implemented using Prolog (Hendriks, 1988). In 1985, an ESPRIT project titled "Generation of Interactive Programming Environments" was embarked upon, in cooperation with INRIA (Sophia Antipolis). The Centaur system (Borras *et al.*, 1989) written in LeLisp became the implementation platform. A first version of the ASF+SDF Meta-Environment was operational in the summer of 1990. The rivalry with the other specification language in Centaur, the Metal (Kahn *et al.*, 1983) and Typol (Kahn, 1987) combination, has since been a fruitful source of inspiration for the development of the ASF+SDF formalism and system.

In a wider perspective, ASF+SDF builds on several other tool generators based on formal language definitions. Some well-known compiler generator examples (based on denotational semantics) are Mosses's (1979) Semantics Implementation System (SIS), or Wand's (1984) and Paulson's (1982) prototyping systems. More recent support systems for language descriptions are, e.g., (Lee and Pleban, 1987; Tofte, 1990; Berry, 1991; Brown *et al.*, 1992; van den Brand, 1992; Michaelson, 1993). One of the first systems for generating syntax-directed editors was Mentor (Donzeau-Gouge *et al.*, 1984). Systems aiming at the generation of integrated environments are the PSG system (Bahlke and Snelting, 1986) and Synthesizer Generator (Reps and Teitelbaum, 1989a), as well as the Gandalf system (Habermann and Notkin, 1986), the Pan language-based system (Ballance *et al.*, 1992), the Eli system dealing with executable specifications for language implementations (Kastens, 1993), and the Language Design Laboratory LDL (Riedewald, 1992). A recently published book by Slonneger and Kurtz (1995) gives an up to date overview of approaches to formal language definitions.

ASF+SDF is an algebraic specification language; a recent survey of algebraic formalisms currently in use is by Wirsing (1995). OBJ (Goguen *et al.*, 1996) is one of the best-known and most influential algebraic specification languages, so let us take a closer look at differences and similarities between OBJ and ASF+SDF. An important difference between OBJ and ASF+SDF is that OBJ supports parameterized modules, views on modules, and theories describing the behavior of modules (the ASF+SDF *formalism* was designed to support parameterization and renaming, but these have not been implemented in the ASF+SDF *system*). Moreover, the rewrite engine of OBJ is more general in that it implements associative commutative matching, whereas ASF+SDF only implements matching modulo associative lists. As a consequence the rewrite engine of OBJ is significantly slower than that of ASF+SDF: in 1992, measurements by Eker (1992) showed a factor four difference. These measurements concerned the interpreted version of ASF+SDF. Current research (see the next section) has also led to an ASF+SDF *compiler*, which generates code that is 50 to 100 times faster than the current rule interpreter.

On the syntactic side, it should be noted that OBJ is order-sorted, whereas ASF+SDF uses *chain*-functions to achieve the injection of smaller sorts into larger ones. ASF+SDF has no automatic retracts. A significant difference is that ASF+SDF in addition to being an algebraic specification formalism, is intended as input language for a programming environment generator. Therefore, the ASF+SDF formalism supports the definition of lexical syntax and (which is impossible in OBJ) empty productions (invisible constants) which can be used to model optional constructs. Moreover, it is more flexible concerning *brackets*. OBJ gives special treatment to parentheses (...), which only serve to group and never occur in abstract syntax trees. In SDF, users can choose their own syntax for brackets (e.g., ⟨...⟩ or {...} pairs). Moreover, parentheses (...) can also be used as genuine functions, for instance as tuple constructors. In OBJ this is forbidden (causing, e.g., problems as described by Martin (1993)). Last but not least, ASF+SDF supports the use of new variables in conditions, i.e., variables not yet occurring in the conclusion of a conditional equation, provided that in each condition at most one side introduces a new variable. In OBJ, conditions cannot introduce new variables.

Other systems supporting the development of algebraic specifications include AS-SPEGIQUE (Voisin, 1986; Bidoit *et al.*, 1989; Choppy and Bidoit, 1992), ACT-ONE (Classen *et al.*, 1993), and OBSCURE (Lehmann and Loeckx, 1993). Features not available in ASF+SDF are proof support as in Larch (Garland and Guttag, 1989), narrowing as in RAP (Hussmann, 1988), completion as in REVEUR4 (Bousdira and Rémy, 1988) or in RRL (Zhang, 1992), or persistence checks as in Perspect (Wiedijk, 1991).

1.5.3 Current and Future Developments

The ASF+SDF formalism and Meta-Environment have been used for a variety of research activities. Their typical application is language design and rapid prototyping of language-specific tools. The advantages of using language prototyping, such as increased reliability, repairability, portability, self-documentation, and reduced time and cost for tool construction are discussed by Herndon and Berzins (1988).

As an example, ASF+SDF has been used to formalize the syntax and operational semantics of the Manifold coordination language (Rutten and Thiébaux, 1992), and to guide the design of the commercially used structure definition language fSDL (Walters *et al.*, 1994). Other applications worth mentioning are the specification of tools supporting the development of action-semantic language definitions (Mosses, 1992; van Deursen, 1994a); the implementation of a program transformation kit based on the Clean language (van den Brand *et al.*, 1995b); the generation of editors, checkers, interpreters, and requirements testers for Message Sequence Charts (Mauw and van der Meulen, 1995); and the definition of a well-formedness checker, simulator, and transformer for the process algebra language μCRL (Hillebrand and Korver, 1995). Recently, Visser (1995b) used ASF+SDF to rethink the design of SDF, thereby specifying a family of syntax definition formalisms.

ASF+SDF has been used in a number of industrial applications, an overview of which is given by van den Brand *et al.* (1996). Many projects have been concerned with the design and prototyping of *domain-specific* languages. An interesting example is the development of *Risla*, a small application language used to describe classes of financial products offered by banks. Commissioned by bank MeesPierson (Rotterdam) and software house CAP Volmac, ASF+SDF has been used to specify the syntax and static semantics of Risla, as well as the generation of COBOL routines from Risla descriptions (Arnold *et al.*, 1995). Three years after its definition, the language Risla is still in daily use at MeesPierson. Recently, the language was redesigned and enhanced, for which ASF+SDF was again used.

Specifying languages and tools is the natural application of ASF+SDF. In addition to that, the ASF+SDF Meta-Environment has been used as a platform to conduct experiments with and to build implementations of new tool generation technology. Examples are the aforementioned incremental scanner, parser and reduction engine generation, the user-interface adaptation language SEAL, and the literate specification facilities. More recently, van den Brand and Visser (1996) extended these to generate language-specific prettyprinters and type setters from SDF syntax definitions. Moreover, Üsküdarlı (1994) has been using the ASF+SDF Meta-Environment to study the possibilities of deriving *visual* tools from algebraic language definitions. In this book we will encounter two more examples of new techniques that were experimentally implemented in the ASF+SDF Meta-Environment: incremental rewriting in Chapter 6, and origin tracking in Chapter 7.

Currently, the rewrite engine of the ASF+SDF Meta-Environment is a rule interpreter written in Lisp. In both Chapter 6 and 7 we will discuss extensions of this rewrite machine. As specifications written in ASF+SDF grew larger (the Pascal specification of Chapter 2, e.g., consists of approximately 75 pages), the need for more efficient rewrite technology based on compilation rather than interpretation became obvious. In their ASF2C project, Kamperman and Walters (1996) have proposed an abstract rewriting machine ARM, which in turn can be translated into C code or native assembly code. The most recent version of this compiler is written in Epic, which can be regarded as a subset of ASF+SDF without user-definable syntax. ASF+SDF specifications are easily mapped to Epic programs. The compiler translates Epic to ARM, and has been bootstrapped. The work on ARM has triggered several interesting extensions of basic rewriting, such as mixing lazy and eager rewriting Kamperman and Walters (1995), and viewing I/O as *narrowing* operations (Walters and Kamperman, 1996b). Reduction results can be stored and retrieved using a *graph exchange language* called GEL (Kamperman, 1994).

To maximize the benefits of the ASF+SDF Meta-Environment as experimental implementation platform, the system must be easily adaptable by people who have not participated in the initial implementation. Therefore, new implementation activities are all written in ASF+SDF itself, using the literate specification facilities for describing the individual components in an intelligible way. Components currently specified include the parser generator, prettyprinter generator, and rewrite rule compiler. Because of the efficiency of the code generated by the ASF2C compiler these specified components can be used directly as the actual implementations.

Connecting the individual components into an integrated system has grown into a separate subject: Bergstra and Klint (1996b, 1996a) have proposed a general *ToolBus* architecture in which several tools can be combined into one. A special ToolBus script, based on process algebra, is used to describe the data communication and control dependencies between the various tools. The document describing the ToolBus is an intriguing example of a complicated, extremely modularized specification, written in ASF+SDF (Bergstra and Klint, 1996a). The use of the ToolBus for implementing a new release of the ASF+SDF Meta-Environment is discussed by (Klint, 1995b).

2

The Static Semantics of Pascal

Arie van Deursen

Abstract   One of the purposes of the ASF+SDF formalism is to simplify the specification of realistic programming languages. In this case study, we describe and evaluate an ASF+SDF specification of the complete static semantics of ISO Pascal. We propose a general layout for specifying typecheckers for large languages. Moreover, we discuss how the syntactic freedom of ASF+SDF can be used to create an easy-to-read description of the static semantics of Pascal that stays as close as possible to the ISO definition.

2.1 Introduction

This book makes a case for the use of algebraic specifications for language description. Specifications first of all serve the purpose of language documentation. Second, they are executable and can be used to obtain a prototype language implementation.

The underlying assumption is that algebraic specifications are indeed attractive for describing languages. It is the validity of this claim that we elaborate on in this chapter. We do so by discussing the specification of the static semantics of the language Pascal (Jensen and Wirth, 1985), as standardized by ISO (1983).

We have chosen Pascal for the following reasons:

- It is a well-known language, making the specification accessible to many readers.

- It is a language that is considerably larger than those specified in earlier case studies involving algebraic language definitions (Bergstra *et al.*, 1989; van der Meulen, 1988), yet of manageable complexity.

- It can be expected that specifications of other imperative languages will have much in common with the specification of Pascal.

- The language is standardized by ISO. A formal specification of the static semantics can contribute to the ongoing debate on the use of formal methods for language standardization (Boom *et al.*, 1989; Kilov, 1995).

- Choosing an *existing* language rather than discussing the design of a new language precludes biasing of the language towards constructs that can be easily specified.

Compared to the state of the art, Pascal's type system is not sophisticated, but for specification purposes it has some interesting characteristics such as name equivalence, polymorphic constants for nil and the empty set, pointer structures, variant records, operator overloading, and predefined functions with varying arity. Readers who would like to see how to specify more modern type systems should take a look at Chapters 3 or 5, which cover object-oriented and multi-level type systems, respectively.

The current chapter aims at solving problems related to the specification of languages of realistic size, of which Pascal is an example. Scaling up language definitions is not at all easy, and requires careful design, the proper abstractions, and a considerable amount of discipline. A technique that helped us is *literate specification*, which encourages extensive documentation – interested readers can obtain both the sources and a PostScript file describing the implementation from *ftp* (the URL is given in the Preface).

The first section of this chapter is introductory, and summarizes the general layout of an algebraically specified typechecker. The core of the chapter is technical in nature, and contains a number of excerpts from the full specification. It covers the representation of types in the Pascal specification, the formulation of context-sensitive properties, the verification of requirements for all language constructs, and a discussion of how to deal with constructs deviating from the general Pascal pattern, such as the checks on the arguments of the `read` procedure, or the restrictions imposed on control variables in for-loops. The last sections provide a comparison of the specification with other existing formal definitions of Pascal, and a discussion of the applicability of the techniques proposed to specifications of other realistic languages.

2.2 Static Semantics in ASF+SDF

A definition of the static semantics of a programming language aims at narrowing the set of all programs generated by a context-free syntax down to those programs that are free of obvious errors, in particular errors that can be detected without executing the program. Typically, these errors involve context-sensitive requirements, for example that all identifiers used must be declared, that procedures must be called with the proper number of arguments, and so on.

The simplest way to characterize the static semantics in an algebraic specification setting is to define a function taking an abstract syntax tree as input and producing

---

module Messages

imports SyntaxProgram
exports
   sorts ERROR ERRORS
   context-free syntax
      ERROR∗   → ERRORS
      "Illegal use of formatted write-parameter."   → ERROR
      "Parameter lists are not congruous."   → ERROR
      ACTUAL-PAR ": must be a variable access." → ERROR
      "Type must be Boolean."   → ERROR
      IDENT ": too few actual parameters."   → ERROR

Module 2.1: Messages. Some of the approximately 50 error messages of the Pascal typechecker. The sorts ACTUAL-PAR and IDENT come from the abstract syntax definition of Pascal, and refer to actual parameters and identifiers, respectively.

---

a Boolean result indicating correctness 'true' or the presence of errors 'false'. Frequently, however, a more accurate diagnostic than just 'false' will be needed, and a function mapping programs to a domain of error messages—indicating *what* is wrong as well— is used. A program is statically correct if and only if it is mapped to the 'true' element of the domain (the empty list of error messages, for example). Note that in ASF+SDF error messages are simply functions defined in a signature, which, thanks to the user-definable syntax, can be made to read like English sentences. An example is found in Module Messages (2.1). The first function of sort ERROR is a simple constant; the last takes an argument indicating for which procedure identifier too few actual parameters were given. Such a mapping has the flavor of a translation from the programming language into the language of errors. It is typically defined inductively over the abstract syntax, i.e., using *syntax-directed translation*. In order to define this mapping, elementary data types representing types, symbol tables, and procedure declarations are needed. Algebraic specifications of these data types can be easily defined, the typical operations being functions with Boolean results to decide type compatibility, type equivalence, assignment compatibility, or inspection and update functions on the symbol table.

Thus, a specification of the static semantics consists of four ingredients: a signature for the *abstract syntax* of the language, a signature for the *error messages*, abstract data types for the necessary *type operations*, and, finally, definitions of the *typecheck functions* mapping syntax to errors using type operations. A simple example of a typechecker is the one for the toy language Pico (Bergstra *et al.*, 1989), which is also discussed in Chapters 4 and 8. For Pico, the ERROR sort just consists of 'true' and 'false', the type operations involve compatibility and the construction of type environments, and there are only five typecheck functions.

In the next sections we will study the type operations and typecheck functions needed for specifying the static semantics of Pascal.

2.3   An Algebra of Pascal Types

To represent Pascal types, we need to know the type identifiers used, and the context in the program in which the type is defined.

Type equivalence in Pascal is based on the place in the program where the types are declared (Fleck (1984) provides a comparison of name and structural type equivalence in Pascal). Stated in ISO terminology: "Each occurrence of a *new-type* shall denote a type that is distinct from any other *new-type*" (ISO, 1983, p.12) (the syntax of Pascal types is given in Appendix 2.A). As an example, variables A1 and A2 in Figure 2.1 are *not* of the same type, whereas B1 and B2 are.

Types may be built from other types, as again shown in Figure 2.1, where the type IndexType is used in the definition of BType. Type identifiers must be declared before they are used, except for components of pointer types[1], in order to facilitate recursively defined types. Because of this, and because type equivalence is name equivalence, we cannot take the simple approach of fully expanding such types. To represent types we use *contexts*, which keep track where in the program a type has been declared, and which identifiers have been defined up to that point.

2.3.1   Contexts

The data type CONTEXT, defined in Module Context (2.2), is a list of entries, each of which is the *defining point* of an identifier (ISO, 1983, 6.2.2.9). Entries are built directly from pieces of abstract syntax from the program, and can define identifiers as constants, types, variables, functions, and procedures. Thus, a context is a list of all identifiers declared up to a certain point.

To model block structure, special entries are used that mark the boundaries of each block. The search functions, for which no equations are shown, simply traverse the context backward, looking for the nearest definition point of a given identifier. The function '*Id* in inner block of *C*?' only checks the most recent block, and is used when verifying that, for example, a new identifier definition does not redefine one introduced in the same block. The 'find' functions yield a context as a result, where the last entry is the defining point of the given identifier *Id*; the preceding entries can be used to look up identifiers used in the definition of *Id*.

A full context starts with the list of *required* identifiers. Module Initial-Types (2.3) shows the block containing all of them. For identifiers whose type can be expressed using Pascal constructs, regular entries can be used, as for

---

[1]The component identifiers must, however, be defined in the same block.

```
type IndexType = 1 .. 10;
    BType = array[IndexType] of char;
var A1 : array[IndexType] of char;
    A2 : array[IndexType] of char;
    B1 : BType;
    B2 : BType;
```

Figure 2.1: A1 and A2 are *not* of the same type; B1 and B2 are.

module Context
Specifies a table containing declarations. Each declaration is represented by an entry as literally occurring in the Pascal text. Moreover, special entries are provided to represent block boundaries and required procedures, functions or types that cannot be expressed within Pascal.
imports Pascal-Syntax Booleans
exports
  sorts CONTEXT ENTRY
  context-free syntax
    "[" {ENTRY ","}* "]"   → CONTEXT

    label LABEL   → ENTRY
    const CONST-DEF   → ENTRY
    type TYPE-DEF   → ENTRY
    var VAR-DECL   → ENTRY
    PROC-FUN-HEADING   → ENTRY
    required-function IDENT → ENTRY
    required-procedure IDENT → ENTRY
    required-type IDENT   → ENTRY
    block-mark   → ENTRY

    add ENTRY to CONTEXT   → CONTEXT
    find IDENT in CONTEXT   → CONTEXT
    find IDENT in inner block of CONTEXT → CONTEXT
    IDENT in CONTEXT "?"   → BOOL
    IDENT in inner block of CONTEXT "?" → BOOL
  variables
    Prefix [0-9]* → {ENTRY ","}*
    Context [0-9]* → CONTEXT

Module 2.2: Context. Contexts containing declared identifiers.

type Boolean $=$ (false, true);   function sin (x : real) : real

For identifiers not typeable using Pascal language constructs, such as writeln, which has an optional file parameter and a varying number of arguments, special entries of the form 'required-function', 'required-procedure', or 'required-type' are used. In Section 2.4.3 we will discuss how these entries are used to check the correct use of required identifiers.

2.3.2 Representing Types

The representation of Pascal types is shown in Module Types (2.4). First of all, a CONTEXT is a TYPE. More precisely, every context which has a 'required-type Id' or a 'type Id = new-type' as its last entry is considered a type. Observe that a new-type is a type constructor and cannot be an identifier (see Appendix 2.A). Contexts with a last entry of the form 'type $Id_1 = Id_2$' are made into a type by looking up the type associated with Id_2 in the preceding entries.

The preceding entries of the context are used to look up components of constructs built from type identifiers[2]. They also guarantee that all new-type occurrences are indeed distinct: the preceding entries form the distinguishing context of the type definition.

Furthermore, it is possible to remove some of the preceding entries, such as constant, label, function, and procedure declarations, from a CONTEXT that is used as a TYPE. Variable and type declarations containing new types as well as type definitions transitively related to the last type entries, cannot be discarded. Since it is not necessary, however, to remove these irrelevant entries, we will not bother about this.

Finally, the actual Id in the last 'type Id = new-type' entry is immaterial; it is the new-type and its position with respect to the preceding entries that determine the type. For that reason, we can represent unnamed types occurring in variable declarations (such as the type of A1 and A2 in the example at the beginning of this section) using some fixed dummy Id: as shown in equation [d4] of Module Type-Operations (2.5), we use identifier dummy for this throughout the specification.

In addition to normally defined Pascal types, Module Types (2.4) introduces two TYPE constructors that are necessary for constants having a polymorphic type not expressible in Pascal: the 'empty-set' for the type of the [] expression, and the 'nil-type' for the constant 'nil'.

Finally, a number of constants are given that are abbreviations for required types, of which only two are shown: 'boolean-type' and 'text-type'. These are simply abbreviations for the expression looking up the type identifiers in the initial block.

---

[2]For looking up pointer type components this is not sufficient: The full block needs to be available as well when extracting pointer components.

---

module Initial-Types

imports Context
exports
  context-free syntax
    required-block → CONTEXT
equations

[i1]   required-block
  = [block-mark,
    required-procedure rewrite, required-procedure put,
    required-procedure reset, required-procedure get,
    required-procedure read, required-procedure write,
    required-procedure readln, required-procedure writeln,
    required-procedure page, required-procedure new,
    required-procedure dispose, required-procedure pack,
    required-procedure unpack,
    required-function abs, required-function sqr,
    required-function trunc, required-function round,
    required-function ord, required-function succ,
    required-function pred, required-function eof,
    required-function eoln,
    required-type integer, required-type real, required-type char,
    type Boolean = (false, true), type text = file of char,
    function sin (x : real) : real, function cos (x : real) : real,
    function exp (x : real) : real, function ln (x : real) : real,
    function sqrt (x : real) : real, function arctan (x : real) : real,
    function chr (x : integer) : char, function odd (x : integer) : Boolean,
    const maxint = 32768,
    block-mark]

Module 2.3: Initial-Types. The required identifiers of Pascal.

---

module Types

imports Context Initial-Types
exports
  sorts TYPE
  context-free syntax
    CONTEXT   → TYPE
    "(" TYPE ")" → TYPE {**bracket**}
    empty-set   → TYPE
    nil-pointer   → TYPE

    boolean-type → TYPE
    text-type   → TYPE
  variables
    T $[0\text{-}9]*$ → TYPE
equations

[t1]	$[Prefix,\ \text{type}\ id_1 = id_2]$	$=$ find id_2 in $[Prefix]$
[t2]	boolean-type	$=$ find `Boolean` in required-block
[t3]	text-type	$=$ find `text` in required-block

Module 2.4: Types. Representation of Pascal types.

2.3.3   Operations on Types

The algebra of Pascal types is completed by defining the operations that are needed to manipulate or classify terms of sort TYPE. Module Type-Operations (2.5) first of all introduces a number of predicates on types. These indicate when a type is *ordinal*, when it is a *string* type, whether it has been designated as *packed*, etc. Mostly, these predicates are defined simply using pattern matching on the last entry in the context. The equations shown only cover the 'true' cases; the 'false' cases are easily covered by means of otherwise-equations.[3]

In addition to this, functions are provided to retrieve components of *structured* types, such as the *index type* of an array, the *host type* of a subrange, or the *component type* of a set. These functions are written in dot notation. Their result value is of sort

---

[3]It is also possible just to omit the false cases – which would give an initial model with non-standard Booleans. In that case, if the predicate is used in a conditional equation, a negative condition must be used to check the falsity of the predicate.

TYPE. Their defining equations use pattern matching to extract the type denoter, and then use a lookup function to find the corresponding TYPE in the preceding entries of the context.

Module Type-Compatibility (2.6) uses the operations of Module Type-Operations (2.5) to define the notion of *compatibility*. Examples are the compatible ranges 1..3 and 2..4, or the string 'aaa', which has a type compatible with array [1..3] of char. In the standard, compatibility is defined as follows (ISO, 1983, 6.4.5):

> Types T_1 and T_2 shall be designated *compatible* if any of the following four statements is true.
>
> 1. T_1 and T_2 are the same type.
>
> 2. T_1 is a subrange of T_2, or T_2 is a subrange of T_1, or both T_1 and T_2 are subranges of the same host type.
>
> 3. T_1 and T_2 are set-types of compatible base-types, and either both T_1 and T_2 are designated packed or neither T_1 nor T_2 is designated packed.
>
> 4. T_1 and T_2 are string types with the same number of components.

The equations of Module Type-Compatibility (2.6) exactly follow this definition. The predicate 'T_1 is the same as T_2?' — for which the equations are not shown — simply checks equality of contexts; moreover it makes sure that any set type is the same as the empty set type, and any pointer type is the same as the nil pointer type[4].

Last but not least, we observe that the actual representation of types is not used in the equations of Module Type-Compatibility (2.6); the abstract functions classifying or decomposing types are used instead. This gives a form of *data hiding*, and allows us to replace our type representation by another one (for example, where we increment a number upon every new-type occurrence in order to avoid having to keep track of all preceding entries in a context).

2.4 Typecheck Functions

The algebra of Pascal types is used to check the requirements on declarations, expressions, and statements as occurring in Pascal programs. The collection of typecheck functions is defined inductively (compositionally) over the abstract syntax of Pascal, and specifies the constraints to be met by each language construct.

---

[4]The standard reads: *The token* nil *does not have a single type, but assumes a suitable* pointer-type *to satisfy the* compatibility *rules, if possible* (ISO, 1983, 6.4.4., note 2).

---

module Type-Operations

imports Types Integers
exports
  context-free syntax
    "is-ordinal?" (TYPE)   → BOOL
    "is-subrange?" (TYPE)   → BOOL
    "is-non-empty-set?" (TYPE)   → BOOL
    "is-empty-set?" (TYPE)   → BOOL
    "is-set-type?" (TYPE)   → BOOL
    "is-string-type?" (TYPE)   → BOOL
    "is-packed?" (TYPE)   → BOOL
    TYPE "." host-type   → TYPE
    TYPE "." comp-type   → TYPE
    TYPE "." index-type   → TYPE
    TYPE "." nr-of-elements   → INT
    TYPE is the same as TYPE "?" → BOOL
hiddens
  context-free syntax
    context-type of TYPE-DENOTER in CONTEXT → TYPE
equations

[c1]   is-subrange?([*Prefix*, type *id* = *const-val*$_1$ .. *const-val*$_2$]) = true
[c2]   is-non-empty-set?([*Prefix*, type *id* = PS set of *type-den*]) = true
[c3]   is-empty-set?(empty-set)   = true
[c4]   is-packed?([*Prefix*, type *id* = packed *struct-type*])   = true

[d1]   [*Prefix*, type *id* = PS set of *type-den*] . comp-type
                   = context-type of *type-den* in [*Prefix*]

[d2]   [*Prefix*, type *id* = PS array[*type-den*$_1$] of *type-den*$_2$] . index-type
                   = context-type of *type-den*$_1$ in [*Prefix*]

[d3]   context-type of *id* in *Context*   = find *id* in *Context*
[d4]   context-type of *new-type* in [*Prefix*] = [*Prefix*, type **dummy** = *new-type*]

Module 2.5: Type-Operations. Elementary type manipulations.

module Type-Compatibility

imports Type-Operations
exports
  context-free syntax
    TYPE and TYPE compatible "?" → BOOL
equations

[c1]
$$\frac{T_1 \text{ is the same as } T_2 \text{ ? } = \text{ true}}{T_1 \text{ and } T_2 \text{ compatible ? } = \text{ true}}$$

[c2a]
$$\frac{\begin{array}{c} \text{is-subrange?}(T_1) = \text{true,} \\ T_1 \text{ . host-type is the same as } T_2 \text{ ? } = \text{ true} \end{array}}{T_1 \text{ and } T_2 \text{ compatible ? } = \text{ true}}$$

[c2b]
$$\frac{\begin{array}{c} \text{is-subrange?}(T_2) = \text{true,} \\ T_2 \text{ . host-type is the same as } T_1 \text{ ? } = \text{ true} \end{array}}{T_1 \text{ and } T_2 \text{ compatible ? } = \text{ true}}$$

[c2c]
$$\frac{\begin{array}{c} \text{is-subrange?}(T_1) = \text{true,} \\ \text{is-subrange?}(T_2) = \text{true,} \\ T_1 \text{ . host-type is the same as } T_2 \text{ . host-type ? } = \text{ true} \end{array}}{T_1 \text{ and } T_2 \text{ compatible ? } = \text{ true}}$$

[c3]
$$\frac{\begin{array}{c} \text{is-non-empty-set?}(T_1) = \text{true,} \\ \text{is-non-empty-set?}(T_2) = \text{true,} \\ \text{is-packed?}(T_1) = \text{is-packed?}(T_2), \\ T_1 \text{ . comp-type and } T_2 \text{ . comp-type compatible ? } = \text{ true} \end{array}}{T_1 \text{ and } T_2 \text{ compatible ? } = \text{ true}}$$

[c4]
$$\frac{\begin{array}{c} \text{is-string-type?}(T_1) = \text{true,} \\ \text{is-string-type?}(T_2) = \text{true,} \\ T_1 \text{ . index-type . nr-of-elements } = T_2 \text{ . index-type . nr-of-elements} \end{array}}{T_1 \text{ and } T_2 \text{ compatible ? } = \text{ true}}$$

Module 2.6: Type-Compatibility. Specification of compatibility of Pascal types.

module Env

An environment is a tuple containing values for the current CONTEXT while type checking a particular program point, a list of errors encountered so far, and a result field containing the type of expressions typechecked. This module introduces some basic functions to ease manipulation of environments. The defining equations for these are not shown.

An environment is built from a number of fields, and in this module three fields (context, errors, and result) are provided. Later modules may introduce other sorts of fields.

imports Types Messages

exports

  sorts FIELD ENV

  context-free syntax

"(" "context:" CONTEXT ")"	→ FIELD
"(" "errors:" ERRORS ")"	→ FIELD
"(" "result:" TYPE ")"	→ FIELD
"[" FIELD* "]"	→ ENV
ENV "." context	→ CONTEXT
ENV "." errors	→ ERRORS
ENV "." result	→ TYPE
set-context of ENV to CONTEXT	→ ENV
ENV "+" ENTRY	→ ENV
add-error "[" ERROR "]" to ENV	→ ENV
set-result of ENV to TYPE	→ ENV

  variables

    E [0-9]* → ENV

Module 2.7: Env. Representation of environments.

2.4.1 Constraint Checking

The typecheck functions collect the errors found while typechecking the constructs used in a Pascal program. To check a construct, the list of identifiers known in the prevailing scope (represented by a CONTEXT) is needed, The result of such a check consists of (1) a list of errors, (2) an updated context (which changes when entering or leaving a block, when processing the declarations of a block, or when encountering a with-statement) and (3) a result type when checking expressions.

All this information is collected in a structure called an *environment*. The signature of an environment is defined in Module Env (2.7). It gives the ENV constructor (which is built from a number of FIELDs) as well as several operations for extracting

module Constraints

imports Type-Compatibility Env Initial-Types Types
exports
  context-free syntax
    TYPE should be boolean in ENV   → ENV
    TYPE should be character or number in ENV → ENV
    TYPE should be
    assignment-compatible with TYPE in ENV   → ENV
equations

[e1]
$$\frac{T \text{ is the same as boolean-type ? } = \text{ true}}{T \text{ should be boolean in } E = E}$$

[e1]
$$\frac{T \text{ is the same as boolean-type ? } \neq \text{ true}}{T \text{ should be boolean in } E = }$$
add-error[Type must be Boolean.] to E

Module 2.8: Constraints. Requirements that will raise error messages if not met.

information from or for updating the information in an environment. All typecheck functions take a language construct and an environment, and compute an updated environment.

In Module Type-Operations (2.5) we encountered a number of predicates, such as 'is-ordinal?(TYPE)'. Given these predicates, we can directly define functions that take an environment, check whether a predicate is true, return the unaltered environment if it is, and return the environment extended with an appropriate error message if it is not. Some examples are shown in Module Constraints (2.8). The signature for three functions is given and for one of them, 'TYPE should be Boolean in ENV', the defining equations are shown. If the given type is indeed Boolean, the environment is not changed; otherwise its list of errors is extended with the message 'Type must be Boolean'. We will refer to these environment-changing functions as *should-be* functions.

A typical example of the use of the should-be functions is given in Module TC-Stats (2.9). The two equations characterize the static semantics of the if-then and the assignment statement. In order to check an if-then, the sub-constructs (the expression and the then-part) are checked. The constraint to be met by the entire

---

module TC-Stats

imports Constraints TC-Exp
exports
  context-free syntax
    stat-tc "[" STATEMENT "]" in ENV → ENV
hiddens
  context-free syntax
    var-at-lhs-tc "[" VARIABLE-ACCESS "]" in ENV → ENV
equations

[1]
$$\frac{\text{expr-tc}\llbracket expr \rrbracket \text{ in } E_1 = E_2, \quad \text{stat-tc}\llbracket stat \rrbracket \text{ in } E_2 = E_3}{\text{stat-tc}\llbracket \text{if } expr \text{ then } stat \rrbracket \text{ in } E_1 =}$$
E_2 . result should be boolean in E_3

[2]
$$\frac{\text{var-at-lhs-tc}\llbracket var\text{-}acc \rrbracket \text{ in } E_1 = E_2, \quad \text{expr-tc}\llbracket expr \rrbracket \text{ in } E_2 = E_3}{\text{stat-tc}\llbracket var\text{-}acc := expr \rrbracket \text{ in } E_1 =}$$
E_3 . result should be assignment-compatible with E_2 . result in E_3

Module 2.9: TC-Stats. Typechecking some statements.

---

if-then is that the type of the expression (denoted by 'E_2.result') should be Boolean. Likewise, the equation dealing with an assignment checks the left-hand side and the right-hand side, and states that their types ('E_3.result' and 'E_2.result') should be assignment-compatible. Checking the left-hand side requires a special typecheck function 'var-at-lhs-tc', since the assignment may involve the return value of a function F, which in Pascal is written as an assignment to identifier F.

Module TC-Stats (2.9) should make the advantages of this approach immediately obvious. One equation is given for each language construct, and the ISO style of stating constraints for each language construct can be followed directly. As an example, for the assignment the ISO standard says that "the value of the expression of the assignment-statement shall be assignment-compatible with the type possessed by the variable denoted by the variable-access" (ISO, 1983, p. 41).

2.4.2 Checking Expressions

About half of the typecheck functions deal with the well-formedness of Pascal *expressions*. This large proportion is mainly due to the wide variety of expressions Pascal supports: they include constants, user-defined or required function calls, access to variables, access to components of arrays, pointers, or records, set constructors, and built-in arithmetic, set, and relational operators.

The typecheck functions for these follow the should-be pattern: for each kind of expression they mention the requirements in the form of should-be conditions. Distinguishing the sort of expression is done by syntactic pattern matching, in combination with Boolean tests on subconstructs or earlier declarations if the distinction is not context-free. For example, an identifier can be a constant, variable, or function without arguments, depending on the declaration of the identifier; likewise, the ↑ operator can denote an access to a file or pointer component, depending on the type of its argument.

The arithmetic, set, and relational operators are overloaded, and almost 50 different cases can be distinguished depending on the types of the arguments. The standard summarizes these 50 cases in three tables, listing the allowed type combinations for the operands, as well as their corresponding result types (ISO, 1983, 6.7.2). The same approach is beneficial in the ASF+SDF specification: rather than giving separate equations for all 50 cases, the operator types have been summarized in tables, which can be made to look exactly like the tables in the standard by exploiting the syntactic freedom of ASF+SDF. Checking a built-in operator amounts to determining the type of the operands, looking up the operator-operands combination in the table, and returning the associated result type if the combination is found or raising an error message otherwise.

2.4.3 Checking Irregular Pascal Features

Most Pascal language constructs are easily checked using the should-be approach. A small number of constructs, however, deviates from the general Pascal pattern. For example, pointer type components and forward procedures or functions use identifiers before they are declared, whereas the general rule is definition before use. Furthermore, all variables can be assigned, with the single exception of those that are used as control variables in for-loops. Statements, in general, do not introduce symbols in the scope; statements prefixed with a jump label, however, have to meet criteria very similar to those imposed on symbol introducing declarations (although the labels must also have been introduced in the declaration part). Last but not least, required procedures and functions can have a varying number of parameters as well as optional parameters with default values—a facility that is not supported for user-defined procedures or functions.

Checking such exceptional features requires gathering extra information, i.e., information that is not in the CONTEXT. For example, labels can only be used by a goto if the block contains exactly one statement that is prefixed by it. This information cannot be extracted from a CONTEXT structure, since that only contains declarations, not statements. Moreover, jumps cannot be arbitrarily placed: one of the allowed cases is that procedures or functions can jump to statements occurring in the statement sequence of the compound statement at the end of the block. In other words, before checking statements in local procedures or functions, the labels used as prefixes in the block statement need to be collected.

The information can then be passed to the typecheck functions as an extra parameter. In our setting, there is an alternative, which is to hide this information in the ENV sort by giving it an extra FIELD (called, e.g., jumpable-labels). This allows equations not needing this information to avoid referring to it, whereas functions requiring it can extract it from the ENV parameter. Observe that if this new FIELD is only used in one module, it can be made *hidden*.

As a last example of how to deal with irregular Pascal features, Module TC-read (2.10) shows how should-be functions are used to check the required function read. The last two equations do the actual checking for the situation that read has one file parameter and one[5] argument to store the value to be read in. These two equations distinguish the cases depending on whether the file parameter is of type text-type. The first two equations check whether the first argument is any file type, and insert the required file variable input (which is of text-type) if it is not. The middle two equations cover the case where not enough actual parameters are given.

From a specification viewpoint, it is almost as difficult to describe checking an optional parameter for a few required procedures as it is to check a general mechanism[6] for allowing user-defined procedures or functions with optional parameters (which are not provided by Pascal).

2.5   Related Work

The Pascal language has been the subject of various earlier formalization projects. Some of these deal exclusively with dynamic semantics, e.g., the axiomatic definition of Hoare and Wirth (1973), or the more recent action semantics of Mosses and Watt (1993). A denotational semantics also covering static semantics is given by Tennent (1977), and by Andrews and Henhapl in VDM (Bjørner and Jones, 1982, Chapter 7). A definition using *predicate rules*, akin to Z, is presented by Duke (1987).

More often, the static semantics are defined by attribute grammars. For instance, definitions have been given in the Synthesizer Specification Language (SSL) (Reps and Teitelbaum, 1989a), in the ALADIN formalism of the GAG system (Kastens

---

[5]The (simple) equation mapping a read of multiple variables to a list of reads of one argument is not shown.

[6]This is done in the *action-semantic* definition of Pascal (Mosses, 1992; Mosses and Watt, 1993). Entries in the list of bindings for required identifiers also contain so-called *modes* for the parameters, which indicate whether procedures have multiple arguments or can insert optional file arguments.

module TC-read

imports Constraints TC-Actual-Pars
exports
  context-free syntax
    tc-read(ACTUAL-PAR-LIST, ENV) $\rightarrow$ ENV
    file-read(ACTUAL-PAR-LIST, ENV) $\rightarrow$ ENV
equations

[r1]
$$\frac{\text{is-file-variable?}(act\text{-}par, E) = \text{true}}{\begin{array}{l}\text{tc-read}((act\text{-}par, act\text{-}par^+), E) = \\ \text{file-read}((act\text{-}par, act\text{-}par^+), E)\end{array}}$$

[r2]
$$\frac{\text{is-file-variable?}(act\text{-}par, E) \neq \text{true}}{\begin{array}{l}\text{tc-read}((act\text{-}par, act\text{-}par^+), E) = \\ \text{file-read}((\textbf{input}, act\text{-}par, act\text{-}par^+), E)\end{array}}$$

[r3]
$$\begin{array}{l}\text{tc-read}(, E) \\ = \text{add-error}[\textbf{read} : \text{too few actual parameters.}] \text{ to } E\end{array}$$

[r4]
$$\frac{\text{is-file-variable?}(act\text{-}par, E) = \text{true}}{\begin{array}{l}\text{tc-read}((act\text{-}par), E) = \\ \text{add-error}[\textbf{read} : \text{too few actual parameters.}] \text{ to } E\end{array}}$$

[r5]
$$\frac{\begin{array}{l}\text{act-par-tc}(filep, E_1) = E_2, \\ E_2 . \text{result is the same as text-type ?} = \text{true}, \\ \text{act-par-tc}(act\text{-}par, E_2) = E_3\end{array}}{\begin{array}{l}\text{file-read}((filep, act\text{-}par), E_1) = \\ E_3 . \text{result should be character or number in } E_3\end{array}}$$

[r6]
$$\frac{\begin{array}{l}\text{act-par-tc}(filep, E_1) = E_2, \\ E_2 . \text{result is the same as text-type ?} \neq \text{true}, \\ \text{act-par-tc}(act\text{-}par, E_2) = E_3\end{array}}{\begin{array}{l}\text{file-read}((filep, act\text{-}par), E_1) = \\ E_3 . \text{result should be assignment-compatible with } E_2 . \text{result in } E_3\end{array}}$$

Module 2.10: TC-read. Typechecking the **read** procedure.

et al., 1982), and using extended attribute grammars (Watt, 1979). None of these attribute grammar formalisms support as much syntactic freedom for function names as ASF+SDF. We feel that, as a result, the ASF+SDF specification is considerably better readable than the others. Concerning the size of the specifications, the description of Watt is remarkably compact. The definitions in SSL and ALADIN are of about the same size as the ASF+SDF specification.

Concerning expressive power of attribute grammars versus algebraic specifications, Courcelle and Franchi-Zannettacci (1982) have proved a one-to-one correspondence between a subclass of algebraic specifications, the so-called *primitive recursive schemes* and a subclass of attribute grammars, the strongly non-circular attribute grammars. This relation is explored further in Chapter 6, where techniques for incremental attribute evaluation are transferred to the algebraic specification domain. The resulting *incremental rewriting* machinery can be used to derive an *incremental* typechecker for Pascal automatically from the specification discussed in this chapter. Incrementality is important in an interactive setting in which large Pascal programs have to be edited. Rather than the complete program, only those parts of it that are affected by a modification are re-checked.

Visser (1992) describes an algebraic formalization (in ASF+SDF) of the static semantics of the object-oriented language Eiffel (Meyer, 1988), a language that is more difficult to typecheck than Pascal. He uses states in a way similar to ours, but extends them with a *context manipulation language*, supporting sequential composition, if-then-else and case statements. His approach has the flavor of translating Eiffel to an intermediate language (the context-manipulation commands) that can be evaluated to yield a list of error messages.

In order to avoid the need to pass states around explicitly (see, e.g., the variables E_1 to E_3 in the equations of Module TC-Stats (2.9)) state-hiding *combinators* can be used. In the approach discussed in this chapter, variables are needed because several components of one state may be needed at more than one place. For example, equation [1] in Module TC-Stats (2.9) assigns a value to E_2 in the first condition, and then uses that value in the second as well as in the resulting should-be function. If we introduce a number of combinators allowing us to sequence various state manipulation as well as to access certain components of states computed in between, we can avoid such use of variables. For *dynamic semantics*, such a combinator approach has been studied extensively in the context of action semantics (Mosses, 1992; Watt, 1991), and it would be interesting to see to what extent the action-semantic combinators can be reused at the static-semantic level.

The specification style of the static semantic definition we gave is rather classical. A function is defined inductively, mapping an abstract tree to a list of errors. In Chapter 4, Dinesh will conduct experiments with the use of abstract interpretation to characterize the static semantics of programming languages. In short, the values of a language are translated into an abstract domain of types, and then evaluated over the new domain using equations like "integer + integer = integer". To illustrate these ideas he uses the language Pico; besides, the language CLaX — a relatively large subset of Pascal — has been specified in this way.

2.6   Concluding Remarks

In this chapter we have studied how to specify a typechecker for ISO Pascal. We concentrated on finding the right abstractions for the algebra of types and the actual typecheck functions. The resulting specification is

- Readable: Distracting details of, e.g., the representation of types are hidden away. Moreover, the syntactic freedom of ASF+SDF has been used to choose meaningful and attractive function names.

- Close in style to the ISO standard: for each language construct it lists the type requirements that are to be fulfilled.

- Extensible: Environments can easily be extended with more information without requiring direct changes to the typecheck functions. As a result, it is fairly easy, for example, to let the same specification generate, besides error messages, intermediate code for use by a compiler backend.

In short, we conclude that the specification of the Pascal typechecker has served its purpose of lending support to the claim that algebraic specifications and ASF+SDF can be used to describe languages in an intelligible way. Nevertheless, there are a number of issues that emerged during specification, and we conclude by discussing these.

To start with a negative point, the modularization constructs[7] of ASF+SDF are inadequate for achieving suitable data hiding. For our specification there is no encapsulation mechanism that causes the representation of Pascal types to be invisible in modules using them. An option might be to make the type representation *hidden*, keeping only the operations on types visible. The effect of this, however, could be that a reduction of a term over a module importing the Pascal types results in a normal form over the hidden signature. The consequences of this (the normal form will not be parseable, for instance) are not acceptable in the current setting: ground normal forms should not contain hidden items. Future versions of ASF+SDF will have to come to terms with this issue. A source of inspiration might be found in the language Opal (Didrich *et al.*, 1994), which supports automatic translations between efficient internal representations and visible abstract ones.

Another problematic issue is the size of the abstract syntax of Pascal. The large number of language constructors makes definition by first-order pattern matching unattractive since too many cases need to be covered. For example, it takes 12 equations to check that a function body contains at least one assignment to the function identifier, because there are so many different structured statements. Resorting to a more applicative form of syntax definition might help here. A more radical solution

---

[7]Sorts, functions and variables can be made hidden or exported. If module M_1 imports M_2, then M_1 can use all exported items of M_2, and M_1 will automatically export all these items.

might be to switch to *higher-order* specifications; an example using higher-order term rewriting is discussed in Chapter 8.

A more positive point is that the tool support provided by the ASF+SDF Meta-Environment — checking syntax, running tests for validating the specification, and generating LATEX code — was very useful during the development. The specification is a terminating, confluent conditional rewrite system, and can be executed as such. Doing this to test the specification has helped to reveal and correct many errors. For our case study, the advantages of executable specifications outweigh the often mentioned problems (over-deterministic specification and the danger to focus on *how* rather than *what*).

A final question is whether executing the specification yields a useful typechecking tool. First of all, in spite of the fact that efficiency played no role at all while writing the specification, the executable version obtained by compilation using the ASF2C compiler (Kamperman and Walters, 1996) has an acceptable performance.

A second point to note, however, is that the output obtained by simply executing the equations as rewrite rules is inadequate in an interactive setting. Typechecking a Pascal program of, say, five pages, simply computes the normal form, e.g., 'Type must be Boolean'. This does not give a clue *where* in the five pages the error was made. Nevertheless, while reading the specification, one intuitively has a very clear picture which statements cause particular errors. Moreover, when executing the rewrite rules "by hand" for a specific program, it is generally quite clear which parts of the source program were responsible for errors. This raises the question whether this information can be extracted *automatically*, while executing the rewrite rules. In Chapter 7 we give an affirmative answer to this question and propose a technique called *origin tracking*, linking reduction results to positions in the initial term.

Appendix

2.A Module SyntaxTypes

The definitions in this module are in accordance with the syntax as specified in section 6.4.1, 6.4.2 and 6.4.3 of the ISO standard.

imports SyntaxConsts

exports

    sorts NEW-TYPE TYPE-DENOTER
           STRUCTURED-TYPE PACKED-STATUS
           FIELD-LIST FIXED-PART VAR-PART VARIANT
           RECORD-SECTION OPT-SEMI-COLON
           SELECTOR FIELDS-DESCRIPTION

    context-free syntax

	→ PACKED-STATUS
packed	→ PACKED-STATUS
IDENT	→ TYPE-DENOTER
NEW-TYPE	→ TYPE-DENOTER
CONST ".." CONST	→ NEW-TYPE
"(" {IDENT ","}+ ")"	→ NEW-TYPE
"↑" IDENT	→ NEW-TYPE
PACKED-STATUS STRUCTURED-TYPE	→ NEW-TYPE
array "[" {TYPE-DENOTER ","}+ "]"	
of TYPE-DENOTER	→ STRUCTURED-TYPE
record FIELD-LIST end	→ STRUCTURED-TYPE
set of TYPE-DENOTER	→ STRUCTURED-TYPE
file of TYPE-DENOTER	→ STRUCTURED-TYPE
	→ FIELD-LIST
FIELDS-DESCRIPTION OPT-SEMI-COLON	→ FIELD-LIST
	→ OPT-SEMI-COLON
";"	→ OPT-SEMI-COLON
FIXED-PART	→ FIELDS-DESCRIPTION
VAR-PART	→ FIELDS-DESCRIPTION
FIXED-PART ";" VAR-PART	→ FIELDS-DESCRIPTION
{RECORD-SECTION ";"}+	→ FIXED-PART
{IDENT ","}+ ":" TYPE-DENOTER	→ RECORD-SECTION
case SELECTOR of {VARIANT ";"}+	→ VAR-PART
IDENT	→ SELECTOR
IDENT ":" IDENT	→ SELECTOR
{CONST ","}+ ":" "(" FIELD-LIST ")"	→ VARIANT

2.B   Module Sorts-and-Vars

Here we list the syntactic sorts and variables used in this chapter.
imports SyntaxTypes
exports
    sorts ACTUAL-PAR IDENT LABEL CONST-DEF
           TYPE-DEF VAR-DECL PROC-FUN-HEADING
           STATEMENT VARIABLE-ACCESS EXPR
    variables

$id[0\text{-}9]*$	$\rightarrow$ IDENT
$type\text{-}den[0\text{-}9]*$	$\rightarrow$ TYPE-DENOTER
$struct\text{-}type[0\text{-}9]*$	$\rightarrow$ STRUCTURED-TYPE
$const\text{-}val[0\text{-}9]*$	$\rightarrow$ CONST
$new\text{-}type[0\text{-}9]*$	$\rightarrow$ NEW-TYPE
$expr[0\text{-}9]*$	$\rightarrow$ EXPR
$stat[0\text{-}9]*$	$\rightarrow$ STATEMENT
$var\text{-}acc[0\text{-}9]*$	$\rightarrow$ VARIABLE-ACCESS
$act\text{-}par[0\text{-}9]*$	$\rightarrow$ ACTUAL-PAR
$act\text{-}par[0\text{-}9]*\text{“+”}$	$\rightarrow$ {ACTUAL-PAR “,”}+
$filep[0\text{-}9]*$	$\rightarrow$ ACTUAL-PAR
$PS\ [0\text{-}9]*$	$\rightarrow$ PACKED-STATUS

3

A Kernel Object-Oriented Language

T. B. Dinesh

Abstract *K*OOL, a *kernel object-oriented language*, is described and its dynamic and static semantics are given in ASF+SDF. *K*OOL is a language with update-able self, with non-strict argument evaluation, and without alias-able state. The specification of its static semantics is derived from its dynamic semantics. This is achieved by taking a copy of the dynamic semantics as starting point and by systematically replacing concrete domain values by more abstract ones. This derivation is aided by the typechecker of the ASF+SDF Meta-Environment, since the type errors reported in the altered specification lead the specifier to accordingly modify the specification of dynamic semantics into a specification of static semantics. Justifying these modifications is easy and feasible in practice. The resulting specification is then extended, in a modular manner, into a typechecker specification.

3.1 Introduction

A formal specification gives a precise description of the syntax and semantics of a language. The syntax of a language can easily be specified, but describing the semantics and justifying the specification of the semantics may prove to be more difficult. It is therefore useful to get some aid in specifying static semantics from the specification of the dynamic semantics of a language. Such a process reduces the effort necessary to justify the consistency of static semantics with respect to dynamic semantics, by localizing the need for justification to the points where they differ. In practice, specifications tend to be large and the process of justification becomes so cumbersome that specifiers often ignore it, which calls for specification styles that encourage the process of justification.

Object-oriented programming has become popular among people who build large software, and the static semantics of object-oriented languages has attracted of considerable interest in the area of the semantics of programming languages (Cardelli,

1984; Bruce, 1994). The kernel of an object-oriented language is generally small and an example of such a language is considered here.

In Section 3.2 we focus on the language $\mathcal{K}$OOL, which is based on objects (dynamic binding) and inheritance with simple expressions that manipulate objects. The syntax module and flattening of the inheritance hierarchy are described in Section 3.3. $\mathcal{K}$OOL objects are described as method dictionaries, with lookup and update operations in Section 3.4 and the value environment that is used during evaluation of κOOL programs is described in Section 3.5. In Section 3.6, the dynamic semantics is specified by first specifying object instantiation.

In Section 3.7, evaluation of the type of an expression is derived using the specification of the dynamic semantics, modulo sub-typing rules. This is done by introducing suitable type-level abstract domains for the value domains used and by attempting to reuse the specification of dynamic semantics. The errors generated in this process indicate the incorrect use of sorts and modifications are needed for the specification to be valid. These modifications can be easily explained by a specifier and this not necessarily informal justification process is feasible even for large specifications. Appendix 3.A contains a listing of all the derived modules for the static semantics of $\mathcal{K}$OOL.

3.2   The Language $\mathcal{K}$OOL

Objects are characterized by their ability to receive messages and execute methods. *Methods* are of two forms: (i) those that simply return an object (these methods are also known as "instance variables") and (ii) those that send messages to other objects, including the object sending the message itself (denoted by *self*).

A *class* is the basic programming unit, the instances of which are objects. Classes are static and can be accessed during compilation, while objects are dynamic and are found at run time. Classes are named and can be defined as a modification of a previously defined class (*inheritance*), using incremental description. This incremental description is done using the '_ subclass of _' operator and is aided by the 'redef _ to _' construct.

A κOOL program consists of a set of classes and an expression. The expression starts the chain of sending messages to objects. An important aspect of κOOL is the notion of substitutability in the presence of dynamic binding. This enables one to substitute a more specific object when a less specific one is expected, thereby aiding smooth upgrading of software (Dinesh, 1992). The type information is generally used to determine substitutability of objects, using the notion of subtypes.

For example, the three classes Bool, True and False, in Figure 3.1, together describe Booleans in κOOL. The two Boolean objects True and False are defined as separate classes each with a uniquely determined instance (they have no instance variables) as in (Goldberg and Robson, 1983). The class False includes a dummy method (flsid) which makes its signature a proper extension of that of class Bool—

```
%% class Bool is used to indicate the common
%% interface between the classes True and False.
%% Class Bool behaves like True by default.
class Bool
  meth cond:Bool(x:Bool,y:Bool) x
  meth and:Bool(y:Bool) self.cond(y,new False)
  meth or:Bool(y:Bool)  self.cond(new True,y)
  meth not:Bool() self.cond(new False, new True)

class True subclass of Bool

%% Class False overrides the 'cond' method behavior.
%% It also defines another method 'flsid'.
class False subclass of Bool
  meth flsid:False() self
  meth cond:Bool(x:Bool,y:Bool) y

class Boolpair
  var one:Bool := new False
  var two:Bool := new True

%% Create an instance of Boolpair and define the
%% instance variable 'one' to be the value of
%% the expression 'new False.and(new True)'.
new Boolpair.one := (new False.and(new True))
```

Figure 3.1: KOOL Bools.

The %% symbol denotes that the rest of the line is a comment.

it is defined only for purposes of illustration. The expression `new False.and(new True)` is "assigned" to the instance variable `one` of an instance of class `Boolpair`. This assigned expression, in conventional Boolean algebra, would be *false ∧ true*. In the KOOL expression, a message `and` is sent to an instance of a `False` class (we call such an instance a `False` object) with an instance of a `True` class. The message `and` invokes the `and` defined in the `False` object, which in turn sends a `cond` message to itself with two arguments—the `True` object it received as an argument and a new `False` object. The `cond` method returns the second argument, which is the object `False` in this case. Thus, the result of evaluation is the object `False`.

3.3   KOOL Syntax

In the module below, we specify a KOOL program 'PROGRAM' as a *list* of classes followed by an expression 'EXP'. Since we do not have any predefined classes or primitive data types, we insist that there is at least one class definition 'CLASS+' in a program.

A class has a name 'CID', instance variable declarations 'VAR*' and method definitions 'METHOD*'. The instance variable declarations also insist that an initial value be specified 'IEXP'. The only way an instance of a class can be created is by using 'new CID', as in prototype based languages. The initialization expression 'IEXP' is a simple 'new CID'. A class can also inherit from another class, using the 'subclass of' operation, giving preference to methods defined in its own class.

A method definition consists of a method name and its return type identifier, formal arguments, their type identifiers and a method body 'EXP'. An expression can be

I. an initialization expression 'IEXP',

II. *self* to refer to the current object environment,

III. 'ID' to refer to formal arguments of a method or to instance variables (with preference to formal argument),

IV. accessing an instance variable of an object 'EXP.ID',

V. updating an instance variable of some object 'EXP.ID := EXP' or

VI. sending a message to an object to invoke a particular method 'EXP.ID({EXP,}*)'.

Updating an instance variable of an object is the only way, in this language, to obtain "different instances" of a class, since 'new CID' always returns identical new instances.

Module KOOLsyntax

imports Layout[5.A.1]

exports

  sorts PROGRAM VAR METHOD EXP CLASS IEXP
         CLASSES REDEF CID ID IDT ARGS

  lexical syntax

    [a-z][a-z0-9]* → ID
    [A-Z][a-z0-9]* → CID

  context-free syntax

CLASSES EXP	→ PROGRAM	{**constructor**}
CLASS+	→ CLASSES	{**constructor**}
class CID VAR* METHOD*	→ CLASS	{**constructor**}
var ID ":" CID ":=" IEXP	→ VAR	{**constructor**}
meth IDT ARGS EXP	→ METHOD	{**constructor**}
ID ":" CID	→ IDT	{**constructor**}
new CID	→ IEXP	{**constructor**}
IEXP	→ EXP	{**constructor**}
self	→ EXP	{**constructor**}
ID	→ EXP	{**constructor**}
EXP "." ID	→ EXP	{**constructor**}
EXP "." ID ":=" EXP	→ EXP	{**left, constructor**}
EXP "." ID "(" {EXP ","}* ")"	→ EXP	{**constructor**}
"(" EXP ")"	→ EXP	{**bracket**}
"(" {IDT ","}* ")"	→ ARGS	{**constructor**}
class CID subclass of CID REDEF* VAR* METHOD*	→ CLASS	
redef ID "to" ID	→ REDEF	

  priorities

    EXP "."ID → EXP > EXP "."ID ":="EXP → EXP >
    EXP "."ID "(" {EXP ","}*")" → EXP

  variables

    V [']*   → VAR
    V "*"[']* → VAR*
    M [']*   → METHOD
    M "*"[']* → METHOD*
    C [01']*   → CLASS
    C "*"[']* → CLASS*
    E [']*   → EXP
    N [0']*   → CID

$$
\begin{array}{ll}
\textit{Redefs} & \rightarrow \text{REDEF}* \\
\textit{Idt } [0']* & \rightarrow \text{IDT} \\
\textit{Args } [0\text{-}9']* & \rightarrow \text{ARGS} \\
\textit{Idt } \text{``*''} & \rightarrow \{\text{IDT ``,''}\}* \\
\text{``}\kappa\text{''} & \rightarrow \text{CLASSES} \\
\textit{Id } [0\text{-}9']* & \rightarrow \text{ID}
\end{array}
$$

equations

The equations [F0] and [F1] below flatten the class hierarchy defined using the '_ subclass of _' construct. This construct aids reuse of methods defined earlier and the maintenance of such programs, since any modification to the inherited class is effective in all classes that inherit it. However, neither the dynamic nor static semantics of κOOL are dependent on the structure of the hierarchy itself.

Rule [F0] removes the 'N' subclass of N' construct by copying all instance variables and methods from the 'super class' N to the (sub)class N'. Methods and instance variables could get multiply defined by this process, however in combination with rules [F2] and [F3] only the lowest ones in the subclass hierarchy survive.

[F0]
$$
\frac{
\begin{array}{l}
C_0 = \text{class } N \; V^* \; M^*, \\
C_1 = \text{class } N' \text{ subclass of } N \; V^{*\prime} \; M^{*\prime}, \\
C_1' = \text{class } N' \; V^{*\prime} \; V^* \; M^{*\prime} \; M^*
\end{array}
}{
C^* \; C_0 \; C^{*\prime} \; C_1 \; C^{*\prime\prime} = C^* \; C_0 \; C^{*\prime} \; C_1' \; C^{*\prime\prime}
}
$$

The notion of 'super class' in object-oriented programming (Goldberg and Robson, 1983) permits one to refer to a method in the super class that has the same name as a method in the (sub)class, say by explicitly using the word 'super'. The flattening process keeps only the method defined in the subclass. To allow one to access a super class method of the same name the 'redef Id to Id'' construct can be used. This allows one to name the method of interest in the super class using a new name which can be used for accessing the super class method of interest (Meyer, 1988)[1]. Redefinition 'redef Id_0 to Id_0'' is handled in rule [F1] by copying the body 'E' of the method Id_0 to a method with the name Id_0'.

[F1]
$$
\frac{
\begin{array}{l}
C_0 = \text{class } N \; V^{*\prime} \; M^{*\prime} \text{ meth } Id_0 : N_0 \; \textit{Args } E \; M^{*\prime\prime}, \\
C_1 = \text{class } N' \text{ subclass of } N \text{ redef } Id_0 \text{ to } Id_0' \; \textit{Redefs } V^* \; M^*, \\
C_1' = \text{class } N' \text{ subclass of } N \; \textit{Redefs } V^* \; M^* \text{ meth } Id_0' : N_0 \; \textit{Args } E
\end{array}
}{
C^* \; C_0 \; C^{*\prime} \; C_1 \; C^{*\prime\prime} = C^* \; C_0 \; C^{*\prime} \; C_1' \; C^{*\prime\prime}
}
$$

The rules [F2] and [F3] choose the instance variables and method definitions that are closer to the 'class _ ...' over those with the same name that appear later by

---

[1]Note that it is still the intention that any message sent to self should actually prefer a method defined in that (sub)class (Cook, 1989). This means that we should not 'rename' the method (i.e., substitute the new name in the body for the old name) but only redefine the response to a message-send. Meyer (1988) provides both renaming and redefining possibilities.

discarding the latter. This in combination with [F0] and [F1] disregards any instance variables or method definitions in the super classes that are over-ridden by new definitions in the (sub)class.

[F2]   class N V^* var Id : $N1$:= new N $V^{*\prime}$ var Id : N_0 := new N' $V^{*\prime\prime}$ M^*
           = class N V^* var Id : $N1$:= new N $V^{*\prime}$ $V^{*\prime}$ M^*

[F3]   class N V^* M^* meth Id : N' $Args'$ E' $M^{*\prime}$ meth Id : N'' $Args''$ E'' $M^{*\prime\prime}$
           = class N V^* M^* meth Id : N' $Args'$ E' $M^{*\prime}$ $M^{*\prime\prime}$

The above equations give the semantics of inheritance and expansion of the 'subclass of' operator by giving rules that equate a hierarchy of classes to a flat list of classes. The implication of this is that inheritance cannot contribute to our synthesis of static semantics and shall not influence the subtype hierarchy.

It is part of the static semantics to ensure that the class, method and instance variable names used are declared and that the classes are uniquely defined. The static semantics will also ensure that all uses conform to their declarations. Such a type correct program will not halt during execution due to undefined messages and will not need any type annotations during run time.

By rules [F0-F3], the KOOL program given earlier in Figure 3.1 is equivalent to the one given in Figure. 3.2

In Section 3.6, the dynamic semantics is given, by which we can evaluate KOOL terms (e.g., the program in Figure 3.1). The evaluation of the example program would result in the following object (see Module KOOLobj[3.4] below), which is an updated instance of class Boolpair:

```
[ one : [flsid : ( )self,
         cond : (x, y) y,
         and : (y)self . cond (y,new False),
         or : (y)self . cond (new True,y),
         not :( )self . cond (new False,new True)
         ],
    two : << new Bool >>
]
```

Note in the above that the value associated with two is not evaluated. This delayed evaluation is explained in Section 3.6.

3.4 KOOL Objects

A class definition is used to create objects that exist during evaluation. A record or a dictionary is a straightforward representation of these objects (Cardelli, 1984).

```
    class Bool
      meth cond : Bool(x : Bool,y : Bool ) x
      meth and : Bool ( y : Bool )
        self . cond(y,new False )
      meth or : Bool ( y : Bool )
        self . cond(new True,y )
      meth not : Bool( )
        self . cond (new False,new True )
    class True
      meth cond : Bool(x : Bool,y : Bool )x
      meth and : Bool( y : Bool )
        self . cond (y,new False )
      meth or : Bool( y : Bool )
        self . cond (new True,y )
      meth not : Bool( )
        self . cond (new False,new True )
    class False
      meth flsid : False( ) self
      meth cond : Bool(x : Bool,y : Bool )y
      meth and : Bool( y : Bool )
        self . cond (y,new False )
      meth or : Bool( y : Bool )
        self . cond (new True,y )
      meth not : Bool( )
        self . cond (new False,new True )
    class Boolpair
      var one : Bool := new False
      var two : Bool := new True

new Boolpair . one := new False
```

Figure 3.2: Flattened KOOL Bools.

Operations are defined over these objects to lookup and update their fields. In order to represent these associations, Module KOOLobj[3.4] presented below introduces a value pair ('VPAIR'). The identifier serves as the named field of an object. An object ('OBJECT') is a list of value pairs which is itself a value (read 'OBJECT → VALUE' as "an 'OBJECT' is a 'VALUE'"). The '_++_' operation effectively removes any duplicate mappings by choosing the leftmost ones (a property of '_++_'—by [EO5] and [EO6]). An interesting aspect, specific to objects in object-oriented programming, is that the method definitions also exist in an object since objects are dictionaries that map the variable names to values and method names to their values, which are method definitions '(ID-LIST) EXP → VALUE'. During evaluation, such a method could be invoked by sending a message to an object. This is called dynamic binding—of a message to a method.

Module KOOLobj
imports KOOLsyntax[3.3] Booleans[5.A.2]
exports
  sorts OBJECT VALUE VPAIR ID-LIST
  context-free syntax

ID ":" VALUE	→ VPAIR	{**constructor**}
"[" {VPAIR ","}* "]"	→ OBJECT	{**constructor**}
OBJECT	→ VALUE	{**constructor**}
"(" ID-LIST ")" EXP	→ VALUE	{**constructor**}
{ID ","}*	→ ID-LIST	{**constructor**}
OBJECT "++" OBJECT	→ OBJECT	{**left**}
lookup ID in OBJECT	→ VALUE	
update ID in OBJECT by VALUE	→ OBJECT	
ID in OBJECT	→ BOOL	

  variables
    Object $[0\text{-}9']*$ → OBJECT
    Object "+" → OBJECT+
    Object "*" → OBJECT*
    Value $[0\text{-}9']*$ → VALUE
    VP "*"$[0\text{-}9']*$ → {VPAIR ","}*
equations
Look up the value of an identifier. Note that if an identifier *Id* is not defined then the lookup reduces to 'lookup *Id* in []'.

[EO0]   lookup *Id* in [*Id* : *Value*, VP*] = *Value*
[EO1]   lookup *Id* in [*Id'* : *Value*, VP*] = lookup *Id* in [VP*]
                      when $Id \neq Id'$

Update an identifier value; if no value is associated then add an association.

[EO2]   update *Id* in [] by *Value* = [*Id* : *Value*]

[EO3]   update Id in $[Id: Value', VP^*]$ by $Value = [Id: Value] + [VP^*]$

[EO4]
$$\frac{Id \neq Id'}{\begin{array}{l}\text{update } Id \text{ in } [Id': Value', VP^*] \text{ by } Value = \\ [Id': Value'] + \text{update } Id \text{ in } [VP^*] \text{ by } Value\end{array}}$$

Appending two 'OBJECT's yields an 'OBJECT'. Associations in the left one are preferred over those in the right 'OBJECT'.

[EO5] $[VP_1^*, Id: Value, VP_2^*] + [VP_3^*, Id: Value', VP_4^*]$
          $= [VP_1^*, Id: Value, VP_2^*] + [VP_3^*, VP_4^*]$

[EO6] $[VP_1^*] + [VP_3^*] = [VP_1^*, VP_3^*]$ **otherwise**

Test if an identifier has an association.

[EO7] Id in $[VP^*, Id: Value, VP^{*\prime}] = $ true
[EO8] Id in $[VP^*]$ $= $ false **otherwise**

3.5 Value Environment

In an object-oriented language, the only interesting environment during program execution is the one associated with *self*. An environment associated with *self* might maintain argument bindings during a method call, other than instance variable bindings.

The activation stack created for maintaining the history of formal to actual argument mappings during the recursive calls of methods is a value environment. This is represented by an object-stack pair using the notation '$_{-}\lfloor_{-}\rfloor$', where stack is denoted by a list of zero or more objects ('OBJECT*'). The use of 'OBJECT' to represent elements of the stack is (i) convenient, since these are special objects (they do not use the method bindings) and (ii) makes it easy to extend κOOL to a language in which updating of methods, with new method definitions during run-time, is possible (Mitchell, 1990a; Dinesh, 1992; Abadi and Cardelli, 1994).

Sort 'VENV' in Module KOOLvenv[3.5] presented below denotes value environments. We need some operations on value environments to lookup and update; to push and pop the 'stack' and to extract the 'object' from it. 'VENV.ID' searches first the most recent bindings in the environment which represent the formal arguments during a method call (rightmost 'OBJECT' in stack) and then the instance variable bindings (the 'Object' in 'Object$\lfloor_{-}\rfloor$'). This search technique gives us static scoping of variable bindings.

Recursion is facilitated by using 'VENV', '$|_{-}|$' and '$_{-}\lfloor_{-}\rfloor$' operations (see Module KOOLeval[3.6] in the next section). The 'pop($_{-}$)' operation shrinks the 'stack' by removing the rightmost 'OBJECT' from the stack. The value operation '$|_{-}|$' extracts the object from an 'activation stack' or the value environment.

Module KOOLvenv
imports KOOLobj[3.4]
exports
  sorts VENV
  context-free syntax
    OBJECT "⌊" OBJECT∗ "⌋" → VENV   {**constructor**}
    "|" VENV "|"   → OBJECT
    pop(VENV)   → VENV
    push(VENV, OBJECT)   → VENV
    VENV "." ID   → VALUE
    VENV "." ID ":=" VALUE → VENV
equations
Lookup an identifier binding in an environment. This is done by the '_ . _' operation,
which looks-up the top of the activation stack for local bindings and then proceeds
to look for the instance variable bindings i.e., looks-up the 'OBJECT' on the left.
Note that the 'OBJECT's used in the stack hold the parameter bindings during a
method invocation, which are always 'OBJECT' 'VALUE's in the case here (between
⌊⌋). These can also be more general when delegation is allowed (Dinesh, 1992).

[EV1]   *Object* ⌊ ⌋ . *Id*   = lookup *Id* in *Object*
[EV2]   *Object* ⌊ *Object*∗ *Object′* ⌋ . *Id* = lookup *Id* in *Object′*
                             when *Id* in *Object′* = true
[EV9]   *Object* ⌊ *Object*∗ ⌋ . *Id*   = lookup *Id* in *Object* **otherwise**

'pop(_)' and 'push(_,_)' operations help maintain a self environment which is a list of
objects, some representing the variable bindings during a recursive call.

[EV3] | *Object* ⌊ *Object*∗ ⌋ | = *Object*
[EV4]   pop(*Object* ⌊ ⌋)   = *Object* ⌊ ⌋
[EV5]   pop(*Object* ⌊ *Object*∗ *Object′* ⌋) = *Object* ⌊ *Object*∗ ⌋
[EV6]   push(*Object* ⌊ *Object*∗ ⌋ , *Object′*) = *Object* ⌊ *Object*∗ *Object′* ⌋

[EV7]   *Object* ⌊ *Object*∗ ⌋ . *Id* := *Value*
          = update *Id* in *Object* by *Value* ⌊ *Object*∗ ⌋

One could require that the *Id* exists before updating and object in [EV7]. In our
case, the typechecker enforces this.

3.6 Dynamic Semantics

Given a *KOOL* program, which is a list of classes followed by an expression, the
dynamic semantics specifies how this expression is evaluated. In order to achieve this,
we need to be able to instantiate a class (make an object, given a class definition)
which can further be modified as it could receive update messages.

Module KOOLc2o
imports KOOLsyntax[3.3] KOOLvenv[3.5]
exports
  context-free syntax
    c2o "_" CLASSES "[" CID "]" → OBJECT
    "≪" IEXP "≫"   → OBJECT {**constructor**}
hiddens
  context-free syntax
    v2o "[" VAR∗ "]"   → OBJECT
    m2o "[" METHOD∗ "]" → OBJECT

    idl(ARGS)   → ID-LIST
  variables
    Ids → {ID ","}∗
equations
'$c2o_\kappa[N]$' creates the 'OBJECT' representation of the class N.[2]

[EC0]
$$\frac{\kappa \ = \ C^* \ \text{class} \ N \ V^* \ M^* \ C^{*\prime}}{c2o_\kappa[N] \ = \ v2o[V^*] + \!\!+ \ m2o[M^*]}$$

Evaluating an initialization expression is delayed until the value is needed. This is done by marking it with the '≪_≫'. Thus, an instance variable can be initialized to be of the same class as that of where it is defined—we refer to this as (potential) *cyclic instantiations*. Cyclic instantiations are handled by delaying the actual instance creation until necessary.

[EC1]   v2o[]   = []
[EC2]   v2o[var $Id : N' :=$ new $N \ V^*$] = [Id : ≪ new N≫] ++ v2o[V^*]

A method body is basically a lambda abstraction in which there could be references to its environment (i.e., a closure). Thus evaluating the definition is delayed until needed.

[EC3]   m2o[]   = []
[EC4]   m2o[meth $Id : N \ Args \ E \ M^*$] = [Id : (idl($Args$)) E] ++ m2o[M^*]

The role of the function 'idl(_)' is to remove the declared type of the formal argument, since the declared types are only interesting for static semantics.

[EC5]   idl(())   =
[EC6]   idl(($Id : N, Idt^*$)) = Id, Ids **when** idl((Idt^*)) = Ids

---

[2]Note that the "ToLaTeX" facility prints an underscore in a function name in the signature as a "subscript" operation in the equations. For example, the function 'c2o _ CLASSES [CID]' prints as '$c2o_\kappa[N]$' where κ and N are variables of sorts 'CLASSES' and 'CID'.

In Module KOOLeval[3.6] presented below, the function '$[\![\_]\!]$' is the evaluation function. This module describes the evaluation of a program, which is the evaluation of an expression in a given context—resulting in an object. Evaluation of an expression results in a value environment 'VENV', rather than an 'OBJECT', which contains some of the argument binding history (i.e., the activation stack). This argument binding history is used during recursion. Module KOOLeval[3.6] imports Module KOOLc2o[3.6], which defines a function 'c2o$_{\text{CLASSES}}$[CID] $\rightarrow$ OBJECT' that is used to make an object from a class identifier and the class definitions (i.e., an instantiation). Evaluation of the initialization expression ('IEXP') uses this function.

Module KOOLeval

imports KOOLsyntax[3.3] KOOLvenv[3.5] KOOLc2o[3.6]
exports
  sorts OBJECT-LIST
  context-free syntax

"[" PROGRAM "]"	$\rightarrow$ OBJECT
"[" EXP "]" "_" CLASSES VENV	$\rightarrow$ VENV
"(" {EXP ","}* ")" "_" CLASSES VENV	$\rightarrow$ OBJECT-LIST
{OBJECT ","}*	$\rightarrow$ OBJECT-LIST **{constructor}**
"[" {ID ","}* "×" {OBJECT ","}* "]"	$\rightarrow$ OBJECT
"≪" EXP "≫" "_" VENV	$\rightarrow$ OBJECT **{constructor}**
OBJECT "!" CLASSES	$\rightarrow$ OBJECT

  variables

Self [0-9']*	$\rightarrow$ VENV
E "*"	$\rightarrow$ {EXP ","}*
Fargs	$\rightarrow$ {ID ","}*
Aargs	$\rightarrow$ {OBJECT ","}*

equations

Evaluation of the program amounts to evaluation of the expression following the class list, with the self environment being initially empty ([EE1]).

[EE1] $$[\![\kappa\ E]\!] = |\ [\![E]\!]_\kappa[]\ \lfloor\ \rfloor\ |$$

Evaluation of the expression 'self' just returns the self environment '*Self*'.

[EE2] $$[\![\text{self}]\!]_\kappa Self = Self$$

Evaluation of *Id* gets its value from the self environment and implies demand evaluation '_!_' in case it is a "lazy" expression. The 'VALUE' returned by *Self.Id* could either be an object or a method definition. Conditions can be used to handle the two cases separately. The condition in [EE3] ensures that the 'VALUE' obtained by *Self.Id* is an 'OBJECT' rather than a method definition. In equation [EE7] a condition ensures that it is a method definition.

[EE3] $\qquad [Id]_\kappa Self = Object \,! \, \kappa \lfloor \, \rfloor$ **when** $Object = Self . Id$

Evaluation of 'new *N*' is creates a new object from the class definition of *N*.

[EE4] $\qquad\qquad\qquad [new\ N]_\kappa Self = c2o_\kappa[N] \lfloor \, \rfloor$

Evaluation of *E.Id* gets the value of the instance variable *Id* of the object resulting by evaluating *E* (rule [EE5]). Note that evaluation of *Id* behaves slightly different from the evaluation of self.*Id*. From rule [EE3], *Id* can be either a formal argument of a method or an instance variable, while in [EE5] *Id* has to be an instance variable.

[EE5] $\qquad\qquad [E . Id]_\kappa Self = [Id]_\kappa | \, [E]_\kappa Self | \lfloor \, \rfloor$

The evaluation of *E.Id := E'* is an object with the instance variable *Id* mapped to the result of evaluating the expression *E'*. The role of '|_|' in rule [EE6] is to extract the 'object' i.e., not consider the parameter binding history in a self environment.

[EE6] $\qquad \dfrac{Self_0 \; = \; [E]_\kappa Self}{[E . Id := E']_\kappa Self \; = \; Self_0 . Id := | \, [E']_\kappa Self |}$

Rule [EE7] specifies the effect of message send. *E'* is the body of the corresponding method and *Fargs* are the formal arguments. The actual arguments, *Aargs*, are evaluated and bound to the formal arguments and the resulting 'OBJECT' is pushed on the current self environment. The body *E'* of the method is evaluated using this new "self environment". The function 'pop(_)' is used to forget the most recent parameter bindings of formal to actual arguments.

[EE7] $\qquad \dfrac{\begin{array}{c} Self' \; = \; [E]_\kappa Self, \\ Self' . Id \; = \; (Fargs)\ E', \\ Aargs \; = \; (E^*)_\kappa Self \end{array}}{[E . Id(E^*)]_\kappa Self \; = \; pop([E']_\kappa push(Self', [Fargs \times Aargs]))}$

To see that the 'pop(_)' here does remove the parameter bindings relevant to the 'push(_,_)' performed at this stage, we need to consider the six different 'EXP' possibilities (see KOOLsyntax) that the variable *E'* may hold. In other words we check the structure of return environments for the rule cases [EE2]-[EE7], using the [EE7] case as hypothesis. The cases are:

- [EE2] *E'* is 'self'. Here the returned environment is the same. Thus the right bindings are popped.

- [EE3]-[EE5] These return environments with no parameter bindings. Thus the pop does not affect these environments.

- [EE6] An update operation updates an instance variable and does not affect the parameter binding stack associated. Thus the right bindings are popped.

- [EE7] Case of message send. Okay—by induction.

A necessary counterpart of allowing lazy instance variable instantiation is to allow lazy evaluation of arguments of a method. This helps prevent inadvertent demands for instantiation.

[EE8] $$()_\kappa Self =$$

[EE9] $$\frac{Aargs = (E^*)_\kappa Self}{(E, E^*)_\kappa Self = \; \ll E \gg_{Self}, Aargs}$$

The rules [EE10] and [EE11] build an object which reflects the binding between the formal and actual arguments, during a message send.

[EE10] $\qquad [\, \times \,] \qquad\qquad\qquad = [\,]$

[EE11] $\qquad [Id, Fargs \times Object, Aargs] = [Id : Object] \mathbin{+\!\!+} [Fargs \times Aargs]$

The rule [EE12] handles the case of evaluating the default value assigned to an instance variable. This is a lazy evaluation since the initialization expression 'IEXP' is not evaluated unless it is necessary. This allows one to specify a class whose objects can have instance variables that are potentially objects of the same class! This effectively accommodates cyclically instantiatable classes in the presence of static typechecking. Similarly rule [EE13], in conjunction with rules [EE8] and [EE9], allows us to achieve non-strict evaluation of arguments.

[EE12] $\qquad \ll$ new $N \gg ! \, \kappa = |\, [\![$new $N]\!]_\kappa [] \, \lfloor \; \rfloor \, |$

[EE13] $\qquad \ll E \gg_{Self} ! \, \kappa \;\; = |\, [\![E]\!]_\kappa Self \,|$

[EE14] $\qquad Object \, ! \, \kappa \qquad\; = Object \quad \textbf{otherwise}$

We note here that even though '$\ll\_\gg$' is a special case of '$\ll\_\gg\_$', we keep these cases distinct for clarity of 'OBJECT's. The first can be present in an 'OBJECT' while the second can only be present in a 'VENV'.

3.7 From Dynamic Semantics to a Typechecker

After specifying the dynamic semantics of κOOL we need to specify the static semantics that is most appropriate for it. Such a static semantic specification would define only the κOOL programs that would not have any "run time" errors as valid— every message-send results in successful method look-up. If we are not careful it is easy to eliminate many κOOL programs, in this process, as invalid (or type incorrect) programs. One needs to justify, in general, why a given static semantics is the intended one for a given dynamic semantics. We take the approach here of synthesizing the specification of static semantics from the dynamic semantics. We proceed, in the next section, by using types as values where types are appropriate abstract interpretations (Marriott, 1993) of the values. After choosing an appropriate abstract representation, the general procedure adopted is to incrementally adjust the given specification of the dynamic semantics to conform to the new selected (abstract) representation.

*K*OOL facilitates type declarations of formal arguments and return types of methods. The type of an instance variable is obtained from the initialization expression. Class names serve as type names. The usual sub-typing rules (Cardelli, 1984) provide sub-typing in *K*OOL (Dinesh, 1992). Informally, an object of a more specific class can be substituted where an object of a less specific class is expected (expectation is indicated by type declaration).

3.7.1 The Type Environment

A type environment has a structure similar to that of the value environment, with the difference that the values in the type environment are types. In our case, the name of a class ('CID' or class identifier) serves as the type of an object of that class and the argument and return type declaration of a method serves as the type of a method, i.e., '"(" CID-LIST ")" CID'.

We need an abstract representation, at the type level, of an object. For instance, the type of a Boolpair 'VALUE' object in Section 3.5 is "Boolpair" and the type of a Boolpair 'OBJECT' is $\boxed{[\text{ one : Bool, two : Bool]}}$ and the analogous representations of a Bool object are: "Bool" and

```
[ cond: ( Bool,Bool ) Bool,
  and : ( Bool ) Bool,
  or  : ( Bool ) Bool,
  not : ( ) Bool ]
```

The corresponding syntax and semantics for Module KOOLtobj[3.4.1] can be obtained by textual substitution, as shown the following table, in a copy of Module KOOLobj[3.4].

Module KOOLobj[3.4]	Module KOOLtobj[3.4.1]
OBJECT → VALUE	CID → VALUE
"(" ID-LIST ")" EXP → VALUE	"(" ID-LIST ")" CID → VALUE

The result of this substitution forces one to substitute appropriately in the semantics by using 'CID' in the 'VALUE' domain where 'OBJECT' was used in Module KOOLobj[3.4] (see Section 3.A.1).

3.7.2 The Static Semantics

We want the static semantics to follow the dynamic semantics not only for the purpose of easing the justification of static semantics with respect to the dynamic semantics but also to increase our confidence in the completeness of static semantics itself. If these are two independent activities, one needs to show why the static semantics specification is the desired one for a given dynamic semantics. We proceed by using types as values where types are appropriate abstract interpretations (Marriott, 1993) of the values.

After choosing an appropriate abstract representation, the general procedure adopted is to copy the other modules (give new names), import the analogous modules (of static semantics) and try to parse the specification. The errors that result during the parsing (indicating wrong use of sorts) dictate the required modifications to the specification. For example, we copy Module KOOLc2o$^{3.6}$ to Module KOOLc2t$^{3.A.3}$, import Module KOOLtenv$^{3.A.2}$ instead of Module KOOLvenv$^{3.5}$ in Module KOOLc2t$^{3.A.3}$ and try parsing it.

In Module KOOLc2t$^{3.A.3}$ some straightforward modifications were necessary to the definition of function 'c2o' so that it now returns an 'OBJECT' which uses type signatures as values. One can compare the modules in Section 3.6 and Section 3.A.3.

Again, we repeat the procedure for Module KOOLeval$^{3.6}$ and obtain an analogous Module KOOLtval$^{3.A.5}$. Module KOOLtval$^{3.A.5}$ (see appendix 3.A.5 of this chapter), thus, evaluates an expression at the "type level" in an analogous manner to that seen in the corresponding Module KOOLeval$^{3.6}$. The following equations differ from the corresponding ones in the KOOLeval$^{3.6}$ specification, in a non-trivial manner, which must be justified:

- The lookup function 'Self . Id' in Module KOOLvenv$^{3.5}$ needs to look into the object structure. However an abstract object is an identifier and not a structure that can be looked-up. An analogous function can be defined for abstract objects by using the class definitions (i.e., function 'Self .$_\kappa$ Id') to help construct the representative object structure.

[TE3] $[\![Id]\!]_\kappa Self = AbsObj \lfloor \ \rfloor$ **when** $AbsObj = Self._\kappa Id$

Subtypes To provide for substitutability of more specific objects where less specific ones were expected, we need to be able to specify when the type information of one class is a subtype of another. We use names to denote classes. The basic strategy is to assume the intended subtype relationship and proceed by checking the associated type environments. This is similar to the idea used for checking the structural similarity of Pascal records by Fleck (1984).

A specification of any suitable subtype notion is permissible. The one we use is given in Section 3.A.4. The specification of the rest of the static semantics only assumes the ability to check subtypes.

- When we compare the equation [TE6] to [EE6] of Module KOOLeval[3.6], we see that the update function 'VENV . ID := VALUE' has been adopted to meet the needs of type evaluation. In KOOLeval[3.6], update returns an updated environment. During type evaluation, we are not interested in updating an environment but in checking if the value being updated conforms to the declaration. This conformance in our case is determined by checking if the type of the update value is a subtype of the exisiting value type. We choose to replace the use of 'update' by conditions that do this check, instead of modifying the function 'update', since checking for subtype satisfaction requires class definitions (i.e., κ). Note that Module KOOLtenv[3.A.2] does not contain 'update' functions analogous to that of Module KOOLvenv[3.5]. Instead this check is done in equation [TE6] which justifies it (compare this to the corresponding equation [EE6] in Module KOOLeval[3.6]), given the rules in Module KOOLsub[3.4.4].

$$[TE6] \quad \frac{Self_0 \;=\; [\![E]\!]_\kappa Self, \qquad \vdash_\kappa | \; [\![E']\!]_\kappa Self \, | \; \leq Self_0 \, ._\kappa Id \;=\; true}{[\![E \,.\, Id := E']\!]_\kappa Self \;=\; Self_0}$$

- Actual argument passing requires a check on whether the types of the arguments being passed are subtypes of what is declared—one cannot assume anything more than what is declared. This is sound, assuming that the body of the method is type consistent (Section 3.7.3). So, during evaluation at the type level we do not need to push on the stack, but we only need to check that the actual argument types are subtypes of formal argument types. This check is done by the condition $Aargs \leq_\kappa Fargs$=true which uses subtype checking as defined in Module KOOLsub[3.4.4].

$$[TE7] \quad \frac{Self' \;=\; [\![E]\!]_\kappa Self, \qquad Self' \, ._\kappa Id \;=\; (Fargs)\, N, \qquad Aargs \;=\; (E^*)_\kappa Self, \qquad Aargs \leq_\kappa Fargs \;=\; true}{[\![E \,.\, Id(E^*)]\!]_\kappa Self \;=\; N \lfloor \; \rfloor}$$

Note that [EE7] could lead to non-termination during evaluation, since it covers the dynamic semantics of recursive method calls (more precisely since the expression being evaluated on the right-hand side need not be a sub-expression of the one on the left-hand side). However, [TE7] clearly terminates provided that subtype checking (the last condition) terminates.

3.7.3 Typechecking

Using Module KOOLtval[3.4.5] which can evaluate an expression at the type level, it is now straightforward to iteratively check all method expressions of the classes in the program. The function 'tc(_)' defined in Module KOOLtc[3.7.3] typechecks each class, while gathering any erroneous constructs (see also Chapter 4). If there are no erroneous constructs, 'tc' returns true. Another module, KOOLerrors[3.7.3], is defined for the purpose of characterizing the κOOL errors. This module is used for presenting the errors in a user-friendly manner as opposed to simply dumping the erroneous constructs.

Let us reconsider the BoolPair example of Figure 3.1. If we modify the class Boolpair and the main expression to

```
%% Classes Bool, True and False as defined earlier

    class Boolpair
        var one:Bool := new Bol
        var two:False := new True

new Boolpair . three := new True
```

and typecheck this κOOL program by means of the term 'errors(tc(Program))', we get three error messages:

```
unknown-class Bol;
undefined-method flsid not-subtype-of ( ) False;
error-in-expression new Boolpair.three := new True
```

Module KOOLtc

imports KOOLtval[3.4.5]

exports

  sorts EROID

    The sort EROID defines an error monoid that uses the *'true'* of Booleans as its identity element.

  context-free syntax

tc(PROGRAM)	→ EROID
tc "_" CLASSES "(" CLASSES ")"	→ EROID
isok "_" CLASSES "(" CID ")"	→ EROID
"[" ARGS "]"	→ OBJECT
BOOL	→ EROID
EROID "∧" EROID	→ EROID {**left**}

  variables

$$
\begin{array}{ll}
Program & \to \text{PROGRAM} \\
Er\ [01]* & \to \text{EROID} \\
V\ \text{"+"} & \to \text{VAR+} \\
M\ \text{"+"} & \to \text{METHOD+}
\end{array}
$$

equations

[TC0] $\qquad$ $\text{tc}(\kappa\ E) \qquad = \text{tc}_\kappa(\kappa) \wedge \text{isok}_\kappa([\![\kappa\ E]\!])$

[TC1] $\qquad$ $\text{tc}_\kappa(C\ C'\ C^*) = \text{tc}_\kappa(C) \wedge \text{tc}_\kappa(C'\ C^*)$

Typechecking a class is basically to walk through its declarations. A class without methods or variable declarations is type correct. A class with variable declarations is type correct, if each of the declarations is correct.

[TC2] $\qquad$ $\text{tc}_\kappa(\text{class } N\ ) \qquad\qquad\qquad = \text{true}$

[TC3] $\qquad$ $\text{tc}_\kappa(\text{class } N \text{ var } Id : N_0 := \text{new } N'\ ) = N' \leq_\kappa N_0$

[TC4] $\qquad$ $\text{tc}_\kappa(\text{class } N\ V\ V^+\ M^*) = \text{tc}_\kappa(\text{class } N\ V) \wedge \text{tc}_\kappa(\text{class } N\ V^+\ M^*)$

A method definition is *type consistent* when the type evaluation value of the method body, using the type declaration of formal arguments, is a subtype of its declaration. The type evaluation of the body, using the class name as the abstract self and the argument declarations as the abstract argument values, results in an environment. The '$\lfloor\_\rfloor$' of which is the type value of the body. [TC6] handles the case of two or more methods in a class.

[TC5] $\text{tc}_\kappa(\text{class } N \text{ meth } Id : N'\ Args\ E) = \lfloor [\![E]\!]_\kappa N \lfloor [Args] \rfloor \rfloor \leq_\kappa N'$

[TC6] $\text{tc}_\kappa(\text{class } N\ V^*\ M\ M^+) \qquad = \text{tc}_\kappa(\text{class } N\ M) \wedge \text{tc}_\kappa(\text{class } N\ V^*\ M^+)$

[TC7] $\text{tc}_\kappa(\text{class } N\ V\ M) \qquad\qquad = \text{tc}_\kappa(\text{class } N\ V) \wedge \text{tc}_\kappa(\text{class } N\ M)$

Convert the argument list into an object format.

[TCa0] $\qquad\qquad$ $[()] \qquad\qquad = []$

[TCa1] $\qquad\qquad$ $[(Id : N, Idt^*)] = [Id : N] \mathbin{+\!\!+} [(Idt^*)]$

A class should be uniquely defined.

[TCok] $\qquad$
$$
\frac{\kappa\ =\ C^* \text{ class } N\ V^*\ M^*\ C^{*\prime},\ \text{ok}_{C^{\bullet}\ C^{*\prime}} N \neq \text{true}}{\text{isok}_\kappa(N)\ =\ \text{true}}
$$

The *true* of BOOL is used as the identity element of the error monoid.

[TEid0] $\qquad\qquad\qquad$ $\text{true} \wedge Er = Er$

[TEid1] $\qquad\qquad\qquad$ $Er \wedge \text{true} = Er$

Module KOOLerrors

imports KOOLtc[3.7.3]

exports

  sorts MSG MSGS MTEXT

  lexical syntax

    $[a\text{-}z\backslash-]+ \to$ MTEXT

  context-free syntax

    errors(PROGRAM) $\to$ MSGS

    msgs(EROID) $\to$ MSGS

    MSGS "++" MSGS $\to$ MSGS

    {MSG ";"}* $\to$ MSGS

    MTEXT $\to$ MSG   {**constructor**}

    MSG MSG $\to$ MSG   {**left, constructor**}

    EXP $\to$ MSG   {**constructor**}

    VALUE $\to$ MSG   {**constructor**}

    CID $\to$ MSG   {**constructor**}

  variables

    $Msg \qquad \to$ MSG

    Msg "*"$[']$* $\to$ {MSG ";"}*

equations

The following rules help reduce the clutter and give readable messages.

[TE1]   errors($Program$) = msgs(tc($Program$))

[TE2a]   msgs($Er_0 \wedge Er_1$)   = msgs(Er_0) ++ msgs(Er_1)

[TE2b]   msgs($Bool_0 \wedge Bool_1$) = msgs($Bool_0$) ++ msgs($Bool_1$)

[TE3a]   msgs(ok$_\kappa$| $[\![E]\!]_{C^\bullet}Self$|) = **error-in-expression** E

[TE3b]   msgs(ok$_\kappa N$)   = **unknown-class** N **otherwise**

[TE4a]   msgs(isok$_\kappa$(| $[\![E]\!]_{C^\bullet}Self$|)) = **error-in-expression** E

[TE4b]   msgs(isok$_\kappa$(N))   = **class-name** N **should-be-unique**

                                            when ok$_\kappa N$ = true

[TE4b]   msgs(isok$_\kappa$(N))   = **unknown-class** N **otherwise**

[TE5a]   msgs($\vdash_{C^\bullet}$| $[\![E]\!]_\kappa Self$| $\leq AbsObj$)   = **subtype-problem** E

[TE5b]   msgs($\vdash_\kappa$c2o$_\kappa[N] \leq Object$)   = **subtype-problem new** N

[TE5c]   msgs($\Gamma \vdash_\kappa Value \leq Value'$)   = $Value$ **not-subtype-of** $Value'$

[TE6]   msgs(tc$_\kappa$(class N subclass of N')) = **unknown-class** N'

[TE7]   msgs(true) = no-errors
[TE8]   msgs($Bool$) = uncatchable-errors   **otherwise**

[TE9a]   lookup Id in [] not-subtype-of $Value$
          = undefined-method Id not-subtype-of $Value$

[TE9b] lookup Id in $c2o_\kappa[N]$ not-subtype-of $Value$ = unknown-class N
[TE9c] unknown-class $|\,[\![E]\!]_{C}\cdot Self\,|$ = error-in-expression E

[TEr1] Msg^* ++ $Msg^{*\prime}$ = Msg^*; $Msg^{*\prime}$
[TEr2] Msg^*; Msg; $Msg^{*\prime}$; Msg; $Msg^{*\prime\prime}$ = Msg^*; Msg; $Msg^{*\prime}$; $Msg^{*\prime\prime}$
[TEr3] Msg^*; uncatchable-errors; $Msg^{*\prime}$ = Msg^*; $Msg^{*\prime}$
                        when Msg; $Msg^{*\prime\prime}$ = Msg^*; $Msg^{*\prime}$

3.8   Conclusions

The dynamic semantics of a kernel object language has been completely specified. We have explained the details of producing a specification of its static semantics, with the help of the ASF+SDF parser/typechecker, by substitution of an abstract domain in place of the value domain used in the dynamic semantics specification. The essential changes that were required to obtain the static semantics have been justified. Justification could otherwise be challenging (Barbuti and Martelli, 1983).

Another advantage of an abstract interpretation style of typechecking is modularity. This is elaborated in Chapter 4.

Doh and Schmidt (1992) extract strong typing rules from action semantics definitions. They use the typing functions of the action combinators to derive the typing functions from a given action semantics definition. They are able to use the built-in domains of action semantics for this process. In our case, we do not assume any built-in domains. If we extend κOOL with some predefined data types, we should also use the specific properties of these data types during the derivation of static semantics.

We could use a test similar to constructor completeness (Kapur *et al.*, 1987) to further aid in the derivation of a typechecker and error-reporter specification. It would be useful to have syntax-directed editing tools to help in the process of abstract domain substitution. Parameterized modules would have also helped towards this. It would also be an interesting exercise to extend the language κOOL so as to allow polymorphic method definitions. In this case, the derivation of static semantics will have to use the context information as well.

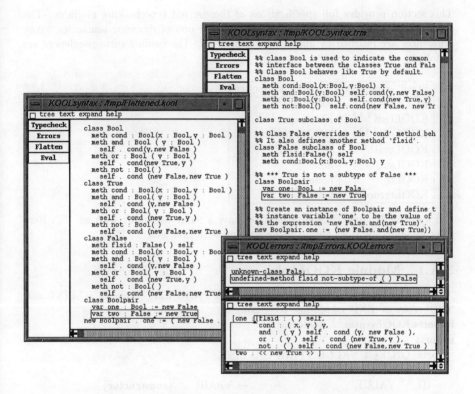

Figure 3.3: Example of the generated KOOL environment.

The KOOLsyntax window in front is the result of pressing the Flatten button which just reduces the term in the KOOLsyntax window behind to its normal form. The KOOLerrors window is the result of pressing the Errors button which applies the function 'errors(_)' to the result of applying function 'tc(_)' to the term in the window. The other window has the result of pressing the Eval button. Note that the term could evaluate even though it has some type errors.

Appendices

3.A   Type Evaluation of an Expression

This section provides full specifications of the derived typechecking modules. The specification is for the most part similar to the one of dynamic semantics. Any differences are justified by appropriate comments. The module correspondences are as follows:

Static semantics	Dynamic semantics
KOOLtobj$^{3.4.1}$	KOOLobj$^{3.4}$
KOOLtenv$^{3.4.2}$	KOOLvenv$^{3.5}$
KOOLc2t$^{3.4.3}$	KOOLc2o$^{3.6}$
KOOLtval$^{3.4.5}$	KOOLeval$^{3.6}$
KOOLsub$^{3.4.4}$	none
KOOLtc$^{3.7.3}$	none
KOOLerrors$^{3.7.3}$	none

Rules in the dynamic semantics modules have a name beginning with an "E". Here the corresponding rules have a name starting with first letter: "T".

3.A.1   Module KOOLtobj

'CID' is used as an abstract value for 'OBJECT'. 'CID-LIST' replaces 'ID-LIST' and 'CID' replaces 'EXP' of Module KOOLobj$^{3.4}$.

imports KOOLsyntax$^{3.3}$ Booleans$^{5.A.2}$

exports

  sorts OBJECT VALUE VPAIR CID-LIST

  context-free syntax

ID ":" VALUE	→ VPAIR	{**constructor**}
"[" {VPAIR ","}* "]"	→ OBJECT	{**constructor**}
CID	→ VALUE	{**constructor**}
"(" CID-LIST ")" CID	→ VALUE	{**constructor**}
{CID ","}*	→ CID-LIST	{**constructor**}
OBJECT "++" OBJECT	→ OBJECT	{**left**}
lookup ID in OBJECT	→ VALUE	
update ID in OBJECT by VALUE	→ OBJECT	
ID in OBJECT	→ BOOL	

  variables

    Object [0-9']* → OBJECT

    Object "+" → OBJECT+

    Object "*" → OBJECT*

Value $[0\text{-}9']* \;\rightarrow$ VALUE
VP "*"$[0\text{-}9']* \rightarrow$ {VPAIR ","}*

equations
None of these rules need modification.

[TO0]	lookup *Id* in [*Id* : *Value*, VP*] = *Value*
[TO1]	lookup *Id* in [*Id'* : *Value*, VP*] = lookup *Id* in [VP*]

when $Id \neq Id'$

[TO2]	update *Id* in [] by *Value* = [*Id* : *Value*]
[TO3]	update *Id* in [*Id* : *Value'*, VP*] by *Value* = [*Id* : *Value*] ++ [VP*]

[TO4]
$$\frac{Id \neq Id'}{\begin{array}{l}\text{update } Id \text{ in } [Id' : Value', VP^*] \text{ by } Value = \\ {[Id' : Value']} \\ +\!\!+ \text{ update } Id \text{ in } [VP^*] \text{ by } Value\end{array}}$$

[TO5]
$$[VP_1^*, Id: Value, VP_2^*] +\!\!+ [VP_3^*, Id: Value', VP_4^*]$$
$$= [VP_1^*, Id: Value, VP_2^*] +\!\!+ [VP_3^*, VP_4^*]$$

[TO6]
$$[VP_1^*] +\!\!+ [VP_3^*] = [VP_1^*, VP_3^*] \quad \textbf{otherwise}$$

[TO7]	*Id* in [VP*, *Id* : *Value*, VP*'] = true
[TO8]	*Id* in [VP*] = false **otherwise**

3.A.2   Module KOOLtenv

An environment is composed of an abstract OBJECT (i.e., CID) and its "activation stack". Also note that some functions that used the structure of OBJECT cannot be defined here now. These will be defined when needed (see Section 3.A.5).
imports KOOLtobj[3.A.1]
exports
  sorts VENV
  context-free syntax
    CID "⌊" OBJECT* "⌋" → VENV {**constructor**}
    "|" VENV "|"   → CID
    pop(VENV)   → VENV
    push(VENV, OBJECT) → VENV
  variables

$AbsObj \rightarrow$ CID

equations

The following equations are modified by replacing variable *Object* by variable *AbsObj*.

[TV3]	$\mid AbsObj \lfloor Object^* \rfloor \mid$	$= AbsObj$
[TV4]	$pop(AbsObj \lfloor \ \rfloor)$	$= AbsObj \lfloor \ \rfloor$
[TV5]	$pop(AbsObj \lfloor Object^* \ Object' \rfloor)$	$= AbsObj \lfloor Object^* \rfloor$
[TV6]	$push(AbsObj \lfloor Object^* \rfloor , Object')$	$= AbsObj \lfloor Object^* \ Object' \rfloor$

3.A.3 Module KOOLc2t

The choice to use 'CID-LIST' as type representation of 'ID-LIST' in Module KOOLtobj[3.A.1] suggests the definition of 'cidl(_)' below instead of the 'idl(_)' defined in Module KOOLc2o[3.6]. Also, '≪ _ ≫' is discarded since typechecking is eager.

imports KOOLsyntax[3.3] KOOLtenv[3.A.2]

exports
  context-free syntax
    c2o "_" CLASSES "[" CID "]" $\rightarrow$ OBJECT

hiddens
  context-free syntax
    v2o "[" VAR∗ "]" $\qquad \rightarrow$ OBJECT
    m2o "[" METHOD∗ "]" $\rightarrow$ OBJECT

    cidl(ARGS) $\qquad\qquad \rightarrow$ CID-LIST

hiddens
  variables
    N "*" $\rightarrow$ {CID ","}∗

equations

$$[TC0] \qquad \frac{\kappa \ = \ C^* \ \text{class} \ N \ V^* \ M^* \ C^{*\prime}}{c2o_\kappa[N] \ = \ v2o[V^*] +\!\!+ m2o[M^*]}$$

The 'VALUE's in an 'OBJECT' are appropriately adjusted. The type of an instance variable is its declaration.

[TC1]	$v2o[]$	$= []$
[TC2]	$v2o[var \ Id : N' := new \ N \ V^*]$	$= [Id : N'] +\!\!+ v2o[V^*]$

The type of a method is the type declaration used.

[TC3]	$m2o[]$	$= []$
[TC4]	$m2o[meth \ Id : N \ Args \ E \ M^*]$	$= [Id : (cidl(Args)) \ N] +\!\!+ m2o[M^*]$

The role of the function 'cidl(_)' is to disregard the identifier associated with a type, of the formal argument, since only the declared types are of interest for static semantics.

[TC5]   cidl(()) =

[TC6] $cidl((Id : N, Idt^*)) = N, N^*$ **when** $cidl((Idt^*)) = N^*$

3.A.4   Module KOOLsub

imports KOOLsyntax[3.3] KOOLtenv[3.A.2] KOOLc2t[3.A.3]
exports
  sorts SUBTYPE
  context-free syntax
    CID "$\leq$" CID $\rightarrow$ SUBTYPE {**constructor**}

    SUBTYPE* "⊢" "_" CLASSES OBJECT "$\leq$" OBJECT $\rightarrow$ BOOL
    SUBTYPE* "⊢" "_" CLASSES VALUE "$\leq$" VALUE $\rightarrow$ BOOL
    ok "_" CLASSES CID $\rightarrow$ BOOL
  variables
    "Γ"['']* $\rightarrow$ SUBTYPE*
hiddens
  context-free syntax
    SUBTYPE* "⊢" CID "$\leq$" CID $\rightarrow$ BOOL
  variables
    Fargs [0-9']* $\rightarrow$ {CID ","}*
equations
Equations [ST1a] to [ST1b] provide for checking the conformance of objects. Every 'OBJECT' should conform to an empty object ([ST1a]). The type of a variable or method name should conform to its corresponding type ([ST1b]).

[ST1a] $\Gamma \vdash_\kappa Object \leq [] = true$

[ST1b] $\Gamma \vdash_\kappa Object \leq [Id : Value, VP^*]$
         $= \Gamma \vdash_\kappa lookup\ Id\ in\ Object \leq Value \wedge \Gamma \vdash_\kappa Object \leq [VP^*]$

The predicate 'SUBTYPE* ⊢ _ $\leq$ _' checks if the SUBTYPE list either already has the given assumption or if it is the reflexive case. Also, on the assumption that no reflexive cases are explicitly assumed, it checks if the contrary is also assumed ([ST2c]). Correctness of [ST2b] and [ST2c] relies on not having duplicate assumptions in Γ.

[ST2a] $\Gamma \vdash N \leq N$ = true
[ST2b] $\Gamma\ N \leq N'\ \Gamma' \vdash N \leq N'$ = true   **when** $\Gamma\ \Gamma' \vdash N' \leq N$ = false
[ST2c] $\Gamma\ N \leq N'\ \Gamma' \vdash N \leq N'$ = false **when** $\Gamma\ \Gamma' \vdash N' \leq N$ = true
[ST2d] $\Gamma \vdash N \leq N'$ = false **otherwise**

Equations [ST3a] to [ST3d] provide the true cases for 'VALUE' comparisons. [ST3a] and [ST3b] handle the 'CID' cases of two 'CID's to be compared. In the first case, the assumption is already part of Γ, in the last it is not yet, and a new assumption is added, for which checking the associated environments is proceeded.

[ST3a] $\qquad \Gamma \vdash_\kappa N \leq N' = \text{true} \quad \textbf{when} \ \Gamma \vdash N \leq N' = \text{true}$

[ST3b] $\qquad \Gamma \vdash_\kappa N \leq N' = \text{ok}_\kappa N \wedge \text{ok}_\kappa N' \wedge N \leq N' \ \Gamma \vdash_\kappa c2o_\kappa[N] \leq c2o_\kappa[N']$
$\qquad\qquad \textbf{when} \ \Gamma \vdash N \leq N' = \text{false}$

The equations [ST3c] and [ST3d] handle the method types. Note that the arguments of the methods are checked for contra-variance ([ST3d]).

[ST3c] $\qquad\qquad \Gamma \vdash_\kappa () \ N \leq () \ N' = \Gamma \vdash_\kappa N \leq N'$

[ST3d] $\qquad\qquad \Gamma \vdash_\kappa (N''', Fargs) \ N \leq (N''', Fargs') \ N'$
$\qquad = \Gamma \vdash_\kappa N''' \leq N'' \wedge \Gamma \vdash_\kappa (Fargs) \ N \leq (Fargs') \ N'$

The predicate 'ok_' is true only if the 'CID' can be instantiated.

[ST4] $\qquad\qquad \text{ok}_\kappa N = \text{true} \quad \textbf{when} \ c2o_\kappa[N] = [VP^*]$

3.A.5 Module KOOLtval

Here we have to consider what might be the most desired analogous representation of evaluating a program at the type level. We have chosen to keep the name of the class 'CID' as the abstract representation of an 'OBJECT' for the result of 'PROGRAM' "evaluation". This requires that appropriate return values for other functions be chosen. We choose 'CID' where 'VALUE' was used in KOOLeval[3.6]. Thus, we have 'CID-LIST' instead of 'VALUE-LIST' of KOOLeval[3.6]. An important function that checks type conformance is introduced that extends the conformance definition to lists of 'CID's. '$\ll$ _ $\gg$_' is discarded—typechecking is eager.

imports KOOLsyntax[3.3] KOOLtenv[3.A.2] KOOLc2t[3.A.3] KOOLsub[3.A.4]

exports

  context-free syntax

"[" PROGRAM "]"	$\rightarrow$ CID
"[" EXP "]" "_" CLASSES VENV	$\rightarrow$ VENV
"(" {EXP ","}* ")" "_" CLASSES VENV	$\rightarrow$ CID-LIST
{CID ","}* "$\leq$" "_" CLASSES {CID ","}*	$\rightarrow$ BOOL
VENV "." "_" CLASSES ID	$\rightarrow$ VALUE

  variables

$$Self\ [0\text{-}9']* \rightarrow \text{VENV}$$
$$E\ \text{``*''} \qquad \rightarrow \{\text{EXP ``,''}\}*$$
$$Fargs \qquad \rightarrow \{\text{CID ``,''}\}*$$
$$Aargs \qquad \rightarrow \{\text{CID ``,''}\}*$$

equations

[TE1] $$[\![\kappa\ E]\!] = \lfloor\ [\![E]\!]_\kappa \text{None}\ \lfloor\ \rfloor\ \rfloor$$

[TE2] $$[\![\text{self}]\!]_\kappa Self = Self$$

[TE3] $$[\![Id]\!]_\kappa Self = AbsObj \lfloor\ \rfloor \quad \textbf{when} \ \ AbsObj \ = \ Self._\kappa Id$$

[TE4] $$[\![\text{new } N]\!]_\kappa Self = N \lfloor\ \rfloor$$

[TE5] $$[\![E\ .\ Id]\!]_\kappa Self = [\![Id]\!]_\kappa \lfloor\ [\![E]\!]_\kappa Self \rfloor\ \lfloor\ \rfloor$$

The rules [TE6] and [TE7] are justified in Section 3.7.2.

[TE6]
$$\frac{Self_0 \ = \ [\![E]\!]_\kappa Self,}{\vdash_\kappa \lfloor\ [\![E']\!]_\kappa Self \rfloor \leq Self_0\ ._\kappa Id \ = \ \text{true}}{[\![E\ .\ Id := E']\!]_\kappa Self \ = \ Self_0}$$

[TE7]
$$\frac{\begin{array}{c}Self' \ = \ [\![E]\!]_\kappa Self, \\ Self'\ ._\kappa Id \ = \ (Fargs)\ N, \\ Aargs \ = \ (E^*)_\kappa Self, \\ Aargs \leq_\kappa Fargs \ = \ \text{true}\end{array}}{[\![E\ .\ Id(E^*)]\!]_\kappa Self \ = \ N \lfloor\ \rfloor}$$

[TE8] $$()_\kappa Self =$$

Again, since we do not want to delay checking arguments, we modify [TE9] for eager evaluation.

[TE9]
$$\frac{Aargs \ = \ (E^*)_\kappa Self}{(E, E^*)_\kappa Self \ = \ \lfloor\ [\![E]\!]_\kappa Self \rfloor, Aargs}$$

The following function helps checking conformance of arguments. Its modification rationale is similar to that of [TE6].

[TE10] $$\leq_\kappa = \text{true}$$

[TE11] $AbsObj, Aargs \leq_\kappa N, Fargs$
                 $= \vdash_\kappa AbsObj \leq N \wedge Aargs \leq_\kappa Fargs$

The equations [EE12]-[EE14] dealt with 'lazy objects' and these are not needed here since typechecking should be eager ('$\ll\_\gg\_$' of KOOLeval[3.6] should be eliminated).

In Module KOOLtenv[3.A.2], we had to delay defining the notion of looking inside an abstract object i.e., a function analogous to 'lookup _ in _' of Module KOOLvenv[3.5]. This can now be defined using 'κ'—the class definitions, to 'concretize' the abstract value and then look inside this concrete object.

[TV8] $AbsObj \lfloor Object^* \ Object \rfloor ._\kappa Id = \text{lookup } Id \text{ in } Object$
                                                   when $Id \text{ in } Object = $ true
[TV9] $AbsObj \lfloor Object^* \rfloor ._\kappa Id \qquad = \text{lookup } Id \text{ in } c2o_\kappa[AbsObj]$ **otherwise**

3.B   A Larger Example

Here we extend the κOOL conditionals of Figure 3.1 with natural numbers and a "clock" which can tick a number of times. The ticker class counts the depth of the instantiations stored in the instance variable `tick`. Observe that the definition of the method `ticks` contains a typing error.

```
%% The classes Bool, True and False are extended here
%% with method ncond. The cond method expects only Bool arguments
%% and it is type-incorrect to pass it Nat arguments. In order to
%% do this we define ncond that accepts Nat arguments.

class Bool
  meth cond:Bool(x:Bool,y:Bool) x
  meth ncond:Nat(x:Nat,y:Nat) x
  meth and:Bool(y:Bool) self.cond(y,new False)
  meth or:Bool(y:Bool)  self.cond(new True,y)
  meth not:Bool() self.cond(new False, new True)

class True subclass of Bool

class False subclass of Bool
  meth flsid:False() self
  meth cond:Bool(x:Bool,y:Bool) y
  meth ncond:Nat(x:Nat,y:Nat) y

%% In the Nat class below, the methods setto, incr and decr
%% are just excercises with complex expressions. incr() emulates
%% succ(), decr() emulates prev() and y.setto(x) emulates x.
```

```
class Nat
  var isz : Bool   := new True
  var pre : Nat := new Nat
  meth iszero:Bool() isz
  meth succ:Nat() (self.pre := self).isz := new False
  meth pred:Nat() self.pre
  meth less:Bool(i:Nat)
    i.iszero().cond(new True, self.pred().less(i.pred()))
  meth setto:Nat(x:Nat) x.iszero()
              .ncond(((self.isz:=new True).pre:=self),
                     ((self.isz:=new False).pre:=(x.pred()))))
  meth incr:Nat() new Nat.setto(self).succ()
  meth decr:Nat() self.iszero().
    ncond(self,(self.isz := (pre.iszero())).pre := (pre.pred()))

class Ticker
  var tick : Ticker := new Ticker
  meth ticks:Ticker(i:Nat)
    i.iszero().ncond(self, self.tick := (self.ticks(i.pred())))

new Ticker.ticks(new Nat.incr().incr().incr())
```

Evaluation of the above program yields the following instance with three "ticks":

```
[tick:
 [tick:
  [tick:
   [tick: << new Ticker >>
   ,ticks:(i)i.iszero().ncond(self,self.tick:=(self.ticks(i.pred())))]
   ,ticks:(i)i.iszero().ncond(self,self.tick:=(self.ticks(i.pred())))]
  ,ticks:(i)i.iszero().ncond(self,self.tick:=(self.ticks(i.pred())))]
 ,ticks:(i)i.iszero().ncond(self,self.tick:=(self.ticks(i.pred())))]
```

Typechecking the complete program yields the following message:

```
error-in-expression
  i.iszero().ncond(self, self.tick:=self.ticks(i.pred()))
```

This expression is the body of the method ticks. It cannot check okay since the "ncond" expects Nat whereas it is passed a Ticker. One can easily fix this by defining a "tcond" similar to "ncond" but with appropriate type declarations for the arguments, i.e., Ticker instead of Nat. This example also indicates a case where the typechecker complains even though there can be no run-time errors!

4

Typechecking with Modular Error Handling

T.B. Dinesh

Abstract Static semantics only determines the validity of a program but is not concerned with the pragmatic issues such as the location in the program where a violation of the static semantics occurred or even a textual explanation of the cause of that violation. A typechecker extends the specification of static semantics with facilities for identifying and presenting the type errors in invalid programs.

We discuss a style of algebraically specifying the static semantics of a language which facilitates the automatic generation of a typechecker and a language specific error reporter. Such a specification can also be extended in a modular manner to yield human-readable error messages.

4.1 Introduction

Static semantics only determines the validity of a program but is not concerned with the pragmatic issues such as the location in the program where a violation of the static semantics occurred or even a textual explanation of the cause of that violation. A typechecker extends the specification of static semantics with facilities for identifying and presenting the type errors in invalid programs. Thus, specifying a typechecker that is useful in practice results in (textually) modifying the specification of static semantics to "knit" in the reporting of the nature and location of type errors. Adding such reporting information about the details of typechecking into the specification of static semantics is a lot of work and is error prone.

We discuss different styles of specifying typecheckers and present a specification style which facilitates the generation of an error reporting tool that automatically locates the erroneous constructs. This specification style advocates the concise and abstract specification of static semantics. A significant advantage of this style is that error handling (providing a summary of type errors) need not be knit in the typechecker specification, but can be specified as a modular extension to the static semantics.

To illustrate our specification style, we use the toy language Pico (Bergstra *et al.*, 1989). Pico programs consist of declarations followed by statements. The syntax and a brief description of Pico can be found in the Appendix 4.A. The small size of Pico allows us to discuss different styles used in the specifications in detail.

In Section 4.2 we examine a "classical" style of specifying static semantics of Pico (Bergstra *et al.*, 1989, Chapter 9), and show how it is modified to serve as a useful typechecker in practice. Then we introduce an alternative style, the *modular errors* style, that helps to achieve this automatically. In Section 4.3 we illustrate the general notion of *origin tracking* which facilitates the automatic generation of an error reporter. In Section 4.4 we discuss *tokenization*, to assure sufficient origins, since the standard notion of *origin tracking* (primary+secondary origins as introduced in Section 7.2) is insufficient for our case. In Section 4.5 we discuss some related work.

4.2   Typechecker Specifications

We first introduce what we refer to as the classical style of specifying static semantics/typechecking[1]. After discussing its problems, in Section 4.2.2, we illustrate what we refer to as the *modular errors* style which introduces types (abstract values) to value domains in the language and interprets the language constructs at the type level. Naur (1965) used this style for typechecking expressions in Algol.

4.2.1   Classical Style

A straightforward specification of a typechecker for Pico was described by Bergstra *et al.* (1989). It was done using a type-environment (sort TENV, see Appendix 4.A), which is a table used to maintain the associations between identifiers and their type declarations. The typechecking was specified as shown in the module below. The function tc(_) returns a BOOL result. Checking the statement series using the type-environment results in a BOOL, and checking whether two types are the same results in a BOOL. Extracting the type of an expression using the type-environment results in a TYPE (either natural or string).

Module Pico-typecheck-old

imports Pico-syntax Type-environments

---

[1]We use the phrases "static semantics" and "typechecking" interchangeably when the specification of static semantics is executable, although the error-handling capabilities of such a specification would be minimal.

exports
  context-free syntax

tc(PROGRAM)	$\rightarrow$ BOOL
tenv(DECLS)	$\rightarrow$ TENV
TENV "[" SERIES "]"	$\rightarrow$ BOOL
TENV "." EXP	$\rightarrow$ TYPE
compatible(TYPE, TYPE)	$\rightarrow$ BOOL

equations

[oTc1a]
$$\frac{\text{tenv}(D)[S] = \text{true}}{\text{tc}(\text{begin } D\ S\ \text{end}) = \text{true}}$$

[oTc1b]
$$\frac{\text{tenv}(D)[S] \neq \text{true}}{\text{tc}(\text{begin } D\ S\ \text{end}) = \text{false}}$$

[oTc2]
$$\frac{Tenv[Stat] = \text{true}, \ Tenv[Stat\text{-}list] = \text{true}}{Tenv[Stat;\ Stat\text{-}list] = \text{true}}$$

[oTc3]
$$Tenv[] = \text{true}$$

[oTc4]
$$\frac{\text{compatible}(Tenv . Id, Tenv . Exp) = \text{true}}{Tenv[Id := Exp] = \text{true}}$$

[oTc5]
$$\frac{Tenv . Exp = \text{natural}, \ Tenv[S_1] = \text{true}, \ Tenv[S_2] = \text{true}}{Tenv[\text{if } Exp \text{ then } S_1 \text{ else } S_2 \text{ fi}] = \text{true}}$$

[oTc6]
$$\frac{Tenv . Exp = \text{natural}, \ Tenv[S] = \text{true}}{Tenv[\text{while } Exp \text{ do } S \text{ od}] = \text{true}}$$

[oTc7]
$$\frac{Tenv . Exp_1 = \text{natural}, \ Tenv . Exp_2 = \text{natural}}{Tenv . Exp_1 + Exp_2 = \text{natural}}$$

[oTc8]
$$\frac{Tenv . Exp_1 = \text{natural}, \ Tenv . Exp_2 = \text{natural}}{Tenv . Exp_1 - Exp_2 = \text{natural}}$$

[oTc9]
$$\frac{Tenv . Exp_1 = \text{string}, \ Tenv . Exp_2 = \text{string}}{Tenv . Exp_1 \parallel Exp_2 = \text{string}}$$

[oTc10] $[Idt^*, Id : Type, Idt^{*\prime}]$. $Id = Type$
[oTc11] $Tenv$. $Nat\text{-}con$ $=$ natural
[oTc12] $Tenv$. $Str\text{-}con$ $=$ string

[oTcTv] $\text{tenv(declare } Idt^*;) = [Idt^*]$

[oTcCa] compatible(natural, natural) $=$ true
[oTcCb] compatible(string, string) $=$ true

Let us consider the equations [oTc1a] and [oTc1b] in this specification. The equation [oTc1a] specifies that typechecking a program is "true" if typechecking the statements, using the type-environment obtained from the declarations, results in "true". However, equation [oTc1b] specifies that if typechecking statements is *not* "true", then the result is "false". Equations such as [oTc1b] are solely used to guarantee that the result of typechecking a program is always equal to either "true" or "false", rather than some non-standard value[2].

The problem with this specification is that generating error messages (which was ignored in the above specification) requires a modification of the specification to handle alternate cases and to keep track of errors (as well as error propagation). The following style of specification, that addressed error handling while typechecking Pico gives an impression of such changes needed. This style was first found in an unpublished 1991 paper of Klint. The following specification is an adaptation (and simplification) of it by van Deursen who uses a similar style for specifying a typechecker for Pascal (Chapter 2).

Note the various (additional) constructs and error sorts introduced in the signature, and the import of Module Pico-type-errors. Error presentation is done by threading the potential error messages into every rule of the static semantic specification.

Module Pico-typecheck-err

imports Pico-syntax Type-environments Pico-error-msgs Pico-type-errors
exports
   context-free syntax
      tc(PROGRAM) $\rightarrow$ ERRORS
      tenv(DECLS) $\rightarrow$ TENV-ERRORS

---

[2] *Non-standard* values are introduced when a new function is defined over an existing sort without giving sufficient equations (i.e., not "sufficiently-complete") to simplify expressions containing that function. In an initial algebra semantics, the definition of such a function introduces new elements for the "undefined cases"—in a partial algebra sense. These additional elements, are known as "non-standard values".

TENV "[" SERIES "]" → ERRORS
TENV "." EXP → TYPE-ERRORS

equations

[eTc1]
$$\frac{\mathrm{tenv}(D) = Tenv : E_1, \ Tenv[S] = E_2}{\mathrm{tc}(\mathrm{begin}\ D\ S\ \mathrm{end}) = E_1\ \&\ E_2}$$

[eTc2] $Tenv[Stat; \ Stat\text{-}list] = Tenv[Stat]\ \&\ Tenv[Stat\text{-}list]$

[eTc3] $Tenv[] = \{\}$

[eTc4]
$$\frac{Tenv . Id = Type_1 : E_1, \ Tenv . Exp = Type_2 : E_2}{Tenv[Id := Exp] = \mathrm{eq\text{-}types}(Id, Type_1, Exp, Type_2, E_1\ \&\ E_2)}$$

[eTc5]
$$\frac{Tenv . Exp = Type : E}{\begin{array}{l} Tenv[\mathrm{if}\ Exp\ \mathrm{then}\ S_1\ \mathrm{else}\ S_2\ \mathrm{fi}] = \\ E\ \&\ Tenv[S_1]\ \&\ Tenv[S_2]\ \&\ \mathrm{eq\text{-}type}(Exp, \mathrm{natural}, Type) \end{array}}$$

[eTc6]
$$\frac{Tenv . Exp = Type : E}{Tenv[\mathrm{while}\ Exp\ \mathrm{do}\ S\ \mathrm{od}] = E\ \&\ Tenv[S]\ \&\ \mathrm{eq\text{-}type}(Exp, \mathrm{natural}, Type)}$$

[eTc7]
$$\frac{Tenv . Exp_1 = Type_1 : E_1, \ Tenv . Exp_2 = Type_2 : E_2}{\begin{array}{l} Tenv . Exp_1 + Exp_2 = \\ \mathrm{natural} : \mathrm{eq\text{-}types}(Exp_1, Type_1, Exp_2, Type_2, E_1\ \&\ E_2) \end{array}}$$

[eTc8]
$$\frac{Tenv . Exp_1 = Type_1 : E_1, \ Tenv . Exp_2 = Type_2 : E_2}{\begin{array}{l} Tenv . Exp_1 - Exp_2 = \\ \mathrm{natural} : \mathrm{eq\text{-}types}(Exp_1, Type_1, Exp_2, Type_2, E_1\ \&\ E_2) \end{array}}$$

[eTc9]
$$\frac{Tenv . Exp_1 = Type_1 : E_1, \ Tenv . Exp_2 = Type_2 : E_2}{\begin{array}{l} Tenv . Exp_1 \parallel Exp_2 = \\ \mathrm{string} : \mathrm{eq\text{-}types}(Exp_1, Type_1, Exp_2, Type_2, E_1\ \&\ E_2) \end{array}}$$

[eTc10] $Tenv . Id = \mathrm{type\ of}\ Id\ \mathrm{in}\ Tenv$

[eTc11] $Tenv . Nat\text{-}con = \mathrm{natural} : \{\}$

[eTc12] $Tenv . Str\text{-}con = \mathrm{string} : \{\}$

[eTcTv] $\text{tenv}(\text{declare } Idt^*;) = [Idt^*] : \{\}$

[eTcE1] $\text{type of } Id \text{ in } [Idt^*, Id : Type, Idt^{*\prime}] = Type : \{\}$

[eTcE2] $\text{type of } Id \text{ in } Tenv = \text{natural} : \{\text{undeclared variable} \ll Id \gg\}$
                                    otherwise

[eTcCa] $\text{compatible}(\text{natural}, \text{natural}) = \text{true}$
[eTcCb] $\text{compatible}(\text{string}, \text{string}) = \text{true}$

This process of extensive specification editing, to convert a static semantics specification into a typechecker, in practice forces a specifier to think of error message generation and appropriate handling of errors at an early stage of the specification process. Note that the result of function tc(_) is a conjunction of error messages. The result of some functions involved in typechecking (e.g., tenv) should now be a pair consisting of a value component (like before) with an additional error component that is to be propagated. This propagated error component (i.e., the eq-type and eq-types functions), reduces to {} in the absence of actual errors. Also note that the erroneous construct itself is passed as an argument to these functions so that one can get a clue on where the type error might be. With origin-tracking, this would lead to good pin-pointing of erroneous constructs. However, in the next section, we see that this propagation of program constructs is not essential in the presence of a suitable origin-tracking mechanism.

4.2.2   *Modular Errors* Style

In a specification of a typechecker, it is desirable to specify only the cases for which the program is considered valid while the erroneous constructs be identified automatically. It is tempting to use partial algebra semantics, which gives "run-time" errors, say by identifying the non-standard values as "undefined". This approach, however, is not what is desired for typechecking a program, since checking a program as "undefined" does not help identify the type error. While typechecking a program, we want to know *what* went wrong (i.e., why it did not typecheck as "true") and *where* it went wrong. Let us first concentrate on extracting the "why" information and then discuss how the "where" information can be extracted (Section 4.4). For this we consider types as the abstract values of the language and interpret the language constructs at the type level.

We start by studying the classical style of specification step by step, with the goal of obtaining a static semantics specification that can be extended in a modular manner to obtain a typechecker. Our first observation is that, by moving the conditions in the equations to the right-hand sides, [oTc1a] and [oTc1b] merges to equation [mTc1]:

[mTc1] $tc(\text{begin } D\ S\ \text{end}) = \text{tenv}(D)[S]$

With this equation, typechecking an erroneous program may result in a non-standard value (not necessarily true or false).

Observing equation [oTc2] in Module Pico-typecheck-old suggests that the condition could be moved to the right-hand side if BOOL provided for an operation where "true" is the identity. Thus we use the conjunction operation "&" and rewrite the equation:

[mTc2] $Tenv[Stat;\ Stat\text{-}list] = Tenv[Stat]\ \&\ Tenv[Stat\text{-}list]$

The next step is to eliminate conditions in equations [oTc4]-[oTc6]. This is done, by delaying the necessary checks, by distribution of the type-environment over the components of a statement, which results in transforming the statements to an abstract representation (see equations [mTc16]-[mTc19] below in Module Pico-typecheck-mod). It is then simple to identify the correct abstract statements. We could thus *inject*[3] statements as non-standard values of Booleans, which means that the type incorrect statements will be non-standard values of sort Booleans.

The need for the compatible predicate in the specification above, as discussed in (Bergstra *et al.*, 1989, Section 9.2)), is basically to avoid accidentally equating the "undeclared variable" cases as type correct. However, this accident is naturally avoided here since the abstract representations have to be explicitly identified as correct.

Note that we are distributing type-environments over the components of expressions, the result of which should be of sort TYPE. Thus we need to inject TYPEs into EXPs. Also, we can keep the specification simple by generalizing the assignment statement to EXP := EXP. This extension to the syntax is only available in typecheck modules and does not affect the syntax of the language Pico itself.

In the following specification statements and expressions evaluate to their abstract values. When the tc function is applied to a program, it either evaluates to true (indicating a type-correct program) or it reduces to a normal form which is a conjunction of type incorrect statements in their abstract form (all expressions in them are also reduced to their normal form).

Module Pico-typecheck-mod

imports Type-environments

---

[3]The ASF+SDF formalism permits writing syntax-less injection functions, e.g., STATEMENT → BOOL. In the world of context-free grammers, such rules are known as *chain* rules. This can be simulated in other formalisms by introducing explicit *injection functions*. E.g., instead of "injecting" statements into Booleans, we could specify a function bool(STATEMENT) → BOOL which acts as an abstraction function that represents statements in Booleans.

exports
  context-free syntax

tc(PROGRAM)	→ BOOL
tenv(DECLS)	→ TENV
TENV "[" SERIES "]"	→ BOOL
TENV "." EXP	→ TYPE
EXP ":=" EXP	→ STATEMENT
STATEMENT	→ BOOL
TYPE	→ EXP

equations

[mTc1] $tc(\text{begin } D\ S\ \text{end}) = \text{tenv}(D)[S]$

[mTc2] $Tenv[Stat;\ Stat\text{-}list] = Tenv[Stat] \ \& \ Tenv[Stat\text{-}list]$

[mTc3] $Tenv[] = \text{true}$

[mTc4] $Tenv[Id := Exp] = Tenv\ .\ Id := Tenv\ .\ Exp$

[mTc5] $Tenv[\text{if } Exp \text{ then } S_1 \text{ else } S_2 \text{ fi}]$
            $= \text{if } Tenv\ .\ Exp \text{ then else fi} \ \& \ Tenv[S_1] \ \& \ Tenv[S_2]$

[mTc6] $Tenv[\text{while } Exp \text{ do } S \text{ od}] = \text{while } Tenv\ .\ Exp \text{ do od} \ \& \ Tenv[S]$

[mTc7] $Tenv\ .\ Exp_1 + Exp_2 = Tenv\ .\ Exp_1 + Tenv\ .\ Exp_2$
[mTc8] $Tenv\ .\ Exp_1 - Exp_2 = Tenv\ .\ Exp_1 - Tenv\ .\ Exp_2$
[mTc9] $Tenv\ .\ Exp_1 \parallel Exp_2 = Tenv\ .\ Exp_1 \parallel Tenv\ .\ Exp_2$

[mTc10a] $[Idt^*,\ Id : Type,\ Idt^{*\prime}]\ .\ Id = Type$
[mTc10b] $Tenv\ .\ Type \qquad\quad = Type$

[mTc11] $Nat\text{-}con = \text{natural}$
[mTc12] $Str\text{-}con = \text{string}$

[mTc13] $\text{natural} + \text{natural} = \text{natural}$
[mTc14] $\text{natural} - \text{natural} = \text{natural}$
[mTc15] $\text{string} \parallel \text{string} \quad = \text{string}$

[mTc16]	natural := natural	= true
[mTc17]	string := string	= true
[mTc18]	if natural then else fi	= true
[mTc19]	while natural do od	= true

[mTcTv]	tenv(declare Idt^*;) = $[Idt^*]$

The techniques used in the above specification are to:

- Extend[4] the syntax to accommodate abstract values, where necessary.
- Avoid conditions in the equations.
- Distribute the type-environment over statements (equations [mTc2]-[mTc6]).
- Distribute the type-environment over expressions ([mTc7]-[mTc9]).
- Evaluate the expressions at an abstract (type) level ([mTc13]-[mTc15]).
- Identify the abstract type-correct statements ([mTc16]-[mTc19]).
- Change the constants to their abstract representation ([mTc11]-[mTc12]).

The equations [mTc13]-[mTc19] are the crux of this style of specification. The other equations help to transform the source program into its abstract form. The equations [mTc13]-[mTc19] identify the type-correct constructs, while others that are not reducible by these equations become *structured error* messages.

The equations [mTc10a]-[mTc12] need some explanation. [mTc10a] handles the case when EXP is an ID and is similar to [oTc10]. [mTc10b] handles the new case, added in Module Pico-typecheck-mod, when EXP is a TYPE (the syntax rule TYPE → EXP). This case was introduced in order to inject abstract values (natural and string) into EXP. [mTc11] and [mTc12] convert constants to their abstract values. Although these equations appear to loop, when they are executed as rewrite rules, they are well defined since the injection of constants into EXP is a different function than the injection of TYPE into EXP. One could split [mTc10b] further to handle the cases of [mTc11] and [mTc12] instead, which would make the abstraction of constants depend on the type environment. Such dependencies can sometimes affect error reporting (see Section 4.4).

We do not go into the details of checking (double) declarations in these different styles. One can easily modify the right-hand side of [mTc1] to also check if the declarations are unique i.e., "tenv(D)[S] & unique(D)" (say by using a function "unique(DECLS) → BOOL").

As an example, the result of applying the tc($\_$) function to the program

```
begin
  declare x : natural,
          s : string;
```

---

[4]Note that the second-order specification style used by Heering (Chapter 8) needs minimal extension.

```
x := 10;
while x do
  x := x - s;
  s := s || "#"
od
end
```

is

```
natural := natural - string
```

This structured error message indicates the following: (1) the program has a type error (did not evaluate to true) (2) the error is in an assignment statement (3) the type of the left-hand side of the assignment is incompatible with the right-hand side and (4) the right argument for a subtraction operation has a string operand.

4.2.3 Readable Messages

The error information produced in the previous section can easily be further processed by a separate module which issues human-readable error messages.

For instance, by applying "msg(_)" to the result of "tc(_)": msg(tc(*Program*)). In the following we assume that this is a two step process. Thus the equations in the Module Pico-mod-errors are used for post-processing to convert the structured errors into more readable structured errors.

Module Pico-mod-errors

imports Pico-typecheck-mod Pico-error-msgs
exports
  context-free syntax
    msg(BOOL)   → ERRORS
    msg(EXP)   → ERRORS
    ERRORS else ERRORS → ERRORS **{left}**
  priorities

    {ERRORS "&"ERRORS → ERRORS} > {else}

equations

[mEr1]	msg(true)	= {}
[mEr2]	msg(*Bool*$_1$ & *Bool*$_2$)	= msg(*Bool*$_1$) & msg(*Bool*$_2$)

[mEr3]	{} else E = E

[mEr4] $$E_1 \text{ else } E_2 = E_1 \quad \textbf{otherwise}$$

[mEr5] $$\text{msg}(\textit{Tenv} . \textit{Id}) = \{\text{undeclared variable} \ll \textit{Id} \gg\}$$

[mEr6] $$\frac{E = \{\ll \textit{Exp}_1 \gg \text{and} \ll \textit{Exp}_2 \gg \text{have unequal type}\}}{\text{msg}(\textit{Exp}_1 + \textit{Exp}_2) = \text{msg}(\textit{Exp}_1) \,\&\, \text{msg}(\textit{Exp}_2) \text{ else } E}$$

[mEr7] $$\frac{E = \{\ll \textit{Exp}_1 \gg \text{and} \ll \textit{Exp}_2 \gg \text{have unequal type}\}}{\text{msg}(\textit{Exp}_1 - \textit{Exp}_2) = \text{msg}(\textit{Exp}_1) \,\&\, \text{msg}(\textit{Exp}_2) \text{ else } E}$$

[mEr8] $$\frac{E = \{\ll \textit{Exp}_1 \gg \text{and} \ll \textit{Exp}_2 \gg \text{have unequal type}\}}{\text{msg}(\textit{Exp}_1 \,\|\, \textit{Exp}_2) = \text{msg}(\textit{Exp}_1) \,\&\, \text{msg}(\textit{Exp}_2) \text{ else } E}$$

[mEr9] $$\text{msg}(\textit{Type} := \textit{Exp}) = \text{msg}(\textit{Type}) \,\&\, \text{msg}(\textit{Exp})$$
$$\text{else } \{\ll \textit{Exp} \gg : \text{required type is } \textit{Type}\}$$

[mEr10] $$\text{msg}(\text{if } \textit{Exp} \text{ then else fi}) = \text{msg}(\textit{Exp})$$
$$\&\, \{\ll \textit{Exp} \gg : \text{required type is natural}\}$$

[mEr11] $$\text{msg}(\text{while } \textit{Exp} \text{ do od}) = \text{msg}(\textit{Exp})$$
$$\&\, \{\ll \textit{Exp} \gg : \text{required type is natural}\}$$

[mEr12] $$\text{msg}(\text{string}) = \{\}$$
[mEr13] $$\text{msg}(\text{natural}) = \{\}$$

The obvious lack of information in a message thus processed, however, is an indication of where in the source program the errors are located. It is mandatory to have information on location of errors in large programs. Generation of this information is often done by keeping track of line numbers in the input program. We claim that error location information can be automatically generated by a programming environment generator and discuss how this is done currently in the ASF+SDF system in Section 4.4.

4.3 Origin Tracking

Origin tracking is a generic technique for relating parts of intermediate terms, which occur during term rewriting, to parts of the initial term. It automatically maintains certain forms of relations between the source and result that can be exploited for generating an error reporter, by using the specification style presented in Section 4.2.2.

Figure 4.1 illustrates some origin relations established in one rewrite rule. Such single step origins are composed to yield origin relations from intermediate terms to

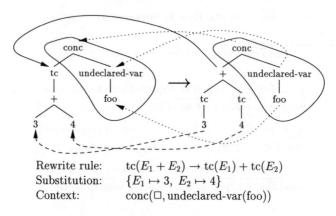

Rewrite rule:	$\mathrm{tc}(E_1 + E_2) \to \mathrm{tc}(E_1) + \mathrm{tc}(E_2)$
Substitution:	$\{E_1 \mapsto 3,\ E_2 \mapsto 4\}$
Context:	$\mathrm{conc}(\square, \mathrm{undeclared\text{-}var}(\mathrm{foo}))$

Dashed arrows:	Origins for Common Variables
Dotted arrows:	Context Origins
Solid arrow:	Origin for Redex-Contractum.

Figure 4.1: Origins established for one rewrite step.

initial term. For a detailed description of origin tracking and its applications, the reader is referred to Chapter 7.

Figure 4.2 shows the use of origin tracking in the ASF+SDF system to find the location of erroneous constructs in a CLaX program (Dinesh and Tip, 1992). Here, function "errors" is applied to a CLaX program in the large window. The resulting type errors are displayed in the small window. These error messages, albeit useful, provide no information regarding the specific constructs of the program that caused it or the position where it originated. Origin tracking in the system provides one with the ability to identify the culprit program constructs by clicking on the desired error and requesting the system to show its origin. Label "step" is defined twice in the program (but a label should be defined uniquely) and in the small window there is an error message that indicates this. By selecting this error message and asking the system to show origins both occurrences of the label **step** that caused this error are high-lighted by the system.

4.4 On Identifying Error Locations

To explain the idea of automating the process of error location identification, we will consider the origin tracking mechanism and modify our specification so that enough origins can be tracked to determine complete information on where the errors are located.

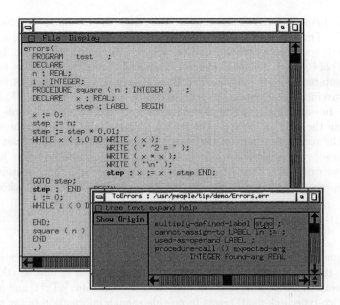

Figure 4.2: Example of a generated environment using origin tracking, for the language CLaX.

We consider equation [oTc11] from the Pico-typecheck-old specification for our discussion.

[oTc11] Tenv.Nat-con = natural

$$\underset{Tenv\quad Nat\text{-}con}{\bigwedge} \quad \longrightarrow \quad natural$$

If we look at this equation for relationships between the left hand side and right hand side, we can hardly see any other than the obvious one indicated by the = symbol (the Redex-Contractum case of Chapter 7). Since the possible terms which match the left side are not program terms (Pico syntax terms), there would be no (transitive) relation from the reduct to any program term.

Now let us compare [oTc11] from Module Pico-typecheck-old to the equations [mTc10b] and [mTc11] from Module Pico-typecheck-mod.

[mTc10b] Tenv.Type = Type

$$\underset{Tenv\quad Type}{\bigwedge} \quad \longrightarrow \quad Type$$

The equation [mTc10b] suggests not only a relationship indicated by the = symbol (as in Redex-contractum case), but also one about the variable *Type*; the variable *Type* on left-hand side and right-hand side are the same (the Common Variables case of Chapter 7). Thus, when this rule is used to rewrite a term, the reduct term could be related to its redex in two ways. First, the Redex-Contractum case, is similar to that for [oTc11] of Pico-typecheck-old and would not lead to relating the reduct to a source program sub-term for our specification. But the second, the Common Variables case could be useful since *Type* on the left-hand side could be a subterm of the source program. In our *modular errors* case **natural** and **string** are two words that can be found in the program source. The second relation could thus help the system in tracking the reduct to a part of the source program; e.g., if the word **natural** has origin to a subterm of the source program (in our case a constant of type natural).

Next we can consider the case of constants of type natural, that equation [oTc11] of Pico-typecheck-old was used for, by considering [mTc11] of Pico-typecheck-mod.

[mTc11] Nat-con = natural

$$\textit{Nat-con} \longrightarrow \text{natural}$$

It is now easy to observe that the necessary relation between a constant and its reduct the word **natural** (type name in our case) exists as desired (the Redex-Contractum case). Handling the constants like this (equations [oTc11] and [oTc12] of Module Pico-typecheck-mod) seems to provide enough information to the system to show automatically the error location information if a constant is involved in causing the error message.

Another situation that is somewhat similar to the case of constants is that of the lexicals of the syntax constructors. E.g., the need to know which ":=" or "-" in the source program appeared in error message discussed earlier. The specification of Module Pico-syntax abstracts away such tokens, i.e., the origin relation for equation [mTc8] in Pico-typecheck-mod is (no relations for the - token):

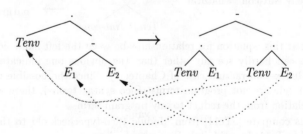

4.4.1 Tokenization

The origin information lost, as illustrated above, can be recoverd either by extending the notion of origin-tracking to a suitable one (see Chapter 7) or by further adopting the specification to suit a particular origin-tracking notion. While experimenting with the CLaX typechecker specification, we tried to adapt the specification in order to obtain meaningful results. We soon noticed that the syntax could be defined slightly differently for processing the origin information. The following modification to the syntax, effectively re-does the implicit structure of operations and statements without asking for changes in the specification of the typechecker. Thus replacing Module Pico-syntax by Module Pico-syntax-new, which uses Module Pico-tokens shown below, provides us with enough of the location information for tracking the origin of error messages.

Module Pico-tokens

exports
  sorts AOP SOP IF THEN ELSE FI WHILE DO OD ASGN
  context-free syntax
      "+"   → AOP
      "−"   → AOP
      "∥"   → SOP
      if   → IF
      then → THEN
      else → ELSE
      fi   → FI
      while → WHILE
      do   → DO
      od   → OD
      ":=" → ASGN

By using the above module, the context-free functions in Module Pico-syntax can be written differently using the sort names in Module Pico-tokens. For example, the function
    EXP "+" EXP → EXP {**left**}
can be written instead as
    EXP AOP EXP → EXP {**left**}
The origin relations for equation [mTc8] now become:

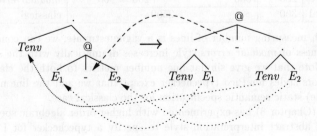

where @ is a nameless function corresponding to the syntax rule for expressions (EXP) just given.

Some of the concrete syntax is converted to abstract syntax for the program constructs, which can now be handled by the origin-tracking mechanism to indicate the location of the error. The rest of the specification need not be altered in any manner.

Of course, it is undesirable to force this *tokenization* on the specifier. But on the brighter side, we also observed that such tokenization does not call for modification of the rest of the specification. Thus, tokenization could be automatically performed by the system and hidden from the user (specifier). Note that we have grouped some operation names into a single sort. This grouping could have some repercussions on priority declarations. This grouping is, however, not essential and will not occur if the tokenization process is automated.

4.5 Related Work

The subject of handling exceptional states in algebraic specifications is not new (Goguen, 1978), however type errors encountered during typechecking are not exceptions per se. Order-sorted algebras (Goguen *et al.*, 1988) allow errors to be dealt in separate sorts. This by itself does not help modularization, whereas our recommended *modular errors* style could be used in that context. Thus specifiers of typecheckers need not be bothered about building the error propagation machinery from the start.

In Section 4.2 we compared the *modular errors* style of specification in detail to what we called the classical style, including the adaptations it needed to cater for error-handling. To give an indication of the conciseness of *modular errors* style, we compare the number of lines of ASF+SDF typechecker specifications for Pico (with and without error handling), CLaX (Dinesh and Tip, 1992) which is a subset of Pascal, and Pascal (Chapter 2).

	syntax	type checker		style used
		static semantics	+ error handling	
Pico	30	35	+ 50 = 85	*modular errors*
Pico	30	35 + 85 = 120		classical
CLaX	280	650	+250 = 900	*modular errors*
Pascal	300	2500		classical

Although measuring number of lines is a vague estimate, we can conclude that the effectiveness of *modular errors* style increases dramatically with the size of the language. Note that we give similar line number metrics to both the classical and modular errors styles for Pico typechecker except that we add the line numbers of (non-reusable) static semantic specification for the classical case.

Heering (Chapter 8) has experimented with higher-order algebraic specifications and uses an abstract interpretation style to specify a typechecker for Pico. This necessitated defining origin-tracking for higher-order TRS (Chapter 9). The general idea of using an abstract interpretation style for specifying typecheckers itself is not new (Naur, 1965) and is likely used by many people. Also, this style appears to be a natural by-product when the static semantics is semi-automatically derived from the dynamic semantics (Chapter 3).

Alternative methods to get an effect similar to that of tokenization are of interest. A notion of *syntax directed* origins discussed in Section 7.5 appears to provide origin information needed for the cases of interest here.

GNU Emacs (Stallman, 1991) and various workbenches extract the line number from a compiler error message and highlight that line in an editor window. In our case, error reporting is language specific and highlighting does not indicate an entire line for some error, but only the offending program constructs.

4.6 Concluding Remarks

The style of typechecking illustrated in this chapter concentrates on specifying only the necessary information, while still providing reasonably good error messages. The style described makes use of the so called non-standard values of an initial algebra specification to generate errors. The result of typechecking is to effectively form a conjunction of the abstract meanings of statements of the language. All type correct statements evaluate to "true" while an incorrect statement reduces to a structured error. This, together with origin tracking, automatically provides information on the location of errors in the source program. The structured errors can be used by a separate module to generate human-readable error messages.

The advocated specification style also allows typechecking over effectively incomplete programs Dinesh and Tip (1992). Incomplete programs can be written in the ASF+SDF system using meta-variables in the input term.

It is an interesting exercise to adopt this style for languages with polymorphic types. Chapter 5 uses a style, similar to modular errors, for typechecking a polymorphic specification language.

Appendices

4.A Pico Language

A Pico program consists of declarations followed by statements and is defined in Chapter 9 of Bergstra *et al.* (1989). All variables are declared to be either of type natural or of type string. Statements may be assignment statements, if-statements and while-statements. Expressions may be a single identifier, addition or subtraction of natural numbers, or concatenation of strings.

The imported modules define the lexical identifiers, constants for natural numbers and strings used in the language. The variables defined in this module are used (since they are exported) in the equations of modules that import Pico-syntax (e.g., Pico-typecheck modules).

Module Pico-syntax

imports Layout[5.A.1] Identifiers Integers Strings Booleans[5.A.2]
exports
    sorts PROGRAM DECLS ID-TYPE SERIES STATEMENT
            EXP TYPE
    context-free syntax

begin DECLS SERIES end	$\rightarrow$ PROGRAM	
declare {ID-TYPE ","}* ";"	$\rightarrow$ DECLS	
ID ":" TYPE	$\rightarrow$ ID-TYPE	
{STATEMENT ";"}*	$\rightarrow$ SERIES	
ID ":=" EXP	$\rightarrow$ STATEMENT	
if EXP then SERIES else SERIES fi	$\rightarrow$ STATEMENT	
while EXP do SERIES od	$\rightarrow$ STATEMENT	
EXP "+" EXP	$\rightarrow$ EXP	{**left**}
EXP "−" EXP	$\rightarrow$ EXP	{**left**}
EXP "||" EXP	$\rightarrow$ EXP	{**left**}
ID	$\rightarrow$ EXP	
NAT-CON	$\rightarrow$ EXP	
STR-CON	$\rightarrow$ EXP	
"(" EXP ")"	$\rightarrow$ EXP	{**bracket**}
natural	$\rightarrow$ TYPE	
string	$\rightarrow$ TYPE	

    variables
        D $\rightarrow$ DECLS
        Idt "*"[']* $\rightarrow$ {ID-TYPE ","}*
        S [12]* $\rightarrow$ SERIES

Stat	→ STATEMENT
Stat-list	→ {STATEMENT ";"}+
Exp [*12'*]∗	→ EXP
Type [*12'*]∗	→ TYPE

4.B Other Modules

Module Type-environments

Specifying a typechecker for Pico is done using a table for type-environments TENV. A table is simply defined as a list with identifier-type pairs.

imports Pico-syntax
exports
  sorts TENV
  context-free syntax
    "[" {ID-TYPE ","}∗ "]" → TENV
  variables
    Tenv → TENV

Module Pico-error-msgs

Both the classical and the modular typechecking style generate the same error messages, which are listed in this module.

imports Layout[5.A.1] Pico-syntax Type-environments
exports
  sorts ERROR ERRORS
  context-free syntax

"{" {ERROR ","}∗ "}"	→ ERRORS	{**constructor**}
ERRORS "&" ERRORS	→ ERRORS	{**left, constructor**}
undeclared variable "≪" ID "≫"	→ ERROR	{**constructor**}
"≪" EXP "≫" ":" required type is TYPE	→ ERROR	{**constructor**}
"≪" EXP "≫" and "≪" EXP "≫"		
have unequal type	→ ERROR	{**constructor**}

  variables

E [*12*]∗	→ ERRORS
E "∗"[*12*]∗	→ {ERROR ","}∗
Error	→ ERROR

equations

[ErM1]	$\{E_1^*\}$ & $\{E_2^*\}$	$= \{E_1^*, E_2^*\}$
[ErM2]	$\{E^*, Error, E_1^*, Error, E_2^*\}$	$= \{E^*, Error, E_1^*, E_2^*\}$

Module Pico-type-errors

The functions introduced in this module are only needed in the classical style. The new sorts introduced make it possible to for functions to yield values that are composed of both a type (or an environment) and a list of errors. The functions checking equality take an extra EXP argument indicating which expression is erroneous.

imports Layout[5.A.1] Pico-syntax Type-environments Pico-error-msgs
exports
    sorts TYPE-ERRORS TENV-ERRORS
    context-free syntax

compatible(TYPE, TYPE)	→ BOOL
eq-type "(" EXP "," TYPE "," TYPE ")"	→ ERRORS
eq-types "(" EXP "," TYPE ","	
EXP "," TYPE "," ERRORS ")"	→ ERRORS
TYPE ":" ERRORS	→ TYPE-ERRORS
TENV ":" ERRORS	→ TENV-ERRORS
type of ID in TENV	→ TYPE-ERRORS

    variables
        T [12]$*$ → TYPE
        E [12]$*$ → ERRORS
equations

[Er1] $\qquad\qquad\qquad$ compatible(T_1, T_2) = false $\quad$ **otherwise**

[Er2] $\qquad\qquad\dfrac{\text{compatible}(T_1, T_2) \;=\; \text{true}}{\text{eq-type}(Exp, T_1, T_2) \;=\; \{\}}$

[Er3] $\quad$ eq-type(Exp, T_1, T_2) = $\{\ll Exp \gg : \text{required type is } T_2\}$ $\quad$ **otherwise**

[Er4] $\qquad\qquad\dfrac{\text{compatible}(T_1, T_2) \;=\; \text{true}}{\text{eq-types}(Exp_1, T_1, Exp_2, T_2, E) \;=\; E}$

[Er5] $\qquad\qquad$ eq-types($Exp_1, T_1, Exp_2, T_2, E$)
$\qquad\qquad = \{\ll Exp_1 \gg \text{ and } \ll Exp_2 \gg \text{ have unequal type}\}$
$\qquad\qquad\qquad\qquad$ **otherwise**

5

Multi-Level Specifications

Eelco Visser

Abstract This chapter introduces a modular, applicative, multi-level equational specification formalism that supports algebraic specification with user-definable type constructors, polymorphic functions and higher-order functions. Specifications consist of one or more levels numbered 0 to n. Level 0 defines the object level terms. Level 1 defines the types used in the signature of level 0. In general, the terms used as types in level n are defined in level $n + 1$. This setup makes the algebra of types and the algebra of types of types, etc., user-definable. The applicative term structure makes functions first-class citizens and facilitates higher-order functions. The use of variables in terms used as types provides polymorphism (including higher-order polymorphism, i.e., abstraction over type constructors). Functions and variables can be overloaded. Specifications can be divided into modules. Modules can be imported at several levels by means of a specification lifting operation. Equations define the semantics of terms over a signature. The formalism also allows equations over types, by means of which many type systems can be described. The typechecker presented in this chapter does not take into account type equations.

The specification, in ASF+SDF, of the syntax, type system and semantics of the formalism is presented in three stages: (1) untyped equational specifications (2) applicative one-level specifications (3) modular multi-level specifications. The definition of a typechecker for stages (2) and (3) is divided into four parts: (a) well-formedness judgements verifying type correctness of fully annotated terms and specifications, (b) non well-formedness rules giving descriptive error messages for the cases not covered under (a), (c) a type assignment function annotating the terms in a plain specification with types, and (d) a typechecking function which checks well-formedness after applying type assignment. These functions are defined uniformly for all levels of a specification.

Aside of defining a new specification formalism, this chapter illustrates the use of ASF+SDF for the design and prototyping of sophisticated specification formalisms.

5.1 Introduction

Algebraic specification and functional programming are closely related paradigms. The foundation of both paradigms is equational logic. Values are represented by *terms* and a program or specification consists of a list of *equations* over these terms Two terms that are equal according to a specification (by means of equational logic) have the same meaning and can replace each other in any context, a property called *referential transparency*.

The paradigms differ in the aim of a program or specification. An algebraic specification defines a class of algebras that satisfy its equations. A functional program on the other hand defines a method to compute a value from an initial value by executing the equations as rewrite rules. However, this difference is mainly one of emphasis; functional programs can be seen as algebraic specifications that satisfy certain restrictions. Almost all specifications in this book can be executed as rewrite systems. In spite of that, there are many technical differences between actual formalisms. These differences can be divided into semantics and type system.

5.1.1 Semantics

The choice of a semantics for a language is based on the set of required program constructs, which may include equations, conditional equations, λ abstraction, let binding, recursion and fixed-point operators, etc. In this chapter we use pure equational logic as the basis for the specification logic.

The operationalization of an equational algebraic specification by means of term rewriting is aimed at determining whether two terms are equal or at finding a normal form for a term. The strategy used to accomplish this is of no importance. Functional programming languages, emphasizing computation rather than specification, incorporate a rewrite strategy (innermost, outermost, lazy) into their semantics. Furthermore, functional languages make a distinction between functions that transform a value into another and constructors that are used to represent data. In algebraic specification this distinction is not made, e.g., the unary minus function '$-$' can be seen either as a constructor (-1) or as a function $(-0 = 0)$.

5.1.2 Type Systems

A *signature* determines which terms are the subject of a specification or program. A *type system* determines the form of signatures and the *well-formed* terms over a signature. Several issues are of importance in the design of type systems.

Term Structure: First-order many-sorted algebraic specifications use a many-sorted algebraic signature to assign types of the form $s_1 \times \cdots \times s_n \to s_0$ to function symbols f. Terms can be formed by application of such function symbols to a list of terms t_i of sort s_i, resulting in terms of the form $f(t_1, \ldots, t_n)$. This function application construct is called *algebraic*. Such a type system is called first-order because no higher-order functions (having functions as arguments) can be defined. A function symbol can only occur in a term when it is applied to the right number of arguments. Other type systems allow higher-order functions and use an *applicative* term structure — application is of the form $t_1\ t_2$, term t_1 applied to term t_2 — to build terms. Applicative term structure is common in functional languages, whereas algebraic specification formalisms generally use first-order term structures.

Overloading: If a function can have a finite number of different types it is said to be *overloaded*. An example of overloading is addition on integers and reals. Overloading is common in frameworks with algebraic term structure, where it is easy to deduce which version of a function is used from the arguments to which it is applied. In applicative frameworks ambiguities caused by overloading are much harder to resolve because functions can occur separate from their arguments. Therefore, overloading was omitted in early functional languages like ML. Most modern functional languages have some restricted form of overloading through type classes (see below).

Polymorphism: Parametric polymorphic functions, which were introduced by Milner (1978) in the functional language ML, can have infinitely many types that are instantiations of one generic type. An example of a polymorphic function is the function that computes the length of a list, which is independent of the contents of lists and can therefore be defined for all possible lists at once. Polymorphic functions have a universally quantified type. For instance the type of length is $\forall \alpha.\text{list}(\alpha) \to \text{int}$.

Restricted polymorphism: For some applications this unrestricted polymorphism is too strong. For instance, the polymorphic equality function with type $\forall \alpha.\alpha \times \alpha \to$ bool also applies to functions, which is undesirable because function equality is not computable. In Standard ML (Milner *et al.*, 1990) the type of the equality function is defined on the subset of the set of all types for which equality is computable. This idea is generalized by Wadler and Blott (1989) by means of *type classes*, which are predicates on types that divide the set of types into subsets with certain properties that can be used to restrict the polymorphism of functions. For instance, if the class eq indicates all types on which equality can be defined, then the type of the equality function can be rephrased as $\forall \alpha.\text{eq}(\alpha) \Rightarrow \alpha \times \alpha \to$ bool to express that the type variable can only be bound to types for which the eq predicate holds, that is, those that are in the eq class. The type classes of Wadler and Blott (1989) are unary predicates on types. Jones (1992) gives a more general formulation of restricted polymorphism in his theory of *qualified types*, in which arbitrary predicates on types are allowed. Special cases of the .theory are type classes, subtyping and extensible records.

Type Operators: In frameworks with polymorphism the language of types becomes a user-definable set of terms and subject to a type system itself. In a first-order framework the type of lists of integers has a name like int-list. In a polymorphic framework one wants to quantify over the type of the contents of lists. By defining a type constructor list (a function from types to types), one can denote lists of integers as list(int) and arbitrary lists as list(A), where A is a variable ranging over types.

Types of Types: The language of types built from type constants and type constructors is itself an algebraic language with a signature. In many-sorted algebraic signatures the only type constructors are $\times$ and $\to$ and the language of types is restricted to types of the form $c_1 \times \cdots \times c_n \to c_0$, where the c_i are type constants. In polymorphic languages like ML the language of types consists of untyped, first-order terms, i.e., all type constructors have a type of the form $\text{type} \times \cdots \times \text{type} \to \text{type}$. For instance, `list` is a type constructor that takes a type and constructs a type, i.e., it is declared as $\text{list} : \text{type} \to \text{type}$. Generalizing the idea of an algebra of type constructors, one can use an arbitrary many-sorted (instead of a one-sorted) signature for the specification of the algebra of types, leading to a two-level signature. Further generalization of this idea leads to a third-level signature that specifies the types of types of types. In this chapter a formalism with multiple levels of signatures is presented.

Higher-Order Polymorphism and Constructor Classes: In Hindley/Milner type systems the quantifier in types can only range over types and not over type constructors. Higher-order polymorphic functions can also quantify over type constructors. With such polymorphism it is natural to extend the notion of a type class to a constructor class which restricts quantification over type constructors (Jones, 1995).

There are many other considerations in the design of type systems. Here we restrict our attention to the ones discussed above. See Section 5.8 for some references to surveys of type systems.

5.1.3 Multi-Level Specifications

In this chapter we present the formalism MLS, a *modular, applicative, multi-level, equational specification formalism with overloading*. Figure 5.1 illustrates several features of this language by means of a two-level specification of lists and trees with polymorphic `size` and `map` functions. The specification imports the specification of the type `nat` of natural numbers with functions `0`, `s` and `(+)`.

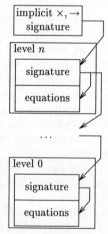

Multi-level: A specification consists of arbitrary many levels of one-level specifications. The terms over the signature at level 0 are the 'object' level terms. The types used in the signature of level 0 are terms over level 1. In general, the types in the signature at level n are terms over the signature at level $n + 1$, as is depicted in the diagram next to this paragraph. The types used in the signature of the highest level are determined by an implicit signature of types consisting only of type constants and the type constructors $\times$ and $\to$.

The sort declarations at level n determine which of the terms at level $n + 1$ can actually be used as type at level n. A term used as type should match one

```
module list-tree
imports nat;
level 1
  signature
    sorts type;
    functions
      (#), (->)  : type # type -> type;
      list, tree : type -> type;
    variables
       A, B : type;
level 0
  signature
    sorts A; list(A);
    functions
      []   : list(A);
      (::) : A # list(A) -> list(A);
      size : list(A) -> nat;
      map  : (A -> B) # list(A) -> list(B);
    variables
      X : A; L : list(A); G : A -> B;
  equations
    size([])      == 0;
    size(X :: L)  == s(size(L));
    map(G, [])    == [];
    map(G, X :: L) == G(X) :: map(G)(L);
  signature
    sorts A; tree(A);
    functions
      []   : tree(A);
      node : tree(A) # A # tree(A) -> tree(A);
      size : tree(A) -> nat;
      map  : (A -> B) # tree(A) -> tree(B);
    variables
      X : A; T : tree(A); G : A -> B;
  equations
    size([])                == 0;
    size(node(T, X, T'))    == s(size(T) + size(T'));
    map(G, [])              == [];
    map(G, node(T, X, T')) == node(map(G)(T), G(X), map(G)(T'))
```

Figure 5.1: Two-level specification of list and tree data types.

of the terms declared as sort. These ideas are illustrated in Figure 5.1. The term
`type # type -> type` in the first function declaration at level 1 is a term over the
implicit signature of the types at the highest level. (Note that $\times$ is written # in
ASCII notation.) The term `list(A)` is a term over the signature at level 1: `list` is a
function from `type` to `type` and `A` is a `type` variable. Furthermore, `list(A)` matches
the sort declarations `A` and `list(A)`. Therefore, `list(A)` can be used in the signature
at level 0 as a type in the declaration of the functions `[]` (empty list), `(::)` (cons)
etc. Level 0, finally, determines the terms for the objects of real interest, such as `[]`,
`s(0) :: []`, and `map(s)(0 :: [])`.

The example in Figure 5.1 shows a two-level specification ($n = 1$). The formalism
supports arbitrarily many levels. The type constructors available at level 1 can be
enriched by means of a third level. In Section 5.5 several examples of three level
specifications are shown.

Polymorphism: Terms over a signature can contain variables. A term with variables used as type in a signature denotes a *polymorphic* type. For instance, `size` is
a function from `list(A)` to `nat`. This means that for any `type` t, `size` applies to
terms of `type list`(t). Quantification is not restricted to types but can also range
over type constructors.

Overloading: Functions can have two or more related, or completely different,
types. This allows the use of function names for different purposes, which is not
possible with polymorphism alone. For instance, the functions `size` and `map` are
defined for both lists and trees. Equations can also be overloaded. For example, the
equations defining the functions `size` and `map` on empty lists and empty trees are
exactly the same. Actually, writing this equation once would have sufficed, because
all possible interpretations of ambiguous equations are taken into consideration.

Applicative: The term structure is applicative, i.e., application is a binary operation on terms. At the functional position an arbitrary term can occur. Functions are
first-class citizens and can be arguments of functions. For instance, the function `map`
has a function as argument, which it applies to all elements of a list or tree.

Observe that the arrow and product constructors for types are considered normal
functions. The arrow in the type of `size` is the same arrow that is declared at level 1
as a binary function on types. There is, however, one difference with other functions:
the arrow and product constructors are related to the operations application and
pairing. For each arrow type, there is a corresponding application operation that
takes a term of type $\tau_1 \rightarrow \tau_2$ and a term of type τ_1 and produces a term of type τ_2.
Similarly for each product type there is a corresponding pairing operation that takes
two terms of types τ_1 and τ_2 and produces a term of type $\tau_1 \times \tau_2$.

Equational: Equational axioms[1] over terms express the semantics of terms. Equational logic can be used for reasoning about terms, whereas term rewriting can be
used to decide equations for appropriate systems of equations or to compute the result

---

[1]The ideas for the multi-level type system in this chapter are also applicable to formalisms with
other logics, e.g., conditional equations, Horn clause logic or even first-order logic.

of defined functions.

Modular: Multi-level specifications can be split into modules by means of a rudimentary module system consisting of module declarations and module references (imports). Operations for manipulating specifications can also be applied to imports, facilitating reuse of specifications at more than one level (see Section 5.5 for examples).

Type Equations: The MLS *formalism* supports equations at all levels of a specification. This means that equations over types can be defined to specify powerful type constructs like recursive types, qualified types, and logical frameworks. However, the typechecker for MLS defined in this chapter does not take into account equations over types. This requires $\mathcal{E}$-unification, which is undecidable in general. For restricted forms of equations typechecking with $\mathcal{E}$-unification seems feasible, and might be incorporated in future versions of the MLS typechecker.

5.1.4   Related Formalisms

The MLS formalism is a generalization of several concepts found in other formalisms. Below we give a brief overview of related formalisms. The landscape of formalisms is summarized by the diagram in Table 5.1.

One-Level Monomorphic Algebraic Languages   The algebraic specification formalisms OBJ (Futatsugi *et al.*, 1985), Pluss (Bidoit *et al.*, 1989) and ASF+SDF (see Chapter 1) have monomorphic many-sorted first-order signatures as type system. The sort space consists of terms of the form $c_1 \times \cdots \times c_n \to c_0$, with the c_i sort constants. A limited form of polymorphism can be obtained by means of overloading and parameterized modules, but polymorphic higher-order functions are not provided. All these formalisms support arbitrary mixfix notation. OBJ provides *order-sorted* signatures, in which an inclusion relation between sorts can be declared. In ASF+SDF, sort inclusion can be simulated by means of syntaxless unary functions (also called injections). The formalisms OLS and MLS considered in this chapter support neither subsorting nor syntaxless functions.

One-Level Monomorphic Applicative Languages   The one-level applicative specification language OLS, defined in Sections 5.3 and 5.4, generalizes the sort space of monomorphic algebraic languages to the closure under $\times$ and $\to$ of the declared sort constants. The extension with respect to the algebraic frameworks discussed above is the support for higher-order functions.

Two-Level Polymorphic Applicative Languages   The type system for polymorphic higher-order functions, known as the Hindley/Milner system, was first described by Hindley (1969) as a type assignment algorithm for expressions in combinatory logic. It was extended by Milner (1978) to languages with local declarations. The functional programming language ML (Gordon *et al.*, 1978) was the first language to incorporate

add. features	algebraic	# levels	applicative	add. features
ol	OBJ, Pluss, AsF+SDF	1	OLS	hof
p, tc	PolySpec	2	ML, Miranda Spectrum, Haskell	hof, p hof, p, tc
p, ol	ATLAS	3	Quest	hof, p, st
p, ol	ATLASII	n	MLS	hof, p, ol

Table 5.1: Several algebraic and functional languages classified according to their number of levels and to their term structure (algebraic vs. applicative). The additional features columns list the presence of: ol: overloading, hof: higher-order functions, p: polymorphism, tc: type classes, st: subtypes.

this type system. For the introduction of type operators, the type system of ML uses a second level of terms consisting of an untyped, first-order signature. All type operators work on one implicit type (kind) of types. ML is not purely functional because it supports side effects through assignments in expressions. Miranda (Turner, 1985) is one of a number of purely functional languages with a Hindley/Milner type system. Haskell is a general purpose, purely functional programming language (Hudak *et al.*, 1992) with a Hindley/Milner type system using one-sorted first-order user-definable type constructors. Overloading, which is not supported in ML and Miranda, is introduced in a restricted form through type classes (see Section 5.1.2), which are the main innovation of the language.

The requirement and design specification language Spectrum (Broy *et al.*, 1993) is an algebraic specification formalism with applicative term structure, a two-level type system and sort classes, which is a variant of type classes. The second level is an unsorted signature. The distinction with functional languages like Haskell is the use of full first-order logic instead of conditional equations.

Two-Level Polymorphic Algebraic Languages The algebraic specification formalism PolySpec of Nazareth (1995) is a two-level formalism, with an untyped second level of type constructors and predicates (sort classes), which are used to constrain polymorphism similarly to type classes.

Both the algebraic and the applicative two-level languages that we have discussed have an untyped second level: all type constructors operate on the single, implicit sort `type`.

Three-Level Applicative Languages Quest is a three level language inspired by second-order typed λ-calculus (Cardelli, 1993). A Quest program introduces objects at three levels: values at level 0, types and type operators at level 1 and kinds at level 2. Instead of the limited universal type quantification of Hindley/Milner type systems, explicit and nested quantification over types is allowed. Universally quantified types, i.e., polymorphic types, have to be instantiated explicitly. For example, the identity function, declared as $id : \forall \alpha.\alpha \rightarrow \alpha$, should first be applied to a type to instantiate the type variable and then to a value, e.g., $id[int](1)$. Cardelli (1993) discusses a rich set of built-in data types including mutable types, array types, exception types, tuple types, option types, recursive types, subtyping, operations at the level of types. Quest does not support overloading.

Three-Level Algebraic Languages The algebraic specification formalism AT-LAS of Hearn and Meinke (1994) is a three-level algebraic specification formalism. The main differences with MLS are: (1) ATLAS has an arrow type constructor for the type of functions and a product type constructor for the type of pairs that are primitive at all levels, and that can be used as first-order types of the form $\tau_1 \times \cdots \times \tau_n \rightarrow \tau$, which means that term structure is algebraic. Higher-order function application can be simulated by means of a user-defined arrow type constructor and a user-defined application operator and by declaring functions as constants of the user defined arrow type. MLS has an applicative instead of an algebraic term structure, which makes higher-order types and functions more naturally definable. (2) An ATLAS specification consists of three levels for the constructors of 'kinds', 'types' and 'combinators' as the different sorts of terms are called. MLS specifications can have arbitrary many levels instead of the fixed three levels of ATLAS, making the definition of the syntax and type system uniform for all levels and enabling specifications with more or fewer than three levels. (3) ATLAS does not have a module system. (4) ATLAS considers ambiguous equations as erroneous. In MLS all well-formed typings of an equation are considered valid. (5) ATLAS specifications can contain rewrite rules at all levels, which are interpreted by the type assignment mechanism. Although the MLS formalism allows equations at all levels, these are not considered by the type assignment algorithm specified in this chapter.

Multi-Level Algebraic Languages ATLASII is a multi-level and modular redesign of ATLAS (Hearn, 1995). Items (1), (4) and (5) above also hold for ATLASII.

Multi-Level Applicative Languages The specification formalism MLS defined in this chapter is an applicative multi-level language with overloading.

5.1.5 Outline

The rest of this chapter presents the multi-level specification formalism MLS by means of a specification in ASF+SDF of syntax, type system and semantics. In order not to introduce too many concepts and technical details at once, the equational specification formalism is presented in three phases, each enhancing the previous one: (1) an untyped formalism, (2) a one-level applicative formalism without overloading or polymorphism, and (3) a multi-level, applicative formalism with polymorphism and overloading.

In Section 5.2 the notions of terms and equations for the untyped language are defined. Specifications are lists of equations over a simple term language with application and pairing.

In Section 5.3 this untyped language is extended to a one-level language, after introducing the notions of types and signatures.

In Section 5.4 a typechecker for this specification language is defined as the composition of a type assignment function and a well-formedness checker. The type assignment function takes a plain term and annotates it with types. The well-formedness checker takes a fully annotated term and verifies its well-formedness. The specification is presented in four parts: *Well-formedness* judgements determine whether a fully annotated term is well-formed according to a signature. The complements of the rules for well-formedness give descriptive *error messages* for non-wellformed terms. A *type assignment* function annotates each subterm of a plain term with a type. A *typechecker* combines type assignment and well-formedness checking.

In Section 5.5 one-level specifications are used to form multi-level specifications. The same syntax for terms, signatures and equations is used at all levels. The usefulness of such multi-level specifications is illustrated with several examples of data type specification in MLS.

In Section 5.7 the type system of multi-level specifications is defined with the same four part structure as for one-level specifications. The same ideas apply to the type system, but are complicated by the addition of multiple levels of signatures, polymorphism and overloading. The most important innovation here is that the types of each level of the specification are well-formed terms over the signature at the next level of the specification. This means that types become typed terms. The same typechecking mechanism is used at all levels.

The appendices of this chapter define a number of tools that are used in the specification. In Appendix 5.A several 'standard' library modules like Layout and Booleans are defined. In Appendix 5.B several utilities on terms such as sets of terms, substitution, matching and unification are defined.

5.2 Untyped Equational Specifications

Equational specifications consist of a list of equations over some term language. Such specifications can be interpreted as a set of axioms for reasoning with equational logic. For many specifications, equality of terms in the context of an equational specification can be made by means of term rewriting. We start with the definition of the term language.

5.2.1   Terms

The *terms* of our specification language are simple applicative terms composed of function symbols (identifiers starting with a lowercase letter, e.g., map, variables (identifiers starting with an uppercase letter, e.g., X), application $(t_1\ t_2)$, and pairing (t_1, t_2). Application is left-associative and has a higher priority than pairing. Pairing is right-associative. For example, map G empty denotes ((map G) empty), not map(G(empty)). Likewise, plus X, Y should be read as (plus X), Y and not as plus(X, Y). In this chapter we will write the argument of an application between parentheses, e.g., map(G)(empty) instead of map G empty. These notations are syntactically equivalent according to the following grammar.

imports Layout[5.A.1]

exports

  sorts Fun Var Term

  lexical syntax

    [a-z0-9][A-Za-z0-9_]* → Fun

    [A-Z][A-Za-z_]*[0-9']* → Var

  context-free syntax

    Var   → Term

    Fun   → Term

    Term Term   → Term **{left}**

    Term "," Term → Term **{right}**

    "(" Term ")" → Term **{bracket}**

  priorities

    Term Term → Term > Term ","Term → Term

  variables

    [xy][0-9']* → Var

    "f"[0-9']* → Fun

    "t"[0-9']* → Term

To accommodate the convention of writing binary functions as infix operators, Appendix 5.B.1 defines syntax for infix operators. The application of a binary operator $\oplus$ to two arguments t_1 and t_2 is written $t_1 \oplus t_2$. By enclosing a binary operator in parentheses it is converted into a prefix function symbol. Using this property an infix application is translated into a prefix application by the equation $t_1 \oplus t_2 = (\oplus)(t_1, t_2)$. For example, in Figure 5.1 the expression size(T) + size(T') is equivalent to (+)(size(T), size(T')) and X :: L is equivalent to (::)(X, L). Furthermore, Appendix 5.B.1 introduces notation to use an arbitrary term as an infix operator, such that a binary function application of the form $t_1(t_2, t_3)$ can be written as $t_2\ .t_1.\ t_3$. Finally, if the functions (::) and [] are used to construct lists, the notation $[t_1, \ldots, t_n]$ can be used to represent a list with a fixed number of elements. This notation is translated to $t_1 :: \ldots :: t_n :: []$. Note that using the $[t_1, \ldots, t_n]$

notation the tail of the list is always [], i.e., can not be a variable or another term. Similarly, tuple terms of the form $<t_1, \ldots, t_n>$ are abbreviations for $t_1 \char94 \ldots \char94 t_n \char94 <>$.

The extension of multi-level signature formalisms with arbitrary mix-fix operators (like if _ then _ else _) leads to a multi-level grammar formalism. Such a formalism leads to extra complications in parsing that are out of the scope of this chapter, and the subject of ongoing research (see (Visser, 1995c) and Section 5.8).

Lists of terms separated by semicolons.

exports
    sorts Terms
    context-free syntax

{Term ";"}*	→ Terms
Terms "++" Terms	→ Terms {**right**}
"(" Terms ")"	→ Terms {**bracket**}

    variables

"t" "*"$[0\text{-}9']$*	→ {Term ";"}*
"t" "+"$[0\text{-}9']$*	→ {Term ";"}+
"ts"$[0\text{-}9']$*	→ Terms

equations

[l-conc] $\qquad\qquad\qquad\qquad\qquad\qquad t_1^* \mathbin{+\!\!+} t_2^* = t_1^*; t_2^*$

5.2.2 Equations

An *equation* is a pair of terms $t_1 \equiv t_2$. In order to avoid confusion between the equality symbol in the object language we are describing and the metalanguage we describe it with, the symbol $\equiv$ is used for specification equations. It is written == in examples. We will refer to the left-hand (right-hand) side t_1 (t_2) of an equation by 'lhs' ('rhs'). An *equational specification* is a list of equations.

imports Binary-Operators[5.B.1] Terms[5.2.1]
exports
    sorts Eq Eqs
    context-free syntax

Term "$\equiv$" Term	→ Eq
{Eq ";"}*	→ Eqs
Eqs "++" Eqs	→ Eqs {**assoc**}
"(" Eqs ")"	→ Eqs {**bracket**}

    variables

"φ"$[0\text{-}9']$*	→ Eq
"φ" "*"$[0\text{-}9']$*	→ {Eq ";"}*
"φ" "+"$[0\text{-}9']$*	→ {Eq ";"}+
"$\mathcal{E}$"$[0\text{-}9']$*	→ Eqs

```
0 + X          == X;
s(X) + Y       == s(X + Y);
map(G)([])     == [];
map(G)(X :: L) == G(X) :: map(G)(L)
```

Figure 5.2: Untyped equational specification of addition on successor naturals and map over cons lists.

equations

[eqs-conc] $\varphi_1^* \mathbin{+\!\!+} \varphi_2^* = \varphi_1^*; \varphi_2^*$

An example specification is shown in Figure 5.2. The first two equations define the addition operation (+) on successor naturals. The last two equations define the function map that applies some function G to all elements of a list represented by means of the functions [] (empty list) and (::) (cons). Observe that some of the parentheses used are optional, e.g., we might as well write G X instead of G(X). Recall that we will use the convention of writing the argument of an application between parentheses.

5.2.3 Equational Logic

A term represents a value. In an equational specification a term represents the same value as all terms to which it is equal. In this view the semantics of a specification is the equality relation on terms that it induces. This relation is determined by the following rules of equational logic together with a list of equations (also called axioms). Two terms t_1 and t_2 are equal according to a set of equations $\mathcal{E}$ if the predicate $\mathcal{E} \vdash t_1 \equiv t_2$ holds. Note that predicates are modeled by means of Boolean functions in ASF+SDF. This entails that the specification of a predicate consists of equations over sort Bool. If P is a Boolean function we will write $P(x)$ in texts when we mean $P(x) = \top$.

The rules of equational logic are the reflexivity, symmetry and transitivity rules of equivalence relations; an axiom rule that declares any equation in $\mathcal{E}$ as axiom; a substitution rule that makes any substitution instance of a derivably equation derivable; and congruence rules. The substitution rule [el-sub] uses the notation $\sigma(t)$ for the application to a term t of a substitution σ that maps variables to terms. (See Appendix 5.B.7 for the definition of substitution.)

imports Equations[5.2.2] Substitution[5.B.7] Booleans[5.A.2]
exports
   context-free syntax
      Eqs "⊢" Eq → Bool

equations

[el-refl]
$$\mathcal{E} \vdash t \equiv t = \top$$

[el-sym]
$$\frac{\mathcal{E} \vdash t_2 \equiv t_1 = \top}{\mathcal{E} \vdash t_1 \equiv t_2 = \top}$$

[el-trans]
$$\frac{\mathcal{E} \vdash t_1 \equiv t_2 = \top, \ \mathcal{E} \vdash t_2 \equiv t_3 = \top}{\mathcal{E} \vdash t_1 \equiv t_3 = \top}$$

[el-ax]
$$\varphi_1^*; t_1 \equiv t_2; \varphi_2^* \vdash t_1 \equiv t_2 = \top$$

[el-sub]
$$\frac{\mathcal{E} \vdash t_1 \equiv t_2 = \top}{\mathcal{E} \vdash \sigma(t_1) \equiv \sigma(t_2) = \top}$$

[el-app]
$$\frac{\mathcal{E} \vdash t_1 \equiv t_3 = \top, \ \mathcal{E} \vdash t_2 \equiv t_4 = \top}{\mathcal{E} \vdash t_1 \ t_2 \equiv t_3 \ t_4 = \top}$$

[el-pr]
$$\frac{\mathcal{E} \vdash t_1 \equiv t_3 = \top, \ \mathcal{E} \vdash t_2 \equiv t_4 = \top}{\mathcal{E} \vdash t_1, t_2 \equiv t_3, t_4 = \top}$$

This specification is not executable as a term rewrite system, because it is non-deterministic and not normalizing. This is not surprising since equational derivability is an undecidable property. To determine whether two terms are equal we can make use of several other techniques. In the following subsection we define an evaluation function that implements a simple rewrite strategy that decides (ground) equality for a large class of specifications.

5.2.4 Term Rewriting

Equational specifications can be interpreted as *term rewriting systems* by directing the equations from left to right. This gives a procedure for deciding derivable equality from a set of equations that constitutes a terminating and confluent rewrite system. *Evaluation* of a term in the context of a specification amounts to finding its *normal form*, if it exists, with respect to the term rewriting system. If $\mathcal{E}$ is a list of equations and t is a term, then $t' = \text{eval}(\mathcal{E})[\![t]\!]$ is the normal form of t under $\mathcal{E}$, i.e., t' has no sub-term that matches the lhs of an equation in $\mathcal{E}$.

There are a number of strategies used to find normal forms. Here we use a simple left-most innermost rewriting algorithm. This strategy is sound with respect to equational logic, i.e., if two terms have the same normal form they are also derivably equal. The strategy is (ground) complete with respect to confluent and strongly normalizing term rewrite systems, i.e., two terms are derivably equal if and only if they have the same normal form.

Evaluation proceeds as follows. The auxiliary function 'step' tries to find a matching equation for a term. If it finds one, the instantiation of its rhs is evaluated. In equation [redex] the list of equations is searched (by means of list matching, see Section 1.4.2) for an equation $t_1 \equiv t_2$ such that the lhs t_1 matches the term t, i.e., such that there is a substitution σ such that $\sigma(t_1) = t$. The substitution is found in the condition $t_1 := t = \sigma$. The substitution σ forms the environment for the evaluation of the rhs of the equation. If no matching equation is found, 'step' just returns its argument (equation [nf]). The function 'eval' itself evaluates a term by first evaluating its direct sub-terms and then applying 'step' to the composition of the resulting normal forms.[2]

imports Matching[5.B.8] Equations[5.2.2]
exports
   context-free syntax

eval "(" Eqs ")" "[" Term "]"	$\rightarrow$ Term
eval "(" Eqs ")" "[" Term "]" "_" Subst	$\rightarrow$ Term
step "(" Eqs ")" "[" Term "]"	$\rightarrow$ Term

equations

[eval-trm]	$\mathrm{eval}(\mathcal{E})[\![t]\!] = \mathrm{eval}(\mathcal{E})[\![t]\!]_{[\,]}$
[eval-var]	$\mathrm{eval}(\mathcal{E})[\![x]\!]_\sigma = \sigma(x)$
[eval-fun]	$\mathrm{eval}(\mathcal{E})[\![f]\!]_\sigma = \mathrm{step}(\mathcal{E})[\![f]\!]$
[eval-app]	$\mathrm{eval}(\mathcal{E})[\![t_1\ t_2]\!]_\sigma = \mathrm{step}(\mathcal{E})[\![\mathrm{eval}(\mathcal{E})[\![t_1]\!]_\sigma\ \mathrm{eval}(\mathcal{E})[\![t_2]\!]_\sigma]\!]$
[eval-pr]	$\mathrm{eval}(\mathcal{E})[\![t_1,\ t_2]\!]_\sigma = \mathrm{step}(\mathcal{E})[\![\mathrm{eval}(\mathcal{E})[\![t_1]\!]_\sigma,\ \mathrm{eval}(\mathcal{E})[\![t_2]\!]_\sigma]\!]$
[redex]	$\mathrm{step}(\mathcal{E})[\![t]\!] = \mathrm{eval}(\mathcal{E})[\![t_2]\!]_\sigma$
	when $\mathcal{E} = \varphi_1^*; t_1 \equiv t_2; \varphi_2^*,\ t_1 := t = \sigma$
[nf]	$\mathrm{step}(\mathcal{E})[\![t]\!] = t$ **otherwise**

The following proposition states that evaluation is sound with respect to derivable equality.

Proposition 5.1 (soundness of evaluation) *If $\mathcal{E}$ constitutes a terminating term rewrite system and* $\mathrm{eval}(\mathcal{E})[\![t]\!]_\sigma = t'$, *then* $\mathcal{E} \vdash \sigma(t) \equiv t'$ *and if* $\mathrm{step}(\mathcal{E})[\![t]\!] = t'$, *then* $\mathcal{E} \vdash t \equiv t'$

Proof: By simultaneous induction on the definition of eval and step.   □

Observe that the specification of evaluation is not sufficiently-complete, because the 'eval' of a non-terminating term cannot be eliminated and thus is a new term constructor. The restriction to terminating rewrite systems in the soundness proposition is necessary because the definition of equational logic does not account for these

---

[2]Note that the underscore _ in the syntax of the function 'eval' is interpreted by the ASF+SDF to LATEX typesetting program by typesetting the next argument, i.e., the substitution, as a subscript.

new term constructors. This could be repaired by introducing an auxiliary sort as the result of evaluation and using conditional equations to define 'eval' as in

$$\frac{\text{eval}(\mathcal{E})\llbracket t_1 \rrbracket = t_1', \text{eval}(\mathcal{E})\llbracket t_2 \rrbracket = t_2'}{\text{eval}(\mathcal{E})\llbracket t_1\ t_2 \rrbracket = \text{step}(\mathcal{E})\llbracket t_1'\ t_2' \rrbracket}$$

The conditions work as 'retracts' and guarantee that the rule only applies if the evaluation of the subterms terminate, thereby avoiding the pollution of the sort Term. However, this gives a more complicated specification that does not have a better termination behavior and adds nothing to our understanding of term rewriting. Therefore, we leave the specification as it is, with the somewhat loose understanding that it says what we intend for terminating specifications.

5.3   One-Level Specifications

The untyped equations of the previous section do not impose a restriction on the set of terms that they describe. Although we have an intuition about the terms that are meaningful with respect to a specification and those that are not, this is not formalized. For instance, the specification in Figure 5.2 clearly manipulates two categories of terms: numbers composed by 0, s and (+) and lists composed by [], (::) and map. However, s(map) + 0 is a valid term over this specification, which has no apparent meaning in our intuition about the specification.

Signatures formalize the intuition about the types of terms in specifications and allow one to check that specifications and terms comply with each other. A signature is a list of declarations of functions and variables that is interpreted as a predicate on terms indicating which terms are well-formed. In this section, we extend the untyped equational specification formalism with signatures, leading to the one-level specification formalism OLS.

5.3.1   An Example

Before giving the syntax of type terms, signatures and specifications we discuss a simple example of a one-level specification. Figure 5.3(a) presents the specification of natural numbers in OLS. The signature part declares the constant nat as a sort and the constant 0, the unary function s and the binary function (+). Furthermore, the signature declares X and Y as nat variables. Together these declarations define the terms of sort nat. The equation part defines the meaning of the binary function (+) in terms of 0 and s.

The signature of this specification is depicted by the *signature diagram* in Figure 5.3(b). The diagram consists an ellipse denoting the set of all terms of sort nat. The arrows denote the functions declared in the signature. The constant 0 is denoted by an arrow without origin. The unary function s is denoted by an arrow from nat to nat; it takes a natural number and produces a new one. The binary function (+)

```
signature
  sorts nat;
  functions
    0    : nat;
    s    : nat -> nat;
    (+) : nat # nat -> nat;
  variables
    X, Y : nat;
  equations
    0 + X    == X;
    s(X) + Y == s(X + Y)
```

(a)

(b)

Figure 5.3: Specification of successor naturals with addition (a) and corresponding signature diagram (b).

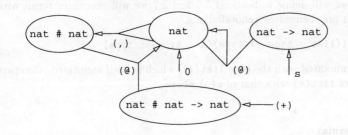

Figure 5.4: Signature diagram of natural numbers in which function and product types and the corresponding application and pairing functions are depicted explicitly. The functions s and (+) are constants of functional types.

takes two natural numbers and produces a new one, which is depicted by the forked arrow.

As we will see, the term structure of one-level specifications is actually applicative. This entails that besides nat, there are two sorts nat -> nat and nat # nat -> nat, i.e., they are sets of terms. The signature diagram in Figure 5.4 depicts this situation. The functions s and (+) are constants of sorts nat -> nat and nat # nat -> nat, respectively. The diagram also shows the role of the implicitly declared pairing (,) and application (@) functions.

5.3.2 Types

A *type* is an expression that denotes a set of terms. Types in many-sorted signatures are composed of constants, such as nat, by means of the type operators product $\times$ and arrow $\rightarrow$. The product type $\tau_1 \times \tau_2$ denotes pairs of terms (t_1, t_2) of type τ_1 and τ_2, respectively. The type $\tau_1 \rightarrow \tau_2$ denotes the type of functions with domain τ_1 and codomain τ_2. The types in polymorphic languages are $\{\times, \rightarrow\}$-types extended with arbitrary terms like list(nat). We will see later that such types can be described by a signature. Anticipating this extension, we use terms extended with the product and arrow operators as types. The variable τ, ranging over terms, will be used to indicate a term used as type.

A *type annotation* of a term is the attachment of a type to each subterm. Annotation is expressed by means of the operator ':'. The term $t : \tau$ denotes the term t annotated with type τ. A term is *fully annotated* if each subterm has a type annotation. For example, the term

        (s : nat -> nat)(0 : nat) : nat

is a fully annotated version of the term s(0). In the context of a signature, a term without annotations is an abbreviation of an annotated term. In the multi-level extension that we will define in Sections 5.5 and 5.7 we will encounter terms with annotations that are themselves annotated, e.g.

        [] : ((list : type -> type)(A : type) : type)

is the term [] annotated with the type list(A), which is itself annotated. Compare the annotation of list(A) with that of s(0) above.

imports Terms[5.2.1]
exports
  context-free syntax
    "nil" $\rightarrow$ Term
    "top" $\rightarrow$ Term
    Term "$\times$" Term $\rightarrow$ Term   {**right**}
    Term "$\rightarrow$" Term $\rightarrow$ Term   {**right**}
    Term ":" Term $\rightarrow$ Term   {**right**}
  priorities
    Term Term $\rightarrow$ Term > Term "$\times$"Term $\rightarrow$ Term > Term "$\rightarrow$"Term $\rightarrow$ Term
    > Term ":"Term $\rightarrow$ Term > Term ","Term $\rightarrow$ Term
  variables
    "τ"$[0\text{-}9']*$ $\rightarrow$ Term
    "τ" "*"$[0\text{-}9']*$ $\rightarrow$ {Term ";"}*
    "τ" "+"$[0\text{-}9']*$ $\rightarrow$ {Term ";"}+

The terms 'nil' and 'top' are auxiliary types that will be used in typechecking. 'nil' denotes the empty type, which is assigned to terms for which no type exists. In our multi-level setting, 'top' will denote the type of top-level types, i.e., terms over the implicit signature on top of a multi-level specification.

The priorities section declares that application has highest priority of all term constructors and that product binds stronger than arrow, which has higher priority than type annotation and pair. For instance, read

```
list : type -> type          as   list : (type -> type)
list A -> nat                as   (list A) -> nat
nat # nat -> nat             as   (nat # nat) -> nat
list : type -> type A : type as   list : ((type -> (type A)) : type)
                and not as   (list : (type -> type)) (A : type)
```

5.3.3 Term Analysis

Recall that we have the following term constructors: variable and function symbols, nil, top, application, pairing, product, arrow and annotation. These are all the constructors we will consider in this chapter. All other functions that produce terms should be such that they can always be eliminated (i.e., the specification is assumed to be sufficiently complete). Assuming this property, a default (otherwise) equation over a function with a term as argument ranges over all constructors for which no other equation is defined, and thus is an abbreviation for a list of equations with those other constructors substituted.

For future use we now define several functions for analyzing terms. The sort TermToTerm is the sort of functions from terms to terms that is defined in Appendix 5.B.3. The basic operation of this sort is the application of a function to a term yielding a term, i.e., TermToTerm(Term) → Term. This approach makes it possible to generically define a function that applies a TermToTerm function to all terms in a list of terms.

imports Term-Functions[5.B.3] Terms[5.2.1] Types[5.3.2] Binary-Operators[5.B.1]
exports
  context-free syntax

spine	→	TermToTerm
fspine	→	TermToTerm
term	→	TermToTerm
type	→	TermToTerm
dom	→	TermToTerm
cod	→	TermToTerm
fun	→	TermToTerm
arg	→	TermToTerm
bterm	→	TermToTerm
bapp	→	TermToTerm

equations
The type assignment functions that will be specified later add annotations to terms. In order to relate a fully annotated term to its underlying plain term, the

function 'spine' removes all annotations from a term. For instance, the spine of
(s : nat -> nat)(0: nat) : nat is s(0).

[sp-ann]	$\text{spine}(t : \tau) = \text{spine}(t)$
[sp-fun]	$\text{spine}(f) = f$
[sp-var]	$\text{spine}(x) = x$
[sp-top]	$\text{spine}(\text{nil}) = \text{nil}$
[sp-top]	$\text{spine}(\text{top}) = \text{top}$
[sp-pr]	$\text{spine}(t_1, t_2) = \text{spine}(t_1), \text{spine}(t_2)$
[sp-app]	$\text{spine}(t_1\ t_2) = \text{spine}(t_1)\ \text{spine}(t_2)$
[sp-prd]	$\text{spine}(t_1 \times t_2) = \text{spine}(t_1) \times \text{spine}(t_2)$
[sp-arr]	$\text{spine}(t_1 \to t_2) = \text{spine}(t_1) \to \text{spine}(t_2)$

The function 'fspine' is the same as 'spine' except that it does not remove the annotation from a function symbol.

[fsp-fun]	$\text{fspine}(f : \tau) = f : \tau$
[fsp-ann]	$\text{fspine}(t : \tau) = \text{fspine}(t)$ **otherwise**

The other equations are the same as for 'spine'. This function is used to translate annotated terms over a signature with overloading to disambiguated plain terms.

The 'term' of an annotated term is the term without its outermost type annotation. The 'type' of a term is its outermost annotation.

[trm-ann]	$\text{term}(t : \tau) = t$
[tp-ann]	$\text{type}(t : \tau) = \tau$

We see that for any term t of the form $t' : \tau$, $\text{term}(t) : \text{type}(t) = t$. To extend this property to arbitrary terms, the 'term' of a term without annotation is defined to be the term itself and the 'type' of a term without annotation is 'top'. To complete the picture it follows that a term with annotation 'top' is equal to the term itself.

[trm]	$\text{term}(t) = t$ **otherwise**
[type]	$\text{type}(t) = \text{top}$ **otherwise**
[top-ann]	$t : \text{top} = t$

Now we have for arbitrary terms

[term-type]	$\text{term}(t) : \text{type}(t) = t$

The functions 'dom' and 'cod' give the *domain* and *codomain* of a function type, respectively. The domain of a term that is not an arrow is nil, its codomain is the term itself. nil is a left unit for arrow. This corresponds to the notion that a constant is a function without arguments. Similarly the functions 'fun' and 'arg' give the *function* and *argument* of an application

[dom-arr] $\text{dom}(t_1 \to t_2) = t_1$	[arg-app] $\text{arg}(t_1\ t_2) = t_2$

[dom]	$\mathrm{dom}(t)$	$=$ nil	**otherwise**	[arg]	$\mathrm{arg}(t)$	$=$ nil	**otherwise**
[cod-arr]	$\mathrm{cod}(t_1 \to t_2)$	$= t_2$		[fun-app]	$\mathrm{fun}(t_1\ t_2)$	$= t_1$	
[cod]	$\mathrm{cod}(t)$	$= t$	**otherwise**	[fun]	$\mathrm{fun}(t)$	$= t$	**otherwise**
[nil-cod]	$\mathrm{nil} \to t$	$= t$		[fun-nil]	$t\ \mathrm{nil}$	$= t$	

We have

[arg-res] $\mathrm{dom}(t) \to \mathrm{cod}(t)\ =\ t$ [arg-res] $\mathrm{fun}(t)\ \mathrm{arg}(t)\ =\ t$

The functions above are combined in the definition of the function 'bterm' that is used to analyze the types of binary functions. It strips the outermost annotation off an arrow term and off its domain.

[bterm1] $\mathrm{bterm}(t) = \mathrm{term}(\mathrm{dom}(\mathrm{term}(t))) \to \mathrm{cod}(\mathrm{term}(t))$

For example,

```
bterm((((nat : type) # (nat : type)) : type -> (nat : type) : type))
= (nat : type) # (nat : type) -> (nat : type)
```

This function will be used for typechecking multi-level specifications. Similarly the function 'bapp' removes the annotations from a binary application

[bapp1] $\mathrm{bapp}(t) = t_1\ (t_2, t_3)$
                     when $\mathrm{term}(t) = t_1'\ t_2'$, $\mathrm{term}(t_1') = t_1$, $\mathrm{term}(t_2') = t_2, t_3$
[bapp2] $\mathrm{bapp}(t) = t$ **otherwise**

For example,

```
bapp(((+) : nat # nat -> nat)((0 : nat, 0 : nat) : nat # nat) : nat)
= (+)((0 : nat), (0 : nat))
```

5.3.4   Syntax of One-Level Specifications (OLS)

A signature is constructed from sort, function and variable declarations.

Declarations   A *function declaration* of the form $f : \tau$ assigns the type τ to function symbol f. For example, the type of the addition operator plus on natural numbers is declared as plus : nat # nat -> nat. An infix operator is declared by declaring its prefix notation as a binary function. For instance, if we use + as an infix operator for addition on natural numbers we would declare (+) : nat # nat -> nat. A *variable declaration* of the form $x : \tau$ assigns type τ to variable symbol x. For instance, the declaration X : nat declares a variable X of type nat. A *sort declaration* consists of a declaration of function symbols to be used as basic types.

imports Terms[5.2.1] Types[5.3.2] Binary-Operators[5.B.1]

exports
  sorts Decl Decls
  context-free syntax
    {Fun ","}+ ":" Term → Decl
    {Var ","}+ ":" Term → Decl
    {Decl ";"}∗   → Decls
    Decls "++" Decls   → Decls {**right**}
  variables
    $[f]$"+"$[0\text{-}9']$∗ → {Fun ","}+
    $[x]$"+"$[0\text{-}9']$∗ → {Var ","}+
    "d"$[0\text{-}9']$∗   → Decl
    "d" "∗"$[0\text{-}9']$∗ → {Decl ";"}∗
    "d" "+"$[0\text{-}9']$∗ → {Decl ";"}+
    "ds"$[0\text{-}9']$∗   → Decls

equations

According to the syntax above, declarations can have the form $f_1, \ldots, f_n : \tau$ declaring in one declaration the function symbols f_i to be of type τ. This notation is merely an abbreviation of a list of declarations $f_i : \tau$ as expressed by the following equations.

[f-decl] $d_1^*; f_1^+, f_2^+ : \tau; d_2^* = d_1^*; f_1^+ : \tau; f_2^+ : \tau; d_2^*$
[v-decl] $d_1^*; x_1^+, x_2^+ : \tau; d_2^* = d_1^*; x_1^+ : \tau; x_2^+ : \tau; d_2^*$
[decls-conc] $d_1^* \mathbin{+\!\!+} d_2^* = d_1^*; d_2^*$

Signatures An atomic signature is constructed from sort, function and variable declarations by the constructors 'sorts', 'functions' and 'variables', respectively. Signatures can be combined by the signature concatenation operator ';'. The projection functions 'S', 'F' and 'V' yield the list of sorts, function declarations, and variable declarations, respectively, of a signature.

exports
  sorts Sig
  context-free syntax
    "sorts" Terms   → Sig
    "functions" Decls → Sig
    "variables" Decls → Sig
                 → Sig
    Sig ";" Sig   → Sig   {**right**}
    "(" Sig ")"   → Sig   {**bracket**}
    "S"(Sig)   → Terms
    "F"(Sig)   → Decls
    "V"(Sig)   → Decls
  variables

"Σ" $[0\text{-}9']* \to$ Sig

equations

Equations [Sig-es], [Sig-ef] and [Sig-ev] express that atomic signatures with empty declaration lists are equivalent to empty signatures.

[Sgel]	; Σ	$= \Sigma$		[Sges]	sorts	$=$	
[Sger]	Σ;	$= \Sigma$		[Sgef]	functions	$=$	
[Sgas]	$(\Sigma_1; \Sigma_2); \Sigma_3$	$= \Sigma_1; \Sigma_2; \Sigma_3$		[Sgev]	variables	$=$	
[S1]	S(sorts ts)	$= ts$		[S4]	S()	$=$	
[S2]	S(functions ds)	$=$		[S5]	S($\Sigma_1; \Sigma_2$)	$=$ S(Σ_1) ++ S(Σ_2)	
[S3]	S(variables ds)	$=$					
[F1]	F(sorts ts)	$=$		[F4]	F()	$=$	
[F2]	F(functions ds)	$= ds$		[F5]	F($\Sigma_1; \Sigma_2$)	$=$ F(Σ_1) ++ F(Σ_2)	
[F3]	F(variables ds)	$=$					
[V1]	V(sorts ts)	$=$		[V4]	V()	$=$	
[V2]	V(functions ds)	$=$		[V5]	V($\Sigma_1; \Sigma_2$)	$=$ V(Σ_1) ++ V(Σ_2)	
[V3]	V(variables ds)	$= ds$					

Specifications An atomic specification is a signature or a list of equations indicated by the functions 'signature' and 'equations', respectively. Specifications are combined by the operator ';'. The projection functions 'Sg' and 'E' give the signature and equations of a specification.

imports Equations[5.2.2]

exports

  sorts Spec

  context-free syntax

    "signature" Sig $\to$ Spec

    "equations" Eqs $\to$ Spec

               $\to$ Spec

    Spec ";" Spec $\to$ Spec **{right}**

    "(" Spec ")" $\to$ Spec **{bracket}**

    "Sg" (Spec) $\to$ Sig

    "E" (Spec) $\to$ Eqs

  variables

    "S" $[0\text{-}9']* \to$ Spec

equations

[Spel]	; S	$= S$		[Spes]	signature	$=$
[Sper]	S;	$= S$		[Spee]	equations	$=$
[Spas]	$(S_1; S_2); S_3$	$= S_1; S_2; S_3$				
[Sg1]	Sg(signature Σ)	$= \Sigma$		[E1]	E(signature Σ)	$=$
[Sg2]	Sg(equations $\mathcal{E}$)	$=$		[E2]	E(equations $\mathcal{E}$)	$= \mathcal{E}$
[Sg3]	Sg()	$=$		[E3]	E()	$=$

[Sg4] $\mathrm{Sg}(\mathcal{S}_1; \mathcal{S}_2)$ $= \mathrm{Sg}(\mathcal{S}_1); \mathrm{Sg}(\mathcal{S}_2)$ [E4] $\mathrm{E}(\mathcal{S}_1; \mathcal{S}_2)$ $= \mathrm{E}(\mathcal{S}_1) + \!\!\!+ \mathrm{E}(\mathcal{S}_2)$

We can extend the TermToTerm functions to apply to all terms in a specification. By means of these functions we can apply the functions 'spine' and 'fspine' to a fully annotated specification in order to get its underlying plain specification. Accordingly, spine($\mathcal{S}$) denotes the underlying plain specification of specification $\mathcal{S}$.

5.3.5 Specification Semantics

The semantics of specifications is defined by means of an extension of equational logic to terms with type annotations.

Typed Equational Logic

Equation [tel-ax] states that an equation $t_1 \equiv t_2$ is an axiom of a specification $\mathcal{S}$ if it is an element of the equations of $\mathcal{S}$. The other rules are the same as in the case of untyped equational logic (Section 5.2.3), except for the congruence rule for annotated terms [tel-ann]. Only terms with the same annotation can be equated if they are equal without annotation. Compare this to the congruence rules for application [el-app] and pairing [el-pr] in Section 5.2.3, where both arguments can be equal modulo the equations in $\mathcal{E}$. In the case of multi-level specifications we will give an equational logic (Section 5.6.4) where equations over types play a role.

imports OLS[5.3.4] Substitution[5.B.7]
exports
    context-free syntax
        Spec "⊢" Eq → Bool
equations

[tel-ax]
$$\frac{\mathrm{E}(\mathcal{S}) = \varphi_1^*; \, t_1 \equiv t_2; \, \varphi_2^*}{\mathcal{S} \vdash t_1 \equiv t_2 \ = \ \mathsf{T}}$$

[tel-ann]
$$\frac{\mathcal{S} \vdash t_1 \equiv t_2 = \mathsf{T}}{\mathcal{S} \vdash t_1 : \tau \equiv t_2 : \tau \ = \ \mathsf{T}}$$

The standard rules for reflexivity, symmetry, transitivity, substitution and congruence for the other binary operators are not shown.

Proposition 5.2 *Typed equational logic over a list of equations $\mathcal{E}$ is type preserving if the equations in $\mathcal{E}$ are type preserving, i.e., if for each $t_1 \equiv t_2 \in \mathcal{E}$, type($t_1$) = type($t_2$) then $\mathcal{E} \vdash t \equiv t'$ implies type(t) = type(t').*

Proof: by induction on derivations. The property clearly holds for [tel-ax], [tel-refl] and [tel-ann] and equality of types is preserved by symmetry, transitivity, substitution and congruence. □

Typed Term Rewriting

In accordance with the rules for typed equational logic, the typed innermost term rewriting function 'eval' applies equations, oriented from left to right, until a term is in normal form. The annotation of a term is not evaluated in equation [eval-ann], because the equations of a specification apply only to object terms and not to types.

imports OLS[5.3.4] Matching[5.B.8]
exports
  context-free syntax
    eval "(" Spec ")" "⟦" Term "⟧" $\rightarrow$ Term
    eval "(" Spec ")" "⟦" Term "⟧" "_" Subst $\rightarrow$ Term
    step "(" Spec ")" "⟦" Term "⟧" $\rightarrow$ Term
equations

[eval-trm] $\text{eval}(\mathcal{S})[\![t]\!] = \text{eval}(\mathcal{S})[\![t]\!]_{[]}$

[eval-ann] $\text{eval}(\mathcal{S})[\![t : \tau]\!]_\sigma = \text{step}(\mathcal{S})[\![\text{eval}(\mathcal{S})[\![t]\!]_\sigma : \sigma(\tau)]\!]$

[redex] $\text{step}(\mathcal{S})[\![t]\!] = \text{eval}(\mathcal{S})[\![t_2]\!]_\sigma$
                when $\text{E}(\mathcal{S}) = \varphi_1^*;\ t_1 \equiv t_2;\ \varphi_2^*,\ t_1 := t = \sigma$

[nf] $\text{step}(\mathcal{S})[\![t]\!] = t$ **otherwise**

The evaluation rules for the other operators are straightforward following Section 5.2.4. Note that recursive applications of eval to the other new operators product and arrow have to be added.

5.4 Typechecking One-Level Specifications

The context-free syntax of specifications defined in the previous section allows many degrees of freedom. In this section we narrow this down to the subset of one-level equational specifications with monomorphic types and no overloading. In Section 5.7 we will extend this to multi-level signatures with polymorphism and overloading. Here we avoid the complications introduced by multi-level specifications to make it easier to explain the architecture and basic ideas of the specification of the type system.

In Section 5.4.2 (Module OLS-WF) the well-formedness of fully annotated specifications is defined. The definition of well-formedness only specifies the correct cases, i.e., it contains a function which yields ⊤ iff the specification is well-formed. It does not deal with erroneous cases. The translation of these to human readable error messages is taken care of in Section 5.4.3 (Module OLS-NWF).

Since fully annotated specifications are difficult to read and write, programmers are not expected to actually write such specifications (although it is possible to supply partial annotations in terms to constrain their typing). Instead, plain specifications without annotations are annotated with types by a type assignment function defined in Section 5.4.4 (Module OLS-TA).

Finally, the typechecker defined in Section 5.4.5 (Module OLS-TC) first applies the type assignment function to a specification and then checks the result for well-formedness. This setup gives a separation between typechecking and type assignment that saves a great deal of bookkeeping and makes the definitions accessible. Moreover, annotated specifications can be used as input for tools other than a well-formedness checker, for instance a theorem prover or term rewriter.

First we define projection functions to find the type of a function or variable in a signature.

5.4.1 Projection

The projection function π yields the type of the first declaration for a variable or function in a list of declarations. The type of a function symbol f in a signature Σ is $\pi_f(\Sigma)$. The type of a variable symbol x in a signature Σ is $\pi_x(\Sigma)$. Observe that variable declarations in a 'functions' section and function declarations in a 'variables' section are ignored.

imports OLS[5.3.4]

exports

  context-free syntax

    "π" "_" Var "(" Decls ")" $\rightarrow$ Term

    "π" "_" Fun "(" Decls ")" $\rightarrow$ Term

    "π" "_" Var "(" Sig ")" $\rightarrow$ Term

    "π" "_" Fun "(" Sig ")" $\rightarrow$ Term

equations

  Looking up a function in a list of declarations. If no declaration is found the term 'nil' is returned.

[p1b] $\pi_f(d^*) = \text{nil}$ **when** $d^* =$

[p2b] $\pi_f(f:\tau; d^*) = \tau$

[p4b] $\pi_f(d; d^*) = \pi_f(d^*)$ **otherwise**

The projection of a variable from a list of declarations is defined similarly.

[p1a] $\pi_x(d^*) = \text{nil}$ **when** $d^* =$

[p2a] $\pi_x(x:\tau; d^*) = \tau$

[p4a] $\pi_x(d; d^*) = \pi_x(d^*)$ **otherwise**

Looking up the type of a function in a signature consists of looking it up in the list of function declarations. The type of a variable is found by looking it up in the list of variable declarations.

[pf] $\pi_f(\Sigma) = \pi_f(\text{F}(\Sigma))$

[px] $\pi_x(\Sigma) = \pi_x(\text{V}(\Sigma))$

```
signature
  sorts nat;
  functions
    0  : nat;
    s  : nat -> nat;
    (+) : nat # nat -> nat ;
  variables
    X : nat; Y : nat;
equations
  ((+) : nat # nat -> nat) ((0 : nat, X : nat) : nat # nat) : nat
  == X : nat;

  ((+) : nat # nat -> nat)
    (((s : nat -> nat) (X : nat) : nat, Y : nat) : nat # nat) : nat
  ==
  (s : nat -> nat) (((+) : nat # nat -> nat)
                    ((X : nat, Y : nat) : nat # nat) : nat) : nat
```

Figure 5.5: A fully annotated one-level specification. This is an annotation of the specification in Figure 5.3.

5.4.2 Well-formedness (OLS-WF)

Well-formedness judgements on terms characterize the well-formed, fully annotated terms over a signature, i.e., given a signature Σ the set $T_{fa}(\Sigma)$ defined as

$$T_{fa}(\Sigma) = \{t \mid t \in \text{Term} \wedge \Sigma \vdash_{\text{term}} t\}$$

is the set of fully annotated terms t that satisfy the well-formedness judgement $\Sigma \vdash_{\text{term}} t$. The plain terms (without annotation) over a signature can be obtained by taking the spines of the well-formed, fully annotated, terms, i.e., the set $T(\Sigma)$ of plain terms over Σ defined as

$$T(\Sigma) = \{\text{spine}(t) \mid t \in \text{Term} \wedge \Sigma \vdash_{\text{term}} t\}$$

In this section we define well-formedness of fully annotated terms. In Section 5.4.4 we define a type assignment function that produces a fully annotated term for a plain term. Figure 5.5 shows a fully annotated specification.

We define not only the well-formedness of terms, but also the well-formedness of signatures and equations. In general, well-formedness judgements define which syntactically correct expressions are well-formed. The well-formedness of fully annotated one-level specifications is defined by means of the following judgements.

imports OLS[5.3.4] Projection[5.4.1] Variables[5.B.6] Error-Booleans[5.A.3] Term-Analysis[5.3.3]

exports

  context-free syntax

    "$\vdash_{\text{spec}}$" Spec $\rightarrow$ EBool

    "$\vdash_{\text{sig}}$" Sig $\rightarrow$ EBool

    "$\vdash_{\text{sorts}}$" Terms $\rightarrow$ EBool

    Sig "$\vdash_{\text{decls}}$" Decls $\rightarrow$ EBool

    Sig "$\vdash_{\text{sort}}$" Term $\rightarrow$ EBool

    Sig "$\vdash_{\text{term}}$" Term $\rightarrow$ EBool

    Sig "$\vdash_{\text{eqs}}$" Eqs $\rightarrow$ EBool

    The well-formedness of a fully annotated specification $\mathcal{S}$ is defined by means of the judgement $\vdash_{\text{spec}} \mathcal{S}$. It is defined in terms of several other judgements of the form $\Sigma \vdash_{\text{r}} r$, which stands for 'construct r (of type r) is correct with respect to signature Σ'. For instance, the judgement $\Sigma \vdash_{\text{term}} t$ determines whether t is a well-formed term with respect to Σ. Equations defining judgements will, in general, have the form

$$\frac{C_1(q, \Sigma), \dots, C_m(q, \Sigma)}{\Sigma \vdash_q q(r_1, \dots, r_n) = \Sigma \vdash_{\text{r}_1} r_1 \wedge \dots \wedge \Sigma \vdash_{\text{r}_n} r_n}$$

to express that a construct q with subconstructs r_i is well-formed if conditions C_i hold for q and Σ and if the subconstructs are well-formed.

    Judgements are functions that yield a term of the sort EBool of error Booleans. This sort is a version of the booleans (defined in Appendix 5.A.3) with a constant $\top$ ('true' or 'correct') but with no constant for 'false' or 'incorrect'. Instead all elements of the sort Error act as values representing incorrectness. Two operations are defined on error Booleans. The symmetric conjunction $\wedge$ yields $\top$ in case both arguments are $\top$ and yields the addition of the errors otherwise. The asymmetric conjunction $\rightsquigarrow$ yields $\top$ if both arguments are $\top$ and otherwise it prefers the error of the left argument.

    In this subsection only the positive cases for the judgements are defined. In the next subsection the other, negative, cases are defined to yield errors that give a description of the well-formedness rule that is violated.

equations

    A specification is well-formed if its signature is well-formed and its equations are well-formed with respect to the signature.

[wf-spec] $\vdash_{\text{spec}} \mathcal{S} = \vdash_{\text{sig}} \Sigma \rightsquigarrow \Sigma \vdash_{\text{eqs}} \text{E}(\mathcal{S})$ **when** $\text{Sg}(\mathcal{S}) = \Sigma$

Signatures   A signature is well-formed if all its sort, function and variable declarations are well-formed.

[wf-srt] $\vdash_{\text{sig}} \Sigma = \vdash_{\text{sorts}} \text{S}(\Sigma) \wedge \Sigma \vdash_{\text{decls}} \text{F}(\Sigma) \wedge \Sigma \vdash_{\text{decls}} \text{V}(\Sigma)$

The terms declared as sorts in the sorts section should be constant terms, i.e., function symbols.

[wf-sort] $\vdash_{\text{sorts}} f = \top$

[wf-sort] $\qquad\qquad\qquad\qquad \vdash_{\text{sorts}} = \top$

[wf-sort-prd] $\qquad\qquad \vdash_{\text{sorts}} \tau_1^+; \tau_2^+ = \vdash_{\text{sorts}} \tau_1^+ \wedge \vdash_{\text{sorts}} \tau_2^+$

A declaration is correct if the type assigned to the function or variable is a well-formed sort (see below) and if the function or variable is not overloaded.

[wf-d-fun] $\qquad\qquad \Sigma \vdash_{\text{decls}} f : \tau = \Sigma \vdash_{\text{sort}} \tau \quad$ **when** $\pi_f(\Sigma) = \tau$

[wf-d-var] $\qquad\qquad \Sigma \vdash_{\text{decls}} x : \tau = \Sigma \vdash_{\text{sort}} \tau \quad$ **when** $\pi_x(\Sigma) = \tau$

[wf-d-cnc] $\qquad\qquad \Sigma \vdash_{\text{decls}} = \top$

[wf-d-cnc] $\qquad\qquad \Sigma \vdash_{\text{decls}} d_1^+; d_2^+ = \Sigma \vdash_{\text{decls}} d_1^+ \wedge \Sigma \vdash_{\text{decls}} d_2^+$

Recall that $\pi_f(\Sigma)$ gives the type of f in Σ. The condition $\pi_f(\Sigma) = \tau$ for a declaration $f : \tau$ expresses that there should be only one declaration for f in the signature. If there are more (with different types), the condition will fail when checking the second declaration because $\pi_f(\Sigma)$ will yield the type of the first declaration.

Sorts Sorts are terms composed by $\times$ and $\rightarrow$ from function symbols, which are the basic sorts. A basic sort should be declared in the sorts section as expressed by the condition of equation [wf-sort-fun].

[wf-sort-fun] $\qquad\qquad \Sigma \vdash_{\text{sort}} f = \top \quad$ **when** $f \in S(\Sigma) = \top$

[wf-sort-prd] $\qquad\qquad \Sigma \vdash_{\text{sort}} t_1 \times t_2 = \Sigma \vdash_{\text{sort}} t_1 \wedge \Sigma \vdash_{\text{sort}} t_2$

[wf-sort-arr] $\qquad\qquad \Sigma \vdash_{\text{sort}} t_1 \rightarrow t_2 = \Sigma \vdash_{\text{sort}} t_1 \wedge \Sigma \vdash_{\text{sort}} t_2$

Terms A term is well-formed if all its subterms are annotated with a type in a correct way corresponding to the signature. Variables and functions are well-formed if their annotation is equal to their declared type in the signature and if that type is a well-formed sort. This additional condition is needed because $\pi_t(\Sigma)$ yields 'nil' if t is not declared. If the annotation is also 'nil', this would wrongly imply that the term is correct. Since 'nil' cannot be a sort, this extra condition is sufficient. A pair is well-formed if its type is the product of the types of its arguments. An application is well-formed if the its type is the codomain of the type of the function and if the type of the argument is equal to the domain of the type of the function.

[wf-var] $\qquad\qquad \dfrac{\pi_x(\Sigma) = \tau, \ \Sigma \vdash_{\text{sort}} \tau = \top}{\Sigma \vdash_{\text{term}} x : \tau \ = \ \top}$

[wf-fun] $\qquad\qquad \dfrac{\pi_f(\Sigma) = \tau, \ \Sigma \vdash_{\text{sort}} \tau = \top}{\Sigma \vdash_{\text{term}} f : \tau \ = \ \top}$

[wf-pr] $\qquad\qquad \dfrac{\text{type}(t_1) \times \text{type}(t_2) = \tau}{\Sigma \vdash_{\text{term}} (t_1, t_2) : \tau \ = \ \Sigma \vdash_{\text{term}} t_1 \wedge \Sigma \vdash_{\text{term}} t_2}$

[wf-app] $\qquad\qquad \dfrac{\text{type}(t_1) = \text{type}(t_2) \rightarrow \tau}{\Sigma \vdash_{\text{term}} t_1 \ t_2 : \tau \ = \ \Sigma \vdash_{\text{term}} t_1 \wedge \Sigma \vdash_{\text{term}} t_2}$

There is no need to check the well-formedness of the types of applications and pairs, because equations [wf-app] and [wf-pr] preserve well-formedness of type annotations. In equation [wf-pr]: if $\mathrm{type}(t_i)$ are well-formed, then their product is also well-formed. In equation [wf-app]: if $\mathrm{type}(t_i)$ are well-formed, then τ must also be well-formed, because it is a subterm of $\mathrm{type}(t_1)$.

Equations An equation is well-formed if both sides have the same type and if all variables used in the right-hand side occur in the left-hand side. The last condition ensures that no new variables are introduced if the equations are interpreted as rewrite rules oriented from left to right.

[wf-eqn]
$$\frac{\mathrm{type}(t_1) = \mathrm{type}(t_2), \ \mathrm{vars}(t_2) \subseteq \mathrm{vars}(t_1) = \top}{\Sigma \vdash_{\mathrm{eqs}} t_1 \equiv t_2 \ = \ \Sigma \vdash_{\mathrm{term}} t_1 \wedge \Sigma \vdash_{\mathrm{term}} t_2}$$

[wf-eqns-empty]
$$\Sigma \vdash_{\mathrm{eqs}} = \top$$

[wf-eqns-conc]
$$\Sigma \vdash_{\mathrm{eqs}} \varphi_1^+ ; \varphi_2^+ \ = \ \Sigma \vdash_{\mathrm{eqs}} \varphi_1^+ \wedge \Sigma \vdash_{\mathrm{eqs}} \varphi_2^+$$

The following proposition states that a well-formed specification preserves types. This means that if two terms are equal according to a well-formed specification (and the rules of equational logic), they have the same type and that the normal form of a term has the same type as the term that is evaluated.

Proposition 5.3 (type soundness) *Well-formed specifications preserve types, i.e., if $\vdash_{\mathrm{spec}} \mathcal{S}$ and $\mathrm{Sg}(\mathcal{S}) \vdash_{\mathrm{term}} t_i$ then $\mathcal{S} \vdash t_1 \equiv t_2$ implies $\mathrm{type}(t_1) \equiv \mathrm{type}(t_2)$. Furthermore, $\mathrm{eval}(\mathcal{S})[t_1] = t_2$ implies $\mathrm{type}(t_1) = \mathrm{type}(t_2)$.*

Proof: By the well-formedness of $\mathcal{S}$ it follows that all equations are type preserving (equation [wf-eqn]) and by Proposition 5.2 it then follows that equational derivations for $\mathcal{S}$ are type preserving. The second part of the proposition follows from the first part and the soundness of evaluation with respect to derivable equality (Proposition 5.1). □

The condition $\mathrm{Sg}(\mathcal{S}) \vdash_{\mathrm{term}} t_i$ implies that the terms t_i are fully annotated. Normally, when considering a specification, we think about equality of plain terms. By means of the function spine and the well-formedness judgements we can characterize the plain terms $\mathrm{T}(\Sigma)$ over a signature (see beginning of this subsection). The following proposition states that well-formed specifications can only equate plain terms for which well-formed full annotations exist.

Proposition 5.4 *If $\vdash_{\mathrm{spec}} \mathcal{S}'$, $\mathcal{S} = \mathrm{spine}(\mathcal{S}')$, $t_1 \neq t_2$ and $\mathcal{S} \vdash t_1 \equiv t_2$, then there are t_1' and t_2' such that $\mathrm{spine}(t_1') = t_1$, $\mathrm{spine}(t_2') = t_2$, $\mathcal{S}' \vdash_{\mathrm{term}} t_{\{1,2\}}'$ and $\mathrm{type}(t_1') = \mathrm{type}(t_2')$.*

```
equations
   0 + X    == Y;
   s(X) + Y == s + (X, Y)
```

(a)

```
equation   "(+)(0, X) == Y" not well-formed :
   variables "Y" of rhs not in lhs ;
application "(+)(s , X , Y )" not well-formed :
   type of argument "(nat -> nat) # nat # nat"
   does not match type of domain "nat # nat"
```

(b)

Figure 5.6:   Non-wellformed specification (a) and errors (b) corresponding to the violations against the well-formedness rules. The signature part of the specification in (a) is not shown here but corresponds to the signature in Figure 5.3(a).

5.4.3   Non-wellformedness (OLS-NWF)

In the previous section we have defined which specifications are well-formed. In this section we look at the cases not covered by the well-formedness rules, which are, by definition, not well-formed. As an example of the type of error messages generated by these rules, Figure 5.6 shows the errors for an incorrect version of equations of the natural numbers specification from Section 5.3. We derive equations for the generation of error messages for non-wellformed specifications by looking at which cases were not covered by the equations above. If we had an equation of the form

$$\frac{C_1(q, \Sigma), \ldots, C_m(q, \Sigma)}{\Sigma \vdash_q q(r_1, \ldots, r_n) = \Sigma \vdash_{\bar{r}_1} r_1 \wedge \ldots \wedge \Sigma \vdash_{\bar{r}_n} r_n}$$

the error case will be of the form

$$\frac{\neg C_1(q, \Sigma) \vee \cdots \vee \neg C_m(q, \Sigma)}{\Sigma \vdash_q q(r_1, \ldots, r_n) = \Sigma \vdash_{\bar{r}_1} r_1 \wedge \ldots \wedge \Sigma \vdash_{\bar{r}_n} r_n \rightsquigarrow \text{"}q\text{" not well-formed}}$$

If either of the conditions does not hold then construct q is not well-formed. But we only want to report this fact if all its sub-constructs are well-formed. Otherwise only the reasons for non-wellformedness of the sub-constructs are reported, which is expressed by the use of the asymmetric conjunction $\rightsquigarrow$. Furthermore, we may choose to generate more precise error messages that are related to the conditions C_i. We then get equations of the form

$$\frac{C_1(q, \Sigma), \ldots, C_{i-1}(q, \Sigma), \neg C_i(q, \Sigma)}{\Sigma \vdash_q q(r_1, \ldots, r_n) = \Sigma \vdash_{\bar{r}_1} r_1 \wedge \ldots \wedge \Sigma \vdash_{\bar{r}_n} r_n \rightsquigarrow \text{"}q\text{" does not have property } C_i}$$

Instead of negating the conditions we can use default equations to deal with the remaining cases.

$$\Sigma \vdash_{\overline{q}} q(r_1, \ldots, r_n) \;=\; \Sigma \vdash_{\overline{r_1}} r_1 \wedge \ldots \wedge \Sigma \vdash_{\overline{r_n}} r_n \rightsquigarrow \text{"}q\text{" not well-formed}$$
$$\textbf{otherwise}$$

imports OLS-WF[5.4.2] SPEC-Errors[5.B.2]
equations

Declarations   No terms other than constants can be declared as sorts.

[wf-sorts'] $\vdash_{\overline{\text{sorts}}} \tau =$ " τ " not a well-formed sort declaration   **otherwise**

[wf-d-fun'] $\Sigma \vdash_{\overline{\text{decls}}} f: \tau =$ function " f " multiply declared   **otherwise**
[wf-d-var'] $\Sigma \vdash_{\overline{\text{decls}}} x: \tau =$ variable " x " multiply declared   **otherwise**

Sorts   A term is a non-wellformed sort if it is a constant that is not declared or if it is a term that is not a constant, product or arrow.

[wf-sort-fun'] $\Sigma \vdash_{\overline{\text{sort}}} f =$ sort " f " not declared   **when** $f \in S(\Sigma) = \bot$
[wf-sort'''] $\Sigma \vdash_{\overline{\text{sort}}} t =$ " t " not a well-formed sort   **otherwise**

Functions and Variables   If the result of looking up a function or variable in the signature is 'nil', it is not declared, otherwise the declared sort is not well-formed.

[wf-fun'] $\Sigma \vdash_{\overline{\text{term}}} f: \tau =$ function " f " not declared   **when** $\pi_f(\Sigma) =$ nil
[wf-fun''] $\Sigma \vdash_{\overline{\text{term}}} f: \tau = \Sigma \vdash_{\overline{\text{sort}}} \tau$ **otherwise**
[wf-var'] $\Sigma \vdash_{\overline{\text{term}}} x: \tau =$ variable " x " not declared   **when** $\pi_x(\Sigma) =$ nil
[wf-var''] $\Sigma \vdash_{\overline{\text{term}}} x: \tau = \Sigma \vdash_{\overline{\text{sort}}} \tau$ **otherwise**

Pair and Application

[wf-pr'] $\Sigma \vdash_{\overline{\text{term}}} (t_1, t_2): \tau = (\Sigma \vdash_{\overline{\text{term}}} t_1 \wedge \Sigma \vdash_{\overline{\text{term}}} t_2)$
$\rightsquigarrow$ pair " spine(t_1, t_2) " not well-formed
otherwise

[wf-app'] $\Sigma \vdash_{\overline{\text{term}}} t_1\, t_2: \tau$
$= (\Sigma \vdash_{\overline{\text{term}}} t_1 \wedge \Sigma \vdash_{\overline{\text{term}}} t_2)$
$\rightsquigarrow$ application " spine$(t_1\, t_2)$ " not well-formed
:: if eq(dom(type(t_1)), nil)
then " spine(t_1) " is not a function
else type of argument " type(t_2)
" does not match type of domain " dom(type(t_1)) "
otherwise

Note that the function 'spine' is used to show a term without its type annotations.

Annotation Terms without annotation or with double annotations are never well-formed.

[wf-term] $\dfrac{\text{type}(t) = \text{top}}{\Sigma \vdash_{\text{term}} t = \text{term } " t " \text{ not well-formed}}$

[wf-ann] $\Sigma \vdash_{\text{term}} (t : \tau_1) : \tau_2$
$= \Sigma \vdash_{\text{term}} t : \tau_1$
$\rightsquigarrow$ annotation of " spine(t) " with " τ_2 " not well-formed
 : should be " spine(τ_1) "

For several constructors in the language of terms we did not formulate any rules because they cannot be used at the level of terms at all.

[wf-term-prd] $\Sigma \vdash_{\text{term}} t_1 \times t_2 : \tau = \text{term } " \text{spine}(t_1 \times t_2) " \text{ not well-formed}$
[wf-term-arr] $\Sigma \vdash_{\text{term}} t_1 \rightarrow t_2 : \tau = \text{term } " \text{spine}(t_1 \rightarrow t_2) " \text{ not well-formed}$
[wf-term-top] $\Sigma \vdash_{\text{term}} \text{top} : \tau = \text{term } " \text{top} " \text{ not well-formed}$
[wf-term-nil] $\Sigma \vdash_{\text{term}} \text{nil} : \tau = \text{term } " \text{nil} " \text{ not well-formed}$

Equations

[wf-eqn'] $\Sigma \vdash_{\text{eqs}} t_1 \equiv t_2$
$= (\Sigma \vdash_{\text{term}} t_1 \wedge \Sigma \vdash_{\text{term}} t_2)$
$\rightsquigarrow$ equation " spine(t_1) $\equiv$ spine(t_2) " not well-formed
 :: if $\neg$ eq(type(t_1), type(t_2))
 then types do not match
 else variables " trms(vars(t_2) / vars(t_1)) " of rhs not in lhs
 otherwise

The following proposition states that the definition of the well-formedness judgement for terms is sufficiently-complete, i.e., all cases are covered by the well-formedness and non-wellformedness rules.

Proposition 5.5 *For any term t and signature Σ, $\Sigma \vdash_{\text{term}} t \in \{\top\} \cup \text{Error}$.*

Proof: by induction on terms. $\qquad\qquad\qquad\qquad\qquad\qquad\qquad\qquad\qquad\qquad\square$

5.4.4 Type Assignment (OLS-TA)

Figure 5.5 shows that it is a tedious task to write fully annotated specifications. In this subsection we define the type assignment function $\text{Wt}(\Sigma)[\![t]\!]$ that annotates a term with types according to signature Σ. Terms for which no typing exists are assigned the 'nil' type. If a term is already partially annotated, these annotations are checked against the derived annotations. In the one-level framework we are currently dealing with there is not much use for such annotations because terms can have at most one type. However, in the multi-level framework terms can be polymorphically typed and we will also allow functions to be overloaded. In such a situation, partial annotations are useful to enforce a more specific type for a term.

imports OLS[5.3.4] Projection[5.4.1] Term-Analysis[5.3.3]

exports

  context-free syntax

  "Wsp" "[" Spec "]" $\rightarrow$ Spec
  "Wt" "(" Sig ")" "[" Term "]" $\rightarrow$ Term
  "We" "(" Sig ")" "[" Eqs "]" $\rightarrow$ Eqs

equations

The function 'Wsp' assigns types to the terms in equations of a specification using its signature.

[wsp]
$$\frac{\Sigma = \mathrm{Sg}(\mathcal{S})}{\mathrm{Wsp}[\![\mathcal{S}]\!] \; = \; \text{signature } \Sigma; \text{equations } \mathrm{We}(\Sigma)[\![\mathrm{E}(\mathcal{S})]\!]}$$

Terms Functions and variables are annotated with their types in the signature. The type of a pair is the product of the types of its arguments. The type of an application is the codomain of the type of the function.

[wt-var]
$$\frac{\pi_x(\Sigma) = \tau}{\mathrm{Wt}(\Sigma)[\![x]\!] \; = \; x : \tau}$$

[wt-fun]
$$\frac{\pi_f(\Sigma) = \tau}{\mathrm{Wt}(\Sigma)[\![f]\!] \; = \; f : \tau}$$

[wt-pr]
$$\frac{\mathrm{Wt}(\Sigma)[\![t_1]\!] = t_3, \; \mathrm{Wt}(\Sigma)[\![t_2]\!] = t_4}{\mathrm{Wt}(\Sigma)[\![t_1, t_2]\!] \; = \; (t_3, t_4) : \mathrm{type}(t_3) \times \mathrm{type}(t_4)}$$

[wt-app]
$$\frac{\mathrm{Wt}(\Sigma)[\![t_1]\!] = t_3, \; \mathrm{Wt}(\Sigma)[\![t_2]\!] = t_4}{\mathrm{Wt}(\Sigma)[\![t_1 \; t_2]\!] \; = \; t_3 \; t_4 : \mathrm{cod}(\mathrm{type}(t_3))}$$

A term that is already partially annotated is handled by first assigning a type to the term without its annotation and then comparing the derived annotation with the given annotation.

[wt-ann]
$$\frac{\mathrm{Wt}(\Sigma)[\![t]\!] = t'}{\mathrm{Wt}(\Sigma)[\![t : \tau]\!] \; = \; \text{if eq}(\mathrm{type}(t'), \tau) \text{ then } t' \text{ else } t' : \tau}$$

In case the given type and the derived type are equal, the annotated term is returned. In case the types are different, the term was inconsistently annotated by the user. To be able to report this, the erroneous annotation is attached to the already annotated term. The resulting term is not well-formed, which will be reported by equation [wf-ann] in Section 5.4.3. Observe that equation [wt-ann] guarantees that we can assign types to fully annotated terms. We have that $Wt(\Sigma)[\![Wt(\Sigma)[\![t]\!]]\!] = Wt(\Sigma)[\![t]\!]$, i.e., type assignment is idempotent.

Terms constructed from 'nil', 'top', '$\times$' and '$\rightarrow$' are assigned the error type 'nil', since these constructors cannot occur in well-formed terms.

[wt-nil]	$Wt(\Sigma)[\![nil]\!] = nil : nil$
[wt-top]	$Wt(\Sigma)[\![top]\!] = top : nil$
[wt-prd]	$Wt(\Sigma)[\![t_1 \times t_2]\!] = Wt(\Sigma)[\![t_1]\!] \times Wt(\Sigma)[\![t_2]\!] : nil$
[wt-arr]	$Wt(\Sigma)[\![t_1 \rightarrow t_2]\!] = Wt(\Sigma)[\![t_1]\!] \rightarrow Wt(\Sigma)[\![t_2]\!] : nil$

Equations Both sides of an equation are assigned types.

[we-eqn-1]	$We(\Sigma)[\![t_1 \equiv t_2]\!] = Wt(\Sigma)[\![t_1]\!] \equiv Wt(\Sigma)[\![t_2]\!]$
[we-eqns-0]	$We(\Sigma)[\![\,]\!] =$
[we-eqns-n]	$We(\Sigma)[\![\varphi_1^+; \varphi_2^+]\!] = We(\Sigma)[\![\varphi_1^+]\!] \mathbin{+\mkern-8mu+} We(\Sigma)[\![\varphi_2^+]\!]$

In Section 5.4.2 we saw that well-formedness judgements identify the fully annotated terms that are well-formed with respect to a signature. The type assignment function defined in this section allows us to produce fully annotated terms from plain terms. The following proposition states that for any plain term the type assignment function finds a well-formed, full annotation if one exists.

Proposition 5.6 (correctness of 'Wt') *The function* Wt *finds a well-formed typing for a term if one exists, i.e., if t is a fully annotated term and $\Sigma \vdash_{\mathsf{term}} t$ then* $Wt(\Sigma)[\![spine(t)]\!] = t$.

Proof: by induction on terms. (Hint: equations [wt-var] until [wt-app] assign types to terms as required by [wf-var] until [wf-app] in Section 5.4.2.) □

5.4.5 Typechecking (OLS-TC)

typechecking can now be defined in terms of type assignment and well-formedness checking. We define three typecheck functions. The first checks a term against a signature, the second checks a list of equations against a signature and the last checks a complete specification. The functions are defined in terms of well-formedness judgements (Section 5.4.2) and type assignment functions (Section 5.4.4).

imports OLS-NWF[5.4.3] OLS-TA[5.4.4]
exports
   context-free syntax
      tc "(" Sig ")" "[" Term "]" $\rightarrow$ EBool

$$\text{tc } \text{``("} \text{ Sig ``)"} \text{ ``[''} \text{ Eqs ``]''} \quad \rightarrow \text{EBool}$$
$$\text{tc } \text{``[''} \text{ Spec ``]''} \qquad\qquad \rightarrow \text{EBool}$$

equations

[tc-terms] $\qquad\qquad tc(\Sigma)[\![t]\!] = \vdash_{\text{sig}} \Sigma \rightsquigarrow \Sigma \vdash_{\text{term}} \text{Wt}(\Sigma)[\![t]\!]$

[tc-eqns] $\qquad\qquad tc(\Sigma)[\![\mathcal{E}]\!] = \vdash_{\text{sig}} \Sigma \rightsquigarrow \Sigma \vdash_{\text{eqs}} \text{We}(\Sigma)[\![\mathcal{E}]\!]$

[tc-spec] $\qquad\qquad tc[\![\mathcal{S}]\!] = \vdash_{\text{spec}} \text{Wsp}[\![\mathcal{S}]\!]$

Now we have seen the complete specification of a typechecker for a monomorphic applicative language. In the next two sections we will repeat this exercise for a multi-level polymorphic specification language.

5.5 Multi-Level Specifications

In the one-level framework of sections 5.3 and 5.4 the algebra of types used for the declaration of functions and variables is the subset of terms consisting of the closure under product ($\times$) and arrow ($\rightarrow$) of a set of sort constants. In such a framework one has higher-order functions (due to the applicative term format) but no polymorphism and no user-definable type constructors.

A *two-level specification* is a pair of specifications, called level 1 and level 0. The signature of the level 1 specification specifies a set of terms (like a one-level signature would) that are used at level 0 as types. In other words the signature at level 1 determines the type algebra of level 0. A type variable can be instantiated to any type. A term that has a type containing variables is polymorphic; it denotes all terms obtained by substituting ground types for type variables. As in the one-level case, the type algebra of signatures at level 1 is determined by the implicit signature generated from the sorts of level 1 and the constructors ($\rightarrow$) and ($\times$).

Multi-level specifications generalize two-level specifications by allowing arbitrary many levels of specifications. The signature at level n uses terms from the signature at level $n+1$ as types and determines the type algebra of the signature at level $n-1$. The types used in the highest level are members of the closure of the sorts at that level under ($\times$) and ($\rightarrow$), i.e., there is an implicit signature at the top that is generated by the sort declarations of the highest level. Figure 5.7 illustrates the concepts of one-level, two-level and multi-level specifications. The arrow from a signature means that the terms over that signature are used at the target of the arrow.

In the next two sections we define the extension of one-level specifications to multi-level specifications. In this section we start with an extensive list of examples that introduce the key ideas of the formalism. The examples are motivated by data type specification. For examples of application of multi-level specification to logical frameworks see (Hearn and Meinke, 1994) and (Hearn, 1995). It is not necessary to read all examples to continue with the rest of the chapter. Indeed for the under-

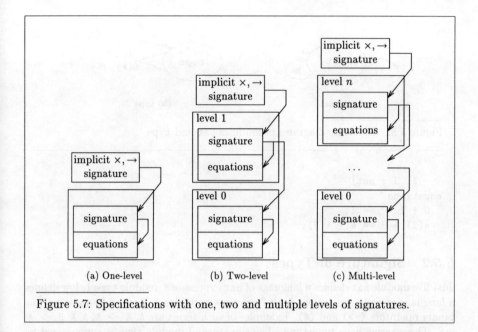

Figure 5.7: Specifications with one, two and multiple levels of signatures.

standing of some of the later examples it might be a good idea to first continue with Section 5.6, where the syntax of multi-level specifications is defined.

5.5.1 Natural Numbers

The running example of sections 5.3 and 5.4, successor naturals with addition, can be specified as a one-level specification. The declaration of sort `nat` generates the implicit sort signature consisting of the basic sort `nat` and the sort operators ($\rightarrow$) and ($\times$). As a consequence, terms like `nat`, `nat -> nat` and `nat # nat -> nat` are sorts that can be used in the signature that declares the functions composing the algebra of natural numbers. The signature is summarized in the diagram in Figure 5.8(a).

```
module nat
level 0
  signature
    sorts nat;
    functions
      0   : nat;
      s   : nat -> nat;
      (+) : nat # nat -> nat;
    variables
```

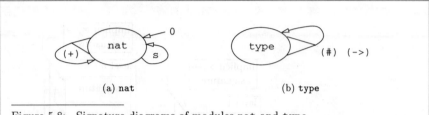

(a) nat   (b) type

Figure 5.8:   Signature diagrams of modules nat and type

```
    I, J : nat;
equations
    0 + I    == I;
    s(I) + J == s(I + J);
```

5.5.2   Signature of Types

Just like module nat defines a language of nat expressions, module type below defines
a language of type expressions built from type variables A, B and C by means of the
binary operators (->) and (#). Examples of such terms are A, A -> A, A # B -> A,
etc. These terms have type type. The signature of module type is summarized by
the diagram in Figure 5.8(b).

```
module type
level 1
  signature
    sorts type;
    functions
      (#), (->) : type # type -> type;
    variables
      A, B, C : type;
```

5.5.3   Functions

The difference between module nat and module type is that the signature of types is
a level 1 signature. This entails that type expressions can be used as sorts at level 0
in signatures of modules that import module type.

The next module function introduces several polymorphic operations on functions. It first imports module type to use type expressions as sorts at level 0. The
sorts declaration declares all expressions over level 1 that match the term A, as sorts.
This means that all terms of type type can be used as sorts, but other terms over

level 1 cannot (because A is a type variable). For instance, A -> A is a type expression, but (->), which is also a term over level 1, is not a type expression. Next, the module defines a number of common functions. The *identity* function i takes any value to itself. The function k creates a *constant function* k(X) that always yields X. The function s is a *duplication* function that copies its third argument. The *composition* G . H of two functions G and H applies G to the result of applying H to the argument of the composition.

All these functions are *polymorphic*. The types of the functions contain type variables, which can be instantiated to arbitrary type expressions. The signature is actually an abbreviation of an infinite signature, declaring each function for each possible instantiation of the type variables. For instance, if nat is a type (as we will define in the next paragraph), then the instantiation i : nat -> nat is the identity function on the natural numbers.

```
module function
imports type;
level 0
  signature
    sorts A;
    functions
      i  : A -> A;
      k  : A -> B -> A;
      s  : (A -> B -> C) -> (A -> B) -> A -> C;
      (.) : (B -> C) # (A -> B) -> A -> C;
    variables
      X : A; Y : B; Z : C; G : A -> B; H : B -> C;
  equations
    i(X)       == X;
    k(X)(Y)    == X;
    s(X)(Y)(Z) == X(Z)(Y(Z));
    (G . H)(X) == G(H(X));
```

Observe that the specification in module function can also be considered as a logical framework in which the types are propositional logic formulas and the types of the functions the axioms of propositional logic, together with the implicit type of the application operator, which represents the modus ponens rule.

5.5.4 Typing Natural Numbers

In module nat_typed, the natural numbers as specified in module nat are incorporated in the world of types by declaring nat as a type constant. This is illustrated by the diagram in Figure 5.9. This provides the polymorphic functionality defined for arbitrary types to natural numbers.

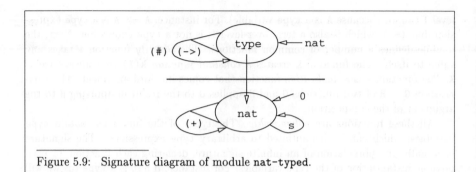

Figure 5.9: Signature diagram of module nat-typed.

```
module nat_typed
imports function, nat;
level 1
  signature
    functions
      nat : type;
```

5.5.5 Cartesian Product

The product A # B of two types A and B is the type of pairs (X, Y) of elements X of A and Y of B. In MLS the pairing constructor function _,_ is implicitly declared as (,) : A # B -> A # B. This means that if at level $n + 1$ a declaration for (#) is given, then at level n the constructor _,_ is defined implicitly. The declaration is implicit because binary infix operators are defined in terms of _,_ by means of the equation $t_1 \oplus t_2 = (\oplus)(t_1, t_2)$. If _,_ would be treated like an ordinary binary operator this would lead to a circular definition $t_1, t_2 = (,)(t_1, t_2) = (,)((,)(t_1, t_2))$

Module **product** defines a number of general functions on products. The projection functions **exl** and **exr** give the left and right elements of a pair. The product G # H of two functions is a function that applies the first function to the first argument of a pair and the second function to the second argument resulting in a new pair. The function **split** takes two functions that split the values of a type C into the components of a pair. For instance, the function **swap** defined as (exr .split. exl) swaps the elements of a pair, i.e., (exr .split. exl)(X, Y) == (Y, X).[3] The function **curry** converts a binary function (a function on pairs) into a *curried* binary function that first takes its first argument and returns a function that when applied to a second argument returns the application of the function to its arguments. The function **uncurry** is the inverse of curry that uncurries a function, i.e., converts it from a curried binary function to a function on pairs. It is defined in terms of dupli-

---

[3]Recall that T1 .T2. T3 can be written as an abbreviation of T2(T1,T2).

cation, projection and composition. Finally, the function `pair` is the curried version of the built-in pairing operator `(,)`.

```
module product
imports function;
level 0
  signature
    sorts A # B;
    functions
      exl     : A # B -> A;
      exr     : A # B -> B;
      (#)     : (A -> B) # (A' -> B') -> (A # A') -> (B # B'));
      split   : (C -> A) # (C -> B) -> C -> A # B;
      curry   : (A # B -> C) -> A -> B -> C;
      uncurry : (A -> B -> C) -> A # B -> C;
      pair    : A -> B -> A # B;
      swap    : A # B -> B # A;
    variables
      X : A; Y : B; Z : C; G : A -> B; H : B -> C;
  equations
    exl(X, Y)          == X;
    exr(X, Y)          == Y;
    (G # H)(X, Y)      == (G(X), H(Y));
    (G .split. H)(X)   == (G(X), H(X));
    curry(G)(X)(Y)     == G(X, Y);
    uncurry(G)         == s(G . exl)(exr);
    pair               == curry(i);
    swap               == (exr .split. exl);
```

5.5.6   Disjoint Sum

The disjoint union or sum A + B of two types A and B contains all elements from A and B. The elements of both types are tagged by means of injection functions `inl` and `inr`, such that their original type can be reconstructed and such that there are no clashes; the union of `bool` and `bool` contains two elements, while the sum `bool + bool` contains the four elements `inl(t)`, `inl(f)`, `int(t)` and `inr(f)`. The sum G + H of two functions G and H is the function that takes the sum of codomains to the sum of the domains of G and H by applying G to left-tagged values and H to right-tagged values. The function `case` applies either of two functions with the same codomain depending on the tag of the value it is applied to.

The signature diagram in Figure 5.10 illustrates the structure of the algebra. Due to polymorphism, the number of sorts of a specification becomes infinite. Therefore,

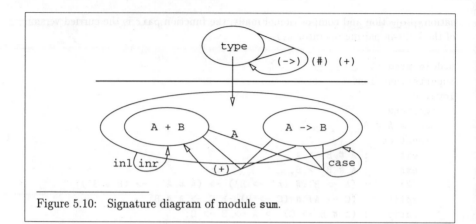

Figure 5.10:   Signature diagram of module sum.

signature diagrams do not provide an accurate description of the structure of the
algebra described by a specification. Nonetheless we will continue to use approximate
signature diagrams to give insight in the examples.

```
module sum
imports function;
level 1
  signature
    functions
      (+) : type # type -> type;
level 0
  signature
    sorts A + B;
    functions
      inl  : A -> A + B;
      inr  : B -> A + B;
      (+)  : (A -> B) # (A' -> B') -> (A + A') -> (B + B')
      case : (A -> C) # (B -> C) -> (A + B) -> C;
    equations
      (G + H)(inl(X))      == inl(G(X));
      (G + H)(inr(Y))      == inr(H(Y));
      (G .case. H)(inl(X)) == G(X);
      (G .case. H)(inr(Y)) == H(Y);
```

5.5.7 Lists

A list is a structure built by the functions [], the empty list, and (::) (cons)
that adds an element to a list. A great number of generic functions have been

defined on lists, see for instance (Bird, 1987, 1989). Here we give some common list functions. The function (*) (map) applies a function G to each element of a list. The function (/) (fold right) takes a pair (G, Z) of a function and a constant to replace the constructors [] and (::) such that (X1 :: ... :: (Xn :: [])) is transformed into (X1 .G. ... .G. (Xn .G. Z)). The function (\) (fold left) is similar to (/) but starts adding the elements at the left side of the list resulting in ((Z .G. X1) .G. ... .G. Xn). The fold operations can be seen as signature morphisms consisting of replacements for the list cons function and the empty list. The function (++) concatenates the elements of two lists. The function size gives the length of a list. The functions (++) and size are defined in terms of the fold functions (/) and (\). Finally, the function zip takes a pair of lists into a list of the pairs of the heads of the lists.[4]

```
module list
imports product, nat_typed;
level 1
  signature
    functions
      list : type -> type;
level 0
  signature
    sorts list(A);
    functions
      []   : list(A);
      (::) : A # list(A) -> list(A);
      (*)  : (A -> B) # list(A) -> list(B);
      (/)  : (A # B -> B) # B -> list(A) -> B;
      (\)  : (A # B -> A) # A -> list(B) -> A;
      size : list(A) -> nat;
      (++) : list(A) # list(A) -> list(A);
      zip  : list(A) # list(B) -> list(A # B);
    variables
      L : list(A);
    equations
      G * []            == [];
      G * (X :: L)      == G(X) :: (G * L);

      (G / Z)([])       == Z;
      (G / Z)(X :: L)   == X .G. ((G / Z)(L));

      (G \ Z)([])       == Z;
```

---

[4]Note that a variable declaration like L : list(A) declares all variables with 'base' L as list(A) variables, e.g., L1, L2 and L' are also declared by this declaration.

```
(G \ Z)(X :: L)        == (G \ (Z .G. X))(L);

size                   == (s . exl) \ 0;
(++)                   == s(((/) . pair(::)) . exr)(exl);

zip([], L)             == [];
zip(L, [])             == [];
zip(X :: L, X' :: L')  == (X, X') :: zip(L, L');
```

5.5.8 Stratified Stacks

All examples we have seen until now use only one sort (type) at level 1. The next module gives an example of a specification that uses an additional sort at level 1.

The data type of stacks can be specified by means of (polymorphic) push, pop and top functions. A well-known disadvantage of the normal formulation is that the top of the empty stack is either undefined or part of the type of stack elements, leading to a pollution of that type. All other operations that use the type have to take account of the top of the empty stack as an additional element. Another solution is to take a default value from the type of stack elements as result of the top of the empty stack. The problem of this solution is that the distinction between failure and success of a partial function is lost.

The solution of Hearn and Meinke (1994) is to 'stratify' the type of stacks. The stack type constructor does not just construct a type from a type, but has a natural number as argument that records the number of elements on the stack. The type operator stack takes a type, which is the type of the elements on the stack, and a nat, which represents the height of the stack. The type of stacks is stratified into stacks with elements of type A and height 0 indicated by the type stack(A,0), stacks of height s(0) indicated by the type stack(A,s(0)), etc. A new type constant error is introduced to represent errors. The usual stack operators are now typed as follows. The empty stack has type stack(A, 0), i.e., is a polymorphic constant for stacks with arbitrary types of elements and with height 0. The push function takes an A element and a stack of A's with height I and produces a stack of A's of height s(I). The operations pop and tops come in two variants, one for empty stacks and one for non-empty stacks. The top of an empty stack (which has type stack(A,0)) results in an error element and not in an A. The error element is not added to the sort of stack elements.

The natural numbers in the types of stacks are used at level 1 while the specification in module nat specifies naturals at level 0. This means that just importing module nat is not enough to reuse the specification. The reuse is achieved by the operation *lift* that increases all levels of its argument specification by 1. The signature diagram in Figure 5.11 gives an overview of the signature in module stratified-stack.

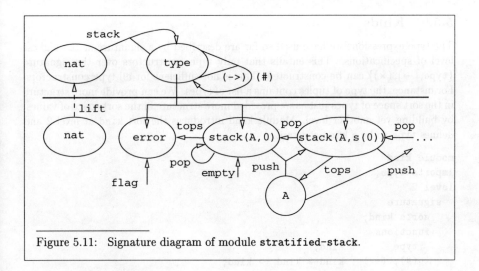

Figure 5.11: Signature diagram of module stratified-stack.

```
module stratified-stack
imports types;
lift(imports nat);
level 1
  signature
    functions
      error : type;
      stack : type # nat -> type;
level 0
  signature
    functions
      flag  : error;
      empty : stack(A, 0);
      push  : A # stack(A, I) -> stack(A, s(I));
      pop   : stack(A, 0)      -> stack(A, 0);
      pop   : stack(A, s(I))   -> stack(A, I);
      tops  : stack(A, 0)      -> error;
      tops  : stack(A, s(I))   -> A;
    variables
      St : stack(A, I);
  equations
    pop(push(X,St))  == St;
    tops(push(X,St)) == X;
    pop(empty)       == empty;
    tops(empty)      == flag;
```

5.5.9   Kinds

The type expressions we have used so far are described by a signature at the highest level of specifications. This entails that only type constructors over the signature $\{\text{type}, (\rightarrow), (\times)\}$ can be constructed. This is not sufficient for all type constructors. For instance, the type of tuples contains a list of types. We can provide more structure in the sort space of types just as we provided more structure in the sort space of values, by building yet another level. Module kind introduces the sort kind at level 2 and defines type to be a kind constant.

```
module kind
imports type;
level 2
  signature
    sorts kind;
    functions
      type       : kind;
      (#), (->) : kind # kind -> kind;
    variables
      K : kind;
level 1
  signature
    sorts K : kind;
```

From here on we can proceed by adding useful kind constructors to level 2 and using them in the signatures at level 1. However, to construct tuples we need lists of types. Since there is not yet a definition of list : kind -> kind, we would have to redo module lists but now one level higher. Since this is a waste of time we use another approach. Module type-type also introduces the constant type at level 2, but uses type itself as its type! The types defined in module type are used as kinds, by lifting the contents of that module. Now we can reuse all type constructors defined so far for level 1 at level 2, by simply lifting their specification.

```
module type-type
lift(imports type);
imports type;
level 2
  signature
    functions
      type : type;
```

5.5.10   Generalized Product

Lists and stacks are homogeneous data types that are parameterized by one sort. All elements of a list or stack are members of the same sort. A tuple on the other

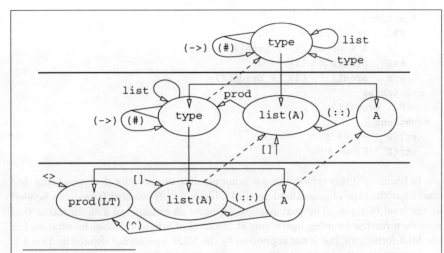

Figure 5.12: Signature diagram of module `generalized-product` with lifted `list` and `type`.

hand is a heterogeneous structure with various types of elements. In the next module we define a type constructor `prod` that constructs a generalized product type from a list of types. To construct a list of types we import the definition of level 0 lists and lift it to the level of types. Now we can use the same polymorphic operations on lists that we defined before. A tuple is constructed by means of the functions `<>` (empty tuple) and `(^)`, which adds an element to a tuple. (Recall from Section 5.2.1 that `<X1, ..., Xn>` is an abbreviation for `X1 ^ ... ^ Xn ^ <>`.) For instance, the tuple `<0, [0], t>` has type `prod([nat, list(nat), bool])`. The first element of a tuple is given by `exl` and the rest by `exr`. Observe that these functions are not partial: they are only well-formed if applied to a non-empty tuple.

```
module generalized-product
imports type-type;
lift(imports list);
level 1
  signature
    functions
      prod : list(type) -> type;
    variables
      LT : list(type);
level 0
  signature
    sorts prod(LT);
```

```
    functions
      <> : prod([]);
      (^) : A # prod(LT) -> prod(A :: LT);
      exl : prod(A :: LT) -> A;
      exr : prod(A :: LT) -> prod(LT);
    variables
      P : prod(LT);
  equations
    exl(X ^ P) == X;
    exr(X ^ P) == P;
```

In Hindley/Milner type systems it is not possible to construct the type of stratified stacks nor the type of generalized products, because only one sort (**type**) can be used at the level of types. The next paragraph shows an example of a specification that goes even further by using operations at the level of types. This can be expressed in the MLS formalism, but is not supported by the MLS typechecker defined Section 5.7.

5.5.11   Generalized Zip

The function `zip` as defined in module `list` above takes a pair of lists into a list of pairs by pairing the heads of both lists until one of the lists is empty. Variants of zip can also be constructed for triples of lists, quadruples of lists and so on. Unzip is the inverse of `zip` that maps a list of products to a product of lists. The following generalized definition of zip takes a generalized product of lists into a list of products by tupling the heads of the lists. For instance, if the argument of `zip` has type `prod([list(nat), list(bool), list(list(bool)))])`, its result has type `list(prod([nat, bool, list(bool)]))`. The declaration of `zip` has to relate the contents of the `list` types in the domain to the types in the codomain. In the declaration below this is achieved by declaring the domain as `prod(list * LT)`. The type constructor `list` is mapped using operator (*) (see module `list`) over the list of types `LT`. This means that the argument of `zip` should be a product with all its arguments of the form `list(A)`. For the example above, we can see that according to the equations for (*) (in module `list`) `prod([list(nat), list(bool), list(list(bool)))])` is equal to `prod(list * [nat, bool, list(bool))])`. This type can be unified syntactically with the domain type of `zip` (take the substitution [LT := [nat, bool, list(bool))]], from which the type of the codomain `list(prod([nat, bool, list(bool)]))` follows.

In order to reflect this in the type assignment for specifications, $\mathcal{E}$-unification has to be used. Given a set of equations $\mathcal{E}$ and two terms t_1 and t_2, an $\mathcal{E}$-unifier is a substitution σ such that $\mathcal{E} \vdash \sigma(t_1) \equiv \sigma(t_2)$. If the t_i are ground terms this question reduces to $\mathcal{E} \vdash t_1 \equiv t_2$. Here $\mathcal{E}$-unification has to be applied to unify the types of actual argument and domain type of the function `zip` given the equations for (*). This problem is undecidable in general (see Jouannaud and Kirchner (1991) for a survey of unification), but for the equations of functions like (*) it seems decidable. However, the type assignment function presented in Section 5.7.5 does not consider equations over types.

```
module generalized-zip
imports generalized-product, list;
level 0
  signature
    functions
      zip   : prod(list * LT) -> list(prod(LT));
      unzip : list(prod(LT)) -> prod(list * LT);
    variables
      L, M, N : list(A);
  equations
    -- empty tuple
    zip(<>) == [];

    -- singleton tuple
    zip(<[]>)    == [];
    zip(<X :: L>) == <X> :: zip(<L>);

    -- pairs of lists
    zip(<[], L>)         == [];
    zip(<L, []>)         == [];
    zip(<X :: L, Y :: M>) == <X, Y> :: zip(<L, M>);

    -- tuples with at least three lists
    zip(L ^ (M ^ (N ^ P))) == zip(L ^ zip(M ^ (N ^ P)));

    unzip([])        == <>;
    unzip(<X> :: L) == <X :: (exl * L)>;
    unzip((X ^ (Y ^ P)) :: L)  == (X :: (exl * L))
                                   ^ unzip((Y ^ P) :: (exr * L));
```

5.5.12 Type Classes

Another example of a specification that uses equations over types, is the following module that models the restriction of the polymorphism of the equality function by means of a type class like mechanism. The module imports module bool that defines the standard operations on the Boolean values t (true) and f (false). At level 1 a unary boolean function (a predicate) eq on types is defined such that the type nat is in the eq class and such that a list type is in the eq class if its content type is in the class. The operator (=>) constrains a type by some boolean condition. At level 0 the equality function eq is now declared with type eq(A) => (A # A -> bool), which expresses that the function only applies to types in the eq class. The function (!) is used to apply a function with a constrained type to an argument. It requires that the condition is equal to t. This ensures that eq cannot be applied to function types or other types not in the eq class.

```
module equality
imports type;
lift(imports bool);
imports list, nat_typed, bool_typed;
level 1
  signature
    functions
      eq    : type -> bool;
      (=>) : bool # type -> type;
  equations
    eq(nat)     == t;
    eq(list(A)) == eq(A);
level 0
  signature
    functions
      (!) : (t => A -> B) # A -> B;
      eq  : eq(A) => (A # A -> bool);
  equations
    eq!(0, 0)         == t;
    eq!(0, s(I))      == f;
    eq!(s(I), 0)      == f;
    eq!(s(I), s(J))   == eq!(I, J);

    eq!([], [])           == t;
    eq!(X :: L, [])       == f;
    eq!([], X :: L)       == f;
    eq!(X :: L, X' :: L') == eq!(X, X') /\ eq!(L, L');
```

Here we conclude our discussion of MLS examples and proceed to formalize the MLS language in the remaining sections.

5.6 Syntax of Multi-Level Specifications

In this section we define the syntax of multi-level specifications, extend these with a module mechanism and define the semantics of multi-level specifications.

5.6.1 Syntax (MLS)

A multi-level specification is either empty, a level composed of a natural number indicating the level and a specification, or a concatenation of multi-level specifications.

imports OLS[5.3.4] Naturals[5.4.4]

exports

  sorts MLS

  context-free syntax

                     $\rightarrow$ MLS

    "level" Nat Spec $\rightarrow$ MLS

    MLS ";" MLS $\rightarrow$ MLS   **{left}**

    "(" MLS ")" $\rightarrow$ MLS   **{bracket}**

  priorities

    Sig ";"Sig $\rightarrow$ Sig > MLS ";"MLS $\rightarrow$ MLS

  variables

    "Γ"$[0\text{-}9']$* $\rightarrow$ MLS

Arrow and Product Functions Since types are terms over a signature, the constructors arrow and product must also be declarable. For this purpose the functions $(\rightarrow)$ and $(\times)$ are introduced with the same notation as used to make other infix operators into prefix functions.

exports

  context-free syntax

    "$(\rightarrow)$" $\rightarrow$ Fun

    "$(\times)$" $\rightarrow$ Fun

Specification Projections As for the OLS case we define several projection functions to decomposing a specification. Most noteworthy is the function 'up' that gives a specification without its lowest level. The projection function π_n gives the specification at level n. The function 'lift' increases the level indicators of all levels by 1. The function 'drop' decreases the indicators of all levels by one and removes the specification at level 0.

exports

  context-free syntax

    "π" "_" Nat "(" MLS ")" $\rightarrow$ Spec

    max(MLS) $\rightarrow$ Nat

    lift(MLS) $\rightarrow$ MLS

    drop(MLS) $\rightarrow$ MLS

    up(MLS) $\rightarrow$ MLS

    top-sig $\rightarrow$ MLS

    decl(Terms, Term) $\rightarrow$ Decls

equations

[ms-assoc]	$\Gamma_1; (\Gamma_2; \Gamma_3) = \Gamma_1; \Gamma_2; \Gamma_3$	[ms-lu]	$; \Gamma = \Gamma$
[ms-el]	level n $=$	[ms-ru]	$\Gamma; = \Gamma$

The projection π_n gives the n-th level of a specification.

[p1] $\pi_n() =$

[p2] $\pi_n(\text{level } n\, \mathcal{S}) = \mathcal{S}$

[p3] $\pi_n(\text{level } m\, \mathcal{S}) = \quad \textbf{when } \mathrm{eq}(n, m) = \bot$

[p4] $\pi_n(\Gamma_1; \Gamma_2) = \pi_n(\Gamma_1); \pi_n(\Gamma_2)$

The function 'max' gives the index of the highest level of a specification. Note that 'max' is also the maximum function on natural numbers.

[max0] $\max() = 0$

[max1] $\max(\text{level } n\, \mathcal{S}) = n$

[max2] $\max(\Gamma_1; \Gamma_2) = \max(\max(\Gamma_1), \max(\Gamma_2))$

Any specification is equal (modulo commutativity of ';') to the concatenation of all levels, i.e., for any specification Γ:

$$\Gamma = \text{level } \max(\Gamma)\ \pi_{\max(\Gamma)}(\Gamma); \ldots ; \text{level } 1\ \pi_1(\Gamma); \text{level } 0\ \pi_0(\Gamma)$$

The function 'lift' increments all levels by one.

[lift1] $\mathrm{lift}() =$

[lift2] $\mathrm{lift}(\text{level } n\, \mathcal{S}) = \text{level } \mathrm{succ}(n)\, \mathcal{S}$

[lift3] $\mathrm{lift}(\Gamma_1; \Gamma_2) = \mathrm{lift}(\Gamma_1); \mathrm{lift}(\Gamma_2)$

The function 'drop' lowers all levels by one level and drops the lowest level.

[drop1] $\mathrm{drop}() =$

[drop2] $\mathrm{drop}(\text{level } 0\, \mathcal{S}) =$

[drop3] $\mathrm{drop}(\text{level } n\, \mathcal{S}) = \text{level } \mathrm{pred}(n)\, \mathcal{S} \quad \textbf{when } \mathrm{zero}(n) = \bot$

[drop4] $\mathrm{drop}(\Gamma_1; \Gamma_2) = \mathrm{drop}(\Gamma_1); \mathrm{drop}(\Gamma_2)$

For π, 'lift' and 'drop' we have (modulo associativity and commutativity of ';')

[lift-drop] $\mathrm{lift}(\mathrm{drop}(\Gamma)); \text{level } 0\ \pi_0(\Gamma) = \Gamma$

A multi-level specification is actually a stack of specifications, with 'drop' as the pop operation and π_0 as top. The term $\mathrm{lift}(\_); \text{level } 0\_$ corresponds to pushing a specification on the stack.

     The constant 'top-sig' is the implicit signature that determines the sorts of the highest signature.

[topsig]   top-sig $=$ level 0 signature functions $(\times), (\rightarrow) : \text{top} \times \text{top} \rightarrow \text{top}$

The operation 'up' is like 'drop' with an extra property. In case level 0 is not the highest level, i.e. max is not equal to 0, then 'up' just drops level 0. If level 0 is the highest level, 'up' is the signature 'top-sig' extended with the sorts of the highest level declared as constants of type 'top'. This is the implicit signature of the types used at the highest level of a specification. Observe that if $\max(\Gamma) = 0$, then after one iteration $\mathrm{up}(\mathrm{up}(\Gamma)) = \mathrm{up}(\Gamma)$.

[up1] $\mathrm{up}(\Gamma) = \text{top-sig; level 0 signature functions } \mathrm{decl}(S(\mathrm{Sg}(\pi_0(\Gamma))), \mathrm{top})$
              when $\mathrm{zero}(\max(\Gamma)) = \top$
[up2] $\mathrm{up}(\Gamma) = \mathrm{drop}(\Gamma)$ **when** $\mathrm{zero}(\max(\Gamma)) = \bot$

The function 'decl' constructs a list of declarations from a list of terms and a sort. It is used in the definition of 'up' above to create a declaration for each sort of the highest level. Only the function constants in the list are declared.

[decl1] $\mathrm{decl}(, \tau) =$
[decl2] $\mathrm{decl}(f, \tau) = f \colon \tau$
[decl3] $\mathrm{decl}(t_1^+; t_2^+, \tau) = \mathrm{decl}(t_1^+, \tau) \mathbin{+\!\!+} \mathrm{decl}(t_2^+, \tau)$
[decl4] $\mathrm{decl}(t, \tau) =$ **otherwise**

5.6.2 Normalization (MLS-Norm)

According to the syntax of signatures and multi-level specifications, specification elements like levels, signatures and declarations can be written in any order and can be repeated. For instance, a specification can contain several sections for `level 0` and a signature can contain several **functions** sections. The function 'norm' below normalizes a specifications such that the levels are presented in decreasing order and specifications consists of one signature section and one equations section. Furthermore, signatures are normalized such that they contain a single sorts, functions and variables section. Finally, redundant declarations, sort declarations and equations are removed.

imports MLS[5.6.1]
exports
  context-free syntax
    $\mathrm{norm}(\mathrm{MLS}) \to \mathrm{MLS}$
    $\mathrm{norm}(\mathrm{Spec}) \to \mathrm{Spec}$
equations

[n-1] $\mathrm{norm}(\Gamma) = \text{level 0 } \mathrm{norm}(\pi_0(\Gamma))$ **when** $\max(\Gamma) = 0$
[n-2] $\mathrm{norm}(\Gamma) = \mathrm{lift}(\mathrm{norm}(\mathrm{drop}(\Gamma))); \text{ level 0 } \mathrm{norm}(\pi_0(\Gamma))$
                              when $\mathrm{zero}(\max(\Gamma)) = \bot$

[n-3] $\text{norm}(\mathcal{S}) = \text{signature } \Sigma'; \text{ equations } \text{E}(\mathcal{S})$
                    when $\text{Sg}(\mathcal{S}) = \Sigma,$
                                 $\Sigma' = \text{sorts } \text{S}(\Sigma);$
                                           $\text{functions } \text{F}(\Sigma);$
                                           $\text{variables } \text{V}(\Sigma);$

[n-4] $d_1^*; \, d; \, d_2^*; \, d; \, d_3^* = d_1^*; \, d; \, d_2^*; \, d_3^*$

[n-5] $\text{sorts } t_1^*; \, t; \, t_2^*; \, t; \, t_3^* = \text{sorts } t_1^*; \, t; \, t_2^*; \, t_3^*$

[n-6] $\text{equations } \varphi_1^*; \, \varphi; \, \varphi_2^*; \, \varphi; \, \varphi_3^* = \text{equations } \varphi_1^*; \, \varphi; \, \varphi_2^*; \, \varphi_3^*$

5.6.3   Modular Multi-Level Specifications (MMLS)

We define a simple modularization scheme based on syntactic inclusion. It adds considerably to the expressive power of the language by the ability to share specifications at more than one level, as we saw in the examples in Section 5.5. A module binds a multi-level specification to a module name. An import is a reference to the body of a module. It denotes the specification that would be obtained by replacing the import by the module body. Name clashes between functions imported from different modules are not problematic, because overloading permits such functions to coexist. Functions from different origins with identical names *and* types are identified. Although this seems a reasonable choice, extension with renaming operators would be useful, but is not further considered here.

imports MLS[5.6.1] MLS-Norm[5.6.2]

exports

  sorts Module Modules

  context-free syntax

    "imports" {Fun ","}*   → MLS

    "module" Fun MLS ";"   → Module

    Module*   → Modules

    Modules "++" Modules   → Modules {**right**}

    π "_" Fun "(" Modules ")" → MLS

  variables

    "M"$[0\text{-}9']*$ → Module

    "M" "*"$[0\text{-}9']*$ → Module*

    "M" "+"$[0\text{-}9']*$ → Module+

equations

  Concatenation of module lists

[mod-cnc] $M_1^* \, ++ \, M_2^* = M_1^* \, M_2^*$

A list of imports denotes the concatenation of the imported specifications.

[imp] $\text{imports } f_1^+, f_2^+ = \text{imports } f_1^+; \text{ imports } f_2^+$

The projection of a module name in a list of modules yields the module body. If more than one module with the same name exists, the bodies are concatenated.

[p1] $\pi_f() =$

[p1] $\pi_f(\text{module } f\,\Gamma;) = \Gamma$

[p3] $\pi_f(\text{module } f'\ \Gamma;) = \quad \textbf{when } \text{eq}(f, f') = \perp$

[p4] $\pi_f(M_1^+\ M_2^+) = \pi_f(M_1^+);\ \pi_f(M_2^+)$

Note that the function π_f is overloaded: lookup of the type of a function in a list of declarations and lookup of a module in a list of modules.

Modules have a simple syntactic replacement semantics. The normalization function 'flat' flattens all modules in a list of modules, by replacing imports by module bodies.

imports Term-Sets[5.B.5]

exports

  context-free syntax

    flat "(" Modules ")" $\to$ Modules

    flat "(" Modules ")" "[" Modules "]" $\to$ Modules

    flat "(" Modules "," TermSet ")" "[" MLS "]" $\to$ MLS

equations

The unary function 'flat', flattens the body of each module in a list of modules with respect to the entire list of modules.

[flat-main] $\text{flat}(M^*) = \text{flat}(M^*)[M^*]$

[flat-mods1] $\text{flat}(M^*)[\![\,]\!] =$

[flat-mods2] $\text{flat}(M^*)[M_1^+\ M_2^+] = \text{flat}(M^*)[M_1^+] + \!\!+ \text{flat}(M^*)[M_2^+]$

[flat-mods3] $\text{flat}(M^*)[\text{module } f\Gamma;] = \text{module } f\ \text{norm}(\text{flat}(M^*, \{\})[\Gamma]);$

An import of a module is replaced by its body. The imports in the body of a module have to be flattened in turn. A loop caused by cyclic imports is prevented by adding the module name to the set of modules already seen (the second argument of function 'flat'). An import is not expanded if a module was already imported (equation [flat-imp2]).

[flat-imp1] $$\frac{f \in \Phi = \perp}{\text{flat}(M^*, \Phi)[\text{imports } f] = \text{flat}(M^*, \Phi \cup \{f\})[\pi_f(M^*)]}$$

[flat-imp2] $$\frac{f \in \Phi = \top}{\text{flat}(M^*, \Phi)[\text{imports } f] =}$$

Imports inside other constructs are replaced by distributing 'flat' over all operators except 'imports'.

[flat-ml0] $\text{flat}(M^*, \Phi)[\Gamma] = \quad \textbf{when } \Gamma =$

[flat-ml1]	$\mathrm{flat}(M^*, \Phi)[\![\Gamma_1; \Gamma_2]\!] = \mathrm{flat}(M^*, \Phi)[\![\Gamma_1]\!]; \mathrm{flat}(M^*, \Phi)[\![\Gamma_2]\!]$
[flat-ml2]	$\mathrm{flat}(M^*, \Phi)[\![\mathrm{level}\ n\ \mathcal{S}]\!] = \mathrm{level}\ n\ \mathrm{flat}(M^*, \Phi)[\![\mathcal{S}]\!]$
[flat-ml3]	$\mathrm{flat}(M^*, \Phi)[\![\pi_n(\Gamma)]\!] = \pi_n(\mathrm{flat}(M^*, \Phi)[\![\Gamma]\!])$
[flat-ml4]	$\mathrm{flat}(M^*, \Phi)[\![\mathrm{lift}(\Gamma)]\!] = \mathrm{lift}(\mathrm{flat}(M^*, \Phi)[\![\Gamma]\!])$
[flat-ml5]	$\mathrm{flat}(M^*, \Phi)[\![\mathrm{drop}(\Gamma)]\!] = \mathrm{drop}(\mathrm{flat}(M^*, \Phi)[\![\Gamma]\!])$
[flat-ml6]	$\mathrm{flat}(M^*, \Phi)[\![\mathrm{up}(\Gamma)]\!] = \mathrm{up}(\mathrm{flat}(M^*, \Phi)[\![\Gamma]\!])$
[flat-ml7]	$\mathrm{flat}(M^*, \Phi)[\![\mathrm{max}(\Gamma)]\!] = \mathrm{max}(\mathrm{flat}(M^*, \Phi)[\![\Gamma]\!])$

The function 'flat' has to consider all projection operations on specifications and has to be extended to all sorts embedded in specifications by means of distribution equations like the ones above. These equations are not shown.

5.6.4 Multi-Level Equational Logic

We redefine equational logic for multi-level specifications. An equation is an axiom if it is an equation at level 0. The equations at higher levels apply to type annotations; in equation [mlel-ann] it is stated that two annotated terms are equal if their term parts are equal and if the annotations are equal with respect to the next level.

imports MLS[5.6.1] Substitution[5.B.7]

exports

  context-free syntax

    MLS "⊢" Eq → Bool

equations

$$[\text{mlel-ax}] \qquad \frac{\mathrm{E}(\pi_0(\Gamma)) = \varphi_1^*;\ t_1 \equiv t_2;\ \varphi_2^*}{\Gamma \vdash t_1 \equiv t_2\ =\ \top}$$

$$[\text{mlel-ann}] \qquad \frac{\Gamma \vdash t_1 \equiv t_2 = \top,\ \mathrm{up}(\Gamma) \vdash \tau_1 \equiv \tau_2 = \top}{\Gamma \vdash t_1 : \tau_1 \equiv t_2 : \tau_2\ =\ \top}$$

The standard rules for reflexivity, symmetry, transitivity, substitution and congruence for the other binary term operators (application, pair, arrow and product) are not shown.

If only free constructors (functions over which no equations are defined) are used in type annotations, then the types τ_i in equation [mlel-ann] have to be syntactically equal. In that case multi-level equational logic reduces to the typed equational logic of Section 5.3.5 and we have

$$\Gamma \vdash t_1 \equiv t_2 = \pi_0(\Gamma) \vdash t_1 \equiv t_2$$

Under the same assumption term rewriting with a multi-level specification reduces to the typed term rewriting of Section 5.3.5. Rewriting of annotated terms in a system with type equations is more complicated because $\mathcal{E}$-matching is needed. Given a set of equations $\mathcal{E}$, term t_1 $\mathcal{E}$-matches term t_2 if there exists a substitution σ such that $\mathcal{E} \vdash \sigma(t_2) \equiv t_1$.

Meinke (1992a) gives an equational logic for two levels of equations similar to the multi-level equational logic above. Meinke (1993) considers the rewrite relation resulting from a set of equations over terms and types by taking the transitive, reflexive closure of the equations considered as rewrite rules in both directions.

5.7 Typechecking Multi-Level Specifications

In this section we define a typechecker for multi-level specifications following the same approach as for one-level specifications. Well-formedness of fully annotated multi-level specifications is defined in Section 5.7.2. Rules for the complementary cases produce error messages for non-wellformed constructs in Section 5.7.3. Type assignment functions, defined in Sections 5.7.4 and 5.7.5, produce a fully annotated specification for a plain specification an example of which is shown in Figure 5.13. Finally, the typechecker is defined in Section 5.7.7 as the composition of type assignment and well-formedness checking.

Typechecking of multi-level specifications differs at several points from typechecking one-level specifications. First of all, types at level n are terms over the signature at level $n + 1$. Secondly, types can be polymorphic. Finally, functions and variables can be overloaded, i.e., have more than one declaration in a signature.

5.7.1 Projection

We define a new projection function that finds the type of a function or variable in a list of declarations. The difference with the projection function from Section 5.4.1 is that the function yields the set of all types that are assigned to the function or variable, instead of the first type. If no declaration exists the empty set is produced. Furthermore, π takes a set of function or variable names as first argument and yields the set of all types for all functions or variables in the set.

imports MLS[5.6.1] Renaming[5.B.10] Term-Sets[5.B.5]

exports

  context-free syntax

    "π" "$\_$" TermSet "(" Decls ")" $\rightarrow$ TermSet

    "π" "$\_$" Var "(" MLS ")" $\rightarrow$ TermSet

    "π" "$\_$" Fun "(" MLS ")" $\rightarrow$ TermSet

equations

  The projection function π_t finds the types of a set of functions or variables in a list of declarations.

[p1] $\pi_\Phi() = \{\}$

[p2] $\pi_\Phi(f : \tau) =$ if $f \in \Phi$ then $\{\tau\}$ else $\{\}$

[p2] $$\pi_\Phi(x:\tau) = \text{if } x \in \Phi \text{ then } \{\tau\} \text{ else } \{\}$$
[p3] $$\pi_\Phi(d_1^+; d_2^+) = \pi_\Phi(d_1^+) \cup \pi_\Phi(d_2^+)$$

The projection function π applied to a specification finds the type of a function or variable in the function or variable declarations of the signature of the lowest level.

[pf] $$\pi_f(\Gamma) = \pi_{\{f\}}(F(Sg(\pi_0(\Gamma))))$$
[px] $$\pi_x(\Gamma) = \pi_{\{x;\ \text{base}(x)\}}(V(Sg(\pi_0(\Gamma))))$$

In case of a variable not only the type of the variable, but also the type of its 'base' (variable without trailing digits or primes; see Appendix 5.B.10) is looked for. This makes it possible to use many variants of a variable with only one declaration. For example, if A : type is declared, then A1, A2, A' : type are implicitly declared as well. This facility encourages a consistent use of variable names.

5.7.2 Well-Formedness (MLS-WF)

As in the one-level case in Section 5.4.2, the well-formedness of fully annotated terms and specifications is defined by several well-formedness judgements—functions that yield an error Boolean value. An example of a fully annotated two-level specification is shown in Figure 5.13.

imports MLS[5.6.1] MLS-Projection[5.7.1] Error-Booleans[5.A.3] SPEC-Errors[5.B.2]
  MLS-TA-Aux[5.7.4] Matching[5.B.8] Term-Analysis[5.3.3]
exports
  context-free syntax
    "$\vdash_{mls}$" MLS $\rightarrow$ EBool
    MLS "$\vdash_{spec}$" Spec $\rightarrow$ EBool
    MLS "$\vdash_{sig}$" Sig $\rightarrow$ EBool
    MLS "$\vdash_{sorts}$" Terms $\rightarrow$ EBool
    MLS "$\vdash_{decls}$" Decls $\rightarrow$ EBool
    MLS "$\vdash_{sort}$" Term $\rightarrow$ EBool
    MLS "$\vdash_{trm}$" Term ":" Term $\rightarrow$ EBool
    MLS "$\vdash_{term}$" Term $\rightarrow$ EBool
    MLS "$\vdash_{eqs}$" Eqs $\rightarrow$ EBool

equations
    A multi-level specification is well-formed if each level is well-formed. The environment in which a specification is checked includes the specification itself because that may contain relevant sort declarations.

[wf-spec-1] $$\vdash_{mls} \Gamma = \Gamma \vdash_{spec} \pi_0(\Gamma) \quad \textbf{when } \max(\Gamma) = 0$$
[wf-spec-1] $$\vdash_{mls} \Gamma = \vdash_{mls} \text{up}(\Gamma) \rightsquigarrow \Gamma \vdash_{spec} \pi_0(\Gamma)$$
$$\textbf{when } \text{zero}(\max(\Gamma)) = \bot$$

```
level 1
  signature
    sorts type ;
    functions
      (->) : type # type -> type ;
    variables
      A : type; B : type; C : type ;
level 0
  signature
    sorts A : type;
    functions
      k : (A : type) -> (( B : type) -> (A : type) : type) : type;
    variables
      X : A : type;
      Y : B : type;
    equations
      ((k : (A : type) -> ((Q : type) -> (A : type) : type) : type)
       (X : A : type) : (Q : type ) -> (A : type) : type)
       (Y : Q : type) : A : type
      == X : A : type
```

Figure 5.13: Example of a fully annotated two-level specification. Observe that the types at level 0 are fully annotated terms over level 1.

A specification is well-formed if both the signature and the equations are well-formed. The errors in the equations generally depend on errors in the signature. Therefore equation [wf-spec] gives precedence to signature errors over equation errors.

[wf-spec] $\qquad\qquad \Gamma \vdash_{\text{spec}} \mathcal{S} = \Gamma \vdash_{\text{sig}} \text{Sg}(\mathcal{S}) \rightsquigarrow \Gamma \vdash_{\text{eqs}} \text{E}(\mathcal{S})$

A signature is well-formed if the sorts section contains well-formed sort declarations and if the function and variable declarations are well-formed.

[wf-sig] $\qquad\qquad \Gamma \vdash_{\text{sig}} \Sigma = \Gamma \vdash_{\text{sorts}} \text{S}(\Sigma) \rightsquigarrow \Gamma \vdash_{\text{decls}} \text{F}(\Sigma) \wedge \Gamma \vdash_{\text{decls}} \text{V}(\Sigma)$

The terms in a sort declaration at level n should be well-formed terms over level $n+1$.

[wf-sorts1] $\qquad\qquad \dfrac{\text{up}(\Gamma) \vdash_{\text{term}} \tau = \top}{\Gamma \vdash_{\text{sorts}} \tau = \top}$

[wf-sorts2] $\qquad\qquad \Gamma \vdash_{\text{sorts}} \tau_1^+; \tau_2^+ = \Gamma \vdash_{\text{sorts}} \tau_1^+ \wedge \Gamma \vdash_{\text{sorts}} \tau_2^+$

[wf-sorts3] $\Gamma \vdash_{\overline{\text{sorts}}} = \top$

A function or variable declaration is well-formed if its type is a well-formed sort.

[wf-decls-vd] $\Gamma \vdash_{\text{decls}} x : \tau = \Gamma \vdash_{\text{sort}} \tau$
[wf-decls-fd]   · $\Gamma \vdash_{\text{decls}} f : \tau = \Gamma \vdash_{\text{sort}} \tau$
[wf-decls-empty] $\Gamma \vdash_{\text{decls}} = \top$
[wf-decls-conc] $\Gamma \vdash_{\text{decls}} d_1^+ ; d_2^+ = \Gamma \vdash_{\text{decls}} d_1^+ \wedge \Gamma \vdash_{\text{decls}} d_2^+$

Sorts A term is a sort at level n if it is a term over level $n + 1$, and if it matches one of the terms declared as sort at level n.

[wf-sort] $$\frac{\text{zero}(\max(\Gamma)) = \bot, \ \{S(Sg(\pi_0(\Gamma)))\} \geqslant t = \top}{\Gamma \vdash_{\text{sort}} t = \text{up}(\Gamma) \vdash_{\text{term}} t}$$

The predicate $\Phi \geqslant t$ (Appendix 5.B.8) tests whether a term t matches one of the elements of a set of terms Φ, in this case the set of sorts declared at level 0.

For a term to be a sort at the highest level it is sufficient to be a term over the next (implicit) level.

[wf-sort] $$\frac{\text{zero}(\max(\Gamma)) = \top}{\Gamma \vdash_{\text{sort}} t = \text{up}(\Gamma) \vdash_{\text{term}} t}$$

Otherwise all terms from the closure of the basic sorts under arrow and product that are used in function and variable declarations, would have to be declared explicitly as sorts.

Terms A complication with respect to the one-level case is that sorts are also annotated, except for the sorts at the highest level. We could solve this problem by introducing two different well-formedness predicates. Instead we use one predicate and the implicit annotation of terms with 'top'. The auxiliary judgement $\vdash_{\text{term.}}$ is introduced to treat explicitly and implicitly annotated terms in the same way. The annotation of a term is constructed explicitly by splitting it in its term and type. This has the effect that terms that are annotated implicitly with 'top' can be treated in the same way as terms with explicit annotations.

[wf-term] $\Gamma \vdash_{\text{term}} t = \Gamma \vdash_{\text{trm}} \text{term}(t) : \text{type}(t)$

The term 'top' has type 'top'. Since 'top' can not be declared as a function, this is the only possible type it can have.

[wf-top] $\Gamma \vdash_{\text{trm}} \text{top} : \text{top} = \top$

The types of functions and variables should be well-formed sorts. The type of a function should match one of the types with which it is declared. If a variable is declared, its type should match one of its declared types. Variables are allowed to be undeclared. The reason for this exception is that the type assignment algorithm has to invent new variables in some cases to prevent name clashes. A result of this choice is that variables can be used without declaration, if some reasonable type can be inferred for it from the context, or if it is given some suitable annotation.

$$[\text{wf-fun}] \quad \frac{\pi_f(\Gamma) \geq \tau = \top}{\Gamma \vdash_{\text{trm}} f : \tau = \top}$$

$$[\text{wf-var}] \quad \frac{\pi_x(\Gamma) = \Phi, \ \Phi \geq \tau \vee \text{empty}(\Phi) = \top}{\Gamma \vdash_{\text{trm}} x : \tau = \Gamma \vdash_{\text{sort}} \tau}$$

A pair is well-formed if its type is the product of the types of its left and right components. An application is well-formed if the type of the argument matches the type of the domain of the type of the function and if the type of the annotation matches the type of the codomain.

$$[\text{wf-pr}] \quad \frac{\text{term}(\tau) = \text{type}(t_1) \times \text{type}(t_2)}{\Gamma \vdash_{\text{trm}} t_1, t_2 : \tau = \Gamma \vdash_{\text{term}} t_1 \wedge \Gamma \vdash_{\text{term}} t_2}$$

$$[\text{wf-app}] \quad \frac{\text{term}(\text{type}(t_1)) = \text{type}(t_2) \to \tau}{\Gamma \vdash_{\text{trm}} t_1 \ t_2 : \tau = \Gamma \vdash_{\text{term}} t_1 \wedge \Gamma \vdash_{\text{term}} t_2}$$

Products and arrows are well-formed if their prefix versions ($\times$) and ($\to$) are declared in the signature as binary functions. The product of the types of the arguments t_1 and t_2 should be the domain and the annotation τ should be the codomain of the declaration of the function. This is checked in the same way as the annotation of a function is checked, by matching the annotation of the function to one of its declarations. Because the type of the product or arrow is reconstructed, it is not clear what the annotations for the product and arrow in the types of ($\times$) and ($\to$) should be. For this purpose, the function 'bterm' (Section 5.3.3) is used to strip the annotation from the the the declared types.

$$[\text{wf-prd}] \quad \frac{\text{bterm}*(\pi_{(\times)}(\Gamma)) \geq \text{type}(t_1) \times \text{type}(t_2) \to \tau = \top}{\Gamma \vdash_{\text{trm}} t_1 \times t_2 : \tau = \Gamma \vdash_{\text{term}} t_1 \wedge \Gamma \vdash_{\text{term}} t_2}$$

$$[\text{wf-arr}] \quad \frac{\text{bterm}*(\pi_{(\to)}(\Gamma)) \geq \text{type}(t_1) \times \text{type}(t_2) \to \tau = \top}{\Gamma \vdash_{\text{trm}} t_1 \to t_2 : \tau = \Gamma \vdash_{\text{term}} t_1 \wedge \Gamma \vdash_{\text{term}} t_2}$$

Equations An equation is well-formed if both sides have the same type, the variables of the rhs are contained in the variables of the lhs and all occurrences of a variable on both sides have the same type.

$$[\text{wf-eqn}] \quad \frac{\text{type}(t_1) = \text{type}(t_2), \ \text{vars}(t_2) \subseteq \text{vars}(t_1) = \top,}{\text{var-types}(\text{avars}(t_1, t_2)) = []}$$
$$\frac{}{\Gamma \vdash_{\text{eqs}} t_1 \equiv t_2 = \Gamma \vdash_{\text{term}} t_1 \wedge \Gamma \vdash_{\text{term}} t_2}$$

[wf-eqns-empty] $\Gamma \vdash_{eqs} = \top$

[wf-eqns-conc] $\Gamma \vdash_{eqs} \varphi_1^+; \varphi_2^+ = \Gamma \vdash_{eqs} \varphi_1^+ \wedge \Gamma \vdash_{eqs} \varphi_2^+$

The following proposition states that equality according to a well-formed specification is type preserving, i.e., a term can only be equal to another term if they have the same type.

Proposition 5.7 (type soundness) *Well-formed specifications preserve types, i.e, let Γ be a fully annotated multi-level specification such that declarations in Γ use only free type constructors, if $\vdash_{mls} \Gamma$ and $\Gamma \vdash_{term} t_i$ then $\pi_0(\Gamma) \vdash t_1 \equiv t_2$ implies* type$(t_1) = $ type(t_2).

Proof: Since Γ is well-formed, all equations in $\pi_0(\Gamma)$ have equal types in the lhs and rhs and typed equational logic is type preserving for equations with that property (Proposition 5.2). □

The following proposition relates equalities over plain terms to equalities over fully annotated terms.

Proposition 5.8 *Equational derivability in a fully annotated specification implies equational derivability in the plain specification: Let Γ be a fully annotated multi-level specification such that declarations in Γ use only free type constructors and such that $\vdash_{mls} \Gamma$, then $\Gamma \vdash t_1 \equiv t_2$ implies* spine$(\Gamma) \vdash$ spine$(t_1) \equiv$ spine(t_2)

In Section 5.7.6 we discuss the requirements for the reverse implication; when does equality in the plain specification preserve types?

5.7.3   Non-wellformedness (MLS-NWF)

The generation of error messages for the non-wellformed cases is very similar to Section 5.4.3, therefore only the case of a non-wellformed application is presented.

imports MLS-WF[5.7.2] SPEC-Errors[5.B.2]

equations

[wf-app'] $\Gamma \vdash_{\mathsf{trm}} t_1\ t_2 : \tau$
$= (\Gamma \vdash_{\mathsf{term}} t_1 \wedge \Gamma \vdash_{\mathsf{term}} t_2)$
$\rightsquigarrow$ application " spine($t_1\ t_2$) " not well-formed
:: if $\neg\ \mathtt{A} \to \mathtt{B} \geq$ term(type(t_1))
then " spine(t_1) " is not a function
else if $\neg$ eq(dom(term(type(t_1))), type(t_2))
then type of argument " type(t_2)
" does not match type of domain " dom(term(type(t_1))) "
else type of result " spine(τ)
" does not match type of codomain " cod(term(type(t_1))) "
otherwise

5.7.4 Preliminaries for Type Assignment (MLS-TA-Aux)

In the next section we will define the type assignment functions for the multi-level
case. First, we define several auxiliary functions that will make the definition of type
assignment easier. The two major complications are overloading and polymorphism.
Overloading caused by multiple declarations of variables and functions leads to multiple fully annotated terms for a single plain term. Therefore, the type assignment
function for terms yields a set of annotated terms instead of a single term. To assign
types to a composite term such as an application, first the subterms are assigned
types, resulting in a pair of sets of terms. Each combination from the two sets can
form a well-formed application. Therefore, each term in the Cartesian product of the
two sets has to be considered.

Join To handle polymorphism correctly, type variables of terms composed by application, pairing etc. have to be renamed before types can be compared, because types
are implicitly universally quantified. The function $\bowtie$ (join) combines the function of
renaming type variables and producing the cartesian product of two sets. Given two
sets Φ_1 and Φ_2 it renames the type variables in the terms in the two sets leading to sets
Φ_3 and Φ_4 such that the type variables are disjunct, i.e., tvars(Φ_3) $\cap$ tvars(Φ_4) = {}.
The operation rn$\Phi[\Phi']$, given a set of variables Φ', produces a renaming of the variables in the set Φ such that they do not occur in Φ' (see Appendix 5.B.10). The result
of the operation is the Cartesian product $\Phi_3 \times \Phi_4$, i.e., the set of all pairs (t_1, t_2) of
elements from $t_1 \in \Phi_3$ and $t_2 \in \Phi_4$ (see also Appendix 5.B.5).

imports Renaming[5.B.10]

exports
  context-free syntax
    TermSet "⋈" TermSet → TermSet {**non-assoc**}
equations

[join]
$$\frac{\text{vars}(\Phi_2) = \Phi_2', \text{ rn tvars}(\Phi_1) \cap \Phi_2'[\text{vars}(\Phi_1) \cup \Phi_2']*(\Phi_1) = \Phi_3, \\ \text{vars}(\Phi_3) = \Phi_3', \text{ rn tvars}(\Phi_2) \cap \Phi_3'[\Phi_2' \cup \Phi_3']*(\Phi_2) = \Phi_4}{\Phi_1 \bowtie \Phi_2 \ = \ \Phi_3 \times \Phi_4}$$

Selection   Once two sets of terms have been joined, the well-formed pairs have to be selected and given a type annotation. This involves tests and type forming operations for each construct applying the test to each element in the set of pairs thereby keeping only the correct ones. This last aspect can be specified generically for all constructs. For each construct we use a function of sort (Term ⇒ Bool × TermSet)[5], which given a term produces a pair of a Boolean value indicating whether the term is well-formed and a set of terms resulting from assigning a type to that term. This function can be mapped over a set of terms resulting from the join of two type-assignments by the function '∗'. It applies the function to each element of the argument set remembering whether a well-formed term was already encountered. If at the end of the list none of the combinations turns out to be well-formed, then the last, non-wellformed one, is returned. This guarantees that type assignment always returns a term. Furthermore, from the non-wellformed term the well-formedness judgements can find out the cause of the error.

imports Term-Analysis[5.3.3] Term-Functions[5.B.3]
exports
  sorts (Bool × TermSet) (Term ⇒ Bool × TermSet)
  context-free syntax

"⟨" Bool "," TermSet "⟩"	→ (Bool × TermSet)
(Term ⇒ Bool × TermSet) "(" Term ")"	→ (Bool × TermSet)
(Term ⇒ Bool × TermSet) "∗" "(" TermSet ")"	→ TermSet
(Term ⇒ Bool × TermSet) "∗" "(" Bool "," TermSet ")"	→ TermSet

  variables
    "G"[0-9']∗ → (Term ⇒ Bool × TermSet)
equations

[mf0] $G*(\Phi) = G*(\bot, \Phi)$
[mf1] $G*(b, \{\}) = \{\}$
[mf2] $G*(b, \{t\}) = $ if $b \wedge \neg\, b'$ then $\{\}$ else Φ **when** $G(t) = \langle b', \Phi \rangle$
[mf3] $G*(b, \{t; t^+\}) = $ (if b' then Φ else $\{\}$) $\cup\, G*(b \vee b', \{t^+\})$
                       when $G(t) = \langle b', \Phi \rangle$

---

[5]Note that we instructed ToLATEX to typeset the sort identifier Term2BoolXTermSet as (Term ⇒ Bool × TermSet)

For functions of sort (Term $\Rightarrow$ Bool $\times$ Eqs), which yield a list of equations instead of a set of terms, similar functions are defined.

Annotation with a Set of Types Due to overloading, the result of assigning a type to a term is a set of terms instead of a single term. This means that the assignment of types in declarations and type annotations also leads to a set of types. These should be translated to lists of declarations and sets of terms, respectively. The following functions can be used to construct the declaration of a function or variable or the annotation of a term with a set of terms. The ambiguity in a declaration is translated to multiple declarations for the function or variable, i.e., $f : \{\tau_1, \tau_2\} = f : \tau_1; f : \tau_2$. The annotation of a term with a set of terms is translated to the set of the term with all the annotations from the set.

imports MLS[5.6.1]

exports

    context-free syntax

        Fun ":" TermSet $\rightarrow$ Decl

        Var ":" TermSet $\rightarrow$ Decl

        Term ":" TermSet $\rightarrow$ TermSet

    priorities

        Term ":" TermSet $\rightarrow$ TermSet $>$ TermSet "$\cup$" TermSet $\rightarrow$ TermSet

[decl1]	$d_1^*; f : \{\}; d_2^* = d_1^*; d_2^*$
[decl2]	$d_1^*; f : \{t\}; d_2^* = d_1^*; f : t; d_2^*$
[decl3]	$d_1^*; f : \{t_1^+; t_2^+\}; d_2^* = d_1^*; f : \{t_1^+\}; f : \{t_2^+\}; d_2^*$
[decl4]	$d_1^*; x : \{\}; d_2^* = d_1^*; d_2^*$
[decl5]	$d_1^*; x : \{t\}; d_2^* = d_1^*; x : t; d_2^*$
[decl6]	$d_1^*; x : \{t_1^+, t_2^+\}; d_2^* = d_1^*; x : \{t_1^+\}; x : \{t_2^+\}; d_2^*$
[trm1]	$t : \{\} = \{t : \text{nil}\}$
[trm2]	$t : \{\tau\} = \{t : \tau\}$
[trm3]	$t : \{t_1^+; t_2^+\} = t : \{t_1^+\} \cup t : \{t_2^+\}$

Variable Type Consistency The function 'var-types' checks whether the types of the variables in a set of terms of the form $x : \tau$ (annotated variables) are consistent, i.e., two occurrences of a variable should have types that are unifiable. If this is the case the function returns a substitution that makes the types of all occurrences of the same variable equal. The functions is used as follows: Given a term t, var-types(avars(t)) either gives $\perp$, which indicates that t contains two occurrences of the same variable with incompatible type annotations or a substitution σ that makes all occurrences of the same variable in t the same.

imports Unification[5.B.9]

exports

    context-free syntax

var-types(TermSet) → Subst$_\perp$
var-eqs(TermSet)   → Eqs

equations

[var-types1]   var-types(Φ) = mgu(var-eqs(Φ))
[var-eqs1]   var-eqs({}) =
[var-eqs2] var-eqs({$x : \tau_1; t_1^*; x : \tau_2; t_2^*$}) = $\tau_1 \equiv \tau_2$ ++ var-eqs({$t_1^*; x : \tau_2; t_2^*$})
[var-eqs2]   var-eqs({$x : \tau_1; t^*$}) = var-eqs({t^*}) **otherwise**

New Variables The function 'new-var' generates a variable name that is not declared in the signature at level 0. Given a set of variables Φ 'nv' picks the first element of Φ that is not declared in Γ. If all variables are declared, the variables in Φ are renamed by prepending an extra letter (Q) to each variable in Φ.

imports MLS-Projection[5.7.1]

exports

  context-free syntax

    new-var "(" MLS ")"   → Term
    nv "(" MLS ")" "(" TermSet "," TermSet ")" → Term

equations

[new-var-0]   new-var(Γ) = nv(Γ)({}, {})
[new-var-1]   nv(Γ)(Φ, {}) = nv(Γ)(Φ', Φ') **when** $\Phi' = $ add(Q, Φ)
[new-var-2] nv(Γ)(Φ, {$x; t^*$}) = if empty($\pi_x(\Gamma)$) then x else nv(Γ)(Φ, {t^*})

5.7.5   Type Assignment (MLS-TA)

The basic ideas for type assignment of multi-level specifications are similar to the one-level case. For instance, the type of an application is the codomain of the first (function) argument. The complications are caused by the multi-level aspect (types are typed terms), overloading and polymorphism. The basic idea in dealing with overloading is to create a set of all possible typings for each term; type assignment function 'Wt' returns a TermSet. When terms are combined all possible combinations of the associated sets have to be considered. The join and select functions of the previous section are applied for this purpose.

Type assignment of multi-level specifications proceeds by first annotating the higher levels and using the resulting annotated specification to assign types to the signature at level 0. The resulting signature can be used to assign types to the equations at level 0.

imports MLS[5.6.1] MLS-TA-Aux[5.7.4] MLS-Projection[5.7.1] Term-Analysis[5.3.3]
    Matching[5.B.8]

exports

  context-free syntax

    "Wm" "[" MLS "]"   → MLS

"Wsp" "(" MLS ")" "[" Spec "]" → Spec
"Wsg" "(" MLS ")" "[" Sig "]" → Sig
"Wd" "(" MLS ")" "[" Decls "]" → Decls
"Ws" "(" MLS ")" "[" Term "]" → TermSet
"Wss" "(" MLS ")" "[" Terms "]" → Terms
"Wtv" "(" MLS ")" "[" Term "]" → TermSet
"Wt" "(" MLS ")" "[" Term "]" → TermSet
"Wts" "(" MLS ")" "[" Terms "]" → Terms
"We" "(" MLS ")" "[" Eqs "]" → Eqs

equations

Assigning types to a specification consists of assigning types to all levels of the signature and using the resulting signature to assign types to the equations.

[wm-1]
$$\frac{\text{zero}(\max(\Gamma)) = \top}{\text{Wm}[\![\Gamma]\!] \ = \ \text{level } 0 \ \text{Wsp}(\text{lift}(\text{up}(\Gamma)))[\![\pi_0(\Gamma)]\!]}$$

[wm-n]
$$\frac{\text{zero}(\max(\Gamma)) = \bot, \ \text{lift}(\text{Wm}[\![\text{up}(\Gamma)]\!]) = \Gamma'}{\text{Wm}[\![\Gamma]\!] \ = \ \Gamma'; \text{level } 0 \ \text{Wsp}(\Gamma')[\![\pi_0(\Gamma)]\!]}$$

A specification is annotated by first annotating the signature using the higher levels and then annotating the equations using the higher levels extended with the annotated signature.

[wsp]
$$\frac{\text{Wsg}(\Gamma)[\![\text{Sg}(\mathcal{S})]\!] = \Sigma, \ \Gamma' = \text{level } 0 \ \text{signature } \Sigma}{\text{Wsp}(\Gamma)[\![\mathcal{S}]\!] \ = \ \text{signature } \Sigma; \text{equations } \text{We}(\Gamma; \Gamma')[\![\text{E}(\mathcal{S})]\!]}$$

Assign types to each section of a signature.

[w-cnc]
$$\frac{\text{sorts } \text{Wss}(\Gamma)[\![\text{S}(\Sigma)]\!] = \Sigma_2, \ \Gamma' = \Gamma; \text{level } 0 \ \text{signature } \Sigma_2}{\begin{aligned}\text{Wsg}(\Gamma)[\![\Sigma]\!] \ = \ &\Sigma_2; \\ &\text{functions } \text{Wd}(\Gamma')[\![\text{F}(\Sigma)]\!]; \\ &\text{variables } \text{Wd}(\Gamma')[\![\text{V}(\Sigma)]\!]\end{aligned}}$$

The sorts in the declarations of sorts, functions and variables are treated as terms over the signature at the next level.

[wd-e] $\text{Wd}(\Gamma)[\![]\!] =$
[wd-fun] $\text{Wd}(\Gamma)[\![f : \tau]\!] = f : \text{Ws}(\Gamma)[\![\tau]\!]$
[wd-var] $\text{Wd}(\Gamma)[\![x : \tau]\!] = x : \text{rn vars}(\Phi)[\{x\}] * (\Phi)$
        when $\text{Ws}(\Gamma)[\![\tau]\!] = \Phi$
[wd-cnc] $\text{Wd}(\Gamma)[\![d_1^+; d_2^+]\!] = \text{Wd}(\Gamma)[\![d_1^+]\!] +\!\!+ \text{Wd}(\Gamma)[\![d_2^+]\!]$

Sorts A sort at level n is a term over level $n + 1$. Only the annotations that match a sort declaration are selected in case a declaration is ambiguous. The function 'srt' selects a term if it matches one of the terms in the set in its first argument.

[ws-1] $\text{Ws}(\Gamma)[\![\tau]\!] = \text{srt}(\{S(\text{Sg}(\pi_0(\Gamma)))\}) * (\text{Wtv}(\text{up}(\Gamma))[\![\tau]\!])$

[sort-1] $\text{srt}(\Phi)(\tau) = \langle \top, \{\tau\} \rangle$ **when** $\Phi \geq \tau = \top$
[sort-2] $\text{srt}(\Phi)(\tau) = \langle \bot, \{\tau\} \rangle$ **otherwise**

A list of sort terms at level n is a list of terms over level $n+1$.

[ws-def] $$\text{Wss}(\Gamma)[\![ts]\!] = \text{Wts}(\text{up}(\Gamma))[\![ts]\!]$$

Terms with Variables   The function 'Wt' defined below assigns types to a term without considering the consistency of the types of variables. The function 'Wtv' first assigns a type to a term using 'Wt' and then applies 'var-types' (Section 5.7.4) to make the types of different occurrences of the same variable equal.

[wt-vars]
$$\frac{\text{Wt}(\Gamma)[\![t]\!] = \Phi, \ \text{var-types}(\text{avars}(\Phi)) = \sigma_\bot}{\text{Wtv}(\Gamma)[\![t]\!] \ = \ \text{if fail?}(\sigma_\bot) \text{ then } \Phi \text{ else } \Downarrow_\bot (\sigma_\bot)*(\Phi)}$$

Functions and Variables   Functions get assigned the type from the declaration in the signature.

[wt-fun] $$\text{Wt}(\Gamma)[\![f]\!] = f \colon \pi_f(\Gamma)$$

The type assignment to variables is somewhat more complicated since undeclared variables are taken into account according to the following rules. Equation [wt-var1] deals with variables in types of the top signature. Equation [wt-var2] finds the set of declared types Φ for a variable x. If Φ is not empty, i.e., the variable is declared, x is annotated with Φ. If there is no declaration (Φ is empty), a new type variable is generated to assign to x, which is assigned a type as a term over the next level. This is necessary to ensure that a term has the right number of annotations.

[wt-var1]
$$\frac{\text{up}(\Gamma) = \text{top-sig}}{\text{Wt}(\Gamma)[\![x]\!] \ = \ \{x\}}$$

[wt-var2]
$$\frac{\text{up}(\Gamma) \neq \text{top-sig}, \ \pi_x(\Gamma) = \Phi,}{\text{if empty}(\Phi) \text{ then } \text{Wt}(\text{up}(\Gamma))[\![\text{new-var}(\text{up}(\Gamma))]\!] \text{ else } \Phi = \{ts\}}{\text{Wt}(\Gamma)[\![x]\!] \ = \ x \colon \{\text{rn vars} *(\ ts)[\{x\}]*(ts)\}}$$

Nil and Top   Nil can not occur in well-formed specifications. Top can only occur as a top-level type.

[wt-nil] $\text{Wt}(\Gamma)[\![\text{nil}]\!] = \{ \text{nil} : \text{nil} \}$
[wt-top] $\text{Wt}(\Gamma)[\![\text{top}]\!] = \{ \text{top} : \text{top} \}$

Auxiliary Functions For the type assignment of non-atomic terms we need the following auxiliary functions.

hiddens

  context-free syntax

srt(TermSet)	$\rightarrow$ (Term $\Rightarrow$ Bool $\times$ TermSet)
app(MLS)	$\rightarrow$ (Term $\Rightarrow$ Bool $\times$ TermSet)
pr(MLS)	$\rightarrow$ (Term $\Rightarrow$ Bool $\times$ TermSet)
arr	$\rightarrow$ (Term $\Rightarrow$ Bool $\times$ TermSet)
prd	$\rightarrow$ (Term $\Rightarrow$ Bool $\times$ TermSet)
ann	$\rightarrow$ (Term $\Rightarrow$ Bool $\times$ TermSet)
eqn	$\rightarrow$ (Term $\Rightarrow$ Bool $\times$ Eqs)
new-arrow(MLS)	$\rightarrow$ Term

equations

Application An application term is assigned the codomain of the type of the function. To this end, both arguments are assigned types and the result terms are joined. The type of the term in the argument position should conform to the argument type of the function.

[wt-app]
$$\mathrm{Wt}(\Gamma)[\![t_1\ t_2]\!] = \mathrm{app}(\Gamma) *((\mathrm{Wt}(\Gamma)[\![t_1]\!] \bowtie \mathrm{Wt}(\Gamma)[\![t_2]\!]) \\ \bowtie \{\mathsf{a} : \text{new-arrow}(\Gamma)\}\ )$$

[app1]
$$\frac{\mathrm{mgu}(\mathrm{type}(t_1) \equiv \tau_1; \mathrm{type}(t_2) \equiv \tau_2) = \sigma}{\mathrm{app}(\Gamma)((t_1, t_2), \mathsf{a} : (\tau_1, \tau_2, \tau_3)) = \langle \top, \{\sigma(t_1\ t_2 : \tau_3)\}\rangle}$$

[app2]
$$\mathrm{app}(\Gamma)((t_1, t_2), \tau) = \langle \bot, \{t_1\ t_2 : \mathrm{nil}\}\rangle$$
$$\textbf{otherwise}$$

The function 'new-arrow' constructs an arrow type with new variables as domain and codomain, annotates it with types and yields a triple of the arrow type, domain and codomain.

[na]
$$\frac{\begin{array}{c}\text{new-var}(\mathrm{up}(\Gamma)) = x,\ x' = \mathrm{prime}(x),\ \tau_0 = x \to x',\\ \text{if } \mathrm{zero}(\mathrm{max}(\Gamma)) \text{ then } \{\tau_0\} \text{ else } \mathrm{Wt}(\mathrm{up}(\Gamma))[\![\tau_0]\!] = \{\tau_1; t^*\}\end{array}}{\text{new-arrow}(\Gamma) = \tau_1, \mathrm{dom}(\mathrm{term}(\tau_1)), \mathrm{cod}(\mathrm{term}(\tau_1))}$$

Pair A pair (t_1, t_2) has the product type $\tau_1 \times \tau_2$ if τ_i is the type of t_i. The product is itself a term over the next level.

[wt-pr]
$$\mathrm{Wt}(\Gamma)[\![t_1, t_2]\!] = \mathrm{pr}(\Gamma)*(\mathrm{Wt}(\Gamma)[\![t_1]\!] \bowtie \mathrm{Wt}(\Gamma)[\![t_2]\!])$$

[pr1]
$$\mathrm{pr}(\Gamma)(t_1, t_2) = \langle \top, \{(t_1, t_2) : \mathrm{type}(t_1) \times \mathrm{type}(t_2)\}\rangle$$
$$\textbf{when}\ \mathrm{zero}(\mathrm{max}(\Gamma)) = \top$$

[pr2]
$$\mathrm{pr}(\Gamma)(t_1, t_2) = \langle \top, t_1, t_2 : \mathrm{Wt}(\mathrm{up}(\Gamma))[\![\mathrm{type}(t_1) \times \mathrm{type}(t_2)]\!]\rangle$$
$$\textbf{when}\ \mathrm{zero}(\mathrm{max}(\Gamma)) = \bot$$

Arrow and Product Arrow and product are defined in terms of application of the functions $(\rightarrow)$ and $(\times)$ to their arguments. After type assignment the binary notation is restored for readability.

[wt-arr] $\quad\quad\quad\quad Wt(\Gamma)[\![t_1 \rightarrow t_2]\!] = arr*(Wt(\Gamma)[\![(\rightarrow)\ (t_1,\ t_2)]\!])$

[arr1] $\quad\quad\quad\quad\quad arr(t) = \langle \top, \{t_1 \rightarrow t_2 : type(t)\}\rangle$
$\quad\quad\quad\quad\quad\quad\quad\quad\quad$ **when** $bapp(t) = (\rightarrow)\ (t_1,\ t_2)$

[arr2] $\quad\quad\quad\quad\quad arr(t) = \langle \bot, \{t\}\rangle$ **otherwise**

[wt-prd] $\quad\quad\quad\quad Wt(\Gamma)[\![t_1 \times t_2]\!] = prd*(Wt(\Gamma)[\![(\times)\ (t_1,\ t_2)]\!])$

[prd1] $\quad\quad\quad\quad\quad prd(t) = \langle \top, \{t_1 \times t_2 : type(t)\}\rangle$
$\quad\quad\quad\quad\quad\quad\quad\quad\quad$ **when** $bapp(t) = (\times)\ (t_1,\ t_2)$

[prd2] $\quad\quad\quad\quad\quad prd(t) = \langle \bot, \{t\}\rangle$ **otherwise**

Annotation A term $t : \tau$ that already has a type annotation τ, has to be assigned a type that conforms with τ and τ itself should be assigned a type as a term at the next level of Γ.

[wt-ann] $\quad\quad\quad Wt(\Gamma)[\![t : \tau]\!] = ann*(Wt(\Gamma)[\![t]\!] \bowtie a : Wt(up(\Gamma))[\![\tau]\!])$

[ann1] $\quad\quad ann(t : \tau_1, a : \tau_2) = \langle \top, \{\sigma(t : \tau_2)\}\rangle$ **when** $mgu(\tau_1 \equiv \tau_2) = \sigma$

[ann2] $\quad\quad ann(t, a : \tau) = \langle \bot, \{t : \tau\}\rangle$ **otherwise**

Lists of Terms

[wt-terms1] $\quad\quad\quad\quad Wts(\Gamma)[\![]\!] =$

[wt-terms2] $\quad\quad\quad\quad Wts(\Gamma)[\![t]\!] = ts$ **when** $\{ts\} = Wt(\Gamma)[\![t]\!]$

[wt-terms3] $\quad\quad Wts(\Gamma)[\![t_1^+;\ t_2^+]\!] = Wts(\Gamma)[\![t_1^+]\!] \;+\!\!+\; Wts(\Gamma)[\![t_2^+]\!]$

Equations An equation is annotated by annotating both sides of the equation. The types of the resulting terms should be unifiable and if this is the case the unifier is applied to both term to make the types equal.

[wt-eqn] $\quad\quad We(\Gamma)[\![t_1 \equiv t_2]\!] = eqn*(Wt(\Gamma)[\![t_1]\!] \bowtie Wt(\Gamma)[\![t_2]\!])$

[eqn1] $\quad\quad eqn(t_1, t_2) = \langle \top, \sigma_2 \circ \sigma_1(t_1 \equiv t_2)\rangle$
$\quad\quad\quad\quad$ **when** $\quad var\text{-}types(avars(t_1, t_2)) = \sigma_1,$
$\quad\quad\quad\quad\quad\quad\quad\quad mgu(\sigma_1(type(t_1) \equiv type(t_2))) = \sigma_2$

[eqn2] $\quad\quad eqn(t_1, t_2) = \langle \bot, t_1 \equiv t_2\rangle$ **otherwise**

[we-eqns-0] $\quad\quad\quad\quad We(\Gamma)[\![]\!] =$

[we-eqns-n] $\quad\quad We(\Gamma)[\![\varphi_1^+;\ \varphi_2^+]\!] = We(\Gamma)[\![\varphi_1^+]\!] \;+\!\!+\; We(\Gamma)[\![\varphi_2^+]\!]$

Correctness The type assignment functions defined above produce a fully annotated specification given an arbitrary plain, partially annotated or fully annotated
specification. Type assignment always succeeds, but the resulting specification is not
necessarily well-formed. The following propositions state that type assignment produces a well-formed result whenever that is possible. The expression $\Phi > t'$ expresses
that t' is an instantiation of one of the terms in Φ. Because we can choose t' arbitrarily as long as it is well-formed the proposition states that Wt finds *all most general
annotations of t*.

Proposition 5.9 (correctness of Wt) *The function* Wt *finds all correct typings
for a term if any exist. Let* Γ *be a multi-level specification with free types such that*
$\vdash_{\mathrm{mls}} \Gamma$. *Given a term t, if there exists a full annotation* t' *of t (*spine$(t') =$ spine(t)*)
such that* $\Gamma \vdash_{\mathrm{term}} t'$ *and if* $\Phi = \mathrm{Wt}(\Gamma)[\![t]\!]$, *then* $\Phi > t'$ *and for all* $t'' \in \Phi$, $\Gamma \vdash_{\mathrm{term}} t''$

Proof: by induction on t. □

If no functions are overloaded, terms have a single full annotation. The previous
proposition states that this single annotation is 'principal', i.e., the most general type
assignment of the term.

Proposition 5.10 *Let* Γ *be a fully annotated multi-level specification with free types
such that* $\vdash_{\mathrm{mls}} \Gamma$ *and such that for each* f, $|\pi_f(\Gamma)| \leq 1$, *then we have* $|\mathrm{Wt}(\Gamma)[\![t]\!]| = 1$.

Similarly, we have that Wm finds a well-formed full annotation for a specification
if one exists.

Proposition 5.11 (correctness of Wm) *If* $\vdash_{\mathrm{mls}} \Gamma$ *then* $\vdash_{\mathrm{mls}}$ Wm$[\![$spine$(\Gamma)]\!]$.

The result of type assignment is an expression over the original language to which
type assignment can again be applied.

Proposition 5.12 *Type assignment is idempotent, i.e.,*

$$\bigcup_{t' \in \mathrm{Wt}(\Gamma)[\![t]\!]} \mathrm{Wt}(\Gamma)[\![t']\!] = \mathrm{Wt}(\Gamma)[\![t]\!].$$

5.7.6 Disambiguation and Confluence

We saw in Section 5.7.2 that well-formedness of a specification ensures that derivable
equality is type preserving. As a corollary, term rewriting with a well-formed specification is type preserving. Furthermore, the type assignment function for multi-level
specifications yields a well-formed annotation of a specification if one exists. However, we have not yet looked at the consequences of overloading resolution by type
assignment for term rewriting. Is the plain term rewrite system the same as the annotated rewrite system? Although this is the case for some specifications, in general
the answer to this question is no.

Non-Confluence Caused by Overloading Due to overloading, the plain term rewrite system (TRS) of a specification can be non-confluent while the annotated TRS is confluent. A TRS is confluent if it does not matter which matching equation is taken for a rewrite step. For example, the following module eqda defines equality on Boolean values and on lists in the style of the data algebra of Bergstra and Sellink (1996). Module list_access extends module list from Section 5.5 with the function empty for testing emptiness of a list and the functions hd and tl, which give the head and tail of a list. The variables X and Y are generic variables.

```
module eqda
imports bool, list_access;
level 0
  signature
    functions
      eq : A # A -> bool;
    equations
      eq(X, Y) == X <-> Y;
      eq(X, Y) == (empty(X) /\ empty(Y))
                        \/ ((~(empty(X)) /\ ~(empty(Y)))
                    /\ (eq(hd(X), hd(Y)) /\ eq(tl(X), tl(Y))));
```

The plain term rewrite system of this module is not confluent because the two eq equations have the same lhs but completely unrelated rhss. For instance, either equation can be used to rewrite the term eq(t,f). Only if the first equation is chosen the expected result is achieved. The TRS of the module becomes confluent if we consider its full annotation. The types of variables X and Y on the rhss force the right types in the lhss. The annotation of eq in the first equation becomes bool # bool -> bool and in the second equation list(A) # list(A) -> bool.

The next example shows that even while the plain TRS is confluent it can have different normal forms than the annotated TRS. The function (/) is used as constructor for positive rational numbers and as defined exclusive or function for the Booleans. When regarded as a plain TRS, rationals of the form X/Y are rewritten anyway.

```
  signature
    functions
      (/)                 : nat  # nat  -> rat;
      (\/), (/\), (/) : bool # bool -> bool;
    equations
      X / Y == (~X /\ Y) \/ (X /\ ~Y)
```

These examples clearly show that, in general, types are needed to disambiguate the equations of specifications. However, in many cases where matching is used and constructors and defined functions do not have overlapping names, overloading is resolved by the choice of constructors in the lhs of an equation. An example is the definition of the generalization of `zip` to generalized products, for which it is not even clear how typed rewriting should be done, but untyped rewriting does not go wrong. Although it is often clear by examination whether types can be discarded, it is not clear how this property can be tested. For rewriting purposes it seems to be sufficient to annotate only functions with their type, i.e., apply function 'fspine' to the specification which removes all annotations except those of functions. It is not clear whether all ambiguities due to overloading are resolved in the fspine of a fully annotated specification.

Ambiguous Equations   Due to overloading an untyped equation can actually denote several typed equations. An example is the equation `size([])` `==` `0` in Figure 5.1. Another example are the overloaded numerical operations in module num below. It is clear that the equations for addition that involve `0` and `s` are valid for both naturals and integers. The type assignment function 'We' produces all annotations of an equation for which the types of lhs and rhs match.

```
module num
level 0
  signature
    sorts nat; int;
    functions
      0   : nat;                 0   : int;
      s   : nat -> nat;          s, p : int -> int;
      (+) : nat # nat -> nat;    (+)  : int # int -> int;
      i   : nat -> int;
    variables
      X, Y : nat; X, Y : int;
  equations
    0    + Y  == Y;          s(p(X)) == X;   i(0)    == 0;
    s(X) + Y  == X + s(Y);   p(s(X)) == X;   i(s(X)) == s(i(X));
    p(X) + Y  == X + p(Y);
```

5.7.7   Typechecking (MLS-TC)

The typecheck function for multi-level specifications is again constructed from a well-formedness predicate and a type assignment function. The main typecheck function checks a multi-level specification. In addition there are two predicates to check terms and equations over a multi-level signature.

imports MLS-TA[5.7.5] MLS-NWF[5.7.3]
exports
   context-free syntax
     tc "⟦" MLS "⟧"   → EBool

$$\text{tc "(" MLS ")" "[" Term "]"} \rightarrow \text{EBool}$$
$$\text{tc "(" MLS ")" "[" Eqs "]"} \rightarrow \text{EBool}$$

equations

[tc-mspec] $\qquad\qquad\qquad tc[\![\Gamma]\!] = \vdash_{\text{mls}} \text{Wm}[\![\Gamma]\!]$

[tc-term] $\qquad\qquad \dfrac{\text{Wm}[\![\Gamma]\!] = \Gamma', \; \text{Wt}(\Gamma')[\![t]\!] = \{t'; t^*\}}{tc(\Gamma)[\![t]\!] = \vdash_{\text{mls}} \Gamma' \rightsquigarrow \Gamma' \vdash_{\text{term}} t'}$

[tc-eqns] $\qquad\qquad \dfrac{\text{Wm}[\![\Gamma]\!] = \Gamma'}{tc(\Gamma)[\![\mathcal{E}]\!] = \vdash_{\text{mls}} \Gamma' \rightsquigarrow \Gamma' \vdash_{\text{eqs}} \text{We}(\Gamma')[\![\mathcal{E}]\!]}$

5.7.8 Typechecking Modular Specifications (MMLS-TC)

Finally, we define typechecking of a list of modules. The approach is rather crude. First all modules are flattened, then the MLS of each module is typechecked. This is of course rather expensive because code is duplicated. Observe that with this approach types and equations are disambiguated *after* being imported. This entails that newly introduced function declarations of existing functions may cause previously unambiguous equations to become ambiguous.

imports MMLS[5.6.3] MLS-TC[5.7.7]

exports
  context-free syntax
    tc "[" Modules "]" $\rightarrow$ EBool
    tcl "[" Modules "]" $\rightarrow$ EBool

equations

[tc-mods] $\qquad\qquad\qquad tc[\![M^*]\!] = tcl[\![\text{flat}(M^*)]\!]$
[tcl-mods1] $\qquad\qquad\qquad tcl[\![\,]\!] = \top$
[tcl-mods2] $\qquad\qquad tcl[\![\text{module } f\Gamma;]\!] = \text{errors in module } " f " :: tc[\![\Gamma]\!]$
[tcl-mods1] $\qquad\qquad tcl[\![M_1^+ \; M_2^+]\!] = tcl[\![M_1^+]\!] \wedge tcl[\![M_2^+]\!]$

This concludes the specification of the syntax, semantics and typechecking of modular multi-level specifications.

5.8 Discussion and Concluding Remarks

5.8.1 Related Work

In Section 5.1 we discussed several formalisms related to the formalism MLS described in this chapter. Here we give some pointers to other related issues.

Type Surveys Cardelli and Wegner (1985) give an informal introduction to types in programming languages including polymorphism, existential types and subtypes. Cardelli (1993) discusses a wide variety of programming features and their types, including mutable types, exception types, tuple types, option types, recursive types and subtypes. Mosses (1993) surveys the usage of sorts in first-order algebraic specification frameworks, discussing order-sorted algebra and partial functions. Mitchell (1990b) gives a survey of type systems for programming languages. Cardelli (1996) provides a more informal introduction to type systems.

Typechecking in AsF+SDF The specification formalism AsF+SDF has been applied to the description or design of several languages. We give some pointers to papers that describe specifications of type systems similar to the one described in this chapter. Hendriks (1989) describes (in the first AsF+SDF specification) the polymorphic type inference algorithm of Milner (1978) in the language Mini-ML. Chapter 2 describes the specification of a typechecker for Pascal. Hillebrand and Korver (1995) give a specification of the well-formedness of μCRL specifications. μCRL is a process specification formalism with a monomorphic algebraic specification language for the specification of data in processes. Vigna (1995, 1996) specifies a typechecker and compiler for the categorical programming language IMP(G). A special feature of the language is the associativity of the built-in type constructors × and +. The typechecker makes extensive use of list matching in AsF+SDF to handle this associativity. In full MLS, associativity of type constructors can be expressed by means of equations over types like $A \times (B \times C) = (A \times B) \times C$. Type checking such specifications requires $\mathcal{E}$-unification.

Polymorphic Typechecking The type inference algorithm of Milner (1978), also described in Damas and Milner (1982), forms the core of all typecheckers for polymorphic languages. The basic idea of that algorithm is also used in the type assignment of terms in multi-level specifications. Although Milner (1978) mentions overloading as a possible orthogonal extension of his type inference algorithm, such an extension is not described in the literature. Ambiguities due to overloading in pure Hindley/Milner systems are difficult to resolve if no restriction on the type(s) of functions is given by means of a signature, because then each occurrence of a function can have a different type. The overloading that is achieved by means of type classes (Wadler and Blott, 1989), or more generally, qualified types (Jones, 1992), is actually not overloading in the sense used in this chapter. Rather, type classes provide the means to restrict the set of types over which the universal quantifier in the type of a polymorphic function ranges and they give an account of 'non-parametric' function definitions of such restricted polymorphic functions.

Types in Algebraic Specification The basic type system of monomorphic many-sorted algebraic specification is explained in any introduction to algebraic specification or universal algebra, see for instance Wechler (1992). Mosses (1993) surveys the many variations and extensions of monomorphic type systems for algebraic specification. Extensions of many sorted algebraic specification where the space of types is defined by means of an algebraic specification have been studied by various authors (Poigné, 1986; Möller, 1987; Meinke, 1992a). Meinke (1992b) develops a theory for universal algebra in higher types. Meinke (1993) gives the operational semantics of ATLAS via term rewriting and proves its equivalence to the denotational semantics (i.e., initial model).

5.8.2 Extensions

The formalism MLS presented in this chapter is a sophisticated specification formalism for abstract data type specification. Some aspects important for specification and execution of specifications have not yet been attended. We discuss several extensions to the formalism and the issues they raise for further research.

Grammars as Signatures   The motivation for this work is to extend the syntax definition formalism SDF of Heering *et al.* (1989). In SDF, context-free grammars are used as monomorphic algebraic signatures, providing flexible notation for functions and constructors. Like normal monomorphic algebraic signatures, SDF does not support polymorphism nor higher-order functions.

The first step towards an extended SDF is made in Visser (1995b), where the design of Heering *et al.* (1989) is rationalized by orthogonally defining its features such that the formalism can be seen as an instance of a family of formalisms. A syntax definition formalism can be created by choosing a set of features. Many features are expressed as conservative extensions of pure context-free grammars by normalizing extended grammars to context-free grammars. As part of this approach, the disambiguation of ambiguous context-free grammars by means of priorities is seen as an instance of a more general view of disambiguation by means of disambiguation filters — functions that select a subset of a set of possible parse trees (Klint and Visser, 1994).

In Visser (1995c) the extension of context-free grammars to two-level grammars and the correspondence of two-level grammars with two-level first-order signatures are studied for the purpose of polymorphic syntax definition — polymorphic notation for algebraic specification.

In this chapter we have abstracted from the use of grammars as signatures, in order to get a clear picture of a multi-level type system without the complications caused by grammars. It is clearly desirable to extend MLS with arbitrary mix-fix operators and disambiguation capabilities like priorities to enhance the notation defined in signatures. However, the generalization of multi-level specifications to multi-level grammars is not straightforward if arbitrary grammars are allowed. The addition of chain and empty productions to signatures makes the parsing problem undecidable in general. Such rules are the cause of infinite ambiguities (sentences can have infinitely many parses) already in context-free grammars. However, in multi-level grammars the set of all parses for a sentence might not be finitely representable. Due to overloading, terms in MLS can have more than one full annotation (the analogon of a parse tree), but always finitely many. It seems possible to generalize MLS to a multi-level grammar formalism with a decidable parsing problem by not allowing chain and empty productions

Implicit Functions ATLAS provides *implicit* functions, which entails that functions declared as {implicit} do not have to be written explicitly in terms (Hearn and Meinke, 1994; Hearn, 1995). This is used, for instance, to hide the explicitly defined application function for user-defined function types. When used for unary functions, this boils down to chain rules of grammars. For example, by introducing an operator inc as

```
inc : nat -> int {implicit}
```

the naturals are embedded in the integers. The equations

```
0    + X == X;
s(X) + Y == s(X + Y)
```

then apply both to naturals and integers. This feature gives rise to infinite ambiguities. Consider the declaration

```
inc : A -> list(A) {implicit};
(++) : list(A) # list(A) -> list(A) {implicit}
```

Given these declarations we can write lists like inc(X) ++ inc(Y) ++ inc(Z) as X Y Z. The problem is that the inclusion operator inc is applicable to any term, i.e., we can interpret X as inc(X), as inc(inc(X)), ... It is clear that this infinite ambiguity is recurrent and could somehow be represented in a finite manner. How this should be achieved is not clear.

In ATLAS only unary and binary functions can be declared as implicit. Implicit constants, which are not allowed in ATLAS, are analogous to empty productions in context-free grammars and make the typechecking problem undecidable. For instance, if we declare

```
empty : list(A) {implicit}
```

then the list X can be interpreted as inc(X), as empty ++ inc(X), as empty ++ inc(X) ++ empty, etc. The implicit constant can be inserted anywhere and arbitrarily many times in the term.

Type Equations Type equations are not interpreted by the type assignment algorithm presented in this chapter. This is a pity, because many type features from programming languages and abstract data types can be expressed in MLS by means of type equations. In Section 5.5.11 the generalization of the `zip` function to arbitrary products of lists is defined by means of functions at the level of types (the map function (*)). In Section 5.5.12 type classes are expressed as type predicates. In the same way the more general qualified types of Jones (1992) can be expressed. There are many other applications of type equations. *Type definitions* of the form

```
parser(A, B) == list(A) -> (B # list(A))
```

can be used to define a type in terms of other types. The original constructor can be eliminated. *Recursive type definitions* of the form

```
list(A) == empty + (A # list(A))
```

can be used to define recursive types. These type constructors can not be eliminated, because the unfolding of the type results in an infinite term. The *associative type constructors* of Vigna (1995, 1996) can be expressed by the equations

```
A # (B # C) == (A # B) # C;
A + (B + C) == (A + B) + C
```

Jones (1992) also discusses *record types* as a special case of qualified types by providing operations for looking up the type of a field in, and for removing a field from a record type.

Simple type definitions can be accounted for by rewriting. For the other cases of type equations $\mathcal{E}$-unification is required. $\mathcal{E}$-unification is undecidable in general [see Jouannaud and Kirchner (1991) for a survey of unification]. However, if the equations are known to belong to a certain class, a solution strategy based on that knowledge might be found. For instance, a simple approach to $\mathcal{E}$-unification led to a unification algorithm that terminates for the unification of the types in the generalization of the `zip` function in Section 5.5.11. All the other examples of type equations mentioned above are embedded in the typechecking of various programming languages. These typecheckers thus use some kind of $\mathcal{E}$-unification optimized for the special case. For instance, Nipkow and Prehofer (1995) describe a typechecking algorithm for type classes in terms of unification with constraint solution. It is an interesting question whether there exists a union of these solutions such that many cases of type equations can be dealt with more generically.

Modules The formalism has a rudimentary modularization scheme based on syntactic inclusion, i.e., imports are expanded before typechecking. How difficult is it to keep the module structure while typechecking? Furthermore, consider using arbitrary terms as module names. An import of a module name provides a term that is at least as specific as a module name. The parameters of the module are determined by matching the actual module name against the declared module name. Function renaming operators applicable to imports would be another useful extension.

Rewriting A first experiment has been conducted with translating the level 0 equations of a multi-level specification to the first-order rewrite rule language of the Epic term rewrite compiler of Walters and Kamperman (1996a). Terms are translated to first-order terms by keeping the same term structure as in the specification, i.e., terms are built by application, pairing, product, arrow and annotation from functions and variables. Research issues here include: When are annotations necessary? The translation is correct for the subset of MLS that uses only free type constructors in declarations. If type equations are allowed, rewriting with type annotations is complicated because matching has to consider type equations. Can this be expressed in the rewrite system itself?

5.8.3 Conclusions

In this chapter we have defined the syntax, semantics and type system of the modular, applicative, multi-level equational specification formalism MLS. Each level of an MLS specification is an applicative equational specification that uses terms over the next level as types. This is a generalization of type systems with two and three levels that have separate definitions for each level. The type system of MLS is orthogonal and uniform (typechecking is the same for each level) and combines parametric polymorphism with overloading. These features form a formalism for the definition of advanced generic data types.

The formalism is completely specified in ASF+SDF. The Meta-Environment made it possible to interactively experiment with design choices and develop the formalism and its prototype implementation in a short period of time (about four months). The typesetting and literate programming facilities provided by the Meta-Environment played an important role in the design process. This chapter demonstrates a number of specification techniques applicable in other specifications, including innermost term rewriting, the separation of well-formedness rules and non-wellformedness rules producing descriptive error messages, type assignment by annotation, module import normalization, and a library of functions on terms, such as sets, substitution, unification and matching.

One of the shortcomings of ASF+SDF is the poor reusability of specifications, due to a lack of abstraction features such as polymorphism and parameterized modules. If ASF+SDF would be equipped with the higher-order functions and polymorphism of MLS, specifications could reuse more standard data types directly. On the other hand, MLS does not provide the syntax definition support of SDF. A formalism that combines the notational facilities of SDF with the typing facilities of MLS into Multi-Level ASF+SDF, will be a powerful tool for designing and prototyping languages.

Appendices

5.A   Library Modules

In this section several modules of common data types are presented.

5.A.1   Layout

exports

  lexical syntax

$[\sqcup \backslash t \backslash n]$	$\rightarrow$ LAYOUT
"%%" $\sim [\backslash n]*$	$\rightarrow$ LAYOUT
"%" $\sim [\% \backslash n]* $ "%"	$\rightarrow$ LAYOUT
"$--$" $\sim [\backslash n]*$	$\rightarrow$ LAYOUT
$\sim [*]$	$\rightarrow$ Aux
"*"$+ \sim [*/]$	$\rightarrow$ Aux
"/*"Aux*"*"$+$"/"	$\rightarrow$ LAYOUT

5.A.2   Booleans

imports Layout[5.A.1]

exports

  sorts Bool

  context-free syntax

"$\top$"	$\rightarrow$ Bool	
"$\bot$"	$\rightarrow$ Bool	
"$\neg$" Bool	$\rightarrow$ Bool	
Bool "$\wedge$" Bool	$\rightarrow$ Bool	**{assoc}**
Bool "$\vee$" Bool	$\rightarrow$ Bool	**{assoc}**
"(" Bool ")"	$\rightarrow$ Bool	**{bracket}**

  priorities

    "$\neg$"Bool $\rightarrow$ Bool $>$ Bool "$\wedge$"Bool $\rightarrow$ Bool $>$ Bool "$\vee$"Bool $\rightarrow$ Bool

  variables

    $[b][0\text{-}9']* \rightarrow$ Bool

equations

[conj-1]	$\top \wedge b = b$	[disj-1]	$\top \vee b = \top$	[neg-1]	$\neg \top = \bot$
[conj-2]	$\bot \wedge b = \bot$	[disj-2]	$\bot \vee b = b$	[neg-2]	$\neg \bot = \top$

5.A.3 Error Booleans

Boolean predicates are either true or false. In case of type checking this is not appropriate. In case the predicate does not hold a more refined value than false should be returned that explains the cause of the error. Error Booleans are a refinement of the normal Booleans with a true value $\top$ and a sort Error to represent the false values.

Errors The error $e_1; e_2$ indicates that both errors e_i occurred. The error $e_1 : e_2$ indicates that error e_1 occurred and that e_2 is an explanation of that error; as in

```
equation "(X :: L) ++ L' == X :: (L1 ++ L2)" not well-formed:
    variables "L1; L2" of rhs do not occur in lhs
```

imports Layout[5.A.1] Booleans[5.A.2]
exports
  sorts Error
  context-free syntax

Error ";" Error	$\rightarrow$ Error {**right**}
Error ":" Error	$\rightarrow$ Error {**right**}
"if" Bool "then" Error "else" Error	$\rightarrow$ Error
"(" Error ")"	$\rightarrow$ Error {**bracket**}

  priorities
    "if"Bool "then"Error "else"Error $\rightarrow$ Error > Error ":"Error $\rightarrow$ Error >
    Error ";"Error $\rightarrow$ Error

equations

[e-assoc1]	$(e_1; e_2); e_3 = e_1; e_2; e_3$
[e-assoc1]	$(e_1 : e_2) : e_3 = e_1 : (e_2; e_3)$
[if-t]	if $\top$ then e_1 else $e_2 = e_1$
[if-f]	if $\perp$ then e_1 else $e_2 = e_2$

Error Booleans An error Boolean value is either $\top$ (correct, true) or an error. The place normally taken by the value false is here represented by the sort of errors. Since it is unclear which error should be indicated by the negation of $\top$, we do not provide negation. The operations on EBool are $\wedge$, $\rightsquigarrow$ and ::. The operator $\wedge$ is a symmetric conjunction that yields $\top$ if both arguments do and otherwise the conjunction of the errors. The operator $\rightsquigarrow$ is an assymetric conjunction that prefers the error in its first argument discarding the error in second. This operator should be used to indicate a dependency between errors. If the well-formedness of a construct depends on the well-formedness of its subconstructs and some conditions, then one can express that the errors in the subconstructs are more important. Finally, the operator :: has $\top$ as right zero and as left unit. If both arguments are errors it yields the explanation of the first by the second.

exports
  sorts EBool
  context-free syntax

"⊤"	→ EBool
Error	→ EBool
EBool "::" EBool	→ EBool {**right**}
EBool "⤳" EBool	→ EBool {**right**}
EBool "∧" EBool	→ EBool {**right**}
"if" Bool "then" EBool "else" EBool	→ EBool
"(" EBool ")"	→ EBool {**bracket**}

  priorities
    "if"Bool "then"EBool "else"EBool → EBool > EBool "::"EBool → EBool >
    EBool "⤳"EBool → EBool > EBool "∧"EBool → EBool
  variables
    "e"$[0\text{-}9']*$ → Error
    "eb"$[0\text{-}9']*$ → EBool

equations

[conj1]	$\top \wedge eb = eb$
[conj2]	$eb \wedge \top = eb$
[conj4]	$e_1 \wedge e_2 = e_1; e_2$
[kill1]	$\top \rightsquigarrow eb = eb$
[kill2]	$e \rightsquigarrow eb = e$
[blck]	$eb :: \top = \top$
[blck]	$\top :: eb = eb$
[blck]	$e_1 :: e_2 = e_1 : e_2$
[if-t]	if $\top$ then eb_1 else $eb_2 = eb_1$
[if-f]	if $\bot$ then eb_1 else $eb_2 = eb_2$

5.A.4 Naturals

imports Booleans[5.A.2]
exports
  sorts Nat
  lexical syntax
    $[0\text{-}9]+$ → Nat
  context-free syntax

succ(Nat)	→ Nat	
pred(Nat)	→ Nat	
Nat "+" Nat	→ Nat	{**left**}
max(Nat, Nat)	→ Nat	

zero(Nat)   → Bool
eq(Nat, Nat)   → Bool
variables
$[mn][0\text{-}9']* \rightarrow$ Nat
"$c*$"$[0\text{-}9']* \rightarrow$ CHAR∗
"$c+$"$[0\text{-}9']* \rightarrow$ CHAR+

The usual equations for the natural numbers are not shown.

5.B Term Utilities

In this section we define several data types and operations on terms.

5.B.1 Binary Operators

imports Types[5.3.2] Terms[5.2.1]
exports
  sorts BinOp
  lexical syntax
    $\sim[' \sqcup \backslash t \backslash n \% () \backslash [\backslash].]* \sim [a\text{-}zA\text{-}Z0\text{-}9' \sqcup \backslash t \backslash n \% () \backslash [\backslash] <>,..] \sim [' \sqcup \backslash t \backslash n \% () \backslash [\backslash]]* \rightarrow$ BinOp
  context-free syntax
    "(" BinOp ")"   → Fun
    "[" "]"   → Fun
    "[" Term "]"   → Term
    "⟨" "⟩"   → Fun
    "⟨" Term "⟩"   → Term
    Term BinOp Term   → Term {**non-assoc**}
    Term "." Term "." Term   → Term {**non-assoc**}
  priorities
    Term Term → Term > {**non-assoc**: Term BinOp Term → Term,
    Term "."Term "."Term → Term} > Term "×"Term → Term
  variables
    "⊕"$[0\text{-}9']* \rightarrow$ BinOp

equations

[bin1]	$t_1 \oplus t_2 = (\oplus)\,(t_1, t_2)$
[bin2]	$t_1\,.t_2.\,t_3 = t_2\,(t_1, t_3)$
[list1]	$[t_1, t_2] = t_1 :: [t_2]$
[list2]	$[t] = t :: [\,]$ **otherwise**
[list1]	$\langle t_1, t_2 \rangle = t_1 \,\hat{}\, \langle t_2 \rangle$
[list2]	$\langle t \rangle = t \,\hat{}\, \langle\,\rangle$ **otherwise**

5.B.2   Errors over Terms and Signatures

To provide errors that convey information related to terms and equations we define several error constructors. An example error is

```
function "(+)" not declared
```

imports Error-Booleans[5.4.3] OLS[5.3.4]
exports
   context-free syntax

"\"" Term "\"" not a well-formed sort declaration	→ Error
sort "\"" Term "\"" not declared	→ Error
"\"" Term "\"" not a well-formed sort	→ Error
sort "\"" Term "\"" matches no sort declaration	→ Error
function "\"" Term "\"" multiply declared	→ Error
variable "\"" Term "\"" multiply declared	→ Error
function "\"" Term "\"" not declared	→ Error
function "\"" Term "\""	
with type "\"" Term "\"" not declared	→ Error
variable "\"" Term "\"" not declared	→ Error
term "\"" Term "\"" not well-formed	→ Error
pair "\"" Term "\"" not well-formed	→ Error
application "\"" Term "\"" not well-formed	→ Error
product "\"" Term "\"" not well-formed	→ Error
arrow "\"" Term "\"" not well-formed	→ Error
annotation of "\"" Term "\""	
with "\"" Term "\"" not well-formed	→ Error
"\"" Term "\"" is not a function	→ Error
type of argument "\"" Term "\""	
does not match type of domain "\"" Term "\""	→ Error
type of result "\"" Term "\""	
does not match type of codomain "\"" Term "\""	→ Error
no declaration for function "\"" Term "\""	
with type "\"" Term "\""	→ Error
equation "\"" Eq "\"" not well-formed	→ Error
types do not match	→ Error
"variables" "\"" Terms "\"" of rhs not in lhs	→ Error
level "\"" Nat "\""	→ Error
should be "\"" Term "\""	→ Error

type "\"" Term "\"" of variable "\"" Term "\""
incompatible with declaration → Error
type "\"" Term "\"" of function "\"" Term "\""
incompatible with declaration → Error
type is "\"" Term "\"" → Error
types of variable "\"" Term "\"" incompatible
"\"" Term "\"" versus "\"" Term "\"" → Error

errors in "module" "\"" Term "\"" → Error

5.B.3 Term Functions

The sort TermToTerm represents functions from terms to terms. The sort is defined in order to reuse several common higher-order operations such as function composition and mapping a function over a list. Furthermore, we define a conditional for terms, list membership, and term equality.

imports Terms[5.2.1] Booleans[5.4.2] Types[5.3.2]
exports
  sorts TermToTerm
  context-free syntax

TermToTerm "(" Term ")"	→ Term
"id"	→ TermToTerm
TermToTerm "∘" TermToTerm	→ TermToTerm {**assoc**}
"if" Bool "then" Term "else" Term	→ Term
TermToTerm "∗" "(" Terms ")"	→ Terms
eq(Term, Term)	→ Bool
Term "∈" Terms	→ Bool

  variables
    "ρ"$[0\text{-}9']\ast$ → TermToTerm

equations

[iden]	$\mathrm{id}(t) = t$
[comp]	$\rho_1 \circ \rho_2(t) = \rho_2(\rho_1(t))$
[id-comp]	$\mathrm{id} \circ \rho = \rho$
[id-comp]	$\rho \circ \mathrm{id} = \rho$
[l-map1]	$\rho\ast() = $
[l-map2]	$\rho\ast(t) = \rho(t)$
[l-map3]	$\rho\ast(t_1^+; t_2^+) = \rho\ast(t_1^+) \mathbin{+\!\!+} \rho\ast(t_2^+)$
[if-t]	if $\top$ then t_1 else $t_2 = t_1$
[if-f]	if $\bot$ then t_1 else $t_2 = t_2$
[eq1]	$\mathrm{eq}(t, t) = \top$
[eq2]	$\mathrm{eq}(t, t') = \bot$ **otherwise**
[l-member0]	$t \in\, = \bot$

[l-member1]	$t \in t' = \mathrm{eq}(t, t')$
[l-member2]	$t \in t_1^+; t_2^+ = t \in t_1^+ \vee t \in t_2^+$

5.B.4   Equation Functions

Map TermToTerm functions over equations and lists of equations.

imports Term-Functions[5.B.3] Equations[5.2.2]
exports
   context-free syntax
      TermToTerm "(" Eq ")"   → Eq
      TermToTerm "∗e" "(" Eqs ")" → Eqs
      "if" Bool "then" Eqs "else" Eqs → Eqs
equations

[map-eq]	$\rho(t_1 \equiv t_2) = \rho(t_1) \equiv \rho(t_2)$
[map-eqs]	$\rho{*}e(\varphi^*) = \quad$ **when** $\varphi^* =$
[map-eqs]	$\rho{*}e(\varphi; \varphi^*) = \rho(\varphi) + \!\!\!+ \, \rho{*}e(\varphi^*)$
[ift]	if $\top$ then $\mathcal{E}_1$ else $\mathcal{E}_2 = \mathcal{E}_1$
[ift]	if $\bot$ then $\mathcal{E}_1$ else $\mathcal{E}_2 = \mathcal{E}_2$

5.B.5   Term Sets

The function {_} creates a 'set' of terms from a list of terms by removing the duplicates from the list. The usual operations on sets are union (∪), intersection (∩), difference (/), emptiness ('empty'), membership (∈) and subset (⊆). The Cartesian product × yields the set of pairs of the elements of two sets.

imports Term-Functions[5.B.3] Terms[5.2.1] Booleans[5.A.2]
exports
   sorts TermSet
   context-free syntax

"{" Terms "}"	→ TermSet	
TermSet "∪" TermSet	→ TermSet	{**left**}
TermSet "∩" TermSet	→ TermSet	{**left**}
TermSet "/" TermSet	→ TermSet	{**left**}
TermSet "×" TermSet	→ TermSet	{**right**}
TermToTerm "∗" "(" TermSet ")"	→ TermSet	
"if" Bool "then" TermSet "else" TermSet	→ TermSet	
trms(TermSet)	→ Terms	
"(" TermSet ")"	→ TermSet	{**bracket**}

empty(TermSet) $\rightarrow$ Bool
Term "$\in$" TermSet $\rightarrow$ Bool
TermSet "$\subseteq$" TermSet $\rightarrow$ Bool

priorities

TermSet "$\times$"TermSet $\rightarrow$ TermSet $>$ TermSet "$/$"TermSet $\rightarrow$ TermSet $>$
TermSet "$\cap$"TermSet $\rightarrow$ TermSet $>$ TermSet "$\cup$"TermSet $\rightarrow$ TermSet $>$
"if"Bool "then"TermSet "else"TermSet $\rightarrow$ TermSet

variables

"Φ"$[0\text{-}9']*$ $\rightarrow$ TermSet

equations

[s-double]	$\{t_1^*;\ t;\ t_2^*;\ t;\ t_3^*\} = \{t_1^*;\ t;\ t_2^*;\ t_3^*\}$
[s-union]	$\{t_1^*\} \cup \{t_2^*\} = \{t_1^*;\ t_2^*\}$
[s-istc1]	$\{\} \cap \Phi = \{\}$
[s-isct2]	$\{t_1^+;\ t_2^+\} \cap \Phi = \{t_1^+\} \cap \Phi \cup \{t_2^+\} \cap \Phi$
[s-isct3]	$\{t\} \cap \Phi =$ if $t \in \Phi$ then $\{t\}$ else $\{\}$
[s-diff1]	$\{\} / \Phi = \{\}$
[s-diff2]	$\{t_1^+;\ t_2^+\} / \Phi = \{t_1^+\} / \Phi \cup \{t_2^+\} / \Phi$
[s-diff3]	$\{t\} / \Phi =$ if $t \in \Phi$ then $\{\}$ else $\{t\}$
[s-prd5]	$\{t_1\} \times \{t_2\} = \{t_1,\ t_2\}$
[s-prd1]	$\{\} \times \Phi = \{\}$
[s-prd3]	$\{t_1^+;\ t_2^+\} \times \Phi = \{t_1^+\} \times \Phi \cup \{t_2^+\} \times \Phi$
[s-prd2]	$\Phi \times \{\} = \{\}$
[s-prd4]	$\Phi \times \{t_1^+;\ t_2^+\} = \Phi \times \{t_1^+\} \cup \Phi \times \{t_2^+\}$
[s-map]	$\rho*(\{ts\}) = \{\rho*(ts)\}$
[s-ift]	if $\top$ then Φ_1 else $\Phi_2 = \Phi_1$
[s-iff]	if $\bot$ then Φ_1 else $\Phi_2 = \Phi_2$
[s-trms]	trms($\{ts\}$) $= ts$
[s-empty1]	empty($\{\}$) $= \top$
[s-empty2]	empty($\{t^+\}$) $= \bot$
[s-member]	$t \in \{ts\} = t \in ts$
[s-subset1]	$\{\} \subseteq \Phi = \top$
[s-subset2]	$\{t\} \subseteq \Phi = t \in \Phi$
[s-subset3]	$\{t_1^+;\ t_2^+\} \subseteq \Phi = \{t_1^+\} \subseteq \Phi \land \{t_2^+\} \subseteq \Phi$

5.B.6 Variables

To extract the variables from a term a family of functions is defined. The functions differ in their treatment of variables and the type annotation operator :, but share their definition for the other operators. To prevent copying the same equations for the four functions, the function names are put in a sort. The generic part of the definition is expressed by means of a 'variable function name' *vs*. The functions are 'var' that yields the set of *all* variables in a term, 'tvars' that yields the set of all type variables, i.e., variables occurring in annotations, 'ovars' that yields all 'object variables', i.e., variables that are not in type annotations, and 'avars' that yields all object variables with their annotation.

imports Term-Sets[5.B.5]

exports

   sorts Vars

   context-free syntax

vars	$\rightarrow$ Vars
tvars	$\rightarrow$ Vars
avars	$\rightarrow$ Vars
ovars	$\rightarrow$ Vars
Vars "(" Term ")"	$\rightarrow$ TermSet
Vars "*(" Terms ")"	$\rightarrow$ TermSet
Vars "(" TermSet ")"	$\rightarrow$ TermSet

   variables

      "vs" $\rightarrow$ Vars

equations

[vs-fun]	$vs(f) = \{\}$
[vs-nil]	$vs(\mathrm{nil}) = \{\}$
[vs-top]	$vs(\mathrm{top}) = \{\}$
[vs-pr]	$vs(t_1, t_2) = vs(t_1) \cup vs(t_2)$
[vs-app]	$vs(t_1 \; t_2) = vs(t_1) \cup vs(t_2)$
[vs-prd]	$vs(t_1 \times t_2) = vs(t_1) \cup vs(t_2)$
[vs-arr]	$vs(t_1 \rightarrow t_2) = vs(t_1) \cup vs(t_2)$
[vs-set]	$vs(\{ts\}) = vs * (\; ts)$
[vs-trms]	$vs * (\;) = \{\}$
[vs-trms-1]	$vs * (\; t) = vs(t)$
[vs-trms-n]	$vs * (\; t_1^+; t_2^+) = vs * (\; t_1^+) \cup vs * (\; t_2^+)$

[vars-var]	$\mathrm{vars}(x) = \{x\}$
[vars-ann-other]	$\mathrm{vars}(t : \tau) = \mathrm{vars}(t) \cup \mathrm{vars}(\tau)$
[ovars-var]	$\mathrm{ovars}(x) = \{x\}$
[ovars-ann]	$\mathrm{ovars}(t : \tau) = \mathrm{ovars}(t)$
[tvars-var]	$\mathrm{tvars}(x) = \{\}$
[tvars-ann]	$\mathrm{tvars}(t : \tau) = \mathrm{tvars}(t) \cup \mathrm{vars}(\tau)$
[avars-ann]	$\mathrm{avars}(x) = \{\}$
[avars-ann]	$\mathrm{avars}(x : \tau) = \{x : \tau\}$
[avars-ann]	$\mathrm{avars}(t : \tau) = \mathrm{avars}(t)$ **otherwise**

5.B.7 Substitution

A substitution is a mapping from variables to terms. When applied to a term all variables occurring in the domain of the substitution are replaced by their result in the substitution. A finite substitution maps only a finite number of variables to other terms than themselves. Finite substitutions are represented by a list of atomic substitutions of the form $x := t$, which express the mapping from variable x to term t. Note that [] is the empty substitution. The application $\sigma(t)$ of a substitution σ to a term t denotes t with each occurrence of a variable x in t replaced by $\sigma(x)$. The union (+) of two substitutions is simply the concatenation of their lists of atomic substitutions. If a conflict arises, i.e., both substitutions contain an assignment to the same variable, the assignment in the first substitution has priority over the second as a result of the definition of $\sigma(x)$ in equations [s-var-i].

imports Term-Functions[5.B.3] Terms[5.2.1] Types[5.3.2]
exports
   sorts ASubst Subst
   context-free syntax

Var ":=" Term	$\rightarrow$ ASubst	
"[" ASubst∗ "]"	$\rightarrow$ Subst	
Subst	$\rightarrow$ TermToTerm	
"⇓"(TermToTerm)	$\rightarrow$ Subst	
Subst "+" Subst	$\rightarrow$ Subst	{**assoc**}
"(" Subst ")"	$\rightarrow$ Subst	{**bracket**}

   variables

"*as*"[0-9']∗	$\rightarrow$ ASubst
"*as*" "∗"[0-9']∗	$\rightarrow$ ASubst∗
"*as*" "+"[0-9']∗	$\rightarrow$ ASubst+
"σ"[0-9']∗	$\rightarrow$ Subst

equations

[s-var-1]	$[x := t \; as^*](x) = t$
[s-var-2]	$[y := t \; as^*](x) = [as^*](x)$ **when** $\mathrm{eq}(x, y) = \bot$
[s-var-3]	$[](x) = x$
[s-fun]	$\sigma(f) = f$
[s-nil]	$\sigma(\mathrm{nil}) = \mathrm{nil}$
[s-top]	$\sigma(\mathrm{top}) = \mathrm{top}$
[s-pr]	$\sigma(t_1, t_2) = \sigma(t_1), \sigma(t_2)$
[s-app]	$\sigma(t_1 \; t_2) = \sigma(t_1) \; \sigma(t_2)$
[s-prd]	$\sigma(t \times \tau) = \sigma(t) \times \sigma(\tau)$
[s-arr]	$\sigma(t \rightarrow \tau) = \sigma(t) \rightarrow \sigma(\tau)$
[s-ann]	$\sigma(t : \tau) = \sigma(t) : \sigma(\tau)$
[s-back]	$\Downarrow(\sigma) = \sigma$
[s-back]	$\Downarrow(\mathrm{id}) = []$

[s-union]	$[as_1^*] + [as_2^*] = [as_1^*\ as_2^*]$
[s-empty]	$[]\circ\sigma = \sigma$
[s-empty]	$\sigma\circ[] = \sigma$
[s-comp-n]	$\sigma\circ[x:=t\ as^*] = [x:=\sigma(t)] + \sigma\circ[as^*]$

Failure Substitutions   A failure substitution is a substitution or the value $\perp$ (fail), which denotes failure for partial functions producing substitutions like matching and unification. The operation $+_\perp$ is the strict extension of $+$ to failure substitutions. The operation is the consistent composition of two substitutions. Two substitutions are consistent if they coincide on the same variable or are undefined.

sorts Subst$_\perp$

context-free syntax

Subst	$\to$ Subst$_\perp$
"$\perp$"	$\to$ Subst$_\perp$
Subst$_\perp$ "$+_\perp$" Subst$_\perp$	$\to$ Subst$_\perp$ {**non-assoc**}
Subst$_\perp$ "$\oplus$" Subst$_\perp$	$\to$ Subst$_\perp$ {**non-assoc**}
Subst$_\perp$ "$\circ_\perp$" Subst$_\perp$	$\to$ Subst$_\perp$ {**non-assoc**}
"if" Bool "then" Subst$_\perp$ "else" Subst$_\perp$	$\to$ Subst$_\perp$
"fail?"(Subst$_\perp$)	$\to$ Bool
"$\Downarrow_\perp$"(Subst$_\perp$)	$\to$ Subst
"(" Subst$_\perp$ ")"	$\to$ Subst$_\perp$ {**bracket**}

variables

"$\sigma_\perp$"$[']*\to$ Subst$_\perp$

priorities

{**non-assoc**: Subst$_\perp$ "$+_\perp$"Subst$_\perp$ $\to$ Subst$_\perp$,   Subst$_\perp$ "$\oplus$"Subst$_\perp$ $\to$ Subst$_\perp$,
Subst$_\perp$ "$\circ_\perp$"Subst$_\perp$ $\to$ Subst$_\perp$} $>$ "if"Bool "then"Subst$_\perp$ "else"Subst$_\perp$ $\to$ Subst$_\perp$

equations

[fs-ift]	if $\top$ then $\sigma_\perp$ else $\sigma_\perp{}' = \sigma_\perp$
[fs-iff]	if $\perp$ then $\sigma_\perp$ else $\sigma_\perp{}' = \sigma_\perp{}'$
[comp1]	$\sigma_1 +_\perp \sigma_2 = \sigma_1 + \sigma_2$
[comp0]	$\sigma_\perp +_\perp \perp = \perp$
[comp0]	$\perp +_\perp \sigma_\perp = \perp$
[comp1]	$\perp \oplus \sigma_\perp = \perp$
[comp2]	$\sigma_\perp \oplus \perp = \perp$
[comp3]	$[] \oplus \sigma_\perp = \sigma_\perp$
[comp4]	$\sigma_\perp \oplus [] = \sigma_\perp$
[comp5]	$[x:=t\ as^*] \oplus \sigma = $ if $\mathrm{eq}(t', x) \vee \mathrm{eq}(t', t)$
	then $[x:=t] +_\perp ([as^*] \oplus \sigma)$
	else $\perp$
	when $\sigma(x) = t'$

[comp]	$\perp \circ_\perp \sigma_\perp = \perp$
[comp]	$\sigma_\perp \circ_\perp \perp = \perp$
[comp]	$\sigma_1 \circ_\perp \sigma_2 = \Downarrow(\sigma_1 \circ \sigma_2)$
[fail-f]	$\text{fail?}(\sigma) = \perp$
[fail-t]	$\text{fail?}(\perp) = \top$
[back-fs]	$\Downarrow_\perp(\sigma) = \sigma$

5.B.8   Matching

A term t matches with a pattern term t', notation $t' := t$, if there exists a substitution σ such that $\sigma(t') = t$. If t matches t', t' is said to more general than t, which is expressed by means of the predicate $\geq$ as $t' \geq t$. If $t' \geq t$ we also say that t is an instance of t'. This relation gives a partial order on terms. A substitution σ is a *renaming* if $\sigma(t) \doteq t$ for any t.

imports Substitution[5.B.7] Term-Sets[5.B.5]

exports

  context-free syntax

    Terms ":=" Terms $\rightarrow$ Subst$_\perp$

    Term "$\geq$" Term $\rightarrow$ Bool

    Term "$>$" Term $\rightarrow$ Bool

    Term "$\doteq$" Term $\rightarrow$ Bool

    TermSet "$\geq$" Term $\rightarrow$ Bool

equations

[m-var]	$x := t = [x := t]$
[m-fun]	$t := t = []$
[m-pr]	$t_1, t_2 := t_3, t_4 = t_1; t_2 := t_3; t_4$
[m-app]	$t_1 \; t_2 := t_3 \; t_4 = t_1; t_2 := t_3; t_4$
[m-prd]	$t_1 \times t_2 := t_3 \times t_4 = t_1; t_2 := t_3; t_4$
[m-pr]	$t_1 \rightarrow t_2 := t_3 \rightarrow t_4 = t_1; t_2 := t_3; t_4$
[m-prd]	$t_1 : t_2 := t_3 : t_4 = t_1; t_2 := t_3; t_4$
[m-trms-0]	$:= \; = []$
[m-trms-n]	$t_1; t_1^+ := t_2; t_2^+ = t_1 := t_2 \oplus t_1^+ := t_2^+$
[no-match]	$t := t' = \perp$ **otherwise**
[m-geq]	$t_1 \geq t_2 = \neg \; \text{fail?}(t_1 := t_2)$
[m-gtr]	$t_1 > t_2 = t_1 \geq t_2 \wedge \neg \; t_2 \geq t_1$
[m-eq]	$t_1 \doteq t_2 = t_1 \geq t_1 \wedge t_2 \geq t_1$
[m-set-0]	$\{\} \geq t = \perp$
[m-set-1t]	$\{t'\} \geq t = t' \geq t$
[m-set-n]	$\{t_1^+; t_2^+\} \geq t = \{t_1^+\} \geq t \vee \{t_2^+\} \geq t$

5.B.9   Unification

Two terms t_1 and t_2 are unifiable if there exists a substitution σ such that $\sigma(t_1) = \sigma(t_2)$. The function 'mgu' yields the most general unifier σ for a set of equations $\mathcal{E}$, such that for each equation $t_1 \equiv t_2$ in $\mathcal{E}$, $\sigma(t_1) = \sigma(t_2)$. The definition is based on the algorithm by Martelli and Montanari (1982). Hendriks (1989) specifies in a similar manner the unification of types in ML. See also Jouannaud and Kirchner (1991) for a survey on unification.

imports Variables[5.B.6] Substitution[5.B.7] Equation-Functions[5.B.4]
exports
  context-free syntax
    mgu(Eqs) $\rightarrow$ Subst$_\perp$
    Term "$\overset{?}{=}$" Term $\rightarrow$ Bool

equations

[u-refl]	$\mathrm{mgu}(t \equiv t) = [\,]$
[u-var]	$\mathrm{mgu}(x \equiv t) = [x := t]$ **when** $x \in \mathrm{vars}(t) = \perp$
[u-var']	$\mathrm{mgu}(t \equiv x) = [x := t]$ **when** $x \in \mathrm{vars}(t) = \perp$
[u-pr]	$\mathrm{mgu}(t_1, t_2 \equiv t_3, t_4) = \mathrm{mgu}(t_1 \equiv t_3; t_2 \equiv t_4)$
[u-app]	$\mathrm{mgu}(t_1\ t_2 \equiv t_3\ t_4) = \mathrm{mgu}(t_1 \equiv t_3; t_2 \equiv t_4)$
[u-prd]	$\mathrm{mgu}(t_1 \times t_2 \equiv t_3 \times t_4) = \mathrm{mgu}(t_1 \equiv t_3; t_2 \equiv t_4)$
[u-arr]	$\mathrm{mgu}(t_1 \rightarrow t_2 \equiv t_3 \rightarrow t_4) = \mathrm{mgu}(t_1 \equiv t_3; t_2 \equiv t_4)$
[u-ann]	$\mathrm{mgu}(t_1 : t_2 \equiv t_3 : t_4) = \mathrm{mgu}(t_1 \equiv t_3; t_2 \equiv t_4)$
[u-es-0]	$\mathrm{mgu}() = [\,]$
[u-es-n]	$\mathrm{mgu}(\varphi_1^+; \varphi_2^+) = \mathrm{mgu}(\Downarrow_\perp(\sigma_\perp)*e(\varphi_2^+)) \circ_\perp \sigma_\perp$
	when $\mathrm{mgu}(\varphi_1^+) = \sigma_\perp$
[u-fail]	$\mathrm{mgu}(\mathcal{E}) = \perp$ **otherwise**
[ueq]	$t_1 \overset{?}{=} t_2 = \neg\ \mathrm{fail?}(\mathrm{mgu}(t_1 \equiv t_2))$

5.B.10   Renaming

It is sometimes necessary to rename variables in a term such that they are disjunct from the variables in another term. To this end several functions are defined to generate new variable names much like the functions in Chapter 1 to rename variables in λ expressions. The function get-fresh produces a fresh variable (not occurring in some set of variables). The function rn $\Phi_1[\Phi_2]$, with Φ_1 and Φ_2 sets of variables, yields a substitution σ_1 that renames the variables in Φ_1 such that none occurs in Φ_2, i.e., $\sigma_1(\Phi_1) \cap \Phi_2 = \emptyset$. The other 'rn' function renames the variables of a term with respect to (the variables of) another term.

imports Variables[5.B.6] Substitution[5.B.7]

exports
  context-free syntax

prime(Var)	→ Var
deprime(Var)	→ Var
base(Var)	→ Var
get-fresh(Var, TermSet)	→ Term
rn TermSet "[" TermSet "]"	→ Subst
rn Term "[" Term "]"	→ Term
add(Var, TermSet)	→ TermSet

hiddens
  variables
    $"c+"[0\text{-}9']* \to$ CHAR+

equations

[prm-var]	$\text{prime}(\text{var}(c^+)) = \text{var}(c^+ \text{ "'"})$
[dprm-var-1]	$\text{deprime}(\text{var}(c^+ \text{ "'"})) = \text{deprime}(\text{var}(c^+))$
[dprm-var-2]	$\text{deprime}(x) = x$ **otherwise**

The function 'base' takes off all trailing digits and primes of a variable. The equations for the function 'base' are not shown.

[add1]	$\text{add}(\text{var}(c_1^+), \{\text{var}(c_2^+)\}) = \{\text{var}(c_1^+ \ c_2^+)\}$
[add2]	$\text{add}(x, \{\}) = \{x\}$
[add3]	$\text{add}(x, \{t_1^+; t_2^+\}) = \text{add}(x, \{t_1^+\}) \cup \text{add}(x, \{t_2^+\})$
[add]	$\text{add}(x, \{t\}) = \{x\}$ **otherwise**

[f-1] $\text{get-fresh}(x, \Phi) = \text{if } x \in \Phi \text{ then get-fresh}(\text{prime}(x), \Phi) \text{ else } x$

[f-3] $\text{rn } \{\}[\Phi] = []$
[f-4] $\text{rn } \{x; t^*\}[\Phi] = [x := y] + \text{rn } \{t^*\}[\{y\} \cup \Phi]$
         when $\text{get-fresh}(\text{deprime}(x), \Phi) = y$

Rename a term with respect to the variables in another term.

[f-5] $\text{rn } t_1[t_2] = \text{rn } \Phi_1 \cap \Phi_2[\Phi_2](t_1)$
         when $\text{vars}(t_1) = \Phi_1, \ \text{vars}(t_2) = \Phi_2$

6

Incremental Typechecking

Emma van der Meulen

Abstract We present a technique for deriving incremental implementations for a
subclass of algebraic specifications, namely, well-presented primitive recursive schemes
with parameters, a class well suited for specifying the static semantics of languages.
We introduce a concept adapted from the translation of well-presented primitive
recursive schemes to strongly non-circular attribute grammars, and store results of
function applications and their parameters as attributes in an abstract syntax tree
of the first argument of the function in question. An attribute dependency graph is
then used to control incremental evaluation. The evaluation technique is based on
a leftmost innermost rewrite strategy. Moreover, we present optimizations to handle
updates in the declarations section of a program in an efficient incremental fashion.
The method has been implemented as part of the rewrite engine of the ASF+SDF
Meta-Environment.

6.1 Introduction

Incremental methods are a significant class of optimization techniques, which are used
in a wide variety of applications. An incremental computation stores the results of
subcomputations, and reuses the results rather than recomputing them. This is espe-
cially effective when a complex computation is performed repeatedly on slightly different inputs, or when computations are performed on large data structures to which
relatively small modifications are made frequently. Standard examples of programs
based on incremental computation are spreadsheet programs and text formatters in
WYSIWYG[1] editors.

Many techniques for incremental computation have been developed, including
incremental algorithms for specific problems as well as techniques of a more general

---

[1]What You See Is What You Get

nature. An overview is given in Ramalingam and Reps (1993). Techniques differ in the way they store and maintain results of subcomputations for later reuse. The stored results must be organized in such a way that they can be retrieved quickly during subsequent computations. A related requirement is that the amount of stored information must be kept within limits.

In interactive programming environments incremental computation is often applied to syntax checking and typechecking. For instance, syntax-directed editors in the ASF+SDF Meta-Environment (Chapter 1) incrementally check whether a text is syntactically correct. After a text has been edited syntax checks are performed only to the modified parts of the program. The idea of incremental *typechecking* is that during typechecking the typecheck results of parts of a program are stored, so that when the program is edited and checked again, those results that were not affected by the change are reused rather than recomputed. Many programming environments generated from attribute grammars offer incremental typecheckers.

In this chapter we present a method for deriving incremental implementations from a subclass of algebraic specifications. This method is used to generate incremental typecheckers and other incremental language tools in the context of the ASF+SDF Meta-Environment. In developing this method we borrow techniques from incremental evaluators for attribute grammars. Courcelle and Franchi-Zannettacci (1982) proved that any well-presented primitive recursive scheme with parameters is equivalent to a strongly non-circular attribute grammar. The result of each function is interpreted as a synthesized attribute of the first argument of the function and its parameters act as the inherited attributes of its output sort. Primitive recursive schemes, in turn, are a subset of algebraic specifications. Following this translation we can transfer techniques developed for attribute grammars to algebraic specifications. In particular we can use attributed trees for storing normal forms for incremental evaluation of terms.

Our strategy has been implemented as part of the term rewriting engine of the ASF+SDF Meta-Environment. In this context, incremental evaluation concerns the application of functions ϕ to the abstract syntax tree T of a text in an editor. During reduction of the term $\phi(T)$, normal forms are stored in attributes of T. When the text is edited subtrees are replaced in the abstract syntax tree T. After each subtree replacement attributes whose value depends on the replaced subtree are marked as unreliable. Let T' be the result of subtree replacements in T. If subsequently the term $\phi(T')$ is reduced, the values of reliable attributes can be used to avoid reduction steps, whereas other attributes obtain a new typecheck value.

Because we do not wish to intrude on the user while he or she is editing, we aim at keeping the process of marking attributes as simple and efficient as possible. For the same reason re-evaluation of the ϕ-value of the modified text takes place only on explicit request by the user. This is possible because our algorithms for incremental evaluation support *multiple subtree replacements*.

Our strategy for incremental evaluation can be thought of as leftmost innermost rewriting with shortcuts and side-effects for updating attributes. This makes it easy to combine incremental evaluation and non-incremental evaluation.

A first implementation of our method for incremental rewriting shows that incremental evaluation is often advantageous, but that attributes containing aggregate values, like symbol tables, give rise to very inefficient incremental evaluation. Since algebraic specifications offer a uniform way of describing data types, and the abstract syntax and semantics of a language are just examples of such data types, an incremental implementation can be generated for each data type as long as its specification is a primitive recursive scheme. We use this idea to refine our incremental algorithm. This *fine-grain* incremental implementation method can typically be applied to a typecheck specification with a table data type with an *incremental* lookup function.

The approach we present is general in the sense that it can be applied to any specification in the class of *layered primitive recursive schemes*, without extending the specification formalism or adding predefined data types. This distinguishes it from techniques in the field of attribute grammars. In attempts to solve the problem of aggregate values in attribute grammars, either a predefined data type is added to the specification formalism, or the attribute grammar formalism is extended, or it is combined with another formalism.

6.2 Preliminaries

6.2.1 Algebraic Specifications

Definition 6.1 An algebraic specification is a pair $\langle \Sigma, E \rangle$ consisting of a signature Σ defining sorts as well as functions over these sorts, and a set of equations E over terms defined by the signature. $\square$

Example 6.2 Module Syntax (6.1) and Module TC (6.2) present part of the typechecker of a simple programming language in ASF+SDF. It will serve as our running example. Each program consists of a (possibly empty) series of variable declarations followed by a series of statements. The functions tcp, tcdecls, tcdecl, tcstms, tcstm and tcexp are introduced to specify the typechecking of, respectively, programs, declarations, statements and expressions. The equations describe how a program is typechecked. According to equation [Tc1] typechecking a program equals checking its statements given the result of checking the declarations. The latter yields a type-environment (a table of variables and types) indicated by the sort TENV. Equations [Tc2], [Tc3] and [Tc4] build an environment from the declarations. Equations [Tc5], [Tc6] and [Tc7] use the environment to check a series of statements and one assignment, which results in a Boolean value. Equations [Tc8]–[Tc11] check the expressions built from variables, integers, strings and the plus operator. $\square$

```
module Syntax
We give the syntax of a simple programming language. To make it easier to see
the structure of the abstract syntax trees, we only use prefix notation for the
various syntactic constructors.
imports Strings Integers Layout Identifiers
exports
  sorts  PROGRAM DECLS DECL TYPE STMS STM EXP
  context-free syntax
    program(DECLS, STMS)  → PROGRAM

    empty-decls            → DECLS
    decls(DECL, DECLS)     → DECLS
    decl(ID, TYPE)         → DECL
    integer                → TYPE
    string                 → TYPE

    single-stm(STM)        → STMS
    stms(STM, STMS)        → STMS
    assign(ID, EXP)        → STM
    e-id(ID)               → EXP
    e-int(INT)             → EXP
    e-str(STR)             → EXP
    plus(EXP, EXP)         → EXP
  variables
    Decls      → DECLS
    Decl       → DECL
    Type       → TYPE
    Stms       → STMS
    Stm        → STM
    Exp [12]*  → EXP
    Id         → ID
    Int        → INT
    Str        → STR
```

Module 6.1: Syntax. Abstract Syntax of a Simple Language.

---

module TC

imports Syntax Booleans Tenv Type-Operations
exports
  context-free syntax
    tcp(PROGRAM)   → BOOL
    tcdecls(DECLS, TENV) → TENV
    tcdecl(DECL, TENV)   → TENV
    tcstms(STMS, TENV) → BOOL
    tcstm(STM, TENV)   → BOOL
    tcexp(EXP, TENV)   → TYPE
equations

[Tc1] $\text{tcp}(\text{program}(Decls, Stms)) = \text{tcstms}(Stms, \text{tcdecls}(Decls, \text{empty-env}))$

[Tc2] $\text{tcdecls}(\text{empty-decls}, Tenv) \qquad\quad = Tenv$
[Tc3] $\text{tcdecls}(\text{decls}(Decl, Decls), Tenv) = \text{tcdecls}(Decls, \text{tcdecl}(Decl, Tenv))$
[Tc4] $\text{tcdecl}(\text{decl}(Id, Type), Tenv) \qquad = \text{tenv}(\text{pair}(Id, Type), Tenv)$

[Tc5] $\qquad\qquad \text{tcstms}(\text{single-stm}(Stm), Tenv) = \text{tcstm}(Stm, Tenv)$

[Tc6] $\qquad\qquad\qquad \text{tcstms}(\text{stms}(Stm, Stms), Tenv)$
$\qquad\qquad = \text{and}(\text{tcstm}(Stm, Tenv), \text{tcstms}(Stms, Tenv))$

[Tc7] $\qquad\qquad\qquad\quad \text{tcstm}(\text{assign}(Id, Exp), Tenv)$
$\qquad\qquad = \text{compatible}(\text{lookup}(Tenv, Id), \text{tcexp}(Exp, Tenv))$

[Tc8] $\qquad\quad \text{tcexp}(\text{e-id}(Id), Tenv) \quad = \text{lookup}(Tenv, Id)$
[Tc9] $\qquad\quad \text{tcexp}(\text{e-int}(Int), Tenv) = \text{integer}$
[Tc10] $\qquad\quad \text{tcexp}(\text{e-str}(Str), Tenv) = \text{string}$

[Tc11] $\qquad\qquad\qquad \text{tcexp}(\text{plus}(Exp_1, Exp_2), Tenv)$
$\qquad = \text{if}(\text{and}(\text{compatible}(\text{tcexp}(Exp_1, Tenv), \text{integer}),$
$\qquad\qquad\qquad \text{compatible}(\text{tcexp}(Exp_2, Tenv), \text{integer})), \text{integer}, \text{error-type})$

Module 6.2: TC. Typechecking the simple language.

Incremental Evaluation

Many algebraic specifications can be implemented as term rewriting systems. Equations are considered as rewrite rules with an orientation from left to right. Evaluating a term means reducing it as far as possible. The result of such a reduction is a *normal form*.

The idea of incremental evaluation of terms is that while evaluating a term we make use of the normal forms of terms that have been stored during a previous reduction of a slightly different term. The naive way of doing this is to store all terms that occur during the reduction process together with their normal form. This would, obviously, take too much space, and require long searches to determine whether a term has been reduced before.

We are looking for a structure in which normal forms can be stored so that they can easily be retrieved and updated. We turn to attribute grammars because they provide such a structure and Courcelle and Franchi-Zannettacci (1982) have proved a correspondence between attribute grammars and a subclass of algebraic specifications.

6.2.2 Attribute Grammars

Definition 6.3 An attribute grammar $\Gamma = \langle G, ATT, R, I \rangle$ consists of a signature G, defining sorts and abstract tree constructors, extended with an attribute system. For each sort X of G two disjoint sets of attributes are defined: the *inherited attributes*, INH(X), and the *synthesized attributes*, SYN(X). ATT is the union of all inherited and synthesized attributes: $ATT = \bigcup_X[\text{INH}(X) \cup \text{SYN}(X)]$. To each abstract tree construct $p : X_1 \times \ldots \times X_n \to X_0$ of G, attribute definition rules R_p are added for specifying the values of the synthesized attributes of the parent X_0 and the values of the inherited attributes of the children X_i ($1 \leq i \leq n$). $R = \bigcup_{p \in G} R_p$. The interpretation I indicates the domain of attribute values. □

Example 6.4 Figure 6.1 and Figure 6.2 show the same typechecker as Module Syntax (6.1) and Module TC (6.2) but now written as an attribute grammar. We have the same program constructors (program, decls, stms, etc.) but now they are extended with attributes and semantic rules. The synthesized attributes tcp, tcstms and tcstm are of type Boolean, tcdecls and tcdecl yield environments, and tcexp returns a type. The interpretation I has been omitted: it would provide the semantics of Boolean functions and type-environments.

The attribute rules describe the typechecking of a program and its substructures. For the constructor program it states that the typecheck value, PROGRAM.tcp, of a program equals the typecheck value of its statements, STMS.tcstms. The value of the inherited attribute of the declarations in this constructor, DECLS.Tenv, is the constant describing the empty type-environment. The value of the inherited attribute for the statements, STMS.Tenv, equals the typecheck value of the declarations, DECLS.tcdecls. □

sorts: PROGRAM DECLS DECL ID TYPE STMS STM EXP

inherited attributes: synthesized attributes
INH(PROGRAM) = ∅   SYN(PROGRAM) = {PROGRAM.tcp}
INH(DECLS)   = {DECLS.Tenv}   SYN(DECLS)   = {DECLS.tcdecls}
INH(DECL)   = {DECL.Tenv}   SYN(DECL)   = {DECL.tcdecl}
INH(STMS)   = {STMS.Tenv}   SYN(STMS)   = {STMS.tcstms}
INH(STM)   = {STM.Tenv}   SYN(STM)   = {STM.tcstm}
INH(EXP)   = {EXP.Tenv}   SYN(EXP)   = {EXP.tcexp}

constructors and semantic rules:
program   : DECLS × STMS → PROGRAM
$$\begin{cases} \text{PROGRAM.tcp} = \text{STMS.tcstms} \\ \text{DECLS.Tenv} = \text{empty-env} \\ \text{STMS.Tenv} = \text{tcdecls} \end{cases}$$

empty-decls :   → DECLS
$$\begin{cases} \text{DECLS.tcdecls} = \text{DECLS.Tenv} \end{cases}$$

decls   : DECL × DECLS₂ → DECLS
$$\begin{cases} \text{DECLS.tcdecls} = \text{DECLS}_2\text{.tcdecls} \\ \text{DECL.Tenv} = \text{DECLS.Tenv} \\ \text{DECLS}_2\text{.Tenv} = \text{DECL.tcdecl} \end{cases}$$

decl   : ID × TYPE   → DECL
$$\begin{cases} \text{DECL.tcdecl} = \text{tenv(pair(ID,TYPE),} \\ \qquad\qquad\qquad \text{DECL.Tenv)} \end{cases}$$

integer   :   → TYPE
string   :   → TYPE

Figure 6.1: Part of a typechecker in an attribute grammar formalism.

single-stm : STM → STMS
$$\begin{cases} \text{STMS.tcstms} = \text{STM.tcstm} \\ \text{STM.Tenv} = \text{STMS.Tenv} \end{cases}$$

stms : $\text{STM} \times \text{STMS}_2$ → STMS
$$\begin{cases} \text{STMS.tcstms} = \text{and(STM.tcstm,STMS}_2\text{.tcstms)} \\ \text{STM.Tenv} = \text{STMS.Tenv} \\ \text{STMS}_2\text{.Tenv} = \text{STMS.Tenv} \end{cases}$$

assign : ID × EXP → STM
$$\begin{cases} \text{STM.tcstm} = \text{compatible(lookup(STM.Tenv,ID),} \\ \qquad\qquad\qquad\qquad\qquad \text{EXP.tcexp)} \\ \text{EXP.Tenv} = \text{STM.Tenv} \end{cases}$$

e-id : ID → EXP
$$\begin{cases} \text{EXP.tcexp} = \text{lookup(EXP.Tenv,ID)} \end{cases}$$

e-int : INT → EXP
$$\begin{cases} \text{EXP.tcexp} = \text{integer} \end{cases}$$

e-string : STRING → EXP
$$\begin{cases} \text{EXP.tcexp} = \text{string} \end{cases}$$

plus : $\text{EXP}_1 \times \text{EXP}_2$ → EXP
$$\begin{cases} \text{EXP.tcexp} = \\ \qquad \text{if(and(compatible(EXP}_1\text{.tcexp, integer),} \\ \qquad\qquad\qquad \text{compatible(EXP}_2\text{.tcexp, integer)),} \\ \qquad\qquad \text{integer, error-type)} \\ \text{EXP}_1\text{.Tenv} = \text{EXP.Tenv} \\ \text{EXP}_2\text{.Tenv} = \text{EXP.Tenv} \end{cases}$$

Figure 6.2: Part of a typechecker in an attribute grammar formalism.

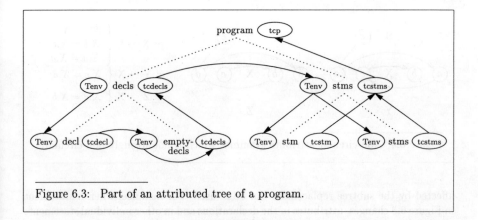

Figure 6.3: Part of an attributed tree of a program.

Attributes can be thought of as labels attached to nodes in the abstract syntax tree and their definition rules as a mechanism for distributing information through the tree. Roughly speaking, inherited attributes are used for distributing information down the tree, while synthesized attributes are used for distributing information up the tree.

Example 6.5 Figure 6.3 shows part of the abstract syntax tree of a program, decorated with attributes in ellipses. Synthesized attributes are displayed on the right-hand side of a tree node, inherited attributes are on the left. The attributes are connected by a *dependency graph* as explained below. □

Definition 6.6 An attribute pair (a, b) belongs to the attribute dependencies D_p of a constructor $p : X_1 \times \ldots \times X_n \to X_0$ if and only if a is used in the definition of b in the attribute definition rules R_p. □

Definition 6.7 The attribute dependency graph D_T of a tree T is the union of all instances of D_p of constructors p in the tree. □

Incremental Attribute Evaluation

Many algorithms for evaluating attribute values in a tree exist and many of them are incremental. The basis of incremental attribute updating is the attribute dependency graph of an abstract syntax tree. The tree represents, for instance, a program in an editor. When the program is edited, a subtree is replaced in the attributed tree. Attributes of the new subtree as well as attributes whose values depend directly or indirectly on them, must be re-evaluated. The value of attributes that are not

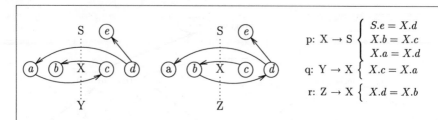

Figure 6.4: Non-circular attribute grammar which is not strongly non-circular.

affected by the subtree replacement can be re-used. For instance, when a statement in Figure 6.3 changes, attributes in the declarations and in other individual statements are not affected.

An attribute grammar is *well-formed* or *non-circular* if for each tree the attribute dependency graph D_T is cycle-free. In that case an evaluation order for attributes of each abstract syntax tree exists. The attribute grammar is called *strongly non-circular* if for each node in each tree an evaluation order of attributes exists that does not depend on the particular subtree rooted at that node. In Figure 6.4 part of an attribute grammar is shown that is not strongly non-circular. The evaluation order of the attributes a, b, c and d at X is either d, a, c, b or c, b, d, a, depending on the constructor applied at X.

An overview of attribute grammars is given by Deransart *et al.* (1988); Paakki (1995). Attribute grammars are widely used for defining the static semantics of programming languages, e.g, in the Cornell Synthesizer Generator (Reps and Teitelbaum, 1989a, 1989b), the FNC-2 system (Jourdan and Parigot, 1991), the GAG-system (Kastens, 1984), the TOOLS system (Koskimies and Paakki, 1990) and the Mjølner/ORM Environment (Magnusson *et al.*, 1990).

6.3 Primitive Recursive Schemes with Parameters

Courcelle and Franchi-Zannettacci (1982) have defined a subclass of algebraic specifications, well-presented primitive recursive schemes with parameters (PRSs), which are equivalent to strongly non-circular attribute grammars. We will use this equivalence to implement incremental rewriting for PRSs.

We first give the definition of the class of primitive recursive schemes as described by Courcelle and Franchi-Zannettacci. In Section 6.3.2 we show the basics of the construction of an attribute grammar from a PRS. This construction is valid only if the PRS is well-presented. In Section 6.3.3 we explain why we need well-presentedness and we define its meaning.

6.3.1 Definition

In the definition below we define a primitive recursive scheme as a 5-tuple $\langle G, S, \Phi,$ $Eq, Eq_\Phi \rangle$. Intuitively, G is a grammar consisting of a set of free constructor functions, describing, for instance, the abstract syntax of a programming language. Φ is a set of functions over this abstract syntax, such as functions for typechecking and compilation of programs. The equations Eq_Φ specify the behavior of these Φ-functions. The specification formed by the remaining signature and equations $\langle S, Eq \rangle$ specifies auxiliary data types for the Φ-functions.

Definition 6.8 (PRS) An algebraic specification is a primitive recursive scheme with parameters if it has the following properties

(i) It can be described by a 5-tuple $\langle G, S, \Phi, Eq, Eq_\Phi \rangle$ such that the signature of the specification is formed by the union of G,S and Φ, and the equations of the specification are the union $Eq \cup Eq_\Phi$. G and S are signatures, and Φ is a set of functions. There are no equations over terms of G in $Eq \cup Eq_\Phi$.[2]

For functions in Φ properties (ii) and (iii) hold:

(ii) The type of the first argument of each ϕ in Φ is a sort in G and the types of all other arguments, called the *parameters of ϕ*, and the type of the output sort are sorts of S. Φ_X indicates the set of all functions of Φ that have the sort X as the type of their first argument.

(iii) For each abstract tree constructor $p : X_1 \times \ldots \times X_n \to X_0$ in G and each function ϕ in Φ_{X_0} there is exactly one *defining* equation $eq_{\phi,p} \in Eq_\Phi$:

$$\phi(p(x_1, \ldots, x_n), y_1, \ldots, y_m) = \tau \qquad (6.1)$$

where τ is a term built from symbols in $S \cup \Phi$ and $\{x_1, \ldots, x_n\} \cup \{y_1, \ldots, y_m\}$.

(a) All x_i and y_j in the left-hand side of equation (6.1) are different variables. Hence, this equation is left-linear.

(b) In equation (6.1) the first argument of any Φ-subterm in τ is an x_i ($1 \le i \le n$). Hence, this equation is strictly decreasing in G.

□

We will use *G-term* to refer to a term of a sort $X \in G$, and *S-term* for a term of sort $S \in S$. On the other hand, we use *Φ-term* to indicate a term of which the head symbol is a function of Φ, and *parameter-term* for the j-th subterm of a Φ-term ($j > 1$). Note that all Φ-terms and parameter terms are S-terms. The k-th parameter of a function $\phi \in \Phi$ is indicated as $par(\phi, k)$.

---

[2]Note that G and S need not be disjoint, however no equations should exist for the shared sorts.

Example 6.9 The specification in Module Syntax (6.1) and Module TC (6.2) is a part of a PRS. The first collection of functions (from program to cat) are abstract tree constructors in G. Φ is the set of typecheck functions {tcp, tcdecls, tcdecl, tcstms, tcstm, tcexp}. All equations shown are Φ-defining equations. $\langle S, Eq \rangle$ consists of the specifications of the Booleans and the Type-environments. They are not shown in the figure.   □

6.3.2   PRS → Attribute Grammar

In the translation from a PRS $\langle G, S, \Phi, Eq, Eq_\Phi \rangle$ to an attribute grammar $\Gamma = \langle G, ATT, R, I \rangle$, the signature G of the PRS will be identified with the signature G of Γ. The set of attributes ATT will be derived from the set of functions Φ and the attribute definition rules R will be derived from the Φ-defining equations Eq_Φ. Finally, $\langle S, Eq \rangle$ is translated into I, the domain of the attribute values.

When constructing the set of attributes we construct SYN(X) for each X in G by adding a synthesized attribute for each function ϕ in Φ_X. INH(X) is constructed by associating an inherited attribute with each parameter $par(\phi, k)$ of each function ϕ in Φ_X. In some cases one inherited attribute is associated with different parameters. We discuss this in Section 6.3.3.

Example 6.10 We translate the specification in Module Syntax (6.1) and Module TC (6.2) into the attribute grammar of Figure 6.1 and Figure 6.2. Synthesized attributes are created for each typecheck function. Inherited attributes DECLS.Tenv, DECL.Tenv, STMS.Tenv, STM.Tenv and EXP.Tenv are created for the parameters of tcdecls, tcdecl, tcstms, tcstm and tcexp respectively.   □

For each constructor $p : X_1 \times \ldots \times X_n \rightarrow X_0$ in G, each Φ-defining equation $eq_{\phi,p}$ yields attribute definition rules R_p for the synthesized attribute ϕ at X_0 and the inherited attributes of children $X_1 \ldots X_n$.

To find the rule for the *synthesized* attribute ϕ at the top node X_0 of constructor p, we replace in a *top-down* traversal of the right-hand side of $eq_{\phi,p}$ all Φ-terms by their associated synthesized attribute, and replace the variables that occur as parameters in the left-hand side by the inherited attributes associated with these parameters.

Example 6.11 As an example, we derive attribution rules for the synthesized attributes tcp, tcdecls and tcstms from the equations

[Tc1]   tcp(program(*Decls,Stms*)) = tcstms(*Stms*,tcdecls(*Decls*,empty-env))
[Tc2]   tcdecls(empty-decls, *Tenv*) = *Tenv*
[Tc3]   tcdecls(decls(*Decl,Decls*), *Tenv*) = tcdecls(*Decls*, tcdecl(*Decl,Tenv*))
[Tc6]   tcstms(stms(*Stm,Stms*), *Tenv*) = and(tcstm(*Stm, Tenv*), tcstms(*Stms, Tenv*))

- From equation [Tc1] we derive the rule for the, synthesized, tcp attribute of PROGRAM in the constructor program: PROGRAM.tcp = STMS.tcstms.

- Equation [Tc2] yields the rule DECLS.tcdecls = DECLS.Tenv, with DECLS.Tenv the inherited attribute for the parameter of tcdecls.

- From equation [Tc3] we derive that DECLS.tcdecls = DECLS$_2$.tcdecls, meaning that the synthesized attribute DECLS.tcdecls of DECLS equals the synthesized attribute of its second child.

- Finally, equation [Tc6] yields STMS.tcstms = and(STM.tcstm, STMS$_2$.tcstms).

The remaining equations are treated in a similar way. □

The attribution rules for *inherited* attributes are derived from the parameter terms in the right-hand sides of Φ-defining equations. In the subterm $\psi(x_i, v_1, \dots, v_l, \dots, v_k)$, of the right-hand side of a defining equation $eq_{\phi,p}$, v_l is the parameter term for the l-th parameter of ψ, at the i-th child of constructor p. The procedure to find the attribution rule for the inherited attribute associated with this parameter is similar to the one for synthesized attributes: Replace in a *top-down* traversal of v_l, all Φ-terms by their associated synthesized attributes, and replace the variables that occur as parameter terms in the left-hand side by the inherited attributes associated with these parameters.

Example 6.12 The first parameter of the function tcstms is its second argument, TENV. The associated inherited attribute of STMS is indicated as STMS.Tenv. The inherited attribute associated with the first parameter of tcdecls is indicated as DECLS.Tenv. From the right-hand side of equation [Tc1] we derive the attribution rules for these inherited attributes in constructor program: STMS.Tenv = DECLS.tcdecls and DECLS.Tenv = empty-env. □

6.3.3 Well-Presentedness

When translating a PRS into an attribute grammar, it is important that a unique rule is created for each attribute. The attribution rule for a *synthesized* attribute of a constructor is always uniquely determined by the right-hand side of the single defining equation for the associated Φ-function, cf. (iii) in Definition 6.8. For inherited attributes, however, different attribution rules can be derived from the parameter terms in the right-hand sides of Φ-defining equations. We have to define an additional property for primitive recursive schemes which guarantees that in the corresponding attribute grammar inherited attributes are uniquely defined. This property is called *well-presentedness*. The example below shows part of a PRS that is *not* well-presented.

Example 6.13 Equations (6.2) and (6.3) below apply to the same constructor p : $X_1 \times X_2 \to X_0$.

$$\phi(p(x_1, x_2), y) = \chi(x_1, f(y)) \tag{6.2}$$
$$\psi(p(x_1, x_2), z) = \chi(x_1, g) \tag{6.3}$$

Let $inh(\phi, 1)$, $inh(\psi, 1)$ and $inh(\chi, 1)$ be the inherited attributes associated with the first parameter (the second argument) of ϕ, ψ and χ, respectively. The equations yield two different rules for $inh(\chi, 1)$ at the first child of constructor p, namely, $inh(\chi, 1) = f(inh(\phi, 1))$ and $inh(\chi, 1) = g$. $\square$

The definition of well-presentedness given below is such that for a well-presented PRS a one-to-one mapping exists between inherited attributes of a grammar constructor and *variable names* for parameter terms in the left-hand side of defining equations. According to property (iv) in Definition 6.15 each parameter term is represented by exactly one variable. Under this condition an inherited attribute associated with a parameter has a unique definition if all the terms for that same parameter in the right-hand sides of defining equations are *identical* according to (v). Property (vi) states that two different parameters with identical definitions must be represented by the same variable in the left-hand side as well. The following example illustrates the case in which two parameter terms are represented by one variable, hence are associated with one inherited attribute.

Example 6.14 Consider a PRS with constructors $p : X_1 \to X_0$, $q : X_2 \to X_1$ and equations

$$\phi(p(x_1), y) = f(\psi(x_1, y), \chi(x_1, y)) \tag{6.4}$$

$$\psi(q(x_2), z) = \xi(x_2, z) \tag{6.5}$$

$$\chi(q(x_2), z) = \xi(x_2, z) \tag{6.6}$$

Equation 6.4 defines the parameters $par(\psi, 1)$ and $par(\chi, 1)$ to be equal for the first child of constructor p. Therefore, we must use one variable, z, to represent both parameters in the left-hand sides of the other equations. As a consequence, the two occurrences in equations 6.5 and 6.6 of the parameter term for ξ at the first child of constructor q are identical. $\square$

Definition 6.15 (Well-Presented) A primitive recursive scheme with parameters is *well-presented* if it has the following properties.

(iv) For any two equations for the same function ϕ

$$\phi(p(x_1, \dots, x_n), y_1, \dots, y_m) = \tau \tag{6.7}$$

$$\phi(q(u_1, \dots, u_{n'}), z_1, \dots, z_m) = \tau' \tag{6.8}$$

the parameters y_j and z_j are identical $(1 \leq j \leq m)$.

(v) In right-hand sides of defining equations $\{eq_{\phi,p}|\phi \in \Phi_{X_0}\}$ for the same abstract tree constructor $p : X_1 \times \ldots \times X_n \rightarrow X_0$, all subterms with the same Φ-function and over the same X_i

$$\ldots \psi(x_i, v_1, \ldots, v_k) \ldots \qquad \ldots \psi(x_i, v_1', \ldots, v_k') \ldots$$

are identical. Hence parameters v_j and v_j' are identical for $1 \leq j \leq k$.

(vi) Two *different* parameters, say the j-th parameter of ψ, denoted $par(\psi, j)$, and the l-th parameter $par(\xi, l)$ of ξ, are represented by the same variable in left-hand sides of defining equations if and only if for each constructor $p : X_1, \ldots, X_n \rightarrow X_0$ the parameter terms v_j and w_l are identical in all occurrences

$$\ldots \psi(x_i, v_1, \ldots, v_k) \ldots \qquad \ldots \xi(x_i, w_1, \ldots, w_{k'}) \ldots$$

in right-hand sides of defining equations $\{eq_{\phi,p}|\phi \in \Phi_{X_0}\}$. Note that these Φ-terms have the same first argument x_i.

□

Definition 6.16 (Well-Presentable) A primitive recursive scheme with parameters is *well-presentable* if it can be turned into a well-presented one by a suitable renaming of variables. □

In their paper, Courcelle and Franchi-Zannettacci give an algorithm for deciding whether a PRS is well-presentable. The algorithm transforms a well-presentable PRS into a well-presented one.

In the sequel we assume that every PRS is well-presented.

6.4   Storage for Incremental Evaluation

Now that we know that a well-presented primitive recursive scheme is equivalent to a strongly non-circular attribute grammar, we can use an attributed tree for storing normal forms during incremental evaluation of terms in a PRS $\langle G, S, \Phi, Eq, Eq_\Phi \rangle$.

We assume that G describes the abstract syntax of some programming language, and that a syntax-directed editor for G exists. If a text in this editor is a G-term (a program) an abstract syntax tree T of this text is maintained. When a function $\phi \in \Phi$ is applied to the program in the editor (ϕ could be a typecheck function or a compilation function) the term $\phi(T)$ is reduced. We want to store normal forms of Φ-terms and parameter terms that occur in this reduction in attributes of the abstract syntax tree T.

In this section we describe the kind of attributes and attribute dependencies that we need for storing information. In Section 6.5 we describe incremental reduction and the updating of the attributes in the stored tree.

6.4.1 Attributes

Attributes in a tree have a name, a value, and a status. The name is derived from the Φ-function they belong to. We usually take the function name ϕ as the name of a synthesized attribute. An inherited attribute is named $inh(\phi, k)$ when it is associated with the k-th parameter $par(\phi, k)$ of ϕ.[3]

The value of an attribute is either void (before computation has taken place) or a normal form.

The status of an attribute indicates if the attribute contains a correct value or not. If it does not, the status is "Initial" (IN) or "TobeEvaluated" (TE). Otherwise it either has status "Unchanged" (UC) or "Changed" (C). For efficiency reasons explained in Section 6.5.2 we need four different status indications rather than just "unreliable" and "reliable".

6.4.2 Attribute Dependencies

Attribute dependencies for a PRS are equal to the ones derived from the equivalent attribute grammar. We derive attribute dependencies directly from Φ-defining equations rather than constructing the attribution rules first, as in Section 6.3.2, and then deriving the attribute dependencies. Figure 6.5 presents the algorithms for deriving attribute dependencies $D_{\phi,p}$ from an equation $eq_{\phi,p}$. If (att_1, att_2) is a pair in $D_{\phi,p}$ then att_1 is a *predecessor* of att_2 and att_2 is a *successor* of att_1.

MAKE-DEP computes from a (sub)term *term* in the right hand side of an equation $eq_{\phi,p}$ the predecessors for the synthesized attribute ϕ at the top of p. For all Φ-terms $\psi(x_i, \dots)$ in *term* that are *not* subterms of another Φ-term, a dependency (ψ_i, ϕ) is added to $D_{\phi,p}$. For all y_k that are not subterms of a Φ-term, a dependency $(inh(\phi, k), \phi)$ is added to $D_{\phi,p}$. In a similar fashion it derives predecessors of inherited attributes of each subtree x_i of p from parameter terms v_l of $\psi(x_i, v_1, \dots, v_k)$.

In addition to dependencies derived from equations, we use transitive dependencies between inherited attributes and their *corresponding* synthesized attributes. The *corresponding* attribute of $inh(\phi, k)$ is the synthesized attribute ϕ at the same tree node[4]. These dependencies reflect that the normal form of a Φ-term depends on the value of its parameter terms. We will use them as shortcuts in the dependency graph during status updating of attributes.

An immediate consequence of the equivalence proved by Courcelle and Franchi-Zannettacci is that the dependency graph D_T is non-circular for all trees T. In their proof they assume a dependency path from each inherited attribute to its *corresponding* synthesized attributes. Hence, adding the transitive dependencies between *corresponding* attributes does not change the non-circularity property.

---

[3] If one inherited attribute is associated with several parameters like $par(\psi, 1)$ and $par(\chi, 1)$, in equations (6.4)–(6.6) in example 6.14, then its name is a set, e.g., $(inh(\psi, 1), inh(\chi, 1))$.

[4] If the name of an inherited attribute is a set $(inh(\psi, 1), inh(\chi, 1))$ then its *corresponding* attributes are ψ and χ.

MAKEDEP-EQ($eq_{\phi,p}$)
let $eq_{\phi,p}$ = a defining equation
$\quad \tau$ = the right-hand side of $eq_{\phi,p}$
$\quad \phi$ = the synthesized attribute associated function ϕ at X_0
$\quad D_{\phi,p}$ = a set of dependencies
in
$\quad D_{\phi,p}$:= MAKEDEP($\tau, \phi, eq_{\phi,p}$)
$\quad$**return** $D_{\phi,p}$
ni

MAKEDEP($term, att, eq_{\phi,p}$)
let $eq_{\phi,p} = \phi(p(x_1, \ldots, x_n), y_1, \ldots, y_m) = \tau$
$\quad term$ = a subterm of τ
$\quad att$ = an attribute in the constructor $p: X_1, \ldots, X_n \rightarrow X_0$,
$\qquad$ either the synthesized attribute ϕ of X_0,
$\qquad$ or an inherited attribute of X_i $(1 \leq i \leq n)$
$\quad D_{\phi,p}$ = a set of dependencies
in
$\quad$**case**
$\quad$• $term = \psi(x_i, v_1, \ldots, v_k)$, $\psi \in \Phi$
$\qquad$**let** ψ_i be the synthesized attribute of function ψ at X_i **in**
$\qquad\quad$ add (ψ_i, att) to $D_{\phi,p}$
$\qquad\quad$ # make dependencies for inherited attributes
$\qquad\quad$ **for** $j = 1$ **to** k
$\qquad\quad$ **do**
$\qquad\qquad$ **let** $inh(\psi, j)$ be the attribute of the j-th parameter of ψ at X_i
$\qquad\qquad$ **in**
$\qquad\qquad\quad D_{\phi,p} := D_{\phi,p} \cup$ MAKEDEP($v_j, inh(\psi,j), eq_{\phi,p}$)
$\qquad\qquad$ **ni od**
$\qquad$**ni**
$\quad$• $term = y_j$, $j \in \{1, \ldots, m\}$
$\qquad$**let** $inh(\phi, j)$ be the attribute of the j-th parameter of ϕ at X_0 **in**
$\qquad\quad$ add $(inh(\phi,j), att)$ to $D_{\phi,p}$
$\qquad$**ni**
$\quad$• $term = f(s_1, \ldots, s_k)$, $f \notin \Phi$
$\qquad$**for** $j = 1$ **to** k **do**
$\qquad\quad D_{\phi,p} := D_{\phi,p} \cup$ MAKEDEP($s_j, att, eq_{\phi,p}$)
$\qquad$**od**
$\quad$**esac**
ni
return $D_{\phi,p}$

Figure 6.5: Algorithms for deducing a dependency graph from an equation.

Example 6.17 Figure 6.3 shows the top of the attributed tree we can use when some closed term tcp(Program) is reduced, where Program is some program with at least one declaration and at least two statements. In Figure 6.9 the same attributed tree is depicted, but it indicates dependencies between *corresponding* attributes as well. Moreover, we omitted the names of the attributes and indicated the status instead. A further explanation of this figure will follow in Section 6.5.2. □

In an attributed tree T we distinguish *upward, horizontal* and *downward* dependencies. *Upward* dependencies run from a synthesized attribute of a subtree T' of T to a synthesized attribute at the parent of T'. *Horizontal* dependencies run from a synthesized attribute of a subtree T' to an inherited attribute of a sibling of T' or of T' itself. The dependency between an inherited attribute and a *corresponding* synthesized attribute is also horizontal. *Downward* dependencies run from an inherited attribute to an inherited attribute at a lower node.

6.5   Incremental Evaluation

Assume T is the attributed abstract syntax tree of a program in an editor.During incremental reduction of a Φ-term $\phi(T)$ we store the normal forms of Φ-terms and parameter terms in attributes of T. After this, the text in the editor can be edited again. As a result of editing subtrees are replaced in T, and attributes that have become unreliable are marked. Let us say that the new abstract syntax tree is T'. When subsequently the user wants to know the ϕ value of the modified program, the term $\phi(T')$ is to be reduced. During reduction of this term, reduction of terms of which the associated attribute value is unaffected is not necessary, since the term can be replaced by the stored attribute value. The status of attributes is updated as well during reduction.

Figure 6.6 presents an overview of the algorithms we use for incremental rewriting. The REDUCE algorithms specify incremental reduction of a term $\phi(T)$ in the presence of an abstract syntax tree T with an attribute dependency graph D_T. They make use of algorithms for storing a normal form in an attribute. These algorithms in turn use propagation algorithms for updating the status of the successors of the attribute in the dependency graph D_T.

In Section 6.5.1 we first describe incremental reduction as specified by the REDUCE algorithms. In Section 6.5.2 we describe how to update the attributes in the stored tree at different stages: before reduction (during editing) when PROPAGATE-TE-UP is applied, during reduction as specified by the STORE algorithms and the PROPAGATE algorithms, and after reduction, when the algorithm RESET-CHANGED is applied.

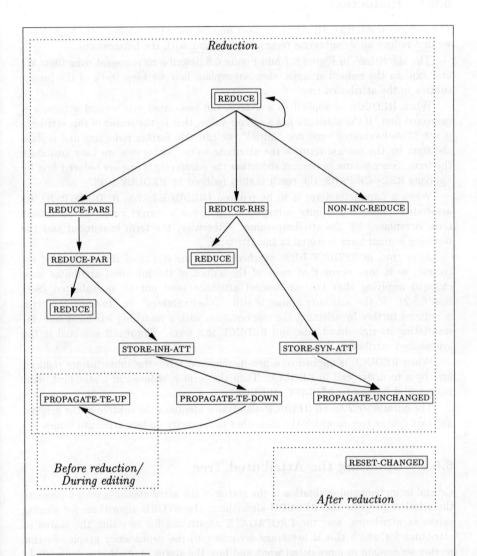

Figure 6.6: Overview of algorithms for incremental rewriting An arrow from algorithm A to algorithm B means that A invokes B.

6.5.1 Reduction

The reduction strategy we use is *leftmost innermost*: when a term is to be reduced we first reduce all its subterms recursively, starting with the leftmost one.

The algorithms in Figure 6.7 and Figure 6.8 describe incremental reduction. We first explain the reduction steps, then we explain how we keep track of the proper subtree in the attributed tree.

When REDUCE is applied to a Φ-term the associated synthesized attribute is inspected first. If the attribute has a correct value, that is, the status of this attribute is not "TobeEvaluated" and not "Initial", we can skip further reduction and replace the term by the normal form in the attribute value. Otherwise we have to reduce the term. Since we use innermost reduction the parameter terms are reduced first by applying REDUCE-PARS, the result is then reduced by REDUCE-RHS.

When a parameter term is to be reduced (REDUCE-PARS, REDUCE-PAR), its associated inherited attribute is inspected. If it has a correct value the parameter term is replaced by the attribute value. Otherwise, the term is reduced and the resulting normal form is stored in the attribute.

After this, in REDUCE-RHS, we check again the status of the synthesized attribute, as it may occur that none of the values of the inherited attributes have changed implying that the synthesized attribute need not be re-evaluated (Section 6.5.2). If the attribute status is still "TobeEvaluated" or "Initial", the term is reduced further by selecting the one equation with a matching left-hand side, instantiating its right-hand side, and REDUCE this term. The result is stored in the synthesized attribute.

When REDUCE is applied to a non-incremental term, the subterms are reduced first by a recursive call to REDUCE. Then the term is reduced in a standard, non-incremental fashion by NON-INC-REDUCE.

The parameter T in all REDUCE algorithms identifies the subtree of the original abstract syntax tree in which the algorithm can directly update attribute values.

6.5.2 Updating the Attributed Tree

Crucial in incremental evaluation is the status of the attributes. Figure 6.6 presents the relation between the REDUCE algorithms, the STORE algorithms for storing values in attributes, and the PROPAGATE algorithms for resetting the status of attributes for which this is necessary according to the dependency graph. In this section we explain in more detail when and how the status of attributes is updated.

Initially, before a function $\phi \in \Phi$ has been applied for the first time to an edit term T attributes in T have an empty value and status "Initial". During reduction of $\phi(T)$, the attribute ϕ of T as well as all its predecessors in the attribute dependency graph of T obtain a (new) value. Their status is then set to "Changed". After reduction all "Changed" attributes are reset to "Unchanged".

```
# In all algorithms T is an  abstract syntax tree
# T is decorated with an attribute dependency graph D_T
# Equations are considered global information

REDUCE(term, T)
let
    T_i = either the top of the tree and equal to T or the
          i-th subtree of T
    S_i = a term p(S'_1, ... , S'_k) which equals T_i
    reduced-term = a term
in case
    • term = φ(S_i, v_1, ... , v_k), φ ∈ Φ
        let φ_i be the synthesized attribute for function φ at T_i
        in if status_{φ_i} ≠ "TobeEvaluated" or "Initial"
           then  reduced-term := value_{φ_i}
           else  reduced-term := REDUCE-PARS(term, T, T_i)
                 reduced-term := REDUCE-RHS(reduced-term, T_i, φ_i)
           fi ni
    • term = f(s_1, ... , s_k), f ∉ Φ
        for j = 1 to k do
            reduced-s_j := REDUCE(s_j, T) od
        reduced-term := NON-INC-REDUCE( f(reduced-s_1, ... , reduced-s_k))
    esac
    return reduced-term
ni


REDUCE-RHS(term, T, φ)
let reduced-term = a term, inst-τ = a term
in
    if status_φ ≠ "TobeEvaluated" or "Initial"
    then  reduced-term := value_φ
    else  term matches equation eq_{φ,p} with right-hand side τ
          inst-τ := instantiated τ
          reduced-term :=  REDUCE(inst-τ, T)
          STORE-SYN-ATT(reduced-term, φ)
    fi
    return reduced-term
ni
```

Figure 6.7: Algorithms used for incremental reduction of a Φ-term.

\# In all algorithms T is an abstract syntax tree
\# T is decorated with an attribute dependency graph D_T
\# T_i is the i-th subtree of T

REDUCE-PARS($term, T, T_i$)
let $term = \phi(S_i, t_1, \ldots, t_m)$ s.t. S_i equals T_i
  $reduced\text{-}term, reduced\text{-}t_j$ = terms
in for $j = 1$ **to** m
    do
      let $inh(\phi, j)$ be the attribute for the j-th parameter of ϕ at T_i
      in
          $reduced\text{-}t_j := $ REDUCE-PAR($t_j, inh(\phi, j), T$)
      ni
    od
    $reduced\text{-}term := \phi(T_i, reduced\text{-}t_1, \ldots, reduced\text{-}t_m)$
    return $reduced\text{-}term$
ni

REDUCE-PAR($parameter\text{-}term, att, T$)
let $parameter\text{-}term, reduced\text{-}parameter$ = terms
  att is an inherited attribute.
in
    if $status_{att} \neq$ "TobeEvaluated" or "Initial"
    then
        $reduced\text{-}parameter\text{-}term := value_{att}$
    else
        $reduced\text{-}parameter\text{-}term := $ REDUCE($parameter\text{-}term, T$)
        STORE-INH-ATT($reduced\text{-}parameter\text{-}term, att$)
    fi
    return $reduced\text{-}parameter\text{-}term$
ni

Figure 6.8: Algorithms for incremental reduction of a parameter term.

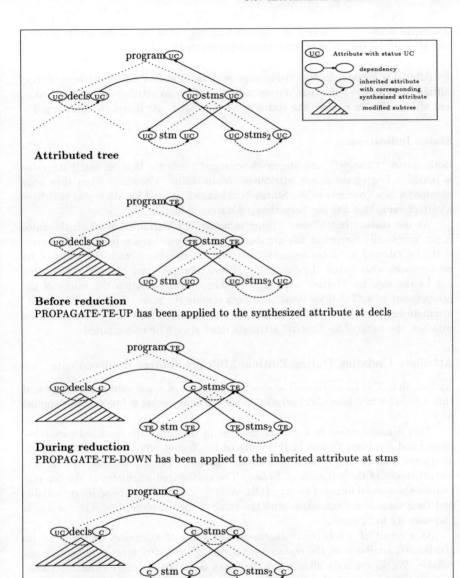

Figure 6.9: Attributed tree at various stages of incremental rewriting.

Example 6.18 The first tree in Figure 6.9 shows the status of the attributes in a tree after initial reduction of some term tcp(Program). □

After this *initial* reduction the storage is updated at four different stages: during editing, right before reduction, during reduction when an attribute gets a new value, and after reduction to reset the status of all "Changed" attributes to "Unchanged".

Status Indications

Both status "Changed" and status "Unchanged" indicate that an attribute value is reliable. During reduction, attributes obtain status "Changed" when they have obtained a new (correct) value. Status "Unchanged" is used for attributes that have a correct value that has not been changed during reduction.

We use status "Initial" and "TobeEvaluated" for attributes of which the value is not necessarily correct in the attributed tree. The difference between the two is that the value of a "TobeEvaluated" attribute is consistent with the value of its predecessors with status "Unchanged", "TobeEvaluated" and "Initial". This need not be the case for "Initial" attributes. When during reduction the values of the predecessors of a "TobeEvaluated" attribute remain the same, the "TobeEvaluated" attribute need not be re-evaluated and its status can be reset to "Unchanged". In contrast, the value of an "Initial" attribute must always be re-computed.

Attribute Updating During Editing; Multiple Subtree Replacements

Assume that T is an attributed abstract syntax tree of a program in an editor and that attributes in T have obtained a value when ϕ or any other Φ-function was applied to T.

After a modification in a part of the text in the editor the modified part is re-parsed and a subtree *Oldsub* in T is replaced by *Newsub*. *Newsub* is decorated with attributes with an empty value and status "Initial". The top node of *Newsub* gets the attributes of the top node of *Oldsub*. The synthesized attributes at the top still contain the normal forms of terms $\chi(Oldsub,\dots)$, $\chi \in \Phi$. They are no longer reliable and their value is not consistent with the value of their predecessors. Their status is therefore set to "Initial".

As a result of a subtree replacement, the value of attributes that depend on synthesized attributes at the replacement node (*affected attributes*) have become unreliable. We do not mark all affected attributes as unreliable before reduction starts. It suffices to do so only for those that are on a path of horizontal and upward dependencies from a synthesized attribute of a replacement node to an attribute at the top, because other affected attributes can be marked during reduction. After the algorithm PROPAGATE-TE-UP in Figure 6.11 has been applied to a synthesized attribute at the top of *Newsub*, all its *horizontal* and *upward* successors have status "TobeEvaluated" or "Initial".

STORE-SYN-ATT($term,\phi$)
let $term$ = the normal form of a Φ-term
$\quad \phi$ is a synthesized attribute
in
$\quad$ **if** $value_\phi \neq term$
$\quad$ **then** $value_\phi := term$
$\qquad\qquad status_\phi :=$ "Changed"
$\quad$ **else** $status_\phi :=$ "Unchanged"
$\qquad\qquad$ PROPAGATE-UNCHANGED(ϕ)
$\quad$ **fi**
ni

STORE-INH-ATT($term,att$)
let $term$ = the normal form of a parameter term
$\quad att$ is an inherited attribute
in
$\quad$ **if** $value_{att} \neq term$
$\quad$ **then** $value_{att} := term$
$\qquad\qquad status_{att} :=$ "Changed"
$\qquad\qquad$ PROPAGATE-TE-DOWN(att)
$\quad$ **else** $status_{att} :=$ "Unchanged"
$\qquad\qquad$ PROPAGATE-UNCHANGED(att)
$\quad$ **fi**
ni

Figure 6.10: Algorithms for storing normal forms in attributes and propagating information to successor attributes.

Example 6.19 The second tree in Figure 6.9 shows the effect of updating an attributed tree in which the declarations have been replaced. $\square$

Editing may proceed and other subtrees will then be replaced in the abstract syntax tree. After each subtree replacement the same procedure is applied. Note that PROPAGATE-TE-UP does not continue if the status of an attribute is already "TobeEvaluated" or "Initial".

Attribute Updating Before Reduction

In case the user of the editor wants to apply a function $\psi \in \Phi$ to the program T', and ψ is a function with parameters, then some term $\psi(T', t'_1, \ldots, t'_m)$ has to be reduced. The parameter terms t'_j can differ from the values of the inherited attributes $inh(\psi, j)$. We therefore mark the associated inherited attributes of the parameters of ψ as "Initial", and apply PROPAGATE-TE-UP from there on. As a result, the synthesized attribute ψ of T either has status "Initial" or status "TobeEvaluated".

Attribute Updating During Reduction

The algorithms STORE-SYNATT and STORE-INHATT in Figure 6.10 are applied when a normal form must be stored in a synthesized or inherited attribute. The new attribute value is compared to the old value and if they are different the status of the attribute is set to "Changed", otherwise it becomes "Unchanged".

A changed inherited attribute of a tree T' can have successor attributes of subtrees of T' (via a *downward* dependency) that are not yet marked as unreliable. After application of PROPAGATE-TE-DOWN all direct and transitive successors at the *top nodes* of the subtrees of T are marked as "TobeEvaluated" or "Initial".

Example 6.20 The third tree in Figure 6.9 shows the effect of applying PROPAGATE-TE-DOWN after the inherited attribute of stms has obtained a new value. □

When an attribute has been re-evaluated, and its value is found not to have changed after all, there is a chance that its successors do not have to be re-evaluated. If the status of a successor is "TobeEvaluated" and it has only "Unchanged" predecessors, its status can be reset to "Unchanged" as well. PROPAGATE-UNCHANGED takes care of this.

This algorithm is the reason why we need two status indications for attributes with a reliable value and two for attributes with an unreliable value. Only "TobeEvaluated" attributes are reset to "Unchanged", but "Initial" attributes are not. Moreover, the status of a "TobeEvaluated" attribute is reset only if all its predecessors have status "Unchanged". Successors of a "Changed" attribute must always be re-evaluated.

Attribute Updating After Reduction

When the reduction process has ended, RESET-CHANGED is applied to reset the status of all "Changed" attributes to "Unchanged", and the status of their direct "TobeEvaluated" successors as well as their *corresponding* attributes to "Initial".[5]

Example 6.21 The last tree in Figure 6.9 shows the attributed tree after reduction has ended, and before RESET-CHANGED is applied. Replacing declarations is a good example to illustrate the propagation algorithms, but it is unfortunate that all attributes had to be re-evaluated because of this modification. Note that after a statement replacement more attribute values can be reused. In Section 6.11 we come back to the consequences of modifying declarations. □

We explain why RESET-CHANGED also resets the status of the "TobeEvaluated" successors of "Changed" attributes. In our running example no "TobeEvaluated" attributes appear when reduction is finished. If a PRS contains two or more

---

[5]For efficiency reasons, "Changed" attributes must be added to a list during reduction. This avoids a search through the whole tree. We have omitted this aspect from the algorithms.

PROPAGATE-TE-UP(ϕ)
let ϕ, ψ, *successor* = attributes in a dependency graph D_T
in for all direct successor attributes *successor* of ϕ
    do when $status_{successor} \neq$ "TobeEvaluated" or "Initial"
      do
          $status_{successor} :=$ "TobeEvaluated"
          if *successor* is a synthesized attribute
          then
              PROPAGATE-TE-UP(*successor*)
          else
              successor is an inherited attribute
              for all its corresponding synthesized attributes ψ
              do $status_\psi :=$ "TobeEvaluated"
                    PROPAGATE-TE-UP(ψ)
              od
        fi
      od od
ni

Figure 6.11: Algorithm for upward propagation of the status "TobeEvaluated", starting at a synthesized attribute.

PROPAGATE-TE-DOWN(*inhatt*)
let *inhatt* = an inherited attribute
    ψ, *successor* = attributes
in for all direct successor attributes *successor* in D_T of *inhatt*
    do when *successor* is an inherited attribute
      and $status_{successor} \neq$ "TobeEvaluated" or "Initial"
      do
          $status_{successor} :=$ "TobeEvaluated"
          for all corresponding synthesized attributes ψ of *successor*
          do $status_\psi :=$ "TobeEvaluated"
              PROPAGATE-TE-UP(ψ)
          od
      od
    od
ni

Figure 6.12: Algorithm for downward propagation of status "TobeEvaluated", starting at an inherited attribute.

\# *att* is an attribute with status "Unchanged" in a dependency graph D_T

PROPAGATE-UNCHANGED(*att*)
let *att* = an attribute with status "Unchanged" in a dependency graph D_T
    successor = an attribute
in
    for all direct successor attributes *successor* in D_T of *att*
    do
    when $status_{successor}$ is "TobeEvaluated"
    do
        when the status of all direct predecessors of *successor* in D_T is "Unchanged"
        do
            $status_{successor}$:= "Unchanged"
            PROPAGATE-UNCHANGED(*successor*)
        od
    od od
ni

Figure 6.13: Algorithm for propagating status "Unchanged".

RESET-CHANGED(*att*)
let *att* = an attribute with status "Changed" in a dependency graph D_T
in
    $status_{att}$:= "Unchanged"
    for all direct successor attributes in D_T of *att*
    do
        $status_{successor}$:= "Initial"
    od
    when *att* is an inherited attribute
    do
        for all corresponding synthesized attributes in D_T of *att*
        do
            $status_{successor}$:= "Initial"
        od
    od
ni

Figure 6.14: Algorithm for resetting the status of a "Changed" attribute.

groups of Φ-functions, for instance, functions for typechecking and for compilation, and the two groups have some functions in common, then a tree is decorated with a dependency graph for each group of functions, and these graphs have common subgraphs. When one group of functions has been evaluated, the attributes for these functions all have status "Unchanged" or "Changed". Attributes associated with other functions can have status "TobeEvaluated", while having a predecessor (in the common subgraph) with status "Changed". The value of these "TobeEvaluated" attributes is not consistent with the value of its "Changed" predecessor. So when the status of a "Changed" attribute is reset to "Unchanged" the status of these "Tobe-Evaluated" successors must be changed to "Initial".

6.6 Copy Dependencies

Often the value of an attribute B is the copy of the value of its predecessor A. In that case we will call B a *copy attribute*. If during incremental reduction an attribute gets a new value, it is compared to the previous one. This may be an expensive operation. The efficiency of incremental evaluation improves when copy attributes share a value with their predecessors, because the old value and the new value have to be compared only once for all copies.

Deriving Copy Dependencies

Attribute dependencies are derived from Φ-defining equations. It is simple to derive copy dependencies as well. Consider the constructor $p : X_1 \times \ldots \times X_n \to X_0$ and the equation $\phi(p(x_1, \ldots, x_n), y_1, \ldots, y_m) = \tau$, with $\psi(x_i, v_1, \ldots, v_k)$ a subterm of the right-hand side τ.

If the head symbol of τ is a Φ-function, i.e., τ equals $\psi(x_i, \ldots)$, then the value of the synthesized attribute for ϕ is a copy of the value of the synthesized attribute for ψ of x_i.

Let $inh(\psi, l)$ $(1 \leq l \leq k)$ be the inherited attribute of X_i associated with the l-th parameter of ψ. Copy predecessors are derived for $inh(\psi, l)$ by analyzing v_l as follows. If $v_l = y_j$ $(1 \leq j \leq m)$ then $inh(\psi, l)$ is a copy of $inh(\phi, j)$ of X_0, the inherited attribute associated with the j-th parameter of ϕ. If $v_l = \xi(x_j, \ldots)$ $(1 \leq j \leq n)$ then $inh(\psi, l)$ is a copy of the synthesized attribute ξ of X_j.

Example 6.22 From equation [Tc1] in the typecheck example of Module Syntax (6.1) and Module TC (6.2) we conclude that the tcp attribute of a program is a copy of the tcstms attribute of its statements, and that the type-environment attribute of the statements subtree of a program is a copy of the tcdecls attribute of the declarations. From equations [Tc5]–[Tc11] it can be concluded that all type-environment attributes of a tree in the statements section are copies of the type-environment attributes at the ancestor of that tree. □

6.6.1 Updating with Copy Dependencies

When a tree is decorated with attributes chains of copy attributes can appear. The *head* of a copy chain in an attribute graph is a non-copy attribute with copy successors. We refer to the direct non-copy successors of the copy attributes as *use* attributes.

If an attribute in a tree is a copy of its predecessor they share the same value and the same status. This means that when a *copy-head* attribute obtains a new value, copies automatically obtain the same new value and the same new status. The non-copy successors of these copies however have to be marked as "TobeEvaluated" as well. This requires dependencies between a *copy-head* and its *use* attributes, as well as an additional algorithm for remote status propagation. We use an approach inspired by Hoover (1986) for creating remote dependencies between a *copy-head* and its *use* attributes. When a tree is decorated each copy attribute obtains information about the *copy-head* and the path from the *copy-head* to itself. The *copy-head* keeps a so-called *copy bypass tree* of all copies that have non-copy successors. They are ordered according to their paths. The dependency established from the copy-head to its *use* attributes is called *non-local*.

Example 6.23 In Figure 6.3 the lower tcdecls attribute is a *copy-head*. Its *use* attributes are the synthesized attributes tcstm at the assign nodes, because they are non-copy successors of the $inh(tcstm, 1)$ attributes. □

The algorithm PROPAGATE-TE-REMOTE is very similar to the PROPAGATE-TE-UP algorithm. Instead of updating the status of all direct successors of an attribute, it marks each *use* attributes of a *copy-head* as "TobeEvaluated" and invokes PROPAGATE-TE-UP for them.

6.6.2 Editing Trees with Non-local Dependencies

During editing, subtrees are replaced in the abstract syntax tree T, and attributes with their incoming and outgoing edges are removed from the attribute dependency graph D_T. After a replacement of a subtree *Oldsub* with a *copy-head* attribute or with *use* attributes, some care must be taken in removing the old non-local dependencies. When a subtree has been removed and one of the nodes contains a *copy-head* attribute there are two possibilities. If all its *use* attributes are inside *Oldsub* these *use* attributes are automatically removed together with the non-local dependencies. If, on the other hand, a *use* attribute exists outside *Oldsub*, a copy attribute at the top node of the *Oldsub* exists that passes on information from the *copy-head* to this *use* attribute. Let us call this attribute *replacement-copy*. The replacement-copy contains a reference to the *copy-head* with the *copy bypass tree*. First, the *copy bypass tree* is pruned at the copy path of the replacement-copy. We then use the copy attributes in this pruned subtree to find the *use* attributes of *copy-head* outside *Oldsub* and remove their remote incoming edges.

Now assume a subtree *Oldsub* has been removed and some node inside this subtree contains a *use* attribute. If the related copy-head is not inside *Oldsub*, again a *replacement-copy* exists at at the top node of *Oldsub*. The replacement-copy contains a pointer to the *copy-head*. First, the *copy bypass tree* is pruned at the copy path of the *replacement-copy*. We then use the copy attributes in this pruned subtree to find the *use* attributes in *Oldsub* and remove their remote incoming edges.

New non-local dependencies are created when *Newsub* is decorated with attributes.

6.7 Layered Primitive Recursive Schemes

For most specifications of typecheckers incremental reduction with or without copy-dependencies is inefficient after a modification in the *declarations* section. Module Syntax (6.1), Module TC (6.2) and Figure 6.3 show that when the declarations are modified, a component in the table in the top tcdecls-attribute is likely to have changed. All attributes in the statement section are successors of this aggregate attribute, hence they all become unreliable and no typecheck results of the statements can be reused.

Algebraic specifications offer a uniform way of describing data types, of which the abstract syntax and semantics of a language are just examples. Therefore, in principle an incremental implementation can be generated for every data type as long as its specification is a PRS. We use this idea to refine our incremental algorithm. The main thing we need to do is find out how attributed terms of auxiliary data types can be connected to the attribute graph of a tree of the main PRS, and how their incremental implementation can be used efficiently.

The fine-grain incremental implementation method can typically be applied to a typecheck specification using a table data type with an *incremental* look-up function. In such a case, a function cache for look-up in this particular table is generated. Direct *definition-use* dependencies are established from entries in the function cache to functionally dependent attributes in a program tree. The cache is updated incrementally when a modification in the symbol table has been detected during attribute evaluation.

The approach we present is general in the sense that it can be applied to any specification in the class of *layered primitive recursive schemes*, without extending the specification formalism or adding predefined data types. This distinguishes it from techniques in the field of attribute grammars. In attempts to solve the problem of aggregate values in attribute grammars, either a predefined data type is added to the specification formalism, or the attribute grammar formalism is extended, or it is combined with another formalism.

6.7.1   Table + look-up as PRS

We will solve the inefficiency caused by multiple dependencies of an aggregate value by extending the incremental technique to functions like the look-up function of the type-environment.

Example 6.24 In Module Tenv (6.3) part of the specification of a type-environment is presented. This algebraic specification is a PRS $\langle G, S, \Phi, Eq, Eq_\Phi \rangle$. G consists of sorts TENV, PAIR, TYPE and ID, and the constructors pair, empty-env and tenv. The constructors for TYPE have been omitted. The elements of Φ are lookup, id-of and type-of. Equations [Tenv1]–[Tenv5] are the Φ-defining equations. The sorts ID and TYPE also serve as the auxiliary data types S, which are used as the output sorts and the parameters of the Φ-functions. Eq is empty. □

For incremental evaluation of a term lookup(Tenv,Id), with TENV a type-environment with at least two identifier-type pairs, we can store the type-environment and decorate it with Id and lookup attributes, as shown in Figure 6.15. After changing Tenv to Tenv', affected attributes are marked as unreliable. When reducing lookup(Tenv',Id), the normal forms in reliable attributes can be reused.

6.7.2 Layered Primitive Recursive Schemes

Informally speaking, a layered PRS is a PRS which contains another PRS. This subPRS in turn can be layered as well. More formally:

Definition 6.25 (Layered PRS) An algebraic specification is a *layered PRS* if it is a PRS, $\langle G_1, S_1, \Phi_1, Eq_1, Eq_{\Phi_1} \rangle$ such that

- The specification of the auxiliary data types $\langle S_1, Eq_1 \rangle$ is also a (possibly layered) PRS $\langle G_2, S_2, \Phi_2, Eq_2, Eq_{\Phi_2} \rangle$.

- If a Φ_2-subterm occurs in the right-hand side τ of a Φ_1-defining equation

$$\phi(p(x_1, \ldots, x_n), y_1, \ldots, y_m) = \tau$$

then the first argument of this Φ_2-subterm is *not* one of x_i $(1 \le i \le n)$.

□

Note that in a layered PRS $S_1 = G_2 \cup S_2 \cup \Phi_2$ and $Eq_1 = Eq_2 \cup Eq_{\Phi_2}$. The second requirement is needed because we allow a limited overlap between S and G (see footnote on page 209). A consequence of this requirement is that, when during reduction of a Φ_1-term with a first argument T, a function $\phi_2(U, \ldots)$ of a different layer is introduced, recursion will shift from T to the new structure U.

A layered PRS is *well-presented* if both $\langle G_1, S_1, \Phi_1, Eq_1, Eq_{\Phi_1} \rangle$ and $\langle G_2, S_2, \Phi_2, Eq_2, Eq_{\Phi_2} \rangle$ are well-presented.

Example 6.26 The specification consisting of the union of the typechecker in Module Syntax (6.1) and Module TC (6.2) and the type-environment in Module Tenv (6.3) is a well-presented layered PRS, with G_1 consisting of the sorts PROGRAM,

---

module Tenv

imports Syntax Booleans Type-Operations
exports
   sorts TENV PAIR
   context-free syntax
      pair(ID, TYPE)   → PAIR   {**constructor**}
      empty-env   → TENV   {**constructor**}
      tenv(PAIR, TENV) → TENV   {**constructor**}

      lookup(TENV, ID) → TYPE
      id-of(PAIR)   → ID
      type-of(PAIR)   → TYPE
   variables
     Pair → PAIR
     Tenv → TENV
equations

[Tenv1] $$\frac{\text{id-of}(Pair) \ = \ Id}{\text{lookup}(\text{tenv}(Pair, Tenv), Id) \ = \ \text{type-of}(Pair)}$$

[Tenv2] $$\frac{\text{id-of}(Pair) \ \neq \ Id}{\text{lookup}(\text{tenv}(Pair, Tenv), Id) \ = \ \text{lookup}(Tenv, Id)}$$

[Tenv3]   lookup(empty-env, *Id*) = error-type

[Tenv4]   id-of(pair(*Id, Type*))   = *Id*
[Tenv5]   type-of(pair(*Id, Type*)) = *Type*

Module 6.3: Tenv. Part of an algebraic specification of a type-environment.

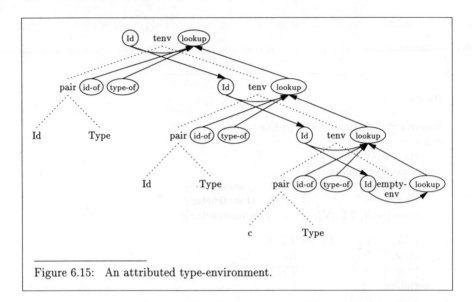

Figure 6.15:   An attributed type-environment.

DECLS, DECL, STMS, STM, EXP, ..., and the related constructor functions. Φ_1 consists of the functions tcp, tcdecls, tcdecl, tcstms, tcstm and tcexp. G_2 consists of the sorts TENV, PAIR, TYPE, ID, the constructors pair, tenv and empty-env, and the Φ_2-functions lookup, id-of, and type-of.   □

6.7.3   Auxiliary Attributed Terms

We will use the properties of a layered PRS to obtain incremental evaluation of the value within Φ_1-attributes, by storing Φ_2-terms that occur in the reduction of a Φ_1-term as *auxiliary attributed terms*: G_2-terms decorated with Φ_2-attributes.

Auxiliary attributed terms can be related to both inherited and synthesized attributes.

Let $\phi(p(x_1, \dots, x_n), y_1, \dots, y_m) = \tau$ be a Φ_1-defining equation with Φ_2-terms in its right-hand side τ. Let $\xi_2(Aux, \dots)$ be such a Φ_2-term. Then Aux is a G_2-term.

- If this Φ_2-term is *not* a subterm of a Φ_1-term, the attributed term Aux is related to the synthesized attribute of function ϕ .

- If this Φ_2-term is a subterm of a Φ_1-term, $\psi(x_i, w_1, \dots, w_m)$ it can only be the subterm of a parameter term, say w_k. the attributed term Aux is then associated with the inherited attribute of the k-th parameter of ψ.

The basic idea of incremental reduction with auxiliary attribute terms is as follows. Auxiliary terms obtain their initial value and are attributed upon reduction of the related Φ_1-term. If the auxiliary term already exists, the differences between the old value and the new value must be computed and subtrees in the old value are replaced to obtain the new value. Next, affected attributes of the auxiliary term are marked as unreliable and so are their direct and transitive successors in the edit tree. Hence, reduction of a Φ_2-term is replaced by a tree difference calculation followed by an updating of the status of attributes.

Clearly, incremental reduction with auxiliary attribute terms can only be profitable if the tree difference calculation is very cheap or if many Φ_1-attributes share one auxiliary term, so that this calculation has to be performed only once. We, therefore, focus on layered PRSs in which auxiliary terms are the values of *copy attributes*.

Example 6.27 In equations [Tc7] and [Tc8] in Module Syntax (6.1) and Module TC (6.2) the function lookup is applied to *Tenv*. If this equation is applied during reduction of some term tcp(Program), a type-environment will appear as an auxiliary term for the attribute tcstm of an assign tree. Moreover, this type-environment is the value of the inherited attribute inh(tcstm,1). This attribute is a copy attribute. □

6.7.4 Multiply Attributed Term with Function Cache

Let the Φ_2-term $\xi_2(Aux, t_1, \dots, t_m)$ occur in the reduction of $\phi(T)$, then Aux is decorated with an attribute graph for ξ_2. If Aux is the value of a copy attribute, for instance a type-environment, it is possible that during the same reduction (of $\phi(T)$) a similar Φ_2-term $\xi_2(Aux, t_1', \dots, t_m')$ $(t_j' \neq t_j)$ occurs, such as lookup(Tenv,X) and lookup(Tenv,Y). The attributes for ξ_2 of Aux already contain a value, but these values are based on the previous parameters $t_1, \dots, t_m$. Therefore, we decorate Aux with an extra attribute graph for ξ_2. During reduction of $\xi_2(Aux, t_1', \dots, t_m')$ values are stored in attributes of this new graph. The result is that Aux is a *multiply attributed term*, i.e., a term which may have any number of attribute graphs for the same incremental function. The values of the inherited attributes at the beginning of each graph, that is, at the top node of the term, differ. To distinguish attributes of different graphs we label them with the values of the inherited attributes at the top.

Synthesized attributes without corresponding inherited attributes are not duplicated for multiple attribute graphs. They can safely be used in all graphs because the values of these attributes is not determined by the value of inherited attributes at the top.

A *hash table* is connected to a multiply attributed tree to allow for fast searching in the list of synthesized attributes at the top. The hash keys are calculated from the name of a function and the values of its parameters. The entries are (pointers to) the corresponding synthesized attributes. In this way we create a *function cache* for operations on the auxiliary term.

Example 6.28 In a program with several identifiers in the statements the single auxiliary term type-environment is used for the lookup of all these identifiers. So, this type-environment is decorated with a different Id-lookup graph for each identifier looked for.

Figure 6.16 shows a multiply attributed type-environment connected to a program term with typecheck attributes. The multiply attributed type-environment is the value shared by the tcdecls attribute and its copy successors. It is also the auxiliary tree for both the synthesized attribute tcstm at the tree assign(X,Exp1) and the tcstm attribute at the tree assign(Y,Exp2). The type-environment is attributed with two lookup-graphs. The function cache for Tenv has entries for the results of lookup X and lookup Y. The functions id-of and type-of have no parameters, so their associated attributes are shared by the two attribute graphs. □

6.8 Fine-Grain Incremental Evaluation

We explain fine-grain incremental evaluation, with multiply attributed terms connected to an attributed term. Function caches and definition-use dependencies are maintained and updated dynamically.

6.8.1 Initial Reduction

Let T be a G_1 term and the attributed abstract syntax tree of a text in an editor. Assume that during the reduction of initial term $\phi(T)$ a term $\phi_2(Aux, par_1, \ldots, par_m)$ occurs and that Aux is the value of an attribute. We check the function cache related to this attribute value.

If an entry for ϕ_2 with parameter values $par_1, \ldots, par_m$ does not exist, then Aux is decorated with a new attribute graph for these parameters, and a key is added to the hash table together with (a pointer to) the new synthesized attribute at the top. The Φ_2-term is reduced and meanwhile the attributes in the new graph obtain a value.

If, on the other hand, the cache for Aux does contain an entry for ϕ_2 with parameter values $par_1, \ldots, par_m$, then the synthesized attribute in the entry contains the normal form of the Φ_2-term and reduction can be avoided.

At each visit to a function cache, attribute dependencies are established between the synthesized attribute in the entry and the attribute in the main tree that uses its information. This edge *replaces* the remote dependency in the main tree from the *copy-head* attribute for Aux to this *use*-attribute.

Example 6.29 We return to the specification in Module Syntax (6.1) and Module TC (6.2) and the picture in Figure 6.16. Here we apply tcp to a program Program with at least two declarations and two statements. During reduction of tcp(Program) equation [Tc7] is applied to reduce tcstm(assign(X,Exp),Tenv), which means that lookup(Tenv,X) must be reduced. If the function cache for Tenv contains no entry for lookup X, Tenv is decorated with attributes for lookup X. While lookup(Tenv,X)

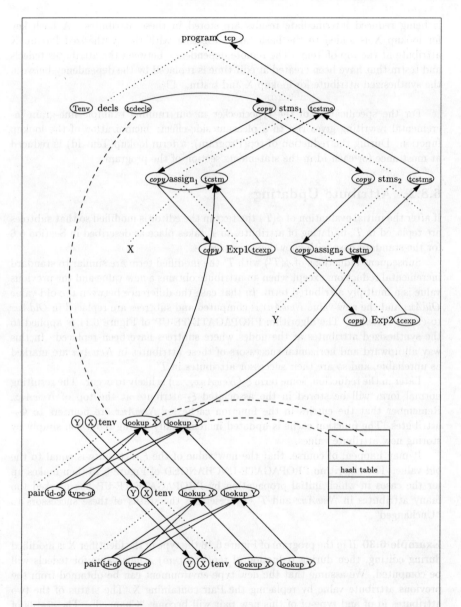

Figure 6.16: Attributed abstract syntax tree of a program. The value of the tcdecls attribute is a multiply attributed term.

is being reduced intermediate results are stored in these attributes. A hash key for lookup X is added to the hash table, together with the synthesized lookup X attribute at the top of Tenv. The remote dependency between the attributes tcdecls and tcstm that have been created at edit time is replaced by the dependency between the synthesized attribute for lookup X and tcstm. $\square$

For the specification of the typechecker in our running example fine-grain incremental rewriting gives rise to a pleasant side-effect: memoization of the lookup function. During the reduction of tcp(Program), a term lookup(Tenv,Id) is reduced at most once for each Id in the statements section of the program.

6.8.2 Attribute Updating

If after the initial evaluation of $\phi(T)$ the text in the editor is modified so that subtrees are replaced in T, updating of attributes in T takes place as described in Section 6.6 for the standard case with copy dependencies.

Subsequent reductions of $\phi(T')$ with T' the modified term are similar to standard incremental reduction, except when an attribute obtains a new value and the previous value is a multiply attributed term. In that case the difference between the old value *OldAux* and the new value *NewAux* is computed and subtrees are replaced in *OldAux* to create *NewAux*. The algorithm PROPAGATE-TE-UP of Figure 6.11 is applied to the synthesized attributes at the nodes where subtrees have been replaced. In this way all upward and horizontal successors of these attributes in *NewAux* are marked as unreliable, and so are their successor attributes in T'.

Later in the reduction, some term $\xi_2(NewAux, \ldots)$ is likely to occur. The resulting normal form will be stored in the associated ξ_2-attribute at the top of *NewAux*. Remember that the entries in the function cache for *NewAux* are pointers to Φ_2-attributes. The function cache is updated incrementally during reduction simply by storing new attribute values.

It may happen, of course, that the new value of the ξ_2-attribute is equal to the old value. The algorithm PROPAGATE-UNCHANGED of Figure 6.13 then makes up for the cases in which initial propagation by PROPAGATE-TE-UP has marked too many attributes in *NewAux* and T', by resetting the status of these successors to "Unchanged".

Example 6.30 If in the program of Figure 6.16 the type of the identifier X is modified during editing, then during reduction of tcp(Program) a new value for tcdecls will be computed. We assume that the new type-environment can be obtained from the previous attribute value by replacing the Pair containing X. The status of the two attributes id-of and type-of of this new pair will become "Changed". The status of their upward successors in the type-environment (the lookup attributes) as well as the successor in the program tree (tcstm and tcstms attributes) will become "Tobe-Evaluated".

The first time the term lookup(Tenv,X) occurs in the reduction its new value will be computed and stored in the synthesized attribute. Every other occurrence of lookup(Tenv,X) will find this new value in the function cache.

The first time the term lookup(Tenv,Y) occurs in the reduction it will be detected that this value has remained the same, so PROPAGATE-UNCHANGED is invoked. □

6.9 Implementation and Measurements

To evaluate the performance of the implementation of the incremental techniques described in the previous chapters, we measured the cost for typechecking Pico programs on the basis of the Pico specification in Module Syntax (6.1) and Module TC (6.2). It is clear from the theoretical description that incremental reduction reduces the *number of rewrite steps*. Since incrementality inevitably comes with time and space overhead for storing additional information, we also discuss the *time* gain of our implementation. It should be noted that the effectiveness of the method depends largely on the particular specification to which it is applied. We believe that the Pico typechecker is a simple example of a large class of typechecking specifications with similar incremental behavior (e.g, most Algol-like languages).

All measurements were performed on a Silicon Graphics workstation, type Iris INDIGO, running under operating system IRIX Release 4.0.5F System V, with 24 MB internal memory. The implementation of the incremental rewriting algorithms is part of the ASF+SDF Meta-Environment (see Chapter 1) which is written in LeLisp. A detailed description of this implementation can be found in van der Meulen (1994).

6.9.1 Basic Implementation

Figure 6.17 shows both the number of rewrite steps for typechecking type-correct programs of various lengths as well as the time spent. It presents graphs for non-incremental typechecking (not-inc), incremental typechecking of a program without using any preliminary information (init-inc), and incremental typechecking after a small modification (inc). We only show measurements for type-correct programs, since our measurements have shown that there is little difference between the type correct and incorrect cases.

Initial Costs

Description of the Test In the test specification the typecheck functions tcp, tcdecls, tcstms, tcstm and tcexp were declared "incremental," i.e., they are considered to be Φ-functions.

We performed measurements on programs with 10 declarations and various numbers of statements. In the test of Figure 6.17 the statements are simple type correct assignments like Id1 := Id2, in which the type of both identifiers is natural. In all

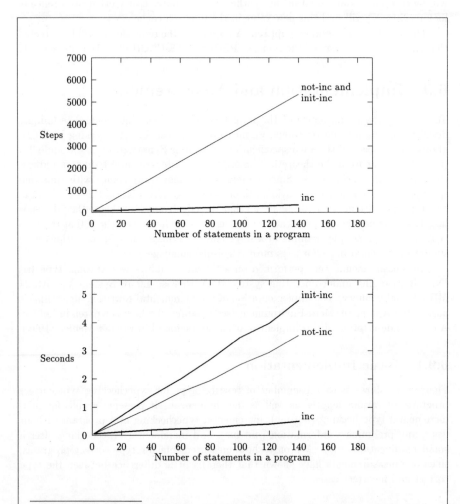

Figure 6.17: Cost of non-incremental typechecking of programs (not-inc), incremental typechecking without making use of previous results (init-inc), and incremental typechecking after a small modification (inc). All programs are type-correct.

programs we modified the last statement by replacing a single identifier by a new un-declared identifier. This modification changed the typecheck value of this statement to compatible(natural,lookup(empty-tenv,Newid)). It also changed the typecheck re-sult of the whole program.

Discussion Initial incremental rewriting is the same as non-incremental rewriting but with some side-effects. So the number of rewrite steps is the same in both cases. The overhead time for initial incremental rewriting is the time needed for the creation of attributes as well as their dependencies, and for storing normal forms in them.

From the difference between the graphs for non-incremental reduction and for initial incremental reduction we can conclude that the overhead for initial incremental reduction for 140 assignments is approximately 1 sec. Apart from the two attributes for tcp and tcdecls, a program with N assignments is decorated with $6N$ attributes. Hence, about 800 attributes can be created in 1 sec.

The number of rewrite steps for incrementally processing a small modification is low because the typechecking of all other statements can be avoided. There is overhead time for attribute updating. This includes time for status propagation, the costs of looking up attributes, and the cost of comparing attribute values. The cost of comparing attribute values depends on the depth in the two trees where the first difference occurs. For checking statements we only need to compare "true" and "false."

The Size of the Modification

We want to know the largest modifications for which incremental processing is still profitable. Figure 6.18 presents the number of rewrite steps and the time needed for processing modifications of various sizes incrementally.

Description of the Test In the test specification the typecheck functions tcp, tcdecls, tcstms, tcstm, tcexp were declared incremental. The test program (Fig-ure 6.18) has 10 declarations and 100 type correct assignments of the form Id1 = Id2. The modifications replace statements at the end of the program by other type correct assignments.

Discussion Clearly the number of rewrite steps for incremental re-checking a pro-gram after a modification of any size is always less than the number of rewrite steps needed for non-incremental typechecking.

When considering the time needed we notice that Figure 6.18 shows that in a program with 100 statements the crossover point is at about 70 statements. This means that incremental processing a modification of less than 70 statements is cheaper than completely checking the modified program of 100 statements. Note that, after completely replacing a program, incremental cost will be equal to the cost of an initial incremental reduction.

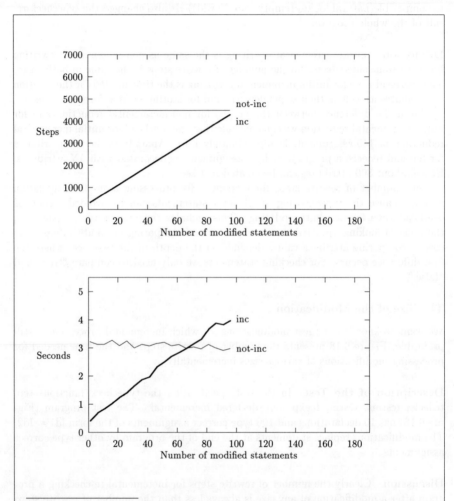

Figure 6.18:   Cost of non-incremental and incremental typechecking of a program after modifications of various sizes. Before and after the modification the program is type-correct.

6.9.2 Fine-Grain Implementation

We now pay special attention to modifications in declarations. Whereas the cost of updating after a modification in the statements is linear in the size of the modification, applying the standard, coarse-grain, incremental technique after a modification in the declarations will always cause the whole statements section to be typechecked again. Fine-grain incrementality is an extension of the standard incremental technique which is meant to remedy this shortcoming.

By declaring the lookup function on type environments as "incremental" a modification in the declaration of an identifier causes a re-check only of the statements and expressions in which this identifier actually occurs.

Initial Costs

Figure 6.19 shows the initial cost for fine-grain incremental reduction and compares it to the cost for non-incremental reduction and standard incremental reduction.

Description of the Test In the test specification the typecheck functions tcp, tcdecls, tcstms, tcstm, tcexp as well as lookup were declared "incremental."

Again we used example programs with 10 declarations and a various number of type correct assignments Id1 = Id2. The use of the 10 declared identifiers is spread evenly over the statements section.

Discussion We already mentioned in Section 6.9.1 that the number of rewrite steps for initial coarse-grain incremental typechecking equals the number of rewrite steps for non-incremental typechecking. Fine-grain incremental typechecking takes less steps due to the fact that the normal form of each "lookup Tenv for Id" is stored in a function cache the first time it occurs. This normal form is used to avoid rewriting of later occurrences of this term.

When considering the time needed we notice that for small programs (less than about 15 assignments) the time for fine-grain reduction exceeds the time for standard incremental reduction. This is caused by the creation of an attribute dependency graph for the lookup function at a Type-environment for each first occurrence of an identifier in the statement section. Observe that in larger programs fine-grain reduction is even faster than non-incremental reduction.

Modifying the Declarations

Figure 6.20 compares the various strategies after changing the first declaration.

Description of the Test We used the same specification and programs as in the previous section. After a program had been checked, we modified the type of its first declaration and re-checked the program.

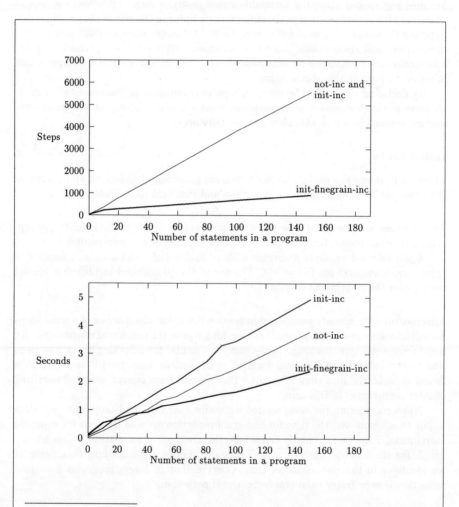

Figure 6.19: Cost of non-incremental (not-inc), coarse-grain incremental (init-inc) and fine-grain incremental (init-finegrain-inc) typechecking of programs without using previous results.

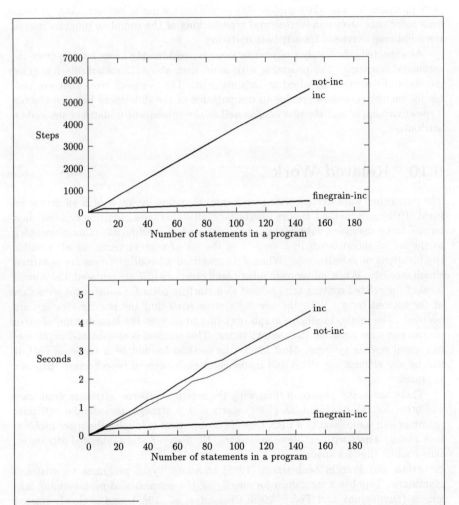

Figure 6.20: Cost of non-incremental (not-inc), coarse-grain incremental (inc) and fine-grain incremental (finegrain-inc) typechecking of programs after the type of one identifier has been modified.

Discussion After a modification in the declarations section, standard coarse-grain incremental reduction takes almost as many rewrite steps as typechecking the complete program, because the complete statements section has to be re-checked. It takes even more time than non-incremental typechecking of the complete program due to the additional overhead for attribute updating.

As expected, the number of rewrite steps is considerably lower for fine-grain incremental rewriting. For programs with more than about 15 statements fine-grain incremental rewriting is indeed an improvement. The overhead costs that are visible for smaller programs are due to computation of the differences between the old Type-environment and the new one, as well as the subsequent updates of the lookup attributes.

6.10 Related Work

The only other work dealing with incremental rewriting we know of is an article by Field (1993). His method applies to arbitrary left-linear term rewriting systems. In a term T to be rewritten, subterms can be designated as *substituends*. Complementary to the set of substituends in a term T is the set of context terms for all possible combinations of substituends. When T is rewritten all context terms are rewritten simultaneously. When subterms in substituend positions in T are replaced, the normal form of the related context term is used as a starting point for subsequent reduction of the altered term. Both the rewrite system itself and the rewrite strategy are adapted. The method relies on graph rewriting to prevent the introduction of extra rewrite steps for reducing the context terms. This method is elegant and applicable to general rewrite systems. Most likely (the method has not been implemented), it will be less efficient for PRSs and incremental evaluation of typecheckers than our approach.

There are many papers dealing with the relation between attribute grammars and other formalisms. Jourdan (1984) starts with a strongly non-circular attribute grammar and compiles it to a PRS. One of his objectives is to solve the space problem that usually arises with attribute grammars. He does not store inherited attributes, thus trading time for space.

Attali and Franchi-Zannettacci (1988) translate Typol programs to attribute grammars. Typol is a formalism for specifying the semantics of programming languages (Despeyroux and Théry, 1989; Clément *et al.*, 1985), and is closely related to Prolog. In order to make incremental and partial evaluation of Typol programs possible, pseudo-circular and strictly decreasing programs are translated into strongly non-circular attribute grammars written in either the Synthesizer Specification Language SSL (Reps and Teitelbaum, 1989a, 1989b) or in Olga, the input formalism of the FNC-2 system (Jourdan *et al.*, 1990; Jourdan and Parigot, 1991). In later papers, Attali and Chazarain (1990); Attali *et al.* (1992) use the relation between attribute grammars and Typol programs to determine a class of Typol programs for which functional evaluators based on pattern matching can be generated. An incremental implementation of these evaluators is based on an attribution of a proof tree. For pseudo-circular and strictly decreasing Typol programs a natural relation exists between parts of the abstract syntax tree of a program in the editor and parts of the corresponding proof tree. When the program is edited subproofs are replaced, and subsequent evaluation computes the values of the attributes of the new parts of the proof tree and all attributes depending on them.

Katayama (1984) describes how strongly non-circular attribute grammars can be translated to procedures, by considering non-terminals as functions mapping inherited attributes to synthesized attributes. He extends his method to general non-circular attribute grammars.

Pugh and Teitelbaum (1989) discuss how function caching can be used for incremental evaluation of attribute grammars that have been translated according to Katayama's scheme. In the resulting procedure, like in ours, the number of attributes that are re-evaluated after a subtree replacement is $O(|Affected| + |paths\_to\_root|)$. This is similar to our results, suggesting that we could just as well have applied function caching directly to our class of algebraic specifications. For efficient implementation of function caching two additional problems have to be solved, however. First, a way of storing function calls must be found, so that pending calls can be compared with entries in the cache in constant time, even when the function calls have large arguments. Secondly, techniques for purging the cache must be developed, so that it will not get filled up with old and useless information.

Pennings et al. (1992); Vogt et al. (1989); Vogt (1993) develop an incremental method for ordered attribute grammars, a subclass of strongly non-circular attribute grammars, based on function caching. In their approach multiple instances of the same tree are shared by means of memoized tree constructors. In this way, comparing function calls with entries in the cache reduces to simple pointer comparison. They do not address the problem of finding a satisfying purging method.

Unlike algebraic specifications, attribute grammars maintain a strict separation between the domains of syntax description and semantics description. In attempts to support aggregate values in attribute grammars either predefined data types are provided or the attribute grammar language is extended or it is combined with another formalism. Hoover and Teitelbaum (1986) describe how symbol tables can be dealt with efficiently in the Synthesizer Generator of Reps and Teitelbaum (1989a). A special class of *finite function* data types, is added to the specification language, and can be used to represent symbol tables. Predefined operations on the data type for construction, updating and lookup have an incremental implementation. In (Reps et al., 1986) the specification language is extended with a mechanism for defining tables and operations on tables. A special relation is defined between attributes whose values are defined by means of predefined table operations like creating, updating and looking up. Horwitz and Teitelbaum (1986) describe attributed grammars augmented with a relational database. Attribute equations can be used to construct and inspect relations Views on relations are updated incrementally.

Higher-order attribute grammars (HAGs) have been designed to remove the separation between the syntax description and the semantic description in attribute grammars (Vogt et al., 1989; Teitelbaum and Chapman, 1990). In implementing higher-order attribute grammars, Vogt et al. (1991); Vogt (1993) use, as we do, the principle of applying incremental methods for operations on programs and their substructures to operations on attributes. An incremental implementation for ordered higher-order attribute grammars is based on caching the results of visit functions for evaluating attributes (Kastens, 1980), rather than on storing attribute values in a tree. A visit function takes as its first parameter a tree and part of the inherited attributes of the root of that tree. It returns a subset of synthesized attributes. An immediate consequence of this is a memoization of attribute values at physically different trees with identical structure. In particular, the visiting results for a type-environment are cached and reused upon later visits to a copy of it. All trees with identical structure are shared. The memoization effect of the method is therefore stronger than ours. Attribute dependencies do not exist in the cache. Therefore there is no way to indentify parts of the tree that need not be visited if an attribute value turns out to be unchanged. If after a modification in the declarations the resulting type-environment has changed the complete statements section has to be revisited. However, re-evaluation of attributes that have not been affected by the change consists of retrieving the values from the cache.

In (van der Meulen, 1994) we present a translation of a *layered* PRS into a strongly non-circular HAG, as well as the translation of a strongly non-circular HAG into an algebraic specification (not necessarily a layered PRS).

6.11 Conclusions

We developed a technique for incremental rewriting for primitive recursive schemes and for layered primitive recursive schemes. It is based on storing normal forms in attributes of a parse tree, and is capable of dealing with multiple subtree replacements. Our point of departure is that the class of well-presented PRSs, like attribute grammars, is a very natural one for specifying the static semantics of languages. Almost all language specifications written in ASF+SDF have the flavor of a PRS, and most are easily transformed into one. Examples are the typechecking of Asple (van der Meulen, 1988), mini-ML (Hendriks, 1989), and Pascal as described in Chapter 2,

For algebraic specifications in the class of layered PRSs a fine-grain incremental implementation can be derived automatically with only small extensions to the algorithms for coarse-grain incremental rewriting. The fine-grain method provides an efficient implementation of functions like the lookup operation on symbol tables in a typechecker. Thus it repairs the common shortcoming that the basic, coarse-grain, incremental implementation presents when dealing with aggregate values.

The design of our algorithms for coarse-grain and fine-grain incremental rewriting has been influenced by our wish to be both efficient and to remain as close as possible to a standard rewrite strategy. The strategy for incremental rewriting can be thought of as leftmost-innermost rewriting with shortcuts and side-effects. The choice for an innermost strategy has been fortunate, since an outermost strategy would not provide such a clear visiting order for attributes. Moreover, it would be more complicated to keep track of the proper subtree in the attributed tree during reduction, and the propagation of status "TobeEvaluated" would have been more greedy.

The fact that our algorithms can handle multiple subtree replacements is relevant because the method has been implemented as part of the rewrite system of the ASF+SDF Meta-Environment. We wanted it to be such that a user can freely edit a program without being bothered by more or less expensive intermediate rewriting. Evaluation of functions applied to the program, takes place only on explicit request by the user.

Related to the previous point is that the algorithms have a *data driven* part and a *demand driven* part. In this it resembles the approach for lazy and incremental attribute updating as proposed by Hudson (1991). The data driven part is the status updating performed by PROPAGATE-TE-UP and is called after each edit action that causes a subtree replacement in the (attributed) abstract syntax tree of the text in the editor. Status propagation is expected to be a very fast operation. The re-evaluation of attributes is demand driven, because only attributes that are visited during rewriting of, for instance, a typecheck term are updated. A tree may be decorated with attributes for typechecking and attributes for compilation, and the user only wants to know the new typecheck value. Attributes for compilation are then not re-evaluated.

The price we pay for remaining close to a standard rewrite strategy is that the algorithm is not *optimal*. An algorithm is called optimal if the number of attributes that are re-evaluated after one ore more subtree replacements is $O(|Affected|)$, with *Affected* the set of attributes getting a new value during re-evaluation. Let *paths_to_root* be the set of attributes on the dependency path from a new subtree or an Affected attribute to the top. These attributes are visited before reduction by PROPAGATE-TE-UP. During reduction the *paths_to_root* attributes of Affected are visited by PROPAGATE-TE-UP if their status is not yet "TobeEvaluated". Consequently, the number of re-evaluated attributes is $O(|Affected| + |paths\_to\_root|)$

Fine-grain incremental rewriting has the same complexity as coarse-grain incremental rewriting. However, as shown by the typecheck example it is more effective. First, because of the memoization of lookup values, and, second, because attributes in the statements section depending on unchanged lookup values are marked as "Unchanged".

Measurements have shown that our incremental method is effective already when applied to medium-sized programs in which changes affecting up to 70 percent of the program are made. The optimization effect of fine-grain incrementality when typechecking new programs or programs in which declarations have been modified, has been convincingly demonstrated.

7

Origin Tracking and its Applications

Arie van Deursen
Paul Klint
Frank Tip

Abstract   Algebraic specifications of programming languages can be used to generate language-specific programming support tools. Tools can be obtained by executing these specifications as term rewriting systems. More advanced tools can be constructed if the term rewriting machinery is extended with *origin tracking*. Origin tracking is a technique which automatically establishes a relation between subterms of a result (normal form) or intermediate value, and their so-called *origins*, which are subterms of the initial term. Origin tracking can be used to associate positional information with messages in error reports, to visualize program execution, and to construct language-specific debuggers. This chapter gives detailed presentations of the definition, implementation, and applications of origin tracking.

7.1   Introduction

Term rewriting is a convenient technique to execute the algebraic language specifications as we encountered them in several chapters of this book. Is it, however, a sufficiently advanced technique? Do we extract the best possible tools from the specifications if all we do is a simple reduction of a term to its normal form?

In this chapter we study a particular technique which aims at generating significantly more sophisticated tools from algebraic language specifications. The underlying idea of this technique, called *origin tracking*,[1] is that we can derive better tools if we have a better understanding *how* the initial term was reduced to its normal form.

---

[1]The notion of origin tracking is *not* related to the origin rule for sort and function symbols in ASF+SDF specifications as discussed in (Bergstra *et al.*, 1989, Section 1.1.7).

Which rewrite rules were used? Which new function symbols were created by which rule? For a single reduction step, were there any subterms occurring in the redex that literally recur in the contractum? And how are subterms propagated over multiple reduction steps?

Answers to questions like these will be given by the *origin tracking* technique. For a reduction $t \to^* t'$, it aims at establishing a relation between a subterm s' of the result t', and subterms s — the *origins* of s' — of the initial term t. The reasons for studying these relations are of an application-oriented nature. We are in particular seeking solutions to the following three problems:

- Associating positional information with messages in error reports.

  In Chapter 2, we studied a specification of the static semantics of Pascal. Executing this specification using plain term rewriting just yields normal forms representing error messages. Can we use the same specification to obtain a typechecker that also indicates *where* in the Pascal program the source of the error is?

- Visualizing program execution.

  A specification of the dynamic semantics of a language, e.g., an operational semantics, can be executed using plain rewriting in order to obtain an evaluator of the language in question. Can we use the same specification to obtain an *animator* for that language, i.e., an evaluator which indicates the statement that is currently being executed in some distinctive way?

- Constructing language-specific debuggers.

  A specification of a translation between a programming language and an assembly language can be executed using term rewriting in order to get a prototype compiler. If we detect an error while running the compiled program, we would like to perform debugging activities (setting breakpoints, inspecting values of variables) in terms of the *source* program rather than in those of the assembly language. Can we use the translation specification to generate such a source-level debugger?

Origin tracking is the way to find a positive answer to these three questions. In this chapter, the principles of origin tracking are presented. After discussing related work and giving a general introduction in the current section, we proceed to give the full definition of origins in Section 7.2. After extending these for *conditional* rewriting in Section 7.3, we discuss various applications in Section 7.4. After that, we discuss two extensions of the basic origin tracking approach: we first present an origin scheme specialized for inductively defined functions in Section 7.5; subsequently, in Section 7.6 we study a notion related to origins tailored towards program slicing applications. We conclude by discussing implementational issues in Section 7.7.

The current chapter discusses origins for first-order conditional rewrite systems. In Chapter 8, higher-order term rewriting systems are introduced, and the corresponding extension of origin tracking can be found in Chapter 9.

7.1.1 Bibliographic Notes

The study of origins was pioneered by Bertot (1990, 1992, 1993). He investigated applications of origin tracking to source-level debugging given a specification in *Natural Semantics* style (Kahn, 1987; Bertot, 1990). Furthermore, he considered the relation between origins for the λ-calculus and for TRSs, and introduced a formal framework for reasoning about origin functions. He focused on orthogonal, unconditional TRSs, where an origin consists of at most one subterm occurrence.

In the theory developed for term rewriting systems, relations between the subterms of an initial term and those of the normal form, have been studied before. Such relations are used in the search for optimal reduction strategies, i.e., strategies that indicate which redex to contract in order to minimize the total number of reduction steps (Huet and Lévy, 1991; Maranget, 1991). So-called *residual maps*, or *descendant relations* are used to keep track of subterm recurrences, and in particular of *redex* recurrences. The origin relation is an extension of these ideas.

The effect obtained automatically from using the origins proposed in Section 7.5 is very similar to that of *subject tracking* in the implementation of the specification language TYPOL (Kahn, 1987; Despeyroux, 1988). TYPOL is a formalism supporting the aforementioned Natural Semantics to define programming languages. A TYPOL judgement is typically defined inductively over the syntax of the language. During execution, the TYPOL implementation maintains a global variable, *subject*, which contains the construct currently being processed. This variable can be used by external tools for such applications as animation and highlighting of error locations. If the TYPOL specification is not purely inductively defined, the special *with-subject* construct can be used to reset the subject.

One of the aims of our origin tracking technique is to produce, in a term rewriting framework, error messages with accurate location information associated with it. In attribute grammars (AGs, see Chapter 6), error messages typically correspond to attributes of type string. The error position is identified by printing the message close to the text position of the grammar node the attribute belongs to. In the Synthesizer Generator (Reps and Teitelbaum, 1989b) unparsing (prettyprinting) rules can be given to indicate where the error message should be printed. If there is no error, the message attribute contains the invisible empty string.

In order to compare this with origin tracking, consider an identifier x of type char in an arithmetic expression like -x, causing a message like `integer instead of char expected`. In an AG approach, this message will be associated with the - node, which gives useful information. In our approach, the message can have origins to (1) the position where the type inconsistency was detected which is the - node as in AGs, (2) the place where x was declared of type `char`, and (3) the actual position where x was used erroneously. Typically, the signature for error messages will include a "_ instead of _ expected" symbol, and origins are associated with both the function and the two arguments.

Although not intended for this purpose, origin tracking could be used to enhance error location in AGs as well, provided the attribute evaluation mechanism is in one way or another based on term rewriting.

The line of research pursued in this chapter was started by van Deursen *et al.* (1993). The applicability of the origin tracking techniques to error location and animation is studied in detail by Dinesh (1993), of which an updated version can be found in this book in Chapter 4, and in (Tip, 1993, 1995b). A notion of origins tailored towards typecheckers and translators as formalized by primitive recursive schemes was proposed by van Deursen (1994b), and is discussed in this book in Section 7.5. The use of an origin-like relation, *dynamic dependence tracking*, for purposes of *program slicing* is covered by Field and Tip (1994); Field *et al.* (1995); Tip (1995c, 1995a), and is summarized in this chapter in Section 7.6. The extension to higher-order term rewriting systems, finally, was first presented by van Deursen and Dinesh (1994), and is discussed in this book in Chapter 9.

7.1.2 Origin Tracking in a Nutshell

Before diving into the details of origin tracking, let us try to obtain an understanding of how origin tracking works. Consider a reduction of a term t_0 to t_n, in a sequence of rewrite steps $t_0 \rightarrow t_1 \rightarrow \cdots \rightarrow t_n$. During such a reduction, we annotate every function symbol occurring in some t_i ($0 \leq i \leq n$) with a set of *occurrences* in the initial term t_0. An occurrence identifies a subterm, and consists of a path from the root to that subterm (an occurrence is a sort of *pointer* or (tree) *address*).

Defining an origin function amounts to describing how origin annotations are affected by each rewrite step $t_i \rightarrow t_{i+1}$ ($0 \leq i < n$). In such a rewrite step, a certain rewrite rule $\alpha \rightarrow \beta$ is applied at a particular occurrence in t_i (the *redex* position). It is below this occurrence that the actual changes in t_i take place; above or next to this redex position (i.e., in the *context*) the term does not change. Therefore, origin annotations in the context simply remain the same. These origins are called *Context Origins*.

The redex part of t_i is changed by $\alpha \rightarrow \beta$ to a new term, the *contractum*. The answer to the question which origins to establish for this contractum is given by an analysis of the rewrite rule. Recall that for a rule $\alpha \rightarrow \beta$ the variables occurring in β must occur in α as well. In other words, every subterm corresponding to a variable occurrence at the right-hand side must occur in the left-hand side. Therefore, we establish relationships between all variable occurrences in the right-hand side, and their counterparts in the left-hand side. These origins are called origins for *Common Variables*.

A picture may help to clarify this. Figure 7.1 shows a single-step reduction. The term

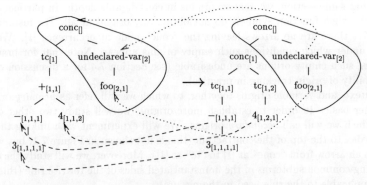

Context: conc($\square$, undeclared-var(foo))
Rewrite rule: tc($E_1 + E_2$) → conc(tc(E_1), tc(E_2))
Substitution: $\{E_1 \mapsto -3, \ E_2 \mapsto 4\}$

Dashed Lines: Origins for Common Variables
Dotted Lines: Context Origins.

The occurrence leading to a function symbol is given as
a subscript of that symbol: for instance, taking the first
son of the second son of the leftmost term leads to "foo",
which is at occurrence [2,1].

Figure 7.1: Origins established for a single rewrite step.

$$\text{conc(tc}(-3 + 4), \text{undeclared-var(foo))}$$

is rewritten to

$$\text{conc(conc(tc}(-3), \text{tc}(4)), \text{undeclared-var(foo))}$$

These two terms are shown in the figure in tree-representation. The context of this
reduction is the term "conc($\square$, undeclared-var(foo))". In the figure, this context
is enclosed in a pear-formed shape for both terms. The origins are indicated by the
arrows. The dotted arrows correspond to origins in the context of the reduction; they
simply point to the same occurrence in the left term. The dashed arrows correspond
to Common Variables. For instance, the two lines from "−" and "3" correspond to
the value (instantiation) of the variable E_1 in the rewrite rule.

In the next section, we make origins more precise by replacing them by sets of
occurrences. The origin associated with the "4" symbol at occurrence $[1, 2, 1]$ at the
right will then become the set $\{[1, 1, 2]\}$.

In that same section, we analyze origins in considerable depth. In particular, we will study when function symbols do not obtain any origins at all. For instance, in Figure 7.1 there are no arrows leaving the "conc" node at occurrence [1]. We will discuss under which conditions such empty origins appear. Note that for practical purposes, such empty origins are undesirable (see Section 7.4 for a discussion of the applicability of origin tracking in practice).

Context- and variable origins together, to which we will refer as *primary* origins, are rather basic. In order to establish more origins, we will study two other origin rules, which we will call *secondary* origins. We will experiment with linking the top of the redex to the top of the contractum (this is not shown in Figure 7.1, but would result in an arrow from "conc" at [1] to "tc" at [1]). Moreover, we will study the effect of relating common subterms of the uninstantiated sides of the rewrite rule (this case is not applicable to the rule used in the picture).

This latter rule may in some cases build unintended relations, for instance between two constants that just happen to occur at both the left- and right-hand side. It will usually be no coincidence that such a common subterm occurs in both sides, however. One of the motivating examples is a rule typically used in a description of the operational semantics of the while statement:

eval-stat(while(E, S), ρ) $\rightarrow$ eval-stat(while(E, S), eval-stat(S, ρ))
when eval-exp(E, ρ) $\rightarrow$ true

The Common Subterms rule identifies "while(E,S)" as a subterm common to both sides of the rewrite rule, and therefore establishes a link between the function symbol, i.e., the "while" symbol, occurring in this common subterm.

7.2   Defining the Origin Function

7.2.1   Preliminaries

In order to make the notion of relations between subterms more precise, we need *occurrences* (paths). An occurrence is either equal to the empty sequence [ ] representing the access path to the root, i.e., the entire term, or to a sequence of integers $[n_1, \ldots, n_m]$ ($m \geq 1$) representing the access path to a proper subterm. Occurrence [1, 2], for example, denotes the second son of the first son of the root, i.e., for term $f(g(a, b), c)$ it denotes subterm b. The subterm of t at occurrence u is written t/u. Occurrences are concatenated by the (associative) $\cdot$-operator. If u, v, w are occurrences and $u = v \cdot w$, then v is *above* u, written $v \preceq u$. Also, if $w \neq []$ then we write $v \prec u$. If neither $v \preceq u$ nor $u \preceq v$ then u and v are *disjoint*, written $u \mid v$. The set of all occurrences in a term t is denoted by $\mathcal{O}(t)$. Subsets of these are $\mathcal{O}_{var}(t)$ for the occurrences of variables in t, and $\mathcal{O}_{fun}(t)$ for the occurrences of function (or constant) symbols in t. The number of elements in a set O of occurrences is written $|O|$.

When we wish to identify the redex occurrence, substitution, and rule of a reduction explicitly, we write $t \xrightarrow{u, \sigma}_r t'$ for the one-step rewrite relation, indicating that rule

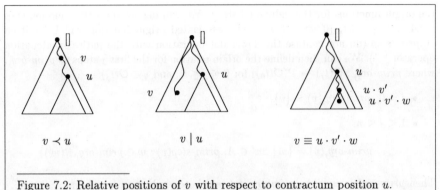

Figure 7.2: Relative positions of v with respect to contractum position u.

r is applied at occurrence u in term t under substitution σ. For multi-step reductions $t_0 \to t_1 \to \cdots \to t_n$ we also write $t_0 \to^* t_n$ $(n \geq 0)$.

Finally, we will write $s \subseteq t$ if s is a subterm of t. Moreover, we require that for each rewrite rule $r : \alpha \to \beta$, every variable occurring in β also occurs in α.

7.2.2 Primary Origins

Let $t \xrightarrow{u,\sigma}_r t'$, where r is a rule $\alpha \to \beta$, be a single reduction step. With each step we associate a function $prim\text{-}step : \mathcal{O}(t') \to \mathcal{P}(\mathcal{O}(t))$ mapping occurrences in t' to sets of occurrences in t (here $\mathcal{P}(S)$ denotes the powerset of S). Let $v \in \mathcal{O}(t')$. We define $prim\text{-}step(v)$ by distinguishing the following cases (see also Figure 7.2):

- (Context)

  If $v \prec u$ or $v \mid u$ then $prim\text{-}step(v) = \{v\}$;

- (Common Variables)

  If $v = u \cdot v' \cdot w$ with $v' \in \mathcal{O}_{var}(\beta)$ the occurrence of some variable X in the right-hand side β of r, and $w \in \mathcal{O}(X^\sigma)$ an occurrence in the instantiation of that variable, then

  $$prim\text{-}step(v) = \{u \cdot v'' \cdot w \mid v'' \in \mathcal{O}_{var}(\alpha),\ \alpha/v'' \equiv X\}$$

  (Note that $v'' \in \mathcal{O}_{var}(\alpha)$ is an occurrence of X in the left-hand side α of r);

- (Otherwise)

  For all other cases $prim\text{-}step(v) = \emptyset$.

The function $prim\text{-}step$ covers single reduction steps. It is generalized to a function $prim\text{-}org^*$ for multi-step reductions $t_0 \to t_1 \to \cdots \to t_n$ $(n \geq 0)$ by considering the origin functions for the individual steps. We will denote the i-th reduction step as $A_i : t_{i-1} \to t_i$ $(0 < i \leq n)$. The associated origin function will be written $A_i.prim\text{-}step$ (do not confuse this lower dot operation with the path concatenation operator "$\cdot$"). We can then define the origin relation for the first j steps as $prim\text{-}org_j$, where $prim\text{-}org_j : \mathcal{O}(t_j) \to \mathcal{P}(\mathcal{O}(t_0))$ for $0 \leq j \leq n$, and $v \in \mathcal{O}(t_j)$:

- $j = 0$: $prim\text{-}org_j(v) = \{v\}$.

- $1 \leq j \leq n$:

$$prim\text{-}org_j(v) = \{w \mid \exists w' \in A_j.prim\text{-}step(v) : w \in prim\text{-}org_{j-1}(w')\}$$

Then $prim\text{-}org^*$ is equal to $prim\text{-}org_n$ for multi-step reduction $t_0 \to^* t_n$.

Given a multi-step reduction $A : t_0 \to t_n$, with associated function $A.prim\text{-}org^*$ and occurrence $u \in \mathcal{O}(t_n)$, the set $O = A.prim\text{-}org^*(u)$ is called *the origin set* of t_n/u, and the elements of O are called *the origins* of t_n/u. Often it is natural to relax the difference between sets and elements. If no confusion is possible, we might, for example, use "subterm s has an origin" to indicate that the origin set of s is non-empty, and "subterm s has multiple origins" to indicate that the origin set of s contains more than one occurrence.

7.2.3   Properties of Primary Origins

In the following properties, let $A : t_0 \to^* t_n$ $(n \geq 0)$ be a multi-step reduction over TRS R. We will not require that t_n is a normal form, so t_n can represent any term occurring in a reduction. We will closely consider the origin function for A, for which we will write $A.prim\text{-}org^*$. We will use an occurrence $v \in \mathcal{O}(t_n)$ in the last term t_n, and its origin $o \in A.prim\text{-}org^*(v) \subseteq \mathcal{O}(t_0)$.

Primary origins are very similar to the better-known *residuals* or *descendants* (Huet and Lévy, 1991), which are used to study the survival of redexes during reductions over so-called *orthogonal* TRSs (left-linear and non-overlapping (Klop, 1992)). We keep track of *all* terms: redexes as well as irreducible subterms. Therefore, we have:

Property 7.1 *Assume R is* orthogonal. *Let $\backslash A$ be Huet and Lévy's residual mapping for reduction A. Then $v \in o\backslash A \Rightarrow o \in A.prim\text{-}org^*(v)$.*

Proof: Immediate from the similarities between the definition of $prim\text{-}step$ (Section 7.2.2) and residual maps (Huet and Lévy, 1991, Definition 2.1). □

For left-linear TRSs, we can say something about the size of the origin sets:

Property 7.2 *Assume R is* left-linear. *Then for every $v \in \mathcal{O}(t_n)$ we have $0 \leq |A.prim\text{-}org^*(v)| \leq 1$.*

Proof: The Context case and Otherwise case cannot introduce origin sets containing more than one origin. The Common Variables case can only yield more than one occurrence if there is a rule $\alpha \to \beta$ using a variable X in β for which there are at least two occurrences $v', v'' \in \mathcal{O}(\alpha)$ with $v' \neq v''$ and $X \equiv \alpha/v' \equiv \alpha/v''$. By left-linearity this cannot happen. $\qquad\square$

For arbitrary TRSs, we can only state that the number of elements in origin sets is bound by the number of nodes in the initial term:

Property 7.3 *For every $v \in \mathcal{O}(t_n)$ we have $0 \leq |A.prim\text{-}org^*(v)| \leq |\mathcal{O}(t_0)|$.*

Proof: Trivial, as the range of $A.prim\text{-}org^*$ is $\mathcal{P}(\mathcal{O}(t_0))$, the elements of which are sets containing at most $|\mathcal{O}(t_0)|$ occurrences. $\qquad\square$

Now consider a subterm occurring in an origin set. If a subterm $s_n \subseteq t_n$ has a subterm $s_0 \subseteq t_0$ as one of its origins, then s_0 can be rewritten to s_n, in zero (syntactic equality) or more steps.

Property 7.4 *For every $o \in A.prim\text{-}org^*(v)$ we have $t_0/o \to^* t_n/v$.*

Proof: By induction on the length n of reduction A.

- If $n = 0$, then $A.prim\text{-}org^*(v) = \{v\}$ for every $v \in \mathcal{O}(t_n)$. So $v = o$ and $t_0 \equiv t_n$, hence $t_0/o \to^* t_n/v$.

- Now assume $n > 0$, and consider reduction $A : t \to^* t_{n-1} \to t_n$.

  We will prove that for every $v_n \in \mathcal{O}(t_n)$ and $v_{n-1} \in A_n.prim\text{-}step(t_n)$ we have either $t_{n-1}/v_{n-1} \to t_n/v_n$ or $t_{n-1}/v_{n-1} \equiv t_n/v_n$.

  We will do so by considering the rule $r : \alpha \to \beta$ applied at step $t_{n-1} \to t_n$, and the position u of the redex in t_{n-1}.

  We will distinguish three cases, depending on how this redex position u is related to v_n:

  - If $v_n \mid u$ then $prim\text{-}step(v_n) = \{v_n\}$ (Context case). As $v_n \mid u$, v_n is independent of this reduction step, and $t_{n-1}/v_n \equiv t_n/v$.

  - If $v_n \prec u$, then again $prim\text{-}step(v_n) = \{v_n\}$ (the Context case again). In this case, v_n is right above the reduction position u. But that means $t_{n-1}/v_n \to t_n/v_n$.

  - If $u \preceq v_n$, then we are within the contractum, for which only the Common Variables case is non-empty. Therefore, assume $v_n = u \cdot v' \cdot w$, where $v' \in \mathcal{O}_{var}(\beta)$ denotes a variable X occurring in the right-hand side. Pick an arbitrary $v'' \in \mathcal{O}_{var}(\alpha)$ such that $\alpha/v'' \equiv X$ (there must be at least one). Then $u \cdot v'' \cdot w \in prim\text{-}step(v)$, which denotes a syntactically equivalent term in the instantiation of X. Hence, $t_{n-1}/u \cdot v'' \cdot w \equiv t_n/u \cdot v' \cdot w$. $\qquad\square$

A careful inspection of the above proof leads to the following property. Let $top(t)$ denote the top symbol f where $t \equiv f(s_1, \cdots s_k)$, $(k \geq 0)$, for terms $s_1, \cdots, s_k$.

Property 7.5 *For every $o \in A.prim\text{-}org^*(v)$ we have $top(t_n/v) = top(t_0/o)$.*

Proof: Similar to the proof of Property 7.4. For the induction step, the cases $v \mid u$ and $u \preceq v$ are trivial, as the terms related by the single origin step, t_{n-1}/v and t_n/v, and $t_{n-1}/u \cdot v'' \cdot w$ and $t_n/u \cdot v \cdot w$ respectively, are syntactically equal and therefore have the same top-symbol. For the $v \prec u$ case, the terms reduce to each other, $t_{n-1}/v \rightarrow t_n/v$, but the reduction takes place strictly below v, so the top-symbols of t_{n-1}/v and t_n/v remain the same. □

We can rephrase this to identify origins that are always empty:

Property 7.6 $A.prim\text{-}org^*(v) = \emptyset$ *if $top(t_n/v)$ is not used in t_0.*

Proof: Immediate from Property 7.5. □

In other words, so-called *created* function symbols, i.e., those introduced during rewriting and not yet part of the initial term always obtain the empty origin (that is, for the primary origins).

Moreover, in practice Property 7.4 will be slightly stronger: Often we will have $t_0/o \equiv t_n/v$ rather than the weaker $t_0/o \rightarrow^* t_n/v$. In particular, this is the case for subterms which are themselves in normal form already. These are simply passed as variable instantiations from the initial term to the result term.

Finally, observe that the converse of Property 7.6 does not hold in general. If a symbol f is used in t_0, then a subterm of the result with top symbol f can still have an empty origin (i.e., the actual occurrence of f in t_n is *created*, not propagated).

7.2.4   Secondary Origins

We extend the definition of primary origins to that of secondary origins by including the redex-contractum and common subterms cases.

Proceeding in the same spirit as before, with reduction step $t \xrightarrow{u,\sigma}_r t'$, where r is a rule $\alpha \rightarrow \beta$, we will associate three more functions with each step, *comm-sub-step*, *redex-contr-step*, and *sec-step*, all mapping occurrences from $\mathcal{O}(t')$ to sets of occurrences from $\mathcal{P}(\mathcal{O}(t))$.

For $v \in \mathcal{O}(t')$, we define *comm-sub-step(v)* as follows:

- (Common Subterms)

  If $v = u \cdot v'$ with $v' \in \mathcal{O}_{fun}(\beta)$ the occurrence of a function symbol (or constant) in the right-hand side β of r, then

$$comm\text{-}sub\text{-}step(v) = \{u \cdot v'' \mid \alpha/v'' \equiv \beta/v'\}$$

  Note that common subterms are extracted from the *uninstantiated* sides α and β. In all other cases $comm\text{-}sub\text{-}step(v) = \emptyset$.

- (Redex-Contractum)

$$redex\text{-}contr\text{-}step(v) = \begin{cases} \{v\} & \text{if } v = u \\ \emptyset & \text{otherwise} \end{cases}$$

- (Secondary Origins)

$$sec\text{-}step(v) = prim\text{-}step(v) \cup comm\text{-}sub\text{-}step(v) \cup redex\text{-}contr\text{-}step(v)$$

The function *sec-step* can be extended to *sec-org**, in a way similar to the generalization of *prim-step* to *prim-org**.

7.2.5 Properties of Secondary Origins

Again, let $A : t_0 \to^* t_n$ $(n \geq 0)$ be a multi-step reduction for a TRS R. Moreover, let $o \in \mathcal{O}(t_0)$ and $v \in \mathcal{O}(t_n)$, and let $A.sec\text{-}org^*$ be the secondary origin function associated with A.

Because of the Redex-Contractum case, we need to consider the right-hand side β of a rule $r : \alpha \to \beta$ a little closer.

Definition 7.7 *Rule r is said to be a* variable-collapse *rule if β consists of a single variable. Rule r is said to be a* term-collapse *rule if $\beta \subseteq \alpha$, i.e., if the entire right-hand side is contained in the left-hand side.*

Note that a variable-collapse rule is a special case of a term collapse rule, because the single variable at the right has to occur in α by the definition of a TRS. A TRS without term-collapse rules is called *non-term-collapsing*.

Moreover, because of the Common Subterms case, we need to classify rules according to their left-hand sides. Recall that a term is *linear* if it does not contain multiple occurrences of the same variable.

Definition 7.8 *A term is* term-linear *if it does not contain multiple occurrences of the same subterm. A TRS consisting only of rules whose left-hand sides are term-linear is called* left-term-linear.

Using these definitions, we can characterize unique origins:

Property 7.9 *Assume R is non-term-collapsing and left-term-linear. Then for every $v \in \mathcal{O}(t_n)$ we have $0 \leq |A.sec\text{-}org^*(v)| \leq 1$.*

Proof: First, since R is non-term-collapsing, the functions *prim-step*, *comm-sub-step*, and *redex-contr-step* cover disjoint cases, i.e., at most one of them is applicable, and hence at most one of them is non-empty. Second, each of them yields at most one origin: *prim-step* because of Property 7.2, *comm-sub-step* since R is left-term-linear, and *redex-contr-step* as it yields, by definition, either $\emptyset$ or a singleton set. □

Property 7.4 remains valid for secondary origins:

Property 7.10 *For every $o \in A.sec\text{-}org^*(v)$ we have $t_0/o \to^* t_n/v$.*

Proof: Along the same lines as the proof of Property 7.4. For the $u \preceq v$ case, we have to make a further distinction for the Redex-Contractum case (for which we obviously have $t_{n-1}/v \to t_n/v$) and the Common Subterms case (for which we have $t_{n-1}/u \cdot v'' \equiv t_n/u \cdot v'$). □

Finally, we will characterize the conditions under which origins are empty. To that end, let us study when a subterm s with top-symbol f is *not* empty:

- The Context or Common Variables case (see also Property 7.6) is applicable when a copy of s is passed from the initial term to the final term; or

- The Redex-Contractum case is used to give f an origin when it occurs as the top-symbol of the right-hand side of some equation; or

- The Redex-Contractum case is used to give f an origin when f is part of the instantiation of a variable, and the right-hand side of the rule consists of just that variable (a collapse rule); or

- The Common Subterms rule is used for a subterm containing s.

To formalize this we need the following notions:

Definition 7.11 *A rewrite rule $r : \alpha \to \beta$ is*

1. *creating f if function symbol f is used in β if and only if it is not used in α;*

2. *re-creating f if function symbol f is used as top of a subterm $s \subseteq \beta$ if and only if $s \subseteq \alpha$.*

Definition 7.12 *A TRS R is top-preserving in f if: every rule $r : \alpha \to \beta$ in R meets the following requirements:*

1. *Function symbol f does not occur as the top symbol of the right-hand side of any rule in R;*

2. *R contains no variable-collapse rules;*

3. *Either all rules in R are creating f; or all rules in R are re-creating f.*

Lemma 7.13 *Let $B : t \to t'$ be a single reduction step in a TRS that is top-preserving in f. Let $w' \in \mathcal{O}(t')$ such that $top(t'/w') = f$. Then for every $w \in B.sec\text{-}step(w')$ we have $top(t/w) = f$.*

Proof: Consider the three constituents of *sec-step*:

- If w' obtains an origin from *prim-step*, then w must point to the same top-symbol f by Property 7.6.

- Rule *comm-sub-step* is only applicable to TRSs that are re-creative. Requirement 3 ensures that either all rules are re-creating f, in which case we have $top(t/w) = f$, or creating f, in which case *comm-sub-step* will not result in an origin for w'.

- w' cannot get an origin from *redex-contr-step*, because at the contractum occurrence the function symbol cannot be f: not as part of an instantiation because of requirement 2; and not as part of the right-hand side because of requirement 1.

$\square$

Property 7.14 *Let f be a function symbol occurring in t_n at occurrence v. $A.sec\text{-}org^*(v) = \emptyset$ if R is top-preserving in f, and f does not occur in t_0.*

Proof: By induction on the length n of reduction A.

- Base case, $n = 0$: As f cannot be both part of term t_n and not part of t_0 if $t_n \equiv t_0$ the condition is always false and the property holds.

- Assume $n > 0$, let $A_{n-1} : t_0 \to^* t_{n-1}$, and let $A_n : t_{n-1} \to t_n$. The induction hypothesis is $A_{n-1}.sec\text{-}org^*(v_{n-1}) = \emptyset$ for every v_{n-1} with $top(t_{n-1}/v_{n-1}) = f$.

  We have to prove that for every $v_{n-1} \in A_n.sec\text{-}step(v)$ we have $top(t_{n-1}/v_{n-1}) = f$. But this follows immediately from Lemma 7.13.

$\square$

Again, the converse does not hold: systems that are both creative and re-creating f may have empty origins as well.

When switching to a *sorted* rewrite system, we can weaken requirement 2 of Definition 7.12 (no collapse rules) to the restriction that there are no collapse rules for variables with the same output-sort as function symbol f.

Note that this last property again states a fact for *created* symbols, i.e., symbols not occurring in the initial term. It states that a created symbol f will be empty if the TRS is top-preserving in f. In Section 7.4 we will discuss the relevance of this property for specifications occurring in practice, and see to what extent empty origins are desirable.

7.3 Conditional Rewrite Rules

Conditional rewrite rules are used to execute conditional equations (Bergstra and Klop, 1986; Klop, 1992). As conditional equations occur very frequently in realistic specifications, and as origin tracking aims at supporting the generation of better tools for realistic specifications, an extension to conditional rewriting is mandatory.

7.3.1 Preliminaries

A conditional rewrite rule takes the form

$$\frac{s_1 \Box t_1, \cdots, s_n \Box t_n}{s_0 \to t_0}$$

with $n \geq 0$, and s_i, t_i $(0 \leq i \leq n)$ terms. We will consider two possibilities for $s \Box t$, namely $s \downarrow_! t$ denoting that s and t reduce to the same normal form, and $s := t$ denoting that the normal form of t matches the pattern s. Conditions using $\downarrow_!$ are called *join*-conditions; those using $:=$ *match*-conditions. We will assume that rewriting in conditions is terminating and confluent.

We will impose the following restrictions on variables (see also (Walters, 1991, p.16), (Hendriks, 1991, p.36)). Let $vars(t)$ be the set of variables used in term t. For a conditional rewrite rule, inductively define V_i $(0 \leq i \leq n)$:

- $V_0 = vars(s_0)$;

- $V_{i+1} = vars(s_{i+1}) \cup V_i$

Now for each condition $s_j \Box t_j$ $(1 \leq j \leq n)$ the following restrictions apply:

- If $s_j \Box t_j$ is a *join*-condition, then $vars(s_j) \subseteq V_{j-1}$ and $vars(t_j) \subseteq V_{j-1}$. In other words, a join condition should not introduce new variables.

- If $s_j \Box t_j$ is a *match*-condition, then $vars(t_j) \subseteq V_{j-1}$, i.e., t_j should not introduce new variables. Moreover, $vars(s_j) \cap V_{j-1} = \emptyset$, i.e., the left-hand side should only contain variables that have not occurred so far.

Finally, we require $vars(t_0) \subseteq V_n$, i.e., the right-hand side should only use variables introduced earlier in conditions or in the left-hand side s_0.

A small example of two conditional rewrite rules is given in Figure 7.3. The first two equations are match-conditions, used to unpack the elements P_1 and P_2, which are pairs consisting of a key and an information field. The third condition uses two variables assigned in the first and the second condition in order to decide whether to insert element P_1 before or after P_2. Although not shown, the right-hand sides of both conclusions are allowed to use variables $Key_{\{1,2\}}$ and $Info_{\{1,2\}}$ as well.

7.3.2 Conditional Origins

As for the unconditional case, origins are defined by focusing on a single reduction step, which can now include subreductions needed to check the conditions. If we are only interested in origins from the normal form to the initial term, and if we only have join-conditions, these subreductions are irrelevant for the origins to be computed; the definition of the previous section directly applies.

$$\text{pair}(Key_1, Info_1) := P_1,$$
$$\text{pair}(Key_2, Info_2) := P_2,$$
$$\text{greater}(Key_1, Key_2) \downarrow_! \text{true}$$

$$\text{insert}(P_1, \text{cons}(P_2, L)) \rightarrow \text{cons}(P_2, \text{insert}(P_1, L))$$

$$\text{pair}(Key_1, Info_1) := P_1,$$
$$\text{pair}(Key_2, Info_2) := P_2,$$
$$\text{less-eq}(Key_1, Key_2) \downarrow_! \text{true}$$

$$\text{insert}(P_1, \text{cons}(P_2, L)) \rightarrow \text{cons}(P_1, \text{cons}(P_2, L))$$

Figure 7.3: Conditional rules inserting elements in increasing order in a list.

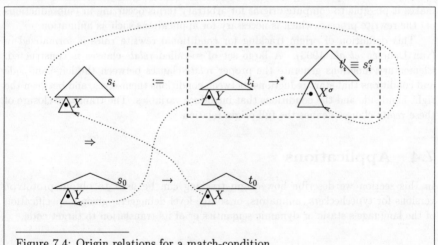

Figure 7.4: Origin relations for a match-condition.

If we also admit match-conditions, we must take subreductions into account. For example, assume the right-hand side t_0 uses a variable X not occurring in the left-hand side s_0, but which is assigned a value by one of the match-conditions $s_i := t_i (1 \leq i \leq n)$. Then we need to compute origins involved in the normalization of t_i.

The origins for the subreduction $t_i \rightarrow^* t_i'$ itself can be computed just as if it were a self-contained reduction. This gives an origin relation between t_i' and t_i. In order to relate it to the left-hand side s_0, Common Subterms and Common Variables relations between s_0 and the initial term t_i of the subreduction can be established.

The last step consists of linking the right-hand side t_0 to the normalized condition side t_i'. This link is made via the introducing condition side s_i. The link between t_0 and s_i can again follow the Common Subterms and Common Variables relations. As s_i and t_i' are syntactically equal under the matching substitution needed to check condition $s_i := t_i$, these can be related by an identity map.

The full sequence of relations is illustrated in Figure 7.4. Starting in the right-hand side t_0, the dotted line can be followed to condition side s_i (finding Common Variable X). Continuing there, we reach the identical position for the instantiated X in the normalized side t_i'. From here we follow origins to the term t_i starting the subreduction. From that initial term we finally reach left-hand side s_0 (finding Common Variable Y).

This picture can be extended to an arbitrary number of match-conditions. This mainly involves extra administration indicating where each variable is introduced (either in the left-hand side or in a match-condition). Moreover, we can use the same techniques to compute origins for subreductions occurring in join-conditions. This makes it possible to compute origins for arbitrary terms occurring in (subreductions of) the rewrite process, which is necessary for applications such as animation.

This definition of origin tracking for conditional rewrite rules is formalized in (van Deursen *et al.*, 1993). A large set of so-called *relate*-clauses is constructed. Elementary functions generate the proper *relate*-clauses between the left-hand side and conditions that start reductions, between conditions themselves, and between the right-hand side and the conditions that introduce variables. The transitive closure of these *relate*-clauses defines the full origin relation.

7.4 Applications

In this section we describe how origin tracking can be used to obtain prototype versions for typecheckers, animators, or source-level debuggers, given a specification of the language's static or dynamic semantics or of its translation to target code.

7.4.1 Improving Error Messages

Error handling is the most straight-forward application of origin tracking. A language developer describes the static semantics as a mapping from the language's abstract

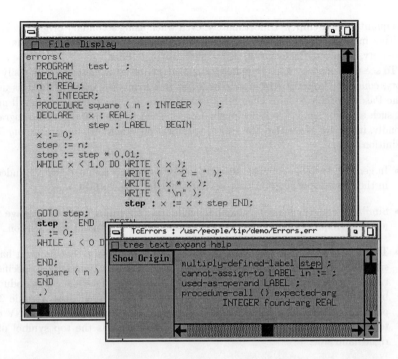

Figure 7.5: Example of a generated environment using origin tracking.

syntax to some domain of error values. Term rewriting is used to execute this specification, which gives a basic tool that can produce a list of error messages indicating *what* is wrong in a program. If term rewriting with origin tracking is used, the error messages are annotated with sets of occurrences in the source program, indicating *where* the errors were made. An *error reporter* can use these sets of occurrences to highlight or color the relevant program parts for each error message.

As an example, Figure 7.5 shows an error reporting application as generated for the language CLaX (a Pascal derivative) taken from (Dinesh and Tip, 1992). In the large window, a CLaX program is shown, for which the programmer has invoked a typecheck. The four error messages for this program are shown in the small window. For each message, the CLaX programmer can ask "Show Origin", in order to detect the source of his error. In the figure, he has done so for the error `multiply-defined-label step`. This caused the two relevant occurrences of `step` in the source program to be highlighted. Note that not *all* occurrences of the identifier `step` are marked, only those related to this particular error message.

Using origins this way naturally raises the questions whether the origin annotations obtained from a typical static semantics definition are (a) non-empty and (b) of good quality if non-empty. Unfortunately, even when using secondary origin tracking, resulting messages far too often have the empty set as their origin. When they are non-empty, however, the occurrences are sufficiently detailed.

To see why primary and secondary origins alone for error messages can easily be empty, consider Property 7.14. Let e be a function symbol of sort ERROR as used in the Pascal specification of Chapter 2 (see Module 2.1, page 33). First of all note that such an error symbol will obviously not yet occur in the initial Pascal program. Secondly, it is easy to see that the Pascal specification is actually *top-preserving in e* (Definition 7.12):

- In general, variable-collapse rules are unlikely to occur (requirement 2); indeed, in the Pascal specification they do not occur for sort ERROR.

- Similarly, equations having a common subterm concerning an error message are unlikely (requirement 1), and they do not occur in the Pascal specification.

- The first requirement for being top preserving in e, namely, that no right-hand side should have e as top-symbol, could be violated by typechecker specifications. For the Pascal specification, however, every error message e is introduced by a special function "add-error ERROR to ENV → ENV" (see Module 2.7, page 42), which takes e and an ENV argument, and produces a new ENV extended with message e. Thus, e is never introduced as the top symbol of a right-hand side.

Therefore, the origins for all error message symbols occurring in Pascal are empty. Luckily, about 40% of the error messages have an argument which is copied from the original abstract syntax tree (an identifier, number, etc.), to which a meaningful origin can be given using the Common Variables case (as for the identifier step in Figure 7.5).

In Section 7.5 we will propose *syntax-directed* origins, which will remedy these problems. Syntax-directed origin tracking creates non-empty origins for *all* created symbols, including error messages.

7.4.2 Visualizing Program Execution

The application of origin tracking to program *animation*, i.e., to the visualization of program execution, is discussed by Tip (1993). His point of departure is a specification of the operational semantics of a programming language that can be executed using (conditional) term rewriting. In this case, one is not interested in origins from the normal form to the initial term (the program to be executed), but in origins from terms occurring *during* rewriting back to the initial term. Particularly interesting are intermediate terms representing certain events taking place during execution. For instance, every time the redex matches a pattern like "eval-stat(S, Env)", a statement is executed. If such a term is contracted, the origin of the first argument exactly indicates *which* statement is currently being executed. Likewise, redex-patterns can be given which correspond to expression evaluation, procedure entry, and the like.

An animator tool asks the language designer to give a set of patterns of interest, and to indicate for each pattern which argument position contains the relevant program construct. Next, the animator tool executes the specification using rewriting. Whenever the redex matches one of the patterns, the origins of the indicated subterm are used to obtain a set of occurrences in the program. These occurrences are visualized using, for instance, highlighting or coloring, and program execution resumes, leading to the next program piece to be visualized, etc.

First of all, note that the origins to be maintained for animation performed this way are mainly origins for terms that represent program pieces, e.g., statements, expressions, and so on. These program pieces literally recur in the initial term, so the Common Variables and Context case can easily provide satisfactory origins.

Secondly, observe that this form of animation does not show any *values* of expressions, variables, parameters, etc. Assume that certain values are computed, and that the terms representing them have non-empty origins. Then they could be shown in the original program at the positions indicated by the origins. So far, no experience exists with the use of origin tracking to obtain such animation facilities. Further research should indicate whether this approach is feasible.

7.4.3 Source-Level Debugging

Finally, we will discuss how origin tracking can be used by a debugger generated automatically from a language specification, a topic covered in more detail by Tip (1995b). We will focus on *breakpoints*, which can be used to stop execution in order to inspect, for example, the values of variables. First, we will explain how a debugger can be derived from the specification of the operational semantics of a programming language; next we will discuss the compiled case. As for animation, the debugger needs to know which patterns correspond to interesting events, such as statement execution, procedure entry, expression evaluation, and so on.

A first possibility are so-called *control* breakpoints, which stop the execution whenever a certain position in the program (such as a particular statement) is reached. The debugging tool asks the programmer to indicate the position in the program where the breakpoint is to be set. It then computes the occurrence O of that position with respect to the initial term of the program execution. Now term rewriting starts, but stops as soon as the redex matches one of the specified patterns, and — most importantly — the origin of the relevant subterm of the pattern contains the breakpoint occurrence O.

A second possibility are *data* breakpoints, stopping execution whenever, for instance, a particular variable is assigned to or referenced. Again the programmer indicates which variable he is interested in, and the debugger tool computes the corresponding occurrence O in the initial term. Execution is stopped whenever the look-up or update function operating on the symbol table is invoked with an actual parameter whose origin set contains the occurrence O.

As for animation, most origins correspond to terms representing parts of the initial program. Therefore, the Common Variables and Context cases are sufficient when deriving debuggers on the basis of a language interpreter.

More challenging is debugging in a compiler context, where the program is translated to some target language. A *source-level* debugger allows the programmer to set breakpoints and inspect the state in terms of the source language, rather than in terms of the target language. Using origin tracking to obtain source-level debuggers basically proceeds in a manner similar to the non-compiled, interpreted case. A first important difference is that the patterns of interest have to be indicated for the evaluation function over the *target* language. Secondly, it is no longer obvious that the arguments of the target evaluation function, such as machine instructions, will have the proper origins to source-level statements (or to the patterns of interest). As for the error handling problems (Section 7.4.1), these machine instructions will often have empty origins, even when secondary origin tracking is used. Again the need for an origin function establishing more relations makes itself felt. This subject will be addressed by the PRS origins discussed in the next section.

7.5 Origins for Primitive Recursive Schemes

Many functions occurring in algebraic specifications are defined by primitive recursion over some structure. This is, in particular, the case for language definitions, where functions characterizing static semantics or compilation are defined by performing a single pass over the syntax, i.e., they are defined by primitive recursion over the abstract syntax. A typical example is the definition of the typecheck functions for Pascal as discussed in Chapter 2.

In Chapter 6 we encountered *primitive recursive schemes* (PRSs) as a formalization of algebraic specifications containing such primitive recursive functions. A PRS is a plain algebraic specification, about which we have extra knowledge concerning the function symbols used. The symbols are partitioned into a set G of functions which are used to construct, e.g., the abstract syntax of a language, and a set Φ of functions which are defined inductively over these constructor functions. The equations defining the Φ-functions have to meet certain criteria.

As PRSs play such a central role in language definitions, and particularly in language definitions to which origin tracking is applicable (static semantics with error handling, compilation with source-level debugging), it is worthwhile to investigate whether it is possible to come up with good origins for specifications in the PRS format.

In this section we start by arguing the need for special origins for PRSs (Section 7.5.1). Within this framework, it is easy to understand "what is going on in a specification", and therefore good origins, the *PRS origins*, can be defined for them (Section 7.5.4). Moreover, these origins can be easily analyzed, and some desirable properties can be proved for them (Section 7.5.4). Larger specifications as occurring in practice seldom meet *all* requirements of a PRS, however. Therefore, we discuss what happens if the requirements are dropped, and how the quality of the origins can be "saved" under those circumstances, giving rise to so-called *syntax-directed* origins (Section 7.5.5). Finally, we discuss how syntax-directed origins can be of use in the various typechecking applications we encountered in this book.

One might argue against the idea of defining origins for PRSs thinking they constitute too limited a class of specifications. This argument, however, is easily refuted by studying definitions of e.g., static semantics, evaluation, translation, and so on. In a first-order formalism it is virtually impossible to specify these without using primitive recursion.

7.5.1 Origins Reconsidered

An Example

Primary origin tracking discussed in Section 7.2.2 establishes only very basic relations. That these can be too basic is illustrated by the example given in Figures 7.6, 7.7 and 7.8, which show the compilation of a simple programming language to assembly language. The equations are taken from (Broy, 1992; van der Meulen, 1988).

The abstract syntax of the source and target language is defined in Figures 7.6 and 7.7. The equations describing the actual translation are shown in Figure 7.8. For the time being, we can ignore the underlining and bold face fonts used for the symbols (see the end of this section). An example reduction is shown in Figure 7.9. The expression "**const**(4) + **const**(3)" is translated to "push(4) @ push(3) @ add @ null" using the function "tr-exp". The dashed lines in Figure 7.9 indicate the primary origin relations established for this reduction. In the first rewrite step, equation [3] is applied. Since variables E_1 and E_2 occur both in its left- and right-hand side, origin relations are established between their instantiations, i.e., between the occurrences of "**const**(4)" and "**const**(3)" respectively. In the remaining rewrite steps, in particular those where equation [2] is applied, only the origins for the constants "3" and "4" survive, as indicated by the dashed lines in the figure.

Limitations

The primary origins established for this small compilation example contain surprisingly little information. Only the copying of the "3" and "4" symbols could be tracked! No origins were established for the "add" or "push" symbols, even though the "+" and "const" nodes occurring in the initial term seem to be good candidates.

This problem is present to an even stronger degree in equation [1]. Origins are established for all variables E, S_1, S_2, and, L, but none of the function symbols in

sorts
  EXP STAT ...
context-free syntax
  "if" EXP "then" STAT "else" STAT "fi"   → STAT
  "const" (INT)   → EXP
  EXP "+" EXP   → EXP
  ...

Figure 7.6: Abstract syntax of simple statements and expressions.

sorts
  ASSEMBLY COMMAND LABEL
context-free syntax
  null   → ASSEMBLY
  COMMAND "@" ASSEMBLY   → ASSEMBLY {**left**}
  cjump(LABEL)   → COMMAND
  jump(LABEL)   → COMMAND
  lab(LABEL)   → COMMAND
  push(INT)   → COMMAND
  add   → COMMAND
  ...
  "1"   → LABEL
  "2"   → LABEL
  "3"   → LABEL
  LABEL ^ LABEL   → LABEL

Figure 7.7: Part of the abstract syntax for a simple assembly language. Individual COMMANDS are sequenced by the cons-like function "_ @ _". The empty sequence is written "null".

context-free syntax

tr-stat(STAT, LABEL)	→ ASSEMBLY
tr-exp(EXP)	→ ASSEMBLY

...

ASSEMBLY ";" ASSEMBLY	→ ASSEMBLY

...

variables

$E[12]^*$	→ EXP	N	→ INT
$S[12]^*$	→ STAT	$Alist[']^*$	→ ASSEMBLY
L	→ LABEL	C	→ COMMAND

equations

[1]   tr-stat(**if** E **then** S_1 **else** S_2 **fi**, L) =

  tr-exp(E)   ;   %% condition
  cjump(L)   @
  tr-stat(S_2, 1ˆL)   ;   %% else part
  jump(3ˆL)   @
  lab(L)   @   %% then part
  tr-stat(S_1, 2ˆL)   ;
  lab(3ˆL)   @
  null

[2]   tr-exp(**const**(N)) = push(N) @ null

[3]   tr-exp(E_1+E_2) = tr-exp(E_1) ; tr-exp(E_2) ; add @ null

[4]   null ; $Alist$ = $Alist$

[5]   (C @ $Alist$) ; $Alist'$ = C @ ($Alist$; $Alist'$)

...

Figure 7.8: Example specification of a simple translation. Equation [1] defines the translation of an **if**-statement. Equations [2] and [3] specify the compilation of expressions. Equations [4] and [5] deal with the "_ ; _" operator used to append two lists of assembly commands.

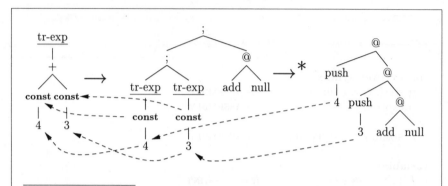

Figure 7.9: Part of a reduction performing the translation of an expression. The dashed lines indicate primary origin relations.

the right hand side, e.g. "jump", "cjump", "lab", ..., are given an origin. This is undesirable since these are the symbols that will occur in the resulting normal form.

In general, the problem is that function symbols introduced in the right-hand side of a rule have the empty set of occurrences as their origin. This is unattractive, since it provides no information why such a function symbol has been created. We will propose an extension which solves this problem. It will establish good origins for function symbols that are created during rewriting in the setting of a primitive recursive scheme.

Observe that secondary origins alone do not resolve this issue. Secondary origins only help if the symbol itself already occurs in the left-hand side, or if the symbol is introduced as the top symbol of the right-hand side. In the example this will only yield one origin from the top @-operator in the result to the tr-exp at the top of the initial term.

7.5.2 Extending Origins

Having noticed the limitations of the existing scheme, one may wonder why it is so difficult to present a suitable extension. Ideally, origins should meet the following requirements:

(A) Origin sets should be small. One would like the origin sets to be as specific as possible. Thus, rather than having an origin which states that this assembly instruction originated from the set of all statements in the source program, one would like to know exactly which statement was responsible for its creation.

(B) However, origin sets should not be *too* small. Having the empty set as origin provides little, if any, information. Moreover, some applications require that multiple origins be established; for error handling purposes one would like to have origins both to a declaration of an identifier and its conflicting use.

(C) Origins should point to deep subtrees. The shorter a path in the initial term, the smaller its information content. For instance, having an origin pointing to the top node of the initial term will only indicate that the normal form somehow has resulted from the initial term. This does not provide very much information.

(D) Origins that point too deeply may be misleading. If, again in an error-handling example, an expression "plus(E_1, E_2)" has incompatible argument types, the origin for a message indicating this should point to either the plus or both the top nodes of E_1 and E_2, but not to a very deep subexpression of E_1 or E_2.

Any extension of origin tracking should be a compromise between these conflicting requirements.

7.5.3 Primitive Recursive Schemes

For a precise definition of a Primitive Recursive Scheme, the reader is referred[2] to Chapter 6, page 208. Informally, the signature of a PRS is split into a set G of tree constructor symbols, a set Φ of functions that are defined inductively over G, and a set S containing auxiliary symbols. In the preceding figures, the G-symbols (introduced in Figure 7.6), are in **boldface**, the Φ-functions (introduced in Figure 7.8) are underlined, and the S-symbols (the ones in Figure 7.7 as well as the ";" operator in Figure 7.8) are in normal font.

A PRS must meet various criteria:

- All Φ-functions take a G-term as their first argument.

- The equations defining the Φ-functions ([1], [2], and [3] in Figure 7.8) must all be of the form:
$$\phi(p(x_1, ..., x_n), y_1, ..., y_m) = \tau$$
where ϕ is a function from Φ, and $p : G_1 \times \cdots \times G_n \to G_0$ is tree constructor over G. The variables $x_1, \ldots, x_n$ range over these G-sorts. The variables $y_1, \ldots, y_m$, which range over $G \cup S$, are called the *parameters* of ϕ.

  Informally, τ is the expression for computing a *synthesized* value for language construct p, using *inherited* information passed through the parameters $y_1, \ldots, y_m$.

- All Φ-defining equations should be *strictly decreasing*, i.e., the only G-terms that are allowed to occur in τ are the variables $x_1, \ldots, x_n$.

- There should be no equations over G: terms over G should be free constructors.

---

[2]Chapter 6 also defines the subclass of *well-presented* PRSs. This notion is not needed in our origins setting.

- All equations in a PRS should be *left linear*, i.e., no variable should occur more than once in a single left-hand side.

7.5.4 Origins in PRSs

The overall effect of a PRS is an inductively defined mapping from G-terms to S-terms. A large G-term (typically the abstract syntax tree of some program) is processed by several Φ-functions. Different Φ-functions operate on different G-constructors p. For instance, there will be one Φ-function to translate an if-statement, another one to translate an assignment, and so on. Now consider a Φ-defining equation $\phi(p(x_1, ..., x_n), y_1, ..., y_m) = \tau$. The right-hand side τ is an expression to compute a particular value (a *synthesized* attribute) for some grammar node p. It consists of:

(1) Variables (the x_i occurring in τ) representing subconstructs of the current node p.

(2) Variables (the y_j occurring in τ) representing global information (the *inherited* attributes).

(3) Function symbols initiating computations over subconstructs of the current node (Φ-functions in τ with some x_i as first argument).

(4) Auxiliary function symbols from S indicating how to "synthesize" the result value from the ingredients mentioned above, or how to construct context information to be passed as parameters to the Φ-functions occurring in τ.

This division is reflected in the origins we will define. The Common Variables case (Section 7.2.2) is used to take care of (1) and (2). For case (3) we have a Φ-function ϕ' operating on a subconstruct, and as origin for ϕ' we will use the origin of the first argument of ϕ', that is, of the relevant x_i. Finally, for case (4) the new function symbols are created when working on the $p(x_1, ..., x_n)$ G-node in the left-hand side; therefore, these new function symbols will obtain the p-node in the left-hand side as their origin.

The origins caused by Φ-functions traversing the abstract syntax tree constitute the backbone of the PRS-origins. The remaining origins, resulting from equations over S, simply propagate these "Φ-origins". This is achieved by giving all new function symbols in the right-hand side of a rewrite rule from E_S an origin to the top symbol of the left-hand side. A precise definition is given in Section 7.5.4.

Example

As an example, once again consider the reduction of "tr-exp(**const**(4) + **const**(3))" by the equations in Figure 7.8. The PRS-origins for this reduction are shown in Figure 7.10. The relations between the constants "3" and "4" in the normal form and the initial term are established because of Common Variable N when applying

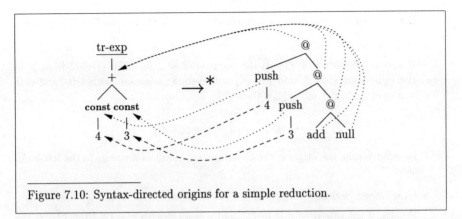

Figure 7.10: Syntax-directed origins for a simple reduction.

equation [2] of Figure 7.8. Note that these origins were the only ones established by the general case of Figure 7.9.

The relations between "push" and "**const**" result from reductions by Φ-defining equation [2]: the S-function symbol "push" gets the G-argument "const(N)" of Φ-function "tr-exp" as origin. Likewise, S-function symbols "_ ; _", "_ @ _", "add" and "null" introduced in Φ-defining equation [3] are given an origin to the "_ + _", which is the G-argument of Φ-function "tr-exp".

Finally, equations [4] and [5] are used to eliminate the concatenation of assembly code operator "_ ; _". New functions introduced within these S-equations receive the top function symbol of the left-hand side as origin. Since in this case the "_ ; _" operators were introduced by equation [3], these origins point to the "+"-function symbol.

Definition

For a PRS $\langle G, \Phi, S, E_\Phi, E_S \rangle$ and term t, let $\mathcal{O}_\Phi(t)$, $\mathcal{O}_G(t)$, and $\mathcal{O}_S(t)$ be the sets of occurrences for function symbols from Φ, G, and S respectively. To define origins for PRSs, we again consider a single reduction step $t = C[\alpha^\sigma] \rightarrow C[\beta^\sigma] = t'$. Let u be the occurrence of the redex position α^σ in $C[\alpha^\sigma]$. The function *prs-org-step* : $\mathcal{O}(t') \rightarrow \mathcal{P}(\mathcal{O}(t))$ maps occurrences in t' to sets of occurrences in t. Define *prs-org-step*(v) by taking the "Common Variables" and "Context" cases of *prim-step* (see Section 7.2.2) together with the following cases, where v is the occurrence of a function (or constant) symbol in β:

- (Φ-Functions)

  If $v = u \cdot v'$ with $v' \in \mathcal{O}_\Phi(\beta)$ the occurrence of a Φ-function symbol in the right-hand side β, then

  $$prs\text{-}org\text{-}step(v) = prs\text{-}org\text{-}step(\ v \cdot [1]\ ).$$

In other words, the origin of a Φ-function is equal to the origin of its G-argument.

- (Synthesizers)

  If $v = u \cdot v'$ with $v' \in \mathcal{O}_S(\beta)$ the occurrence of a function symbol from S in the right-hand side β, and $r \in E_\Phi$ a Φ-defining equation with left-hand side $\alpha \equiv \phi(p(x_1, ..., x_n), y_1, ..., y_m)$, then

$$prs\text{-}org\text{-}step(v) = \{u \cdot [1]\}.$$

  In other words, the origin is the G-term $p(x_1, ..., x_n)$ as it occurs in the left-hand side.

- (Auxiliary Symbols)

  Finally, if the rule $\alpha \to \beta$ is in E_S, and $v = u \cdot v'$ with $v' \in \mathcal{O}_G(\beta) \cup \mathcal{O}_S(\beta)$ the occurrence of a function symbol from G or S in the right-hand side β, then

$$prs\text{-}org\text{-}step(v) = \{u\}.$$

  In other words, the origin is the top-symbol of the left-hand side.

At first sight the definition of *prs-org-step* for the Φ-Functions case may seem a little dangerous since *prs-org-step* appears at both sides of the equality sign. However, the first argument of a Φ-function must — by definition of a PRS — be a G-term, for which the *prs-org-step* function is directly defined in the remaining cases. When we know that rule r actually is a Φ-defining equation $\phi(p(x_1, ..., x_n), y_1, ..., y_m) = \tau$ we can make an even stronger statement: A Φ-function ϕ' occurring at position v in right-hand side τ must — again by definition of a PRS — have one of the x_i ($1 \leq i \leq n$) as its first argument. The occurrence of that x_i in the left-hand side is $[1, i]$, so for this case we can define *prs-org-step* alternatively as $prs\text{-}org\text{-}step(v) = \{u \cdot [1, i]\}$.

The function *prs-org-step* can be extended to a function *prs-org** covering multi-step reduction as in the case of the extension of *org-step* to *org** (see Section 7.2.2).

Properties of PRS Origins

In Section 7.5.2 we mentioned the four requirements (A), (B), (C), and (D) for extensions of origin tracking. As for the size of the origin sets (requirements (A) and (B)), we observe that origin sets always contain exactly one element in pure PRSs:

Property 7.15 *Let t, t' be terms, $A : t \to^* t'$ a reduction in a PRS, and let $A.prs\text{-}org^*$ be the origin function for this reduction. For all $v \in \mathcal{O}(t')$ we have $|A.prs\text{-}org^*(v)| = 1$.*

Proof: This follows from the fact that (1) PRSs are left-linear, (2) none of the various cases for function symbol origins in PRSs overlap, and (3) every individual case yields exactly one origin. $\qquad \square$

This means that requirement (A), to keep the origin sets small, is met as they always consist of exactly one element. However, its counterpart (B), not to make them too small, is only partly met. On the positive side, no empty origins will occur (which contrasts with the primary or secondary origins, see Properties 7.6 and 7.14). On the negative side, situations were multiple origins are desirable (for example, an origin to both the use of an identifier and to its definition point) are treated in an unsatisfactory manner.

PRS origins try to achieve the proper depth (requirements (C) and (D)) by focusing on the G-terms. Created function symbols get an origin to the G-argument of the *closest* surrounding Φ-function. More precisely, assume we are reducing t by applying a rule $\phi(p(x_1, \dots, x_n), y_1, \dots, y_m) = \tau$. Function symbols created when reducing τ further will have an origin to a subterm of $p(x_1, \dots, x_n)$. Existing function symbols that are passed around in variables $x_1, \dots, x_n, y_1, \dots, y_m$ simply maintain their origins.

Property 7.16 *Let t, t' be terms, $t \not\equiv t'$, let $A : t \rightarrow^* t'$ be a reduction in a PRS, and let $A.prs\text{-}org^*$ be the origin function for this reduction. Assume that the top operator of t is a Φ-function, and let $A.prs\text{-}org^*(v') = \{v\}$ for all $v' \in \mathcal{O}(t')$. Then either*

- *v is is an occurrence in one of the y_j, i.e., $[j] \preceq v$, with $j \geq 2$, and $t'/v = t/u$;*

- *or v is an occurrence in the G-argument of ϕ, i.e., $[1] \preceq u$.*

Proof: Immediate from the definition of *prs-org-step* and the fact that t has a Φ-function as its top node. □

As an example, assume we are typechecking or translating an expression using a Φ-function ϕ expecting the expression as its G-argument, and with a single parameter $SymT$ representing a symbol table of a sort from S. All function symbols *created* while reducing $\phi(E, SymT)$ will have an origin pointing to E, and not to a subterm of the symbol table.

7.5.5 Extension to Syntax-Directed Origin Tracking

In the previous sections we have proposed origins for pure PRSs, and we have formulated some desirable properties. To assess the usefulness of these origins, we would like to see how they work on the various typechecking specifications we encountered in earlier chapters. A problem is that although these specifications are very similar to PRSs, they do not meet all criteria listed in Section 6.3. To solve this, we use this section to extend origins for pure PRSs to arbitrary TRSs. Provided that the latter resemble a PRS, the new origins — called *syntax-directed* origins — will still be of high quality.

Thus, we extend PRS specifications to conditional rewriting, relax the requirements for PRSs, and then discuss the usefulness of permitting *layered* PRSs. In the next section we assess the usefulness of these extensions for the various typechecking specifications described in this book, and discuss a complicated example — taken from Chapter 5 — in full detail.

Conditional Rewriting

The extension of PRSs to conditional term rewrite systems (CTRS) is described in (van der Meulen, 1994, Chapter 3). In short, the restrictions making a CTRS into a conditional PRS involve the Φ-defining equations only. Terms occurring in the condition sides of conditional Φ-defining equations should meet the same criteria as the right-hand sides of non-conditional defining equations (i.e., they should not introduce new G-terms). Defining PRS-origins for the conditional case along the lines of Section 7.3 is then straightforward.

Relaxing the PRS Requirements

- The requirement that is eliminated most easily is that the recursion proceeds over the *first* argument of Φ-functions. In ASF+SDF one could indicate which functions are Φ-functions by extending their context-free syntax declaration with an SDF attribute like $\{\mathbf{syn\text{-}dir}(i)\}$, indicating that this function is syntax-directed over the ith argument. With this extension, meaningful origins can be obtained for specifications Pico-typecheck-old and Pico-typecheck-err as discussed in Chapter 4. The four Φ-functions are tc(PROGRAM), tenv(DECLS), TENV "[" SERIES "]", and TENV "." EXP, of which the last two have their syntactic argument at the second position.

- The requirement that Φ-defining equations are strictly decreasing in G ensures proper termination of recursively called Φ-functions. When defining the operational semantics of languages featuring recursion or while loops, however, termination cannot be guaranteed, and hence strictly decreasing specifications are not possible. A typical example is the evaluation of the while statement, for which an equation was given in Section 7.1.2, page 254. Another interesting example is given in Chapter 3, which discusses the dynamic semantics of an object-oriented language called KOOL. Module KOOLeval (Section 3.6) defines the function "[" EXP "]" CLASSES VENV by case distinction over the syntactic argument EXP. Equation [EE7] covers the case where KOOL methods are called recursively. The second condition of this equation looks up the corresponding method body E' of a method call in the given class definitions, and then proceeds to evaluate it using $[\![E']\!] \cdots$ in the right-hand side τ of the equation. In other words, the Φ-function in τ has a G-argument that does not originate from the G-argument $[\![E.Id(E^*)]\!]$ in the left-hand side.

  Thus, lifting the requirement that Φ-defining equations should be decreasing makes syntax-directed origins applicable to animation of definitions of operational semantics. The extension of the origin definition required is that new G-terms introduced in right-hand sides τ of Φ-defining equations obtain an origin to the G-term at the left. In the KOOL example above, the origin of E' comes from an assignment condition introducing new variables.

- Φ-defining equations are required to have a linear left-hand side of the form $\phi(p(x_1, ..., x_n), y_1, ..., y_m)$. In practice, other forms may occur, such as $\phi(x, y_1, ..., y_m)$ (no syntactic constructor), $\phi(p(q(x_1), r(x_2)), y_1, ..., y_m)$ (more complex syntactic patterns), $\phi(p(x_1, ..., x_n), s(y))$ (patterns at parameter positions), or non-linear left-hand sides.

These patterns can be safely permitted, if all symbols created in right-hand sides of Φ-defining equations are given an origin to the top of the G-argument of the Φ-function at the left. In addition to this, the Common Subterms origins can now also be of use in Φ-defining equations[3] if the right-hand side contains a subterm that literally recurs in the left-hand side.

In the next section, we will discuss the specification of the well-formedness checker of the MLS language covered in Chapter 5. Most equations in Module OLS-NWF (5.4.3) fall in one of the categories listed above: equation [wf-term] is conditional over the syntactic argument and does not have a specific syntactic constructor, equation [wf-ann] has a nested pattern (two *annotations*) of which the deepest one recurs (Common Subterm) in the right-hand side. Most of the other equations in this module also have nested patterns to which the Common Subterms case is applicable.

- Finally, we consider permitting equations over G-terms. Most specifications discussed in this book use such equations to eliminate various syntactic constructs, such as modularization features (Chapter 5), inheritance operations (Chapter 3), or redundant constructs offering alternative ways to write equivalent sentences (Section 5.3.4). Origins can be established for these by treating equations over G-terms in the same way as equations over S terms.

With this extension, origins can be established for specification Pico-typecheckmod (Section 4.2.2). In this specification, the distinction between grammar G-terms and "semantic" S-terms is blurred, since, e.g., the syntactic sort EXP is extended with TYPE. The functions mapping Pico to an abstract type domain are ordinary Φ-functions; the equations giving the abstract interpretation over the new domain are over $S \cup G$. Using syntax-directed origins in this setting makes the use of *tokenization* unnecessary.

Observe that these relaxed requirements are not necessarily compatible with incremental rewriting as defined in Chapter 6, but from an origin tracking point of view they are very useful.

---

[3]Common Subterms will also be useful in equations over S-terms, as an extension of the Auxiliary Symbols case.

Layered PRSs

So far, we assumed implicitly that there is a single G-signature consisting of the grammar of a language, and a single set of Φ-functions defined inductively over G. A large specification, however, will consist of many data types each with several functions defined inductively over a set of constructors. Many of these can be regarded as PRSs. In Chapter 6 (page 229), van der Meulen has extended PRSs to so-called *layered* PRSs, which gives the formal basis for dealing with multiple PRSs. The definition of PRS origins does not require any adaptation to cover layered PRSs. The usefulness of regarding definitions of auxiliary data types as sub-PRSs is illustrated in the next section, where we discuss the specification of Chapter 5 from the viewpoint of origin tracking.

7.5.6   Assessment

The result of extending PRS origins to syntax-directed origins yields a powerful mechanism for obtaining meaningful origins. Certain functions are attributed with {**syn-dir**(i)}, indicating that their ith argument conveys useful origin information; all symbols created while reducing such a function yield an origin to this argument.

For the specification of the Pascal typechecker in Chapter 2, all error messages, including the 60% not covered by primary origin tracking as discussed in Section 7.4, receive an origin to the Pascal language construct typechecked while discovering the error message. Although it would be interesting to take a detailed look at the Pascal example, the specification is *very* close to a true PRS, hence it is not surprising that syntax-directed origins yield good results.

A far more interesting example — because it is not so similar to a PRS — is the specification of the typechecker for the MLS formalism discussed in Chapter 5. The full specification is given there, as well as an example of a non-wellformed input term together with the error messages computed for that term (Figure 5.6, page 135). In Figure 7.11 we have repeated the erroneous term[4], where we have attached symbolic labels to various nodes in the abstract syntax tree. The two error messages for this term produced by the typechecker are given in Figure 7.12. The labels in this figure are used to represent the syntax-directed origins established[5]; they refer to the labels in Figure 7.11. The error messages consist of several words or quoted sentences derived from the input term. Each symbol has an origin to the input term. The origins for the symbols +, 0, X, Y, nat, -> as well as the last occurrence of # are obtained using Common Subterms, the remaining symbols are (re)created and obtain their origin

---

[4]There is a danger of confusion since this term happens to be a one-level specification, which is very similar to an ordinary ASF+SDF specification. The language typechecked may look like ASF+SDF, but this is irrelevant for the origins established.

[5]If we would strictly follow the definition, these labels would be (lengthy) paths from the root of the term to the node at which the labels are attached.

```
signature
   sorts nat;
   functions
      0^{0.1} : nat^{0.2};
      s^{s.1} : nat^{s.2} ->^{s.3} nat^{s.4};
      (+^{a.1})^{a.2} : nat^{a.3} #^{a.4} nat^{a.5} ->^{a.6} nat^{a.7};
   variables
      X^{v.1}, Y^{v.2} : nat^{v.3};
   equations
      (0^{e.1} +^{e.2} X^{e.3})^{e.4}  ==^{e.5} Y^{e.6};
      (s^{f.1}(X^{f.2}) +^{f.3} Y^{f.4})^{f.5} ==^{f.6} (s^{f.7} +^{f.8} (X^{f.9}, Y^{f.10})^{f.11})^{f.12}
```

Figure 7.11: A specification with two non-wellformed equations. At various nodes in the abstract syntax tree, symbolic labels have been added as superscripts.

```
equation^{e.5} " (+^{e.2})^{e.4}(0^{e.1}, X^{e.3})^{e.4} ==^{e.5} Y^{e.6} "^{e.5}
   not^{e.5} well-formed^{e.5} :
   variables^{e.5} "Y^{e.6}" of^{e.5} rhs^{e.5} not^{e.5} in^{e.5} lhs^{e.5} ;
application^{f.12} "(+^{f.8})^{f.12}(s^{f.7} ,^{f.12} X^{f.9} ,^{f.11} Y^{f.10} )^{f.12}"^{f.12}
   not^{f.12} well-formed^{f.12} :^{f.12}
   type^{f.12} of^{f.12} argument^{f.12}
   " (nat^{s.2} ->^{s.3} nat^{s.4}) #^{f.12} nat^{v.3} #^{f.11} nat^{v.3} "^{f.12}
   does^{f.12} not^{f.12} match^{f.12}
   type^{f.12} of^{f.12} domain^{f.12}
   " nat^{a.3} #^{a.4} nat^{a.5} "^{f.12}
```

Figure 7.12: The error messages produced by the typechecker. The attached labels are the syntax-directed origins established. They refer to the labels given in the previous figure.

from syntax-directed origin tracking. To understand the various origins, an analysis of several equations discussed in Chapter 5 is necessary. The most relevant issues are:

- Errors are lists of words or quoted erroneous terms. The origins for each word refer to the place where the error was detected. The two messages given are created in Module OLS-NWF (5.4.3), equation [wf-eqn'] for the equation with the wrong variable, and equation [wf-app'] for the non-wellformed application.

- The top-level typechecking module is Module OLS-TC (5.4.5), which invokes two PRS functions; one for performing the *type assignment* (Module OLS-TA (5.4.4)), and one for checking the well-formedness given the annotations (Module OLS-WF (5.4.2) and Module OLS-NWF (5.4.3)).

- Infix operators (like +) are rewritten to prefix notation by equation [bin1] from Module Binary-Operators (5.B.1). This equation rewrites the term 0 + X to (+)(0, X), and similarly for all other occurrences of (+). Symbols created by this reduction (the brackets around + and the ',' product constructor) obtain an origin to the top at the left, which is the (invisible) operator 'Term BinOp Term' from module Binary-Operators.

- The 'type', 'spine', 'dom', etc. operators manipulate terms with annotations. All these are defined inductively over the structure of terms, and reconstruct operators in such terms. To get the proper origins for these re-created symbols, it is important to view these functions as sub-PRSs. As an example, equation [sp-arr] in Module Term-Analysis (5.3.3) rebuilds the arrow in its right-hand side. Its origin should be the arrow at the left, which is achieved by making spine a Φ-function (or actually, the 'TermToTerm(Term)' function, which is syntax-directed on the second argument).

- The types of functions (+ or s) are obtained by the Common Variables rule. Their type is retrieved by equation [p2b] from Module Projection (5.4.1) and equation [wt-fun] from Module OLS-TA (5.4.4).

- The declaration X, Y:nat is rewritten to X:nat, Y:nat using equation [v-decl] from Module OLS (5.3.4) (observe that this is an equation between the syntactic constructors). Therefore, the two occurrences in the type of argument ... part of the second message of the nat type derived for the X and the Y share the same origin to the single occurrence of nat in the variable part of the signature.

- The product type operator # is created while inferring the type annotations in equation [wt-pr] from Module OLS-TA (5.4.4). It is created while processing the ',' product constructor, and hence obtains an origin to the ',' in question.

This example illustrates how syntax-directed origins can help to provide origin information for error messages that refer to inferred type information. The example shown is relatively simple, since it does not yet include any polymorphic type inference. Such polymorphism is supported by the specification given in Chapter 5, and meaningful origins are obtained for such inferred types as well. This raises the question whether syntax-directed origin tracking could be of help when clarifying error messages for Standard ML, a well-known problem discussed in the literature (Wand, 1986; Johnson and Walz, 1986; Beaven and Stansifer, 1993). Further research is needed here, yet the results obtained for the multi-level specification language of Chapter 5 are promising.

7.6 Dynamic Dependence Tracking

Dynamic dependence tracking is a technique similar to origin tracking in the sense that, in both cases, static analyses of rewrite rules form the basis for constructing relationships between terms that occur in a rewriting process. However, whereas origin tracking is focused on keeping track of the origin of a particular subterm, dynamic dependence tracking is concerned with the question of which function symbols need to be present in order for a rewrite rule to be applicable, and how function symbols are affected by the application of a rewrite rule. More precisely, dynamic dependence tracking defines how applications of rewrite rules cause *creation* of new function symbols, and *residuation* (i.e., moving around or copying) of existing function symbols. In Section 7.6.1 below, dynamic dependence tracking will be presented informally. The reader is referred to (Field and Tip, 1994; Tip, 1995a) for further details.

The main application of dynamic dependence tracking is *program slicing*, a method for isolating computational threads in programs proposed by Weiser (1979). Program slicing has been suggested as a valuable tool for debugging (Kamkar *et al.*, 1992; Agrawal *et al.*, 1993), dataflow testing (Duesterwald *et al.*, 1992; Kamkar *et al.*, 1993), software maintenance (Gallagher and Lyle, 1991), program understanding (Field *et al.*, 1995), and a variety of other applications (see (Kamkar, 1995; Tip, 1995c) for overviews of program slicing and its applications). By applying dynamic dependence tracking to specifications of the semantics of programming languages, various semantically well-founded notions of program slices can be defined in a uniform way. Slicing is discussed in more detail in Section 7.6.2.

7.6.1 Dynamic Dependence Relations

The following two rewrite rules for integer arithmetic will serve as an example to present dynamic dependence tracking informally:

```
[A1]  intmul(0, X)            = 0
[A2]  intmul(intmul(X, Y), Z) = intmul(X, intmul(Y, Z))
```

By applying these rules, the term intsub(3, intmul(intmul(0, 1), 2)) may be rewritten as follows (subterms affected by rule applications are underlined):

$$
\begin{aligned}
t_0 &= \text{intsub(3, \underline{intmul(intmul(0, 1), 2)})} &&\longrightarrow {}^{[A2]} \\
t_1 &= \text{intsub(3, \underline{intmul(0, intmul(1, 2))})} &&\longrightarrow {}^{[A1]} \\
t_2 &= \qquad\qquad \text{intsub(3,0)}
\end{aligned}
$$

By carefully studying this example reduction, we can make the following observations:

- The outer context intsub(3, ●) of t_0 ('●' denotes a missing subterm) is not affected by any rule, and therefore reappears in t_1 and t_2.

- The occurrence of variables X, Y, and Z in both the left-hand side and the right-hand side of [A2] causes the respective subterms '0', '1', and '2' of the underlined subterm of t_0 to reappear in t_1.

- Variable X only occurs in the left-hand side of [A1]. Consequently, the subterm (of t_1) intmul(1, 2) matched against X does not reappear in t_2. In fact, we can make the stronger observation that the subterm matched against X is *irrelevant* for producing the constant 0 in t_2: the "creation" of subterm '0' in t_2 only requires the presence of the context intmul(0, ●) in t_1.

The above observations are the basis for the dynamic dependence relation. It is based on notions of *creation* and *residuation* defined for single rewrite-steps. The former involves function symbols produced by rewrite rules whereas the latter corresponds to situations where symbols are moved around, copied, or not affected by rewrite rules.[6]. Figure 7.13 shows all creation and residuation relations for the example reduction discussed above.

Roughly speaking, the dynamic dependence relation for a multi-step reduction r consists of the transitive closure of creation and residuation relations for the individual rewrite steps in r. It is defined as a relation on generalized *contexts*, i.e., connected sets of function symbols in a term. The fact that c is a *subcontext* of a term t is denoted $c \sqsubseteq t$. For any reduction r that transforms a term t into a term t', a *term slice* with respect to some $c' \sqsubseteq t'$ is defined as the subcontext $c \sqsubseteq t$ that is found by tracing back the dynamic dependence relations from c'. It can be proved that this term slice c satisfies the following properties:

1. c can be rewritten to a term $d' \sqsupseteq c'$ via a reduction r', and

2. r' is a *subreduction* of the original reduction r. Intuitively, r' contains a subset of the rule applications in r.

This situation is illustrated in Figure 7.14. In cases where no confusion arises, we will write $c = SliceOf(c')$ to indicate that c is the term slice with respect to c' for some reduction $r : t \rightarrow^* t'$, $c \sqsubseteq t$, and $c' \sqsubseteq t'$.

---

[6]The notions of creation and residuation become more complicated in the presence of so-called *left-nonlinear* rules and *collapse rules*

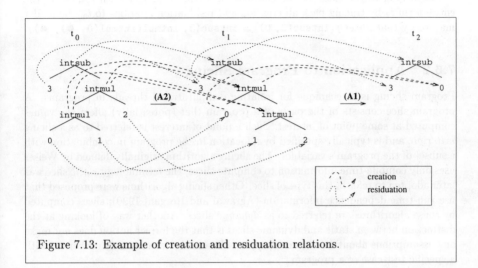

Figure 7.13: Example of creation and residuation relations.

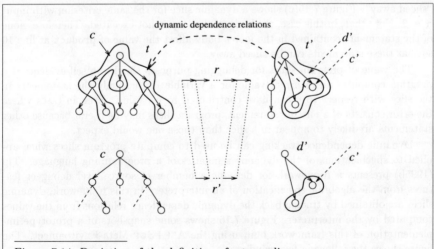

Figure 7.14: Depiction of the definition of a term slice.

Returning to the example, we can determine the term slice with respect to the entire term t_2 by tracing back all creation and residuation relations to t_0; the reader may verify that $SliceOf$(intsub(3, 0)) = intsub(3, intmul(intmul(0, ●), ●)).

7.6.2 Application to Program Slicing

Program slicing is a technique for isolating computational threads in programs. A program slice consists of the parts of a program that (potentially) affect the values computed at some point of interest. Such a point of interest is referred to as a slicing *criterion*, and is typically specified by a location in the program in combination with a subset of the program's variables. The slicing algorithm originally defined by Weiser uses only compile-time information to compute slices; the terminology *static* slice was later adopted to refer to this type of slice. Other slicing algorithms were proposed that use run-time dependence information (Agrawal and Horgan, 1990); slices computed by these algorithms are referred to as *dynamic* slices. Another way of looking at the distinction between static and dynamic slices is that the former notion does not make any assumptions about a program's inputs, whereas the latter is only concerned with a specific test-case of a program.

Figure 7.15(a) shows an example program that asks for a number n, and computes the sum and product of the first n positive numbers. Figure 7.15(b) shows a static slice of this program with respect to criterion (line 10, product). As can be seen in the figure, all computations not relevant to the value of product at line 10 have been "sliced away". Figure 7.15(c) shows a dynamic slice for the same criterion with input n = 0. Note that, in this case, the body of the loop is not executed. Therefore, none of the statements contained in the loop's body affect the value of product at line 10 so that these statements can be sliced away.

The value of program slices for debugging purposes should be self-evident: if a program computes an incorrect value for a variable v, then only the statements in the slice with respect to v can have contributed to v's value. Even in cases where the error consists of a missing statement, program slices may be useful because other statements are likely to appear in a slice than those one would expect.

Dynamic dependence tracking can be used to compute program slices when applied to specifications of the dynamic semantics of a programming language. Tip (1995b) presents a framework for deriving a number of source-level debugger features from the algebraic specification of an interpreter. In this framework, dynamic slices are obtained by tracing back the dynamic dependence relations from the values computed by the interpreter. Figure 7.16 shows some snapshots of a prototype implementation of this framework built using the ASF+SDF Meta-Environment. The figure shows the following four windows:

1. The top left window shows an example program, which is a variation of the example program of Figure 7.15.

```
(1)    read(n);           read(n);              read(n);
(2)    i := 1;            i := 1;               i := 1;
(3)    sum := 0;
(4)    product := 1;      product := 1;         product := 1;
(5)    while i<=n do      while i<=n do         while i<=n do
       begin              begin                 begin
(6)      sum := sum + i;
(7)      product := product*i;   product := product*i;
(8)      i := i + 1         i := i + 1
       end;               end;                  end;
(9)    write(sum);
(10)   write(product)     write(product)        write(product)

           (a)                   (b)                    (c)
```

Figure 7.15: **(a)** An example program. **(b)** Static slice of the program with respect to criterion (10, product). **(c)** Dynamic slice of the program with respect to criterion (10, product) for input n = 0.

2. The top right window displays the values computed by executing this program. Observe that the expression 'product : 120' has been selected in this window.

3. In the bottom left window, the term slice with respect to the selected subterm, 'product : 120', is displayed. In this window, the '<?>' subterms represent the holes '●' in the term slice. Note that the values assigned to variable sum are irrelevant.

4. In the bottom right window, the term slice of (3) has been postprocessed to obtain a more conventional-looking dynamic slice.

Field *et al.* (1995) present a framework where programs are translated to an intermediate representation called Pim (Field, 1992; Bergstra *et al.*, 1996). Pim consists of a directed acyclic graph representation of a program, together with an equational logic. A subsystem of this equational logic defines a rewriting semantics for a program's Pim representation. This rewriting semantics can be used to execute programs, but it is also capable of performing various kinds of analyses by simplifying the program's Pim graph. These analyses include certain aspects of partial evaluation, symbolic execution, and optimization techniques similar to those used in optimizing compilers.

By applying dynamic dependence tracking to Pim's rewriting semantics, various kinds of program slices can be obtained. This approach to computing slices is distinguished by two important characteristics. First, in many cases the program slices are more accurate than those computed by "traditional" slicing algorithms, due to the various optimizations the rewriting process carries out on Pim graphs. Second, it

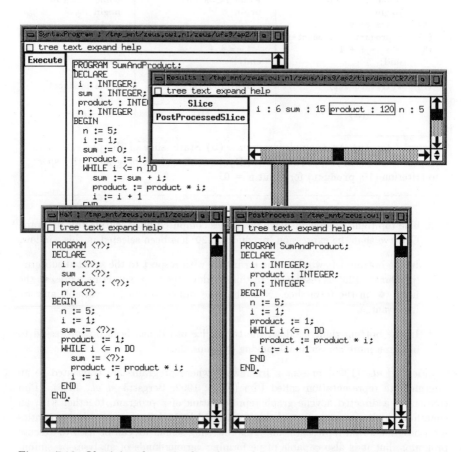

Figure 7.16: Obtaining dynamic slices by applying dynamic dependence tracking to a specification of an interpreter.

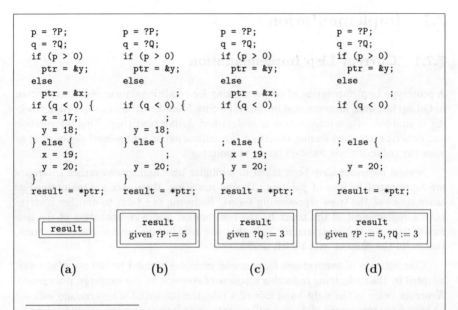

Figure 7.17: **(a)** Example program (= static slice). **(b)** Constrained slice with ?P := 5. **(c)** Constrained slice with ?Q := 3. **(d)** Constrained slice with ?P := 5, ?Q := 3 (= dynamic slice).

allows for the computation of *constrained slices*. The notion of a constrained slice is a generalization of the traditional notions of static and dynamic slices; it allows the user to specify any set of constraints on a program's inputs.

Figure 7.17(a) shows an example program written in a subset of C. In this program, the expressions '?P' and '?Q' represent unknown expressions or inputs. The static slice with respect to the final value of variable `result` consists of the entire program. Figures 7.17(b) and (c) show two constrained slices of the program with respect to the final value of `result`. In (b), the slice is computed for ?P := 5, but no assumptions about the value of ?Q are made. Note that in this case `ptr` cannot be aliased to `x`, so that the assignments to `x` can be sliced away. In (c), the assumption ?Q := 3 is made. In this case, `ptr` can be aliased to either `x` or `y`, but the statements in the first branch of the second conditional will never be executed, and can be eliminated. Finally, in Figure 7.17(d) a slice is computed for the constraint ?P := 5, ?Q := 3. Since all inputs are constrained, this is equivalent to a traditional dynamic slice. Such *parametric* slicing clearly can be valuable in program understanding tools, because it allows one to experiment with the effect of each input.

7.7   Implementation

7.7.1   Current Lisp Implementation

A prototype implementation of origin tracking for conditional term rewriting written in LeLisp has been incorporated in the ASF+SDF Meta-Environment. If origin tracking is enabled, origin information is maintained during rewriting. This information can either be accessed during rewriting (for animation or source-level debuggers) or after the reduction has finished (error pinpointing).

Several measures have been taken to minimize time and space overhead. Origins are represented by sets of pointers. During rewriting, these sets are maintained as annotations of the trees representing terms. Reducing one term to another involves both a replacement of the redex by the contractum, and a computation of the new annotations for the contractum. Note that the annotations outside the contractum, that is, in the context, can be left unchanged.

Computation of annotations for common variables is eased by the use of *sharing*, adopted by the underlying reduction machine of ASF+SDF. For example, if a variable X occurs twice in the right-hand side of a rule, the instantiated contractum will not be built from two *copies* of X, but will contain — as long as this can safely be done — two pointers to the old tree instead. For left-linear rules, this sharing behavior is fully consistent with the origins to be established, which implies that no annotations in the instantiations of variables need to be updated. In other words: the implementation for the Common Variables case comes — for most rewrite rules — for free. For non-leftlinear rules, the implementation has to merge the origin sets of the variables in the left-hand sides into one new set.

In order to minimize the time lost in origin computations during rewriting, the common variables and common subterm relations are computed in advance ("compile time") for each rule. Although storing this information involves some space overhead, it significantly reduces the origin computations, in particular for conditional rules with complicated patterns that are often applied.

These measures are sufficient to bring the loss of efficiency to an acceptable level. So far, it seems that using origin tracking involves an increase in reduction time by at most a factor 2. We expect to be able to reduce this overhead further in the near future. For instance, if one is only interested in origins for the normal form (error handling applications), there is no need to maintain origins for join-conditions. The current implementation does not allow the disabling of such computations. Moreover, in some cases we are only interested in origins for particular sorts, for instance, only for sorts used in error messages. This may significantly reduce the total amount of bookkeeping needed. Again, the current implementation does not yet feature such sort selections.

7.7.2 Executable Specifications of Origin Tracking

It is desirable to acquire further insight in the implementational aspects of origin tracking. This has been done by developing ASF+SDF specifications that describe certain operational aspects of origin tracking. Most of this work is in a preliminary state and is only partially documented. We summarize here three different approaches that can be classified according to the following two criteria:

- How are the rewrite rules executed? The first two approaches extend the interpretation of rewrite rules with origin tracking, while in the third approach the rewrite rules are transformed to include origin tracking. In the first two approaches the rewrite rule interpreter has to be extended, in the third approach the transformed set of rewrite rules can be executed by a standard rewrite rule implementation.

- Where are the origin sets stored? In the first approach, they are kept separate from the term being reduced. In the second approach, the syntactic structure of terms is extended with an annotation operator that permits the direct attachment of origin sets to (sub)terms. In the third approach, a new function symbol is introduced that adds origin sets to each of the original function symbols.

Approach #1: An extended rewrite rule interpreter. Recall that the formalization of origin tracking as given in this chapter proceeds in two stages. First, relations are defined for elementary reduction steps $t_0 \rightarrow t_1$. Next, these relations are extended to reduction sequences $t_0 \rightarrow t_1 \rightarrow ... \rightarrow t_n$ ($n \geq 1$). In particular, relations are established between subterms of an intermediate term t_i, and subterms of the initial term t_0.

In Appendix B of (van Deursen, 1994a) an ASF+SDF specification is given along these lines. In fact, it is a faithful translation of the definitions of Sections 7.2, 7.3, and 7.5 into ASF+SDF. This approach requires an interpreter for rewrite rules that is extended with origin propagation. Applying the (specified) normalization function to a given a term and a set of rewrite rules as in:

```
normalize(
    rev(cons(one, cons(two, nil))),
    { rev(nil)              -> nil,
      rev(cons(E,L))        -> append(rev(L),cons(E,nil)),
      append(nil,L)         -> L,
      append(cons(E,L1),L2) -> cons(E,append(L1,L2))
    })
```

will yield *two* results: the normal form cons(two, cons(one, nil)) as well as a map of the form

$$\{[1] \mapsto \{[1,2,1]\}, [2,1] \mapsto \{[1,1]\}, [2,2] \mapsto \{\}, [2] \mapsto \{\}, [] \mapsto \{[]\}\}$$

relating the normal form to the original term. The two in the normal form, for instance, is related to the two in the initial term by $[1] \mapsto \{[1,2,1]\}$.

Approach #2: A rewrite rule interpreter for labeled terms. In an actual implementation using pointers and data sharing, the *memory address* where each subterm is stored may act as a unique identification for it. In that setting, a possible view on origin tracking is that primary origins determine which subterms in the normal form and in the initial term can be identified because they are stored at the same memory address.

This view has been formalized in Klint (1995c) by annotating each subterm of the initial term with a unique label and defining how these labels are propagated during rewriting. First, the syntactic structure of terms has to be extended to represent *origin sets*: sets of labels of the form $\{L_1, L_2, ...\}$, where the labels L_i are arbitrary identifiers. Next, the syntactic form of terms is extended with an annotation operator in order to permit the use of origin sets as labels for (sub)terms. Typically, a term f(a, g(b)) may be (partially) labeled as

```
{lab1} : f(a, g({lab2, lab3} : b)).
```

Finally, the definitions of the functions that manipulate terms are extended in order to properly preserve origin sets.

It turns out that in this approach the relations *Common Variables*, and *Context* become implicit since they are taken care of by the labeling. This observation was also made in our prototype implementation in LeLisp (Section 7.7.1). Applying the same rewrite rules as above to the labeled term

```
rev(cons({a}:one, cons({b}:two,cons({c}:two,nil))))
```

will yield an appropriately labeled normal form:

```
cons({c}:two, cons({b}:two, cons({a}:one, nil)))
```

We did not label *all* subterms of the initial term in this example. For instance, its root was not labeled and as a result there is no origin associated with the root of the normal form.

By removing all origin sets one obtains the same normal form as is obtained by ordinary rewriting. If the initial term would have been reduced using ordinary rewriting, the two occurrences of the constant two would have become indistinguishable. Using origin tracking, the different origins of these two constants are explicitly indicated in the normal form itself.

Approach #3: Transformation of rewrite rules. Tip has specified a transformational approach to origin tracking that also uses annotated terms. Rather than extending the interpretation of term rewriting systems with origin tracking he transforms a given TRS into a new one that includes origin tracking. Typically, all terms are annotated using a "wrapper" function of the form $o(\_,\_)$ with a function symbol as first argument and a set of paths as second argument. The term `rev(cons(one, cons(two, nil)))` is, for instance, transformed into

```
$o(rev($o(cons($o(one, $set((1 1), $empty)),
           $o(cons($o(two, $set((1 2 1), $empty)),
                   $o(nil, $set((1 2 2), $empty))),
              $set((1 2), $empty))),
        $set((1), $empty))),
    $set(( ), $empty))
```

Here, a single path is written in a Lisp-like notation and the functions `$set` and `$empty` are auxiliary functions that are introduced during the transformation; they are used to construct sets of path.

The rewrite rules are transformed accordingly and have to deal with the `$o` wrappers as well. For instance, the rule

```
append(nil,L)  -> L
```

is transformed into

```
$o(append($o(nil, Z0_1), $o(L_2,Z0_2)), Z0) ->
$o(L_2, $union(Z0_2, Z0))
```

The names of the 'Z' variables that match the origin information (the second argument of `$o`) are derived from the path of the subterm in question in the original term. The `$union` function constructs the union of origin sets. For equations that are not left-linear additional measures are needed to merge origin information and to ensure that multiple variable occurrences at the left-hand side indeed match the same value (modulo origin information).

In approach #2 the origins sets are manipulated by the rewrite rule interpreter while in approach #3 all manipulations of origins sets are expressed by rewrite rules.

Future directions. The experience with the current prototype implementation of origin tracking combined with the ideas explored in the three approaches just described gives some guidance for more efficient implementations of origin tracking. Some issues are:

(1) A transformational approach has the advantage that an implementation of term rewriting can be re-used without any modification. However, preliminary measurements suggest that using rewriting for the manipulation of origin sets increases the number of rewrite steps by more than four orders of magnitude compared to standard rewriting without origin tracking.

(2) The overhead of functions for manipulating origin sets is substantial. They should be implemented in a very efficient manner.

(3) Once origins have been computed, they should be represented in a *standard format* to permit tools to use them.

The reconciliation of items (1) and (2) may be hard to achieve. The problems involved are, however, similar to the ones that are encountered when replacing rewrite rules defining, for instance, an arithmetic operation by an external function that implements the same operation more efficiently. One direction we want to explore is to add external functions for the manipulation of origin sets to an existing rewrite machine.

8

Second-Order Term Rewriting
Specification of Static Semantics:
An Exercise

Jan Heering

Abstract The static semantics of the simple programming language Pico is expressed using second-order rewrite rules in addition to first-order ones. The specification has a highly non-deterministic character and does not use a type environment. Furthermore, it supports error recovery and the early detection of errors in incomplete programs.

8.1 Introduction

8.1.1 Higher-Order Term Rewriting

In some cases, the associative lists available in ASF+SDF (Section 1.2.5, p. 7) may be used to avoid unnecessary traversal of structures and thus raise the abstraction level of a specification. See for instance the specification in Figure 1.1 (p. 10) and the associated discussion in Section 1.4.2. There is no reason why this should only be interesting for lists. In this chapter we show how second-order term rewriting rules may serve a similar purpose in a setting where associative list matching would only be applicable after a rather artificial conversion of programs to lists.

A higher-order rewrite system consists of a signature and a set of rewrite rules as usual, except that both of them may be higher-order. A higher-order signature defines the abstract syntax of a language of typed λ-terms whose semantics is given by the rewrite rules of the specification in conjunction with the built-in rules of α-, β- and η-conversion for typed λ-terms. The latter are similar to their untyped counterparts, which were explained in Section 1.3.3. For reasons to be explained we do not allow

λ-terms $\lambda x.t$ such that x is not a free variable of t, i.e., *we do not allow vacuous abstraction*.

Higher-order term rewriting uses *higher-order matching* (matching of typed λ-terms) as its basic computational primitive. We give an example of *second*-order matching, which is all we need in this chapter.

sorts S BOOL
context-free syntax
    a → S
    f(S) → S
    g(S) → S
    if(BOOL, S, S) → S
variables
    $[XY]$ → S
    $F(S)$ → S (second-order variable F)
    $B[']*$ → BOOL

and the second-order rewrite rule

$$\text{if}(B, F(X), F(Y)) = F(\text{if}(B, X, Y)). \tag{8.1}$$

The left-hand side of (8.1) matches

$$\text{if}(B', g(f(a)), g(f(f(a))))$$

in three different ways, namely, for

$$
\begin{array}{llll}
F = \lambda V.g(f(V)) & X = a & Y = f(a) & B = B' \\
F = \lambda V.g(V) & X = f(a) & Y = f(f(a)) & B = B' \\
F = \lambda V.V & X = g(f(a)) & Y = g(f(f(a))) & B = B'.
\end{array}
$$

Thus, just like associative list matching (Section 1.4.2), higher-order matching need not be unitary but may yield many solutions. In this particular case, substitution in the right-hand side of (8.1) followed by β-conversion yields respectively

$$
\begin{array}{l}
g(f(\text{if}(B', a, f(a)))) \\
g(\text{if}(B', f(a), f(f(a)))) \\
\text{if}(B', g(f(a)), g(f(f(a)))).
\end{array}
$$

Obviously, the last solution may cause a loop during rewriting.

This chapter is rather informal. The full definition of higher-order term rewriting is not needed for the case study at hand and is given in Chapter 9. Our specification formalism will be an *ad hoc* extension of ASF+SDF with second-order variables.

Higher-order matching is the special case of higher-order unification in which only one of the terms involved is instantiated. Since higher-order unification is available in λProlog, an extension of Prolog to typed λ-terms (Nadathur and Miller, 1988), it is a suitable vehicle for experiments with higher-order term rewriting (Felty, 1992; Heering, 1992).

8.1.2 Some Issues in the Specification of Static Semantics

Our point of departure is the observation that most first-order static semantics specifications introduce unnecessary dependences. For instance, the declaration and use of an identifier in a program can be related only indirectly, the declaration information being inherited from the enclosing construct rather than the declarations section itself. This is typically the way attribute grammars or primitive recursive schemes (Chapter 6) are structured. Although static analysis of such a specification may allow an implementation to optimize the attribute evaluation order, it would be better not to have to specify any dependence if it does not matter.

In view of this, our first two desiderata for static semantics specifications are:

(A) No unnecessary dependences;

(B) No type environment.

Since it is to be expected that execution of a specification in this style is not hampered by incorrect or missing parts in the program being checked, we mention another desirable property:

(C) Early detection of errors in incomplete programs containing editor place holders (meta-variables) (Section 1.4.1).

Keeping these issues in mind, we construct a second-order term rewriting specification for the static semantics of the toy language Pico (Chapter 4) in the next section. Recovery from undeclared variables will be added in Section 8.3.

A first-order static semantics specification that does not use a type environment (although for a different reason) has been given by Walters (1989).

8.2 Basic Static Semantics of Pico

The syntax of Pico is shown in Figure 8.1. The sorts ID, NATURAL, and STRING occurring in it are imported from modules Identifiers, Naturals, and Strings respectively. These are not shown.

The basic static semantics of Pico is shown in Figure 8.2. All of its equations (rewrite rules) are first-order, except (8.2). First of all, it should be noted that typechecking proceeds by transformation of the program itself. Hence, there is no explicit typecheck predicate in the syntax, but the result of program normalization indicates whether the program is statically correct or not. Since there is no type environment, the typecheck predicate is not needed to distribute the declaration information. This is similar to the evaluation of a boolean or arithmetic expression, which is just rewritten to normal form without an explicit evaluation function being necessary.

Typechecking proceeds as follows. For the time being we assume there are no multiply declared variables in the program to be typechecked. Equation (8.2) involves

```
module Pico-syntax
imports Layout Identifiers Naturals Strings
exports
sorts PROGRAM DECLS DECL SERIES STATEMENT EXPR TYPE
context-free syntax
        begin DECLS SERIES end   → PROGRAM
        declare {DECL "," }* ";"  → DECLS
        ID ":" TYPE              → DECL
        {STATEMENT ";" }*        → SERIES
        ID ":=" EXPR             → STATEMENT
        if EXPR then SERIES else SERIES fi → STATEMENT
        while EXPR do SERIES od → STATEMENT
        EXPR "+" EXPR            → EXPR {assoc}
        EXPR "−" EXPR            → EXPR {left}
        EXPR "‖" EXPR            → EXPR {assoc}
        ID                       → EXPR
        NATURAL                  → EXPR
        STRING                   → EXPR
        "(" EXPR ")"             → EXPR {bracket}
        natural                  → TYPE
        string                   → TYPE
```

Figure 8.1: Syntax of Pico.

the second-order variable *Series*. According to its declaration in the **variables**-section, it is of type ID → SERIES. The variables D_1 and D_2 are list variables of type {DECL "," }*. Equation (8.2) picks up a declaration $X : \tau$ in the list of declarations by means of associative list matching, and, since we do not allow vacuous abstraction (Section 8.1.1), it picks up at least one occurrence of identifier X in the statements section by means of second-order matching. It then replaces the occurrence(s) of X with type τ, or rather with the corresponding identifier tp(τ), where the tp-function converts types into identifiers.

The replacement of items with their type is continued by equations (8.3) and (8.4). These apply to constants and do not need access to the declarations section of the Pico program. Note that their left- and right-hand sides are terms of sort EXPR rather than NATURAL or STRING, since EXPR is the only sort that can be assigned to both sides.

The remaining equations eliminate parts of the Pico program that are statically correct. Equation (8.5) deletes an assignment statement whose left- and right-hand

module Pico-typecheck
imports Pico-syntax (Figure 8.1)
exports
context-free syntax
$\quad$ tp(TYPE) $\quad \to$ ID
variables $Series$(ID) $\quad \to$ SERIES
$\quad D[0-9]* \quad \to$ {DECL "," }*
$\quad S[0-9']* \quad \to$ {STATEMENT ";" }*
$\quad X \qquad\qquad \to$ ID
$\quad \tau \qquad\qquad \to$ TYPE
$\quad n \qquad\qquad \to$ NATURAL
$\quad \sigma \qquad\qquad \to$ STRING

equations

$$
\begin{array}{l}
\text{begin} \\
\quad \text{declare } D_1, X : \tau, D_2; \\
\quad Series(X) \\
\text{end}
\end{array}
=
\begin{array}{l}
\text{begin} \\
\quad \text{declare } D_1, X : \tau, D_2; \\
\quad Series(\text{tp}(\tau)) \\
\text{end}
\end{array}
\qquad (8.2)
$$

$$n = \text{tp(natural)} \qquad (8.3)$$

$$\sigma = \text{tp(string)} \qquad (8.4)$$

$$S_1; \text{tp}(\tau) := \text{tp}(\tau); S_2 = S_1; S_2 \qquad (8.5)$$

$$S_1; \text{if tp(natural) then } S \text{ else } S' \text{ fi}; S_2 = S_1; S; S'; S_2 \qquad (8.6)$$

$$S_1; \text{while tp(natural) do } S \text{ od}; S_2 = S_1; S; S_2 \qquad (8.7)$$

$$\text{tp(natural)} + \text{tp(natural)} = \text{tp(natural)} \qquad (8.8)$$

$$\text{tp(natural)} - \text{tp(natural)} = \text{tp(natural)} \qquad (8.9)$$

$$\text{tp(string)} \parallel \text{tp(string)} = \text{tp(string)} \qquad (8.10)$$

Figure 8.2: Basic static semantics of Pico.

sides have the same type, and equations (8.6) and (8.7) remove the skeleton of an if- or while-statement whose expression part has the correct type tp(natural). Expressions are evaluated by equations (8.8)–(8.10). If the program is correct, its statements section is completely eliminated, yielding the normal form

$$\text{begin declare } \cdots \text{; end.}$$

If it is incorrect, the normal form contains remnants of offending statements. These can be related to the parts of the program they originated from by a suitably extended origin tracking facility. Such an extension is discussed in Chapter 9. Furthermore, equations converting the normal form into a set of user-friendly diagnostic messages can be added to the specification in a straightforward way as explained in Chapter 4.

For instance, let P be the (statically incorrect) Pico program

> begin
> declare a : natural, b : string;
> while a do $b := a$ od
> end.

The character of second-order matching is such that an identifier X can be picked up by the left-hand side of (8.2) in the statements section *regardless of the depth at which it occurs*. Using associative list matching, this could only have been achieved after a rather artificial conversion of Pico programs to lists. The left-hand side of equation (8.2) matches P in four different ways. Apart from the values of the list variables D_1 and D_2, the solutions are

$$X = a \quad \tau = \text{natural} \quad Series = \lambda U.\ \text{while } U \text{ do } b := U \text{ od}$$
$$X = a \quad \tau = \text{natural} \quad Series = \lambda U.\ \text{while } U \text{ do } b := a \text{ od}$$
$$X = a \quad \tau = \text{natural} \quad Series = \lambda U.\ \text{while } a \text{ do } b := U \text{ od}$$
$$X = b \quad \tau = \text{string} \quad Series = \lambda U.\ \text{while } a \text{ do } U := a \text{ od},$$

where U is a bound variable of sort ID. Hence, after a single application of (8.2) the possible results are

> begin
> declare a : natural, b : string;
> while tp(natural) do b := tp(natural) od
> end

> begin
> declare a : natural, b : string;
> while tp(natural) do b := a od
> end

> begin
> declare a : natural, b : string;
> while a do b := tp(natural) od
> end

> begin
> declare a : natural, b : string;
> while a do tp(string) := a od
> end.

The normal form of P is

> begin
> declare a : natural, b : string;
> tp(string) := tp(natural)
> end,

where the non-standard statement

$$\text{tp(string)} := \text{tp(natural)}$$

is a remnant of the incorrect statement $b := a$. The skeleton of the while-statement is correct and has been eliminated by (8.7). The second-order matching strategy actually used does not matter.

Pico-typecheck not only works well on complete Pico programs but also on incomplete ones containing editor place holders (requirement (C), Section 8.1.2). For instance, Pico-typecheck reduces

> begin
> declare a : natural, b : natural;
> while a do ⟨STATEMENT⟩; $b := a$ od
> end,

where ⟨STATEMENT⟩ is a place holder of sort STATEMENT, to

> begin
> declare a : natural, b : natural;
> ⟨STATEMENT⟩
> end.

Whether a statically correct value will be substituted for the place holder remains to be seen, so it is retained in the normal form. Everything else is eliminated. In a first-order specification without associative lists, substitution of types in the statement $b := a$ would require an inductive argument on the possible substitutions of the place holder preceding it, and would very probably be blocked.

Finally, multiply declared variables cause ambiguity (non-confluence) if they are actually used in the statements section. For instance, the program

> begin
> declare a : natural, a : string;
> $a := a$
> end.

has three different normal forms, reflecting the ambiguity in the declared type of a. Hence, the program has ambiguous static semantics, just like a sentence might be syntactically ambiguous (Section 1.2.3). One way of disambiguating it would be to delete the declarations of multiply declared variables altogether during typechecking and apply the recovery procedure discussed in the next section.

The non-confluence of Pico-typecheck does not mean it is incorrect, but only that its interpretation as an algebraic specification requires an appropriate notion of semantics. Since our viewpoint in this book is primarily an operational one based on term rewriting, this is beyond our present scope and we refer the interested reader to (Hussmann, 1993).

module Pico-recover
imports Pico-typecheck   (Figure 8.2)
variables $Series$(STATEMENT) $\rightarrow$ SERIES
           $Series$(EXPR) $\rightarrow$ SERIES
           E $\rightarrow$ EXPR
           ξ $\rightarrow$ CHAR+

equations

$$
\begin{array}{l}
\text{begin} \\
\quad \text{declare } D; \\
\quad Series(\text{id}(\xi) := \text{tp}(\tau)) \\
\text{end}
\end{array}
\;=\;
\begin{array}{l}
\text{begin} \\
\quad \text{declare } D, \text{id}(\xi) : \tau; \\
\quad Series(\text{tp}(\tau) := \text{tp}(\tau)) \\
\text{end}
\end{array}
\qquad (8.11)
$$

$$
\begin{array}{l}
\text{begin} \\
\quad \text{declare } D; \\
\quad Series(\text{tp}(\tau) := \text{id}(\xi)) \\
\text{end}
\end{array}
\;=\;
\begin{array}{l}
\text{begin} \\
\quad \text{declare } D, \text{id}(\xi) : \tau; \\
\quad Series(\text{tp}(\tau) := \text{tp}(\tau)) \\
\text{end}
\end{array}
\qquad (8.12)
$$

$$
\begin{array}{l}
\text{begin} \\
\quad \text{declare } D; \\
Series(\text{if id}(\xi) \text{ then } S \text{ else } S' \text{ fi}) \\
\text{end}
\end{array}
\;=\;
\begin{array}{l}
\text{begin} \\
\quad \text{declare } D, \text{id}(\xi) : \text{natural}; \\
Series(\text{if tp}(\tau) \text{ then } S \text{ else } S' \text{ fi}) \\
\text{end}
\end{array}
\qquad (8.13)
$$

$$
\begin{array}{l}
\text{begin} \\
\quad \text{declare } D; \\
\quad Series(\text{while id}(\xi) \text{ do } S \text{ od}) \\
\text{end}
\end{array}
\;=\;
\begin{array}{l}
\text{begin} \\
\quad \text{declare } D, \text{id}(\xi) : \text{natural}; \\
\quad Series(\text{while tp}(\tau) \text{ do } S \text{ od}) \\
\text{end}
\end{array}
\qquad (8.14)
$$

$$
\begin{array}{l}
\text{begin} \\
\quad \text{declare } D; \\
\quad Series(\text{id}(\xi) + E) \\
\text{end}
\end{array}
\;=\;
\begin{array}{l}
\text{begin} \\
\quad \text{declare } D, \text{id}(\xi) : \text{natural}; \\
\quad Series(\text{tp}(\tau) + E) \\
\text{end}
\end{array}
\qquad (8.15)
$$

$$
\begin{array}{l}
\text{begin} \\
\quad \text{declare } D; \\
\quad Series(E + \text{id}(\xi)) \\
\text{end}
\end{array}
\;=\;
\begin{array}{l}
\text{begin} \\
\quad \text{declare } D, \text{id}(\xi) : \text{natural}; \\
\quad Series(E + \text{tp}(\tau)) \\
\text{end}
\end{array}
\qquad (8.16)
$$

Figure 8.3: Recovery from undeclared variables (preliminary version).

equations

$$
\begin{array}{l}
\text{begin} \\
\quad \text{declare } D; \\
\quad Series(\text{id}(\xi) - E) \\
\text{end}
\end{array}
=
\begin{array}{l}
\text{begin} \\
\quad \text{declare } D, \text{id}(\xi) : \text{natural}; \\
\quad Series(\text{tp}(\tau) - E) \\
\text{end}
\end{array}
\qquad (8.17)
$$

$$
\begin{array}{l}
\text{begin} \\
\quad \text{declare } D; \\
\quad Series(E - \text{id}(\xi)) \\
\text{end}
\end{array}
=
\begin{array}{l}
\text{begin} \\
\quad \text{declare } D, \text{id}(\xi) : \text{natural}; \\
\quad Series(E - \text{tp}(\tau)) \\
\text{end}
\end{array}
\qquad (8.18)
$$

$$
\begin{array}{l}
\text{begin} \\
\quad \text{declare } D; \\
\quad Series(\text{id}(\xi) \parallel E) \\
\text{end}
\end{array}
=
\begin{array}{l}
\text{begin} \\
\quad \text{declare } D, \text{id}(\xi) : \text{string}; \\
\quad Series(\text{tp}(\tau) \parallel E) \\
\text{end}
\end{array}
\qquad (8.19)
$$

$$
\begin{array}{l}
\text{begin} \\
\quad \text{declare } D; \\
\quad Series(E \parallel \text{id}(\xi)) \\
\text{end}
\end{array}
=
\begin{array}{l}
\text{begin} \\
\quad \text{declare } D, \text{id}(\xi) : \text{string}; \\
\quad Series(E \parallel \text{tp}(\tau)) \\
\text{end}
\end{array}
\qquad (8.20)
$$

Figure 8.4: Recovery from undeclared variables (preliminary version) (cont.).

8.3 Recovery from Undeclared Variables

Undeclared variables cannot be eliminated by Pico-typecheck (Figure 8.2), and are left in the statements section of the normal form. In addition to these, the normal form may contain the non-standard identifiers tp(natural), tp(string), or even tp($\langle$TYPE$\rangle$) with editor place holder $\langle$TYPE$\rangle$. Module Pico-recover shown in Figure 8.3 and 8.4 adds declarations for variables occurring in the statements section regardless of any declarations already present. It picks up a standard identifier id(ξ) with sufficient context to determine its type, and adds the corresponding declaration to the declarations section. For instance, if a value of type τ is assigned to a variable id(ξ), equation (8.11) adds a declaration id(ξ) : τ to the program. The other equations are similar. We note that variable *Series* is overloaded. It is of type STATEMENT $\rightarrow$ SERIES as well as of type EXPR $\rightarrow$ SERIES. For more details on the implicitly defined lexical constructor function id, which is of type CHAR+ $\rightarrow$ ID, see Section 1.2.4.

We have neglected the fact that a declaration may already be present for id(ξ), and that an undeclared variable should not be added to the declarations section more than once. These closely related cases are taken care of by the negative condition

$$(\forall\, D_1\, \tau'\, D_2)[\text{declare } D; \neq \text{declare } D_1, \text{id}(\xi) : \tau', D_2;],$$

module Pico-recover
imports Pico-typecheck (Figure 8.2)
variables $Series(\text{STATEMENT}) \rightarrow \text{SERIES}$
$Series(\text{EXPR}) \rightarrow \text{SERIES}$
$E \rightarrow \text{EXPR}$
$\xi \rightarrow \text{CHAR+}$
$\tau' \rightarrow \text{TYPE}$

equations

$$\frac{(\forall\, D_1\, \tau'\, D_2)[\text{declare } D; \neq \text{declare } D_1, \text{id}(\xi) : \tau', D_2;]}{\begin{array}{lcl} \text{begin} & & \text{begin} \\ \quad \text{declare } D; & & \quad \text{declare } D, \text{id}(\xi) : \tau; \\ \quad Series(\text{id}(\xi) := \text{tp}(\tau)) & = & \quad Series(\text{id}(\xi) := \text{tp}(\tau)) \\ \text{end} & & \text{end} \end{array}} \qquad (8.21)$$

$\cdots$

$\cdots$

Figure 8.5: Recovery from undeclared variables.

which has to be added to every equation. It is evaluated by attempting an associative list match of the right-hand side with the declarations section. The match should fail for the condition to succeed. (We note that this type of negative condition is not supported by the current version of the ASF+SDF system, but it could easily be added.) As a result we obtain the specification shown in Figure 8.5.

Pico-recover is not confluent. For instance, the program

$$\begin{array}{l} \text{begin} \\ \quad \text{declare } b : \text{string}; \\ \quad \text{while } a \text{ do } b := a \text{ od} \\ \quad \text{end}, \end{array}$$

with undeclared variable a, normalizes either to

$$\begin{array}{l} \text{begin} \\ \quad \text{declare } b : \text{string}, \ a : \text{natural}; \\ \quad \text{tp}(\text{string}) := \text{tp}(\text{natural}) \\ \quad \text{end}, \end{array}$$

or to

```
begin
  declare b : string, a : string;
  while tp(string) do od
end.
```

If an undeclared variable is used inconsistently, the implementation adds one of the possible declarations for it. Hence, the non-confluence reflects the non-deterministic character of the recovery process.

Origin Tracking for Higher-Order Term Rewriting Systems

Arie van Deursen

T.B. Dinesh

Abstract   The experiments with the use of second-order rewrite rules for the definition of the typechecking of the simple imperative language described in the previous chapter revealed a need to extend origin tracking to higher-order term rewriting systems. In this chapter we discuss how origin information can be maintained for β-reductions and η-expansions during higher-order rewriting. We give a definition of higher-order origin tracking and illustrate its suitability using the second-order typechecker definition as an example.

9.1   Introduction

Many first-order specifications of programming languages are more deterministic than desirable. Typically, a considerable amount of specification effort is invested in writing functions to extract information from programs (concerning, e.g., declaration and use of identifiers), functions which have to be defined inductively over the syntax of the language. For realistic languages having a larger grammar, these functions tend to be uninteresting, and distract readers from the more essential parts of the specification.

In Chapter 8, Heering studied the use of *second-order* specifications as a solution to this over-specification problem. He came up with an example specification of the static semantics of a small language, for which he needed neither an explicit program traversal nor the construction of a program environment (symbol table).

One of his observations was that when turning this higher-order specification into an executable typechecker, "a suitably extended origin tracking facility" was mandatory (see Section 8.2). This raises the question whether the notion of origin can be extended to the higher-order case, which is the topic we will be studying in this chapter. It has turned out that origin tracking in higher-order systems is considerably more complicated. This extra complexity mainly arises because equality in the higher-order case is modulo $\beta\bar{\eta}$-conversion rather than simple syntactic equivalence.

We start this chapter by defining higher-order rewriting and giving a small example. Next, we present primary origins for the higher-order case in Section 9.3, and extensions to secondary origins in Section 9.4. In Section 9.5 we mention related work and draw some conclusions.

Note that this chapter is complementary to Section 7.5, which deals with origins for Primitive Recursive Schemes (PRSs). A PRS is a formalization of a set of functions defined inductively over a set of grammar constructors. In a first-order setting, it is difficult to avoid such functions, which effectively encode how to traverse a syntax tree from top to bottom in order to retrieve information only available at the leaf nodes of the tree. Therefore, PRSs will occur frequently in first-order specifications, and establishing good origins for them is important. In a higher-order setting, by contrast, λ-abstractions are used to abstract from the actual structure of the syntax trees, thus avoiding the need for PRSs. This role is taken over by rewrite rules over higher-order terms. Finding good origins for these higher-order rules is the theme of this chapter.

9.2 Higher-Order Term Rewriting

For the definition of Higher-Order Term Rewriting Systems, we follow Wolfram (1993). The main difference with the first-order case is that terms in higher-order term rewriting systems are constructed according to the simply-typed λ-calculus (Church, 1940).

9.2.1 The Simply-Typed λ-Calculus

The set of *type symbols* T consists of *elementary* type symbols from T_0 and of *functional* type symbols $(\alpha \to \beta)$, where $\alpha, \beta \in T$. We may abbreviate a type $(\alpha_1 \to (\alpha_2 \to (\cdots \to (\alpha_n \to \beta)\cdots)))$ to $(\alpha_1, \ldots, \alpha_n \to \beta)$. *Terms* are built using *constants* and *variables*, each of which has an associated type symbol. The type of t is written $\tau(t)$. If x is a variable with $\tau(x) = \alpha$, and t a term with $\tau(t) = \beta$, then the *abstraction* $(\lambda x.t)$ is a term of type $(\alpha \to \beta)$. If t, t' are terms with $\tau(t) = (\alpha \to \beta)$ and $\tau(t') = \alpha$, then the *application*[1] $(t\ t')$ is a term of type β. Application is left-associative.

Occurrences in λ-terms are defined as for first-order terms, by representing abstraction as a node with one son and application as a node with two sons. As an example, Figure 9.1 shows all occurrences in the term (add $((\lambda N.N)$ zero) zero). Again, $\mathcal{O}(t)$ is the set of all occurrences in t.

---

[1] We use $@(t, t')$ alternatively, when there is a need to make the application operator explicit, as in Figure 9.1. We also use $t(t')$ in the context of term rewriting, as in Figure 9.2.

All occurrences of x in $(\lambda x.t)$ are said to be *bound*. Non-bound occurrences are *free*. A term is *closed* if it does not contain free variables, *open* otherwise. Bound variables can be renamed according to the rule of α-conversion. A *replacement* of a term t at occurrence u by subterm s is denoted by $t[u \leftarrow s]$. A *substitution* σ is a mapping from variables to terms. Application of a substitution σ to a term t, written t^σ, has the effect that all free occurrences of variables in the domain of σ are replaced by their associated term. Following the *variable convention* (Barendregt, 1984), bound variables are renamed if necessary.

Let x be a variable, t_1, t_2 terms, and let substitution $\sigma = \{x \mapsto t_2\}$. Then the term $((\lambda x.t_1)\, t_2)$ is a β-*redex* and can be transformed to t_1^σ by β-reduction. A term without β-redex occurrences is said to be in β-*normal form*. All simply-typed λ-terms have a β-normal form, which is unique up to α-conversion. A β-normal form always has the form

$$(\lambda x_1.(\lambda x_2.\cdots (\lambda x_n.\{(\cdots ((H\, t_1)\, t_2)\cdots t_m)\})\cdots))$$

where $x_1, \ldots, x_n$ are variables, $t_1, \ldots, t_m$ terms in β-normal form, H a constant or a variable, $m, n \geq 0$. We will sometimes write this as $\lambda x_1 \cdots x_n.H(t_1, \ldots, t_m)$. In such a term, H is called the *head*, $H(t_1, \ldots, t_m)$ is called the *matrix*, and $\lambda x_1 \cdots x_n$ is called the *binder*.

The rule of η-reduction states that terms of the form $\lambda x.(t\, x)$ can be transformed to just t, provided that x does not occur freely in t. Its counterpart is $\bar\eta$-expansion: if a head H of a β-normal form $\lambda x_1 \cdots x_n.H(t_1, \ldots, t_m)$ is of type $(\alpha_1, \ldots, \alpha_{m+k} \to \beta)$ $(k > 0)$, then clearly as H expects more arguments, we can add these as extra abstractions. The term above can be $\bar\eta$-expanded to $\lambda x_1 \cdots x_n y.H(t_1, \ldots, t_m, y)$, where y is a fresh variable of type α_{m+1}. Every term has an $\bar\eta$-normal form.

Let χ be any of $\{\alpha, \beta, \eta, \bar\eta\}$. If t can be transformed to t' by performing a χ-reduction at occurrence u, we write this as $t \rhd_{\chi,u} t'$, or alternatively as $t' \lhd_{\chi,u} t$, where we may omit occurrence u. Repeated χ-reduction is written $t \rhd_\chi^* t'$. Since $\rhd_\alpha^*$ is a symmetric relation, we will sometimes write it as $=_\alpha$. The $\beta\bar\eta$-normal form of t is indicated by $t\!\downarrow_{\beta\bar\eta}$. The relation $t =_{\beta\bar\eta} t'$ holds if and only if $t\!\downarrow_{\beta\bar\eta} =_\alpha t'\!\downarrow_{\beta\bar\eta}$.

9.2.2 Higher-Order Rewrite Steps

If p, q are (open) simply-typed λ-terms of the same type and in $\beta\bar\eta$-normal form, and if every free variable in q also occurs in p, then $p \to q$ is a (higher-order) rewrite rule. A reduction $t \xrightarrow{u,\sigma}_r t'$, where t, t' are closed λ-terms in $\beta\bar\eta$-normal form, σ is a substitution, $r : p \to q$ is a rewrite rule, and u is an occurrence in $\mathcal{O}(t)$ denoting the redex position, is possible if:

- The types of the redex and the left-hand side of the rule are the same:
$$\tau(t/u) = \tau(p)$$

- The instantiated left-hand side is $\beta\bar\eta$-equal to the redex:
$$\{p^\sigma\}\!\downarrow_{\beta\bar\eta} =_\alpha \{t/u\}\!\downarrow_{\bar\eta}$$

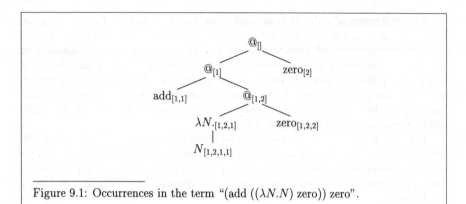

Figure 9.1: Occurrences in the term "(add $((\lambda N.N)$ zero)) zero".

- Replacement of the redex by the instantiated right-hand side followed by $\beta\overline{\eta}$-normalization yields the result t':

$$\{t[u \leftarrow q^\sigma]\}\downarrow_{\beta\overline{\eta}} =_\alpha t'$$

Notice the variety of $\{\alpha, \beta, \overline{\eta}\}$-conversions involved in the application of one rule. This turns out to have consequences for the definition of origins. Also note that matching the redex against a left-hand side may yield more than one substitution. For origin tracking purposes, however, we are not concerned with finding matches; we assume that in some way it has been decided to apply a rewrite rule under a given substitution (see also Section 9.4.3).

9.2.3 Example

Consider the second-order term rewriting specification of a simple typechecker shown in Figure 9.2. The specification is equivalent to the one given in Chapter 8, but for reasons of clarity it uses prefix syntax rather than distfix notation. The objective of this specification is to replace all simple expressions (identifiers, string or natural constants) by a term "tp(τ)", where τ is the type of that simple expression (see equations [1], [2], and [3]). Next, type correct expressions are reduced to their type (equation [4]). Finally, type correct statements are eliminated (equation [5]). The resulting normal form only contains the incorrect statements.

Take the initial term P_1:

```
program(
    decls( decl(n,natural),  decls( decl(s,string), emptydecls) ),
    stats( assign(s, plus(id(n),id(n))), emptystats )   )
```

It can be reduced according to equation [1] with, e.g., the substitution[2] σ_1:

$$
\begin{aligned}
\{ \quad \mathcal{D} \;&\mapsto\; \lambda Decl.\ \text{decls}(Decl,\ \text{decls(decl(s,string),\ emptydecls))}, \\
\mathcal{S} \;&\mapsto\; \lambda Id.\ \text{stats(assign(s,plus(id}(Id),\text{id}(Id)\text{)), emptystats)}, \\
X \;&\mapsto\; \text{n}, \\
\tau \;&\mapsto\; \text{natural} \quad \}
\end{aligned}
$$

Applying this rule replaces occurrences of "n" by "tp(natural)", which results in a term P_2:

```
program(
   decls( decl(n,natural),  decls( decl(s,string), emptydecls) ),
   stats( assign(s, plus(id( tp(natural) ),
                      id( tp(natural) ))), emptystats )  )
```

Next, equation [1] can be applied again, this time replacing "s" by "tp(string)", yielding a P_3. Finally, equation [4] can be used to replace the "plus" expression by a representation of its type (natural) resulting in P_4, which is the normal form of P_1.

Initially, we are allowed to apply equation [1] to P_1, since under substitution σ_1, the left-hand side of equation [1] produces a new term P_1'', which after two β-reductions (one for $\mathcal{D}$ and one for $\mathcal{S}$) is exactly equal to term P_1.

To construct the result P_2 of this one-step reduction, we first apply σ_1 to the right-hand side of equation [1], producing some term P_2''. Then two more β-reductions transform P_2'' to its β-normal form, which results in the desired P_2. We can summarize this first single-step rewrite by:

$$
P_1 \;\lhd_\beta\; P_1' \;\lhd_\beta\; P_1'' \equiv l_1^{\sigma_1} \;\rightsquigarrow\; r_1^{\sigma_1} \equiv P_2'' \;\rhd_\beta\; P_2' \;\rhd_\beta\; P_2
$$

where $\rightsquigarrow$ denotes the replacement of the instantiated left-hand side by the instantiated right-hand side, and l_1 and r_1 are the left- and right-hand side of equation [1]. Our definition of origins also follows this "flow" where origin relations between P_2 and P_1 are defined using elementary origin definitions between the pairs $P_2 - P_2'$, $P_2' - P_2''$, etc.

9.3 Higher-Order Origins

We define origins for higher-order rewriting by (i) indicating how origins are to be established for $\rhd_\alpha$, $\rhd_\beta$, $\rhd_\eta$, and $\rhd_{\overline{\eta}}$ conversion; then (ii) describing how the inverses

---

[2]It is necessary to avoid vacuous abstraction of *Decl* in the assignments of $\mathcal{S}$ and $\mathcal{D}$ in accordance with Chapter 8.

sorts: PROG DECLS DECL STAT STATS ID TYPE EXP ...

functions:

program	: DECLS, STATS	$\rightarrow$ PROG
decls	: DECL, DECLS	$\rightarrow$ DECLS
emptydecls	:	$\rightarrow$ DECLS
decl	: ID, TYPE	$\rightarrow$ DECL
natural	:	$\rightarrow$ TYPE
string	:	$\rightarrow$ TYPE
stats	: STAT, STATS	$\rightarrow$ STATS
emptystats	:	$\rightarrow$ STATS
assign	: ID, EXP	$\rightarrow$ STAT
plus	: EXP, EXP	$\rightarrow$ EXP
id	: ID	$\rightarrow$ EXP
nat	: NAT	$\rightarrow$ EXP
str	: STRING	$\rightarrow$ EXP
...		
tp	: TYPE	$\rightarrow$ ID

variables:

$\mathcal{D}$	: DECL $\rightarrow$ DECLS		X	: ID
τ	: TYPE		$\mathcal{S}$	: ID $\rightarrow$ STATS
S	: STATS		N	: NAT
R	: STRING			

equations:

[1] program($\mathcal{D}$(decl(X,τ)), $\mathcal{S}(X)$) = program($\mathcal{D}$(decl(X,τ)), $\mathcal{S}$(tp(τ)))

[2] nat(N) = id(tp(natural))

[3] str(R) = id(tp(string))

[4] plus(id(tp(natural)), id(tp(natural))) = id(tp(natural))

[5] stats(assign(tp(τ), id(tp(τ))), S) = S

Figure 9.2: Part of a static semantics specification.

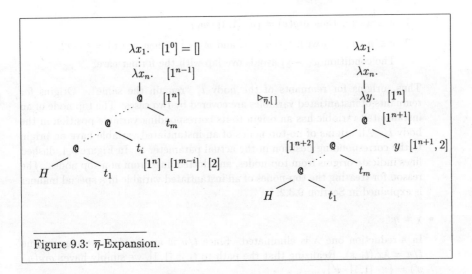

Figure 9.3: $\overline{\eta}$-Expansion.

$\triangleleft_\beta$ and $\triangleleft_{\overline{\eta}}$ can be dealt with; and (iii) explaining how origin relations can be set up between the left- and right-hand side of a rewrite rule. In this section we give a very basic definition of what we will call *primary higher-order origins*. In the next section we discuss various proposals and heuristics to extend these origins.

We use the following notational conventions. For a term t and variable x, we write $\mathcal{O}_{fvars}(t)$ for all free variable occurrences in t, $\mathcal{O}_{fvars(x)}(t)$ for the occurrences of x in t that are free, and $\mathcal{O}_{bfun}(t)$ for the application, abstraction, or constants as well as the bound variable occurrences in t. Moreover, we abbreviate occurrences of a series of n b-branches as $[b^n]$. For example, for a β-normal form $\lambda x_1 \cdots x_n.H(t_1, \ldots, t_m)$, the path to λx_j is $[1^{j-1}]$ $(1 \le j \le n)$ and the path to t_i is $[1^n] \cdot [1^{m-i}] \cdot [2]$. The left-hand side of Figure 9.3 shows a term in β normal form, and some path abbreviations.

9.3.1 Conversions

Let t, t' be terms, $u \in \mathcal{O}(t)$, and let χ be any of $\{\alpha, \beta, \eta, \overline{\eta}\}$. Given $t \triangleright_{\chi,u} t'$, we define $org(v)$ for $v \in \mathcal{O}(t')$. First, if $v \mid u$ or $v \prec u$ then $org(v) = \{v\}$. Otherwise,

- $\chi = \alpha$:

  α-Conversion does not change the term structure, so we simply have $org(v) = \{v\}$.

- $\chi = \beta$:

  Since t/u is a β-redex, we have $t/u \equiv ((\lambda x.t_1)\, t_2)$. Note that in t/u, the path to t_1 is $[1,1]$, and to t_2 is $[2]$. Now let $w_1 \in \mathcal{O}(t_1), w_2 \in \mathcal{O}(t_2)$. We distinguish two cases:

1. $v \equiv u \cdot w_1$: then $org(v) = \{u \cdot [1,1] \cdot w_1\}$.

2. $v \equiv u \cdot w_1 \cdot w_2$ with $t_1/w_1 = x$, and $w_2 \succ [\,]$: then $org(v) = \{u \cdot [2] \cdot w_2\}$. The condition $w_2 \succ [\,]$ avoids overlap with the former case.

Thus, origins for remnants of the body t_1 "remain the same". Origins for remnants of instantiated variables are covered by two cases: The top node of an instantiated variable has an origin to its corresponding variable position in the body t_1. All origins of no-top nodes of an instantiated variable have an origin to the corresponding position in the actual parameter t_2. In Figure 9.4, dashed lines indicate origins from top-nodes, and dotted lines from non-top nodes. The reason for treating the top-nodes of an instantiated variable in a special manner is explained in Section 9.3.2.

- $\chi = \eta$:

  In η-reduction one λ is eliminated. Since t/u is an η-redex, we can assume $t/u = \lambda x.(t_1\ x)$. Realizing that the path to t_1 is $[1,1]$, we simply have: $org(u \cdot v') = \{u \cdot [1,1] \cdot v'\}$.

- $\chi = \bar{\eta}$:

  In η-expansion, an extra λ is added. The origins of the old parts point to the same old parts, while the origin of the new λ is the empty set:

  Since t/u is an $\bar{\eta}$-redex, we have $t/u = \lambda x_1 \cdots x_n.H(t_1, \ldots, t_m)$. We distinguish three cases for $v = u \cdot v'$:

  1. For $v' \preceq [1^{n-1}]$, $org(u \cdot v') = \{u \cdot v'\}$.

  2. For $v' \in \{[1^n], [1^{n+1}], [1^{n+1}, 2]\}$, $org(u \cdot v') = \emptyset$.
     Figure 9.3 shows, using tree representations, the occurrences $[1^n]$, $[1^{n+1}]$ and $[1^{n+1}, 2]$ introduced by $\bar{\eta}$-expansion.

  3. For $v' \succeq [1^{n+2}]$, $org(u \cdot [1^{n+2}] \cdot v'') = \{u \cdot [1^{n+1}] \cdot v''\}$ where $v' \equiv [1^{n+2}] \cdot v''$.

Assume that we have an origin function O mapping occurrences of t' to sets of occurrences in t. Then O is said to be *unitary* if its result values are always sets containing exactly one element, and *unique* if they contain at most one element. If an occurrence can have the empty set as origin, we say O is *forgetful*. If several occurrences in t' have an origin to the same node in t, we may refer to O as *many-to-one*, while its counterpart, where an origin set can contain more than one path, is called *one-to-many*. Finally, if for every $v \in \mathcal{O}(t')$ we have $O(v) = \{v\}$, then we say O is *identical*.

Thus, the origin function is identical for α, unitary for η, forgetful for $\bar{\eta}$ and unitary as well as many-to-one for β. None of these is one-to-many, which is fortunate, since in Section 7.5.2 we concluded that it was advisable to keep the origin sets small.

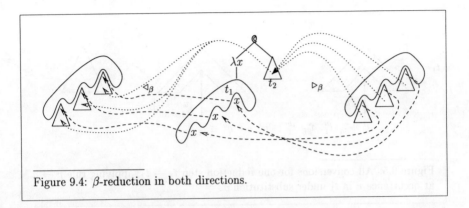

Figure 9.4: β-reduction in both directions.

9.3.2 Equality Modulo $\beta\bar{\eta}$-Conversions

In Section 9.2.3 we discussed reversed β and $\bar{\eta}$-reductions that need to take place during higher-order rewriting. In order to obtain origins for these reversed reductions, the origin functions for $\rhd_{\{\alpha,\beta,\eta,\bar{\eta}\}}$ defined in the previous section can easily be inverted, thus yielding origin functions for $\lhd_{\{\alpha,\beta,\eta,\bar{\eta}\}}$. Note that, from an origin tracking point of view, the inverse of η-reduction is $\bar{\eta}$-expansion.

Since the origin function is *identical* for α-conversion, performing several α-conversions in one direction or another does not affect the origins. This is not the case for $\bar{\eta}$ or β reduction. Since β-reduction is many-to-one, its inverse must be one-to-many. As can be seen from Figure 9.4, this may lead to a growth of the origin sets. Consider a conversion $t \lhd_\beta t' \rhd_\beta t''$, where $t' = ((\lambda x.t_1)\ t_2)$, and $t, t'' = t_1^{\{x \mapsto t_2\}}$, then the origins from t'' to t' will cause all instantiated occurrences of x to be related to the same t_2 in t'; the origins of t' to t in turn will link this t_2 to all instantiated occurrences of x in t. Thus, transitively, one occurrence of t_2 in t'' has origins to *all* occurrences of t_2 in t. This is illustrated by the dotted lines in Figure 9.4. Note that the definition of the origin function for the β reduction (case 1), relates the *top node* of t_2, via the xs occurring in t_1 to its position in t (dashed lines of Figure 9.4).

Since the origins for $\bar{\eta}$ conversions are unique this problem does not arise for $\bar{\eta}$ conversions. However, the $\rhd_{\bar{\eta}}$ are forgetful, so checking for $\bar{\eta}$-equality may result in loss of some origin information (in particular in the binders).

9.3.3 Left- and Right-Hand Sides

We define the relations between the instantiated left and right-hand side of a rewrite rule, where we assume that these are instantiated but not yet $\beta\bar{\eta}$-normalized. We closely follow the first-order case defined in Section 7.2.2.

Let $p \to q$ be a rewrite rule, and σ a substitution. The function $org : \mathcal{O}(q^\sigma) \to \mathcal{P}(\mathcal{O}(p^\sigma))$, for a path $v \in \mathcal{O}(q^\sigma)$, is defined as follows:

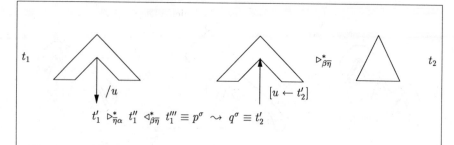

Figure 9.5: All conversions for one reduction step $t_1 \to t_2$, applying rule $p \to q$ at occurrence u in t_1 under substitution σ.

- (Common Free Variables)

  If $v \equiv v' \cdot w$ with $v' \in \mathcal{O}_{fvars}(q)$ denoting some variable X in the right-hand side, and $w \in \mathcal{O}(X^\sigma)$ an occurrence in the instantiation of that variable. Then:

  $$org(v) = \{v'' \cdot w \mid q/v' \equiv p/v'', \ v'' \in \mathcal{O}_{fvars(X)}(p)\}$$

  Thus, v'' denotes an occurrence of X in left-hand side p.

- (Function Symbols)

  If $v \in \mathcal{O}_{bfun}(q)$, then $org(v) = \emptyset$.

This is obviously a forgetful definition, but this situation is improved in Section 9.4. As in the first-order case, it is also possibly one-to-many (in the case of non-left-linearity).

Note that the common free variables case results in the same origins as in the common variables case of Section 7.2.2, when the specification does not use the higher-order features. The Context case will be dealt with in the next section.

9.3.4 Rewrite Steps

Knowing both how to establish origins for α-, β-, and $\bar{\eta}$-conversions in either direction and to set up origins between the instantiated left- and right-hand side, we can obtain the origins for one complete reduction step $t_1 \to t_2$. Figure 9.5 summarizes the work to be done for one reduction, following the description of Section 9.2.2.

Note that in general the situation is slightly more complicated than in the example of Section 9.2.3

$$P_1 \lhd_\beta P_1' \lhd_\beta P_1'' \equiv l_1^{\sigma_1} \rightsquigarrow r_1^{\sigma_1} \equiv P_2'' \rhd_\beta P_2' \rhd_\beta P_2$$

where the rewrite rule is applied at the root of P_1 which has the effect that Figure 9.5 can be reduced to just "one level": The context is empty ($u = []$), and consequently the term t/u is already a $\bar{\eta}$-normal form, hence the result need not be put back into the context (in the figure, $[~[] \leftarrow t_2'~]$ is just equal to t_2').

9.3.5 Example

Consider reduction $P_1 \rightarrow P_2$ as presented in Section 9.2.3. Most occurrences in P_2 have their intuitive origin; mainly because they also occur in bodies of the instantiations of $\mathcal{D}$ and $\mathcal{S}$ in substitution σ_1. However, some origins are lost; in particular for nodes occurring in the right-hand side of rule [1]. Thus, symbols "program", "decl" (for the declaration of n), and "tp" do not have an origin. Moreover, rule [1] is non-linear in X, and therefore the X-occurrence in the declaration at the right-hand side has an origin to the occurrence in the statement as well as in the declaration. Thus, the single n in P_2 has origins to all occurrences of n in P_1 (this does not seem intuitive). All occurrences of "natural" in P_2 have their origin to the declaration it came from (this is reasonable).

Now consider the entire reduction $P_1 \rightarrow^* P_4$, where normal form P_4 is:

```
program( decls( decl(n,natural), decls( decl(s,string), emptydecls) ),
         stats( assign( tp(string),
                plus(id( tp(natural) ),id( tp(natural) ))),
                emptystats ) )
```

In this case, more origins are lost. In particular, the two "decl" nodes have empty origins, and the reduction according to rule [4] did not establish any origins, so "tp(natural)" does not have any origins.

9.4 Extensions

The origins in the previous example were acceptable, but not yet of sufficient quality to be useful in practice. In this section we present some extensions of the origin function. Some of these extensions are of a heuristic nature, based on frequently occurring forms of (higher-order) rewrite rules.

9.4.1 Extended Contexts

Taking a close look at equation [1] of Figure 9.2, we see that its intention is to identify some context "program(...)" in which a certain term (the identifier denoted by X) is to be replaced by another term (in this case tp(τ)). This context is exactly the same in the left- and right-hand side of the rewrite rule.

It seems reasonable to extend the notion of a context to cover such similarities within rewrite rules as well. Considering a rewrite rule $p \rightarrow q$, we can look for a (possibly empty) *common context* C and *holes* (terms) $h_1, \ldots, h_m$ and $h'_1 \ldots h'_m$ ($m \geq 0$) such that $p =_\alpha C[h_1, \ldots, h_m]$ and $q =_\alpha C[h'_1, \ldots, h'_m]$, where $h_j \neq_\alpha h'_j$ for all $1 \leq j \leq m$. We are actually looking for the biggest of such contexts which contain the smallest possible number of holes where none of the holes h_j, h'_j ($1 \leq j \leq m$) start with a non-empty context $\overline{C}$ such that $h_j =_\alpha \overline{C}[\overline{h}_1, \ldots \overline{h}_n]$ and $h'_j =_\alpha \overline{C}[\overline{h}'_1, \ldots \overline{h}'_n]$. As an example, equation [1] of Figure 9.2 has a common context $C =$ "program($\mathcal{D}(\text{decl}(X,\tau))$, $\mathcal{S}(\square)$)", where the hole h_1 at the left is equal to "X", and h'_1 at the right to "tp(τ)".

For every node in this extended context, the origin should point only to its corresponding occurrence in the same context at the left-hand side. Note that, as a consequence, the common variables case should *not* apply to variables occurring in the common context. For example, in equation [1], the origin of X at the right will only point to its counterpart under the "decl" at the left and not to the X in the statements. Moreover, when trying to find origins for a node in a hole h'_j, it is reasonable to focus on origins that can be found within the corresponding hole h_j. Only if it is impossible to find origins there, an origin can be looked for in the rest of the left-hand side.

There is, however, a minor catch in this. If two consecutive holes h_j and h_{j+1} are only separated by an application in the context C, i.e., if they actually occur as @(h_j, h_{j+1}) at the left and as @(h'_j, h'_{j+1}) at the right, then it is more natural to regard these two as a single hole $H = $ @(h_j, h_{j+1}) instead of the two holes h_j and h_{j+1}. As an example, equation [2] in applicative form reads as @(nat,N) = @(id, @(tp, natural)). It would be counter-intuitive to regard the top-application as a common context @$(\square, \square)$ with two holes: $h_1 = $ nat, $h'_1 = $ id, and $h_2 = N$, $h'_2 = $ @(tp, natural).

Note that this new extended context case will be useful in the first-order case as well.

9.4.2   Origins for Constants

Let $p \equiv C[h_1, \ldots, h_m] \rightarrow C[h'_1, \ldots, h'_m] \equiv q$ be a rewrite rule with the common context C and m ($m \geq 0$) holes. We define origins for constants occurring in the h'_j ($1 \leq j \leq m$) according to the following three cases:

1. Head-to-Head

   The origin for the occurrence of the head symbol of a hole h'_j at the right is the occurrence of the head symbol of that same hole h_j at the left. For example, the "tp" symbol in equation [1] is linked to the occurrence of X in the statements at the left. This head-to-head rule corresponds to the "redex-contractum" rule of the first-order origins as described in Section 7.2.4. Note that if the head symbol at the right is a free variable, the common variables case is applicable as well. This can, in general, have the effect that the origin set for the head symbols consist of more than one path.

2. Common Subterms

   If a term s is a subterm of both h'_j and h_j, then these occurrences of s are related. For example, the subterm "tp(natural)" at the right of equation [4] (Figure 9.2) is related to both occurrences of "tp(natural)" at the left. Note that these common subterms are identified in the *un-instantiated* left- and right-hand side. This rule can in rare cases lead to unintended connections, but has already proven its usefulness for the first-order case, as discussed in Sections 7.2.4 and 7.5.5. The common subterms behave slightly differently in the higher-order case, due to the applicative form of the λ-terms. In the first-order case, function symbols were only related if all arguments were identical at the left and right. In the higher-order case, function symbols are constants. Each constant F in h'_j is related to all occurrences of F in h_j. This effect is similar to the *tokenization* discussed in Chapter 4.

   If for a subterm s of h'_j no occurrences of s can be found in h_j, then the entire left-hand side p can be used to find a common subterm occurrence of s.

3. Any-to-All.

   If after application of the head-to-head and common subterms case there are still constants in h'_j with empty origins, these obtain the set of all constant occurrences from the left-hole h_j as their origin. For example, in equation [2], the subterms "tp(natural)" and "natural" relate to both "nat(N)" and "N".

9.4.3 Abstraction and Concretization Degree

Let us end our discussion with an interesting observation. Recall from Section 9.3.2 that $\lhd_\beta$ conversions are one-to-many. Assume that $t' \lhd_\beta t$ with $t \equiv ((\lambda x.t_1)\ t_2)$. It would be useful to call the number of free occurrences of x in t_1 the *abstraction degree* of $\lambda x.t_1$, and the number of occurrences of term t_2 in t_1 the *concretization degree*. When trying to find a matching substitution σ in order to apply a rewrite rule, freedom exists concerning the abstraction and concretization degree. For example, if σ assigns to F a value T with abstraction degree $N > 0$ and concretization degree $M \geq 0$, then an alternative match σ' can also be possible which assigns to F a term T' with abstraction degree $N - 1$ and concretization degree $M + 1$. The problems with $\lhd_\beta$ are minimized if matches with abstraction degree 1 are preferred over those with a higher abstraction degree.

In practice, however, such a preference may be somewhat problematic. First, a substitution with a lower degree of abstraction may not even exist. Second, the repeated application of a substitution with abstraction degree 1 need not yield the same result as a single application with a higher abstraction degree. Finally, repeated applications may be more expensive in terms of run-time behavior, than a single application with a high abstraction degree.

9.4.4 Example

With these extensions, suitable origins for the example in Section 9.2.3 are obtained. We assume that equation [1] is applied with substitutions of abstraction degree 1 only. The extended contexts assure that "program" and "decl" are linked. Moreover, the effect of linking variables in contexts only to the same occurrence in the context, guarantees that the n and s in the declaration have the proper unitary origin. Furthermore, relating heads of holes guarantees that the "tp" nodes get the right origin to the variable they were substituted for. Likewise, the application of equation [4] results in "plus" as the origin of "tp". Finally, common subterms results in "tp(natural)" to be linked to both occurrences of "tp(natural)" in the "plus" expression (equation [4]).

The example given here is only part of the specification discussed in Chapter 8. The origins with extensions create the proper relations for the full specification as well.

9.5 Concluding Remarks

In this chapter we have studied how the notion of origin tracking can be extended to term rewriting systems containing bound variables. It turned out that the extra β and η conversions and expansions cause a considerable extra complication. Nevertheless, it has been possible to come up with a scheme that works satisfactory for the full typechecking example given in Chapter 8 (which we have shown in part).

We have discussed origins in the liberal setting for higher-order term rewriting proposed by Wolfram (1993). Nipkow (1991) discusses a more restrictive definition where the rewrite rules have to satisfy several syntactic constraints. Obviously, the same origin function can be applied in Nipkow's HRSs. The nicer matching behavior of Nipkow's HRSs will probably have a favorable effect on the origins. Note, however, that equation [1] of our example does not satisfy Nipkow's constraints.

Origin tracking is a technique grown out of practical need. Full assessment of higher-order origin tracking is only possible when more higher-order specifications of programming languages are available. An interesting application area might also be found in second-order *program transformations*, as discussed in the landmark paper by Huet and Lang (1978). We expect higher-order origin tracking to be a useful device when executing such specifications using higher-order rewriting.

An interesting area for further research might be a closer study of the various labeling schemes for λ-calculus discussed, e.g., by Lévy (1975). His labels contain much more structure than our occurrences, which might be used to encode more information in structures representing origins. Moreover, a better understanding of the exact relationship with the various descendance or residual relations would be beneficial (van Oostrom, 1994; van Oostrom and van Raamsdonk, 1994). An interesting comparison between residuals and labels for the λ-calculus and term rewriting systems is discussed by Bertot (1992).

References

Abadi, M. and Cardelli, L. (1994). A theory of primitive objects: Untyped and first-order systems. In M. Hagiya and J. C. Mitchell, editors, *Theoretical Aspects of Computer Software (TACS '94)*, volume 789 of *Lecture Notes in Computer Science*, pages 296–320. Springer-Verlag.

Abadi, M., Cardelli, L., Currien, P.-L., and Lévy, J.-J. (1990). Explicit substitutions. In *Principles of Programming Languages (POPL '90)*, pages 31–46. ACM.

Agrawal, H. and Horgan, J. R. (1990). Dynamic program slicing. *SIGPLAN Notices*, **25**(6), 246–256. *Proceedings of the ACM SIGPLAN '90 Conference on Programming Language Design and Implementation*.

Agrawal, H., DeMillo, R. A., and Spafford, E. H. (1993). Debugging with dynamic slicing and backtracking. *Software — Practice and Experience*, **23**, 589–616.

Arnold, B. R. T., van Deursen, A., and Res, M. (1995). An algebraic specification of a language for describing financial products. In M. Wirsing, editor, *ICSE-17 Workshop on Formal Methods Application in Software Engineering*, pages 6–13. IEEE.

Attali, I. and Chazarain, J. (1990). Functional evaluation of strongly noncircular Typol specifications. In P. Deransart and M. Jourdan, editors, *Attribute Grammars and Their Applications (WAGA '90)*, volume 461 of *Lecture Notes in Computer Science*, pages 157–176. Springer-Verlag.

Attali, I. and Franchi-Zannettacci, P. (1988). Unification-free execution of Typol programs by semantic attribute evaluation. In R. A. Kowalski and K. A. Bowen, editors, *Logic Programming: Fifth International Conference*, volume 1, pages 160–177. MIT Press.

Attali, I., Chazarain, J., and Gilette, S. (1992). Incremental evaluation of Natural Semantics specifications. In M. Bruynooghe and M. Wirsing, editors, *Programming Language Implementation and Logic Programming (PLILP '92)*, volume 631 of *Lecture Notes in Computer Science*, pages 87–99. Springer-Verlag.

Baeten, J. C. M., Bergstra, J. A., Klop, J. W., and Weijland, W. P. (1989). Term rewriting systems with rule priorities. *Theoretical Computer Science*, **67**, 283–301.

323

Bahlke, R. and Snelting, G. (1986). The PSG system: From formal language definitions to interactive programming environments. *ACM Transactions on Programming Languages and Systems*, **8**, 547–576.

Ballance, R. A., Graham, S. L., and van de Vanter, M. L. (1992). The Pan language-based editing system. *ACM Transactions on Software Engineering and Methodology*, **1**, 95–127.

Barbuti, R. and Martelli, A. (1983). A structured approach to static semantics correctness. *Science of Computer Programming*, **3**, 279–311.

Barendregt, H. P. (1984). *The Lambda Calculus: Its Syntax and Semantics*. North-Holland.

Beaven, M. and Stansifer, R. (1993). Explaining type errors in polymorphic languages. *ACM Letters on Programming Languages and Systems*, **2**, 17–30.

Bergstra, J. A. and Klint, P. (1996a). The Discrete Time ToolBus. In M. Wirsing, editor, *Algebraic Methodology and Software Technology (AMAST '96)*, volume xxx of *Lecture Notes in Computer Science*. Springer-Verlag. To appear. Full version: Technical Report P9502, Programming Research Group, University of Amsterdam.

Bergstra, J. A. and Klint, P. (1996b). The ToolBus coordination architecture. In P. Ciancarini and C. Hankin, editors, *Coordination Languages and Models (CO-ORDINATION '96)*, volume 1061 of *Lecture Notes in Computer Science*, pages 75–88. Springer-Verlag. Full version: Technical Report P9408, Programming Research Group, University of Amsterdam.

Bergstra, J. A. and Klop, J. W. (1986). Conditional rewrite rules: Confluence and termination. *Journal of Computer and System Sciences*, **32**, 323–362.

Bergstra, J. A. and Sellink, M. P. A. (1996). Sequential data algebra primitives. Technical Report P9602, Programming Research Group, University of Amsterdam.

Bergstra, J. A., Heering, J., and Klint, P., editors (1989). *Algebraic Specification*. ACM Press/Addison-Wesley.

Bergstra, J. A., Dinesh, T. B., Field, J., and Heering, J. (1996). A complete transformational toolkit for compilers. In H. R. Nielson, editor, *Programming Languages and Systems (ESOP '96)*, volume 1058 of *Lecture Notes in Computer Science*, pages 92–107. Springer-Verlag. Full version: Technical Report RC 20342, IBM T. J. Watson Research Center, Yorktown Heights, and Technical Report CS-R9601, Centrum voor Wiskunde en Informatica (CWI), Amsterdam.

Berry, D. (1991). *Generating Program Animators from Programming Language Semantics*. Ph.D. thesis, University of Edinburgh.

Bertot, Y. (1990). Implementation of an interpreter for a parallel language in Centaur. In N. Jones, editor, *Third European Symposium on Programming (ESOP '90)*, volume 432 of *Lecture Notes in Computer Science*, pages 57–69. Springer-Verlag.

Bertot, Y. (1992). Origin functions in lambda-calculus and term rewriting systems. In J.-C. Raoult, editor, *17th Colloquium on Trees in Algebra and Programming (CAAP '92)*, volume 581 of *Lecture Notes in Computer Science*, pages 49–65. Springer-Verlag.

Bertot, Y. (1993). A canonical calculus of residuals. In G. Huet and G. Plotkin, editors, *Logical Environments*, pages 140–163. Cambridge University Press.

Bidoit, M., Gaudel, M.-C., and Mauboussin, A. (1989). How to make algebraic specifications more understandable: An experiment with the PLUSS specification language. *Science of Computer Programming*, **12**, 1–38.

Bird, R. S. (1987). An introduction to the theory of lists. In M. Broy, editor, *Logic of Programming and Calculi of Discrete Design*, pages 3–42. Springer-Verlag.

Bird, R. S. (1989). Algebraic identities for program calculation. *The Computer Journal*, **32**, 122–126.

Bjørner, D. and Jones, C. B. (1982). *Formal Specification and Software Development*. Prentice-Hall.

Boom, H. J., Nielsen, C. B., McGettrick, A. D., Mosses, P. D., Rattray, C., Tennent, R. D., and Watt, D. A. (1989). A view of formal semantics. *Computer Standards and Interfaces*, **9**, 3–9.

Borras, P., Clément, D., Despeyroux, Th., Incerpi, J., Kahn, G., Lang, B., and Pascual, V. (1989). Centaur: The System. *SIGPLAN Notices*, **24**(2), 14–24. *Proceedings of the ACM SIGSOFT/SIGPLAN Software Engineering Symposium on Practical Software Development Environments*. The Centaur Tutorial is available at URL: http://www.inria.fr/croap/centaur/tutorial/main/main.html.

Bousdira, W. and Rémy, J. L. (1988). REVEUR4: A laboratory for conditional rewriting. In S. Kaplan and J.-P. Jouannaud, editors, *Conditional Term Rewriting Systems (CTRS '88)*, volume 308 of *Lecture Notes in Computer Science*, pages 253–257. Springer-Verlag.

van den Brand, M. G. J. (1992). *Pregmatic: A Generator for Incremental Programming Environments*. Ph.D. thesis, Katholieke Universiteit Nijmegen.

van den Brand, M. G. J. and Visser, E. (1996). Generation of formatters for context-free languages. *ACM Transactions on Software Engineering and Methodology*, **5**, 1–41.

326 · *References*

van den Brand, M. G. J., van Deursen, A., Dinesh, T. B., Kamperman, J. F. Th., and Visser, E., editors (1995a). *ASF+SDF '95: A Workshop on Generating Tools from Algebraic Specifications*, Technical Report P9504. Programming Research Group, University of Amsterdam.

van den Brand, M. G. J., Eijkelkamp, S. M., Geluk, D. K. A., Meijer, H., Osborne, H. R., and Polling, M. J. F. (1995b). Program transformations using ASF+SDF. In van den Brand *et al.* (1995a), pages 29–52.

van den Brand, M. G. J., van Deursen, A., Klint, P., Klusener, S., and van der Meulen, E. A. (1996). Industrial applications of ASF+SDF. In M. Wirsing, editor, *Algebraic Methodology and Software Technology (AMAST '96)*, volume xxx of *Lecture Notes in Computer Science*. Springer-Verlag. To appear.

Brown, D. F., Moura, H., and Watt, D. A. (1992). Actress: Action semantics directed compiler generator. In U. Kastens and P. Pfahler, editors, *Compiler Construction (CC '92)*, volume 641 of *Lecture Notes in Computer Science*, pages 95–109. Springer-Verlag.

Broy, M. (1992). Experiences with software specification and verification using LP, the Larch Proof Assistant. Technical Report 93, DEC Systems Research Center.

Broy, M., Facchi, C., Grosu, R., Hettler, R., Hussmann, H., Nazareth, D., Regensburger, F., Slotosch, O., and Stølen, K. (1993). The requirement and design specification language Spectrum, An informal introduction. Version 1.0. Technical Report TUM-I9311 and TUM-I9312, Fakultät für Informatik, Technische Universität München.

Bruce, K. B. (1994). A paradigmatic object-oriented programming language: Design, static typing and semantics. *Journal of Functional Programming*, **4**, 127–206.

Cardelli, L. (1984). Semantics of multiple inheritance. In G. Kahn, D. B. MacQueen, and G. Plotkin, editors, *Semantics of Data Types*, volume 173 of *Lecture Notes in Computer Science*, pages 51–68. Springer-Verlag.

Cardelli, L. (1993). Typeful programming. Technical report, DEC Systems Research Center. Earlier version in E. J. Neuhold and M. Paul, editors, *Formal Description of Programming Concepts*, pages 51–136. Springer-Verlag, 1991.

Cardelli, L. (1996). Type systems. Draft. To appear in *CRC Handbook of Computer Science and Engineering*.

Cardelli, L. and Wegner, P. (1985). On understanding types, data abstraction, and polymorphism. *ACM Computing Surveys*, **17**, 471–522.

Choppy, C. and Bidoit, M. (1992). Integrating ASSPEGIQUE and LP. In U. Martin and J. M. Wing, editors, *First International Workshop on Larch*, Workshops in Computing, pages 69–85. Springer-Verlag.

Church, A. (1940). A formulation of a Simple Theory of Types. *Journal of Symbolic Logic*, **5**, 56–68.

Classen, I., Ehrig, H., and Wolz, D. (1993). *Algebraic Specification Techniques and Tools for Software Develoment. The ACT Approach*, volume 1 of *AMAST Series in Computing*. World Scientific.

Clément, D., Despeyroux, J., Despeyroux, Th., Hascoet, L., and Kahn, G. (1985). Natural Semantics on the computer. Technical Report 416, INRIA Sophia Antipolis.

Cook, W. (1989). Denotational semantics of inheritance. Technical Report CS-89-33, Brown University.

Courcelle, B. and Franchi-Zannettacci, P. (1982). Attribute grammars and recursive program schemes I and II. *Theoretical Computer Science*, **17**, 163–191 and 235–257.

Damas, L. and Milner, R. (1982). Principal type-schemes for functional programs. In *Principles of Programming Languages (POPL '82)*, pages 207–212. ACM.

Deransart, P., Jourdan, M., and Lorho, B. (1988). *Attribute Grammars: Definitions, Systems and Bibliography*, volume 323 of *Lecture Notes in Computer Science*. Springer-Verlag.

Dershowitz, N. and Jouannaud, J.-P. (1990). Rewrite systems. In J. van Leeuwen, editor, *Handbook of Theoretical Computer Science, volume B*, pages 243–320. Elsevier Science Publishers.

Despeyroux, Th. (1988). Typol: A formalism to implement Natural Semantics. Technical Report 94, INRIA Sophia-Antipolis.

Despeyroux, Th. and Théry, L. (1989). Typol — User's guide and manual. In *The CENTAUR Documentation Version 0.9, volume I — User's Guide*. INRIA Sophia Antipolis. The most recent version is available in the Centaur Tutorial at URL: http://www.inria.fr/croap/centaur/tutorial/main/main.html.

van Deursen, A. (1994a). *Executable Language Definitions: Case Studies and Origin Tracking Techniques*. Ph.D. thesis, University of Amsterdam.

van Deursen, A. (1994b). Origin tracking in primitive recursive schemes. Technical Report CS-R9401, Centrum voor Wiskunde en Informatica (CWI), Amsterdam.

van Deursen, A. and Dinesh, T. B. (1994). Origin tracking for higher-order term rewriting systems. In J. Heering, K. Meinke, B. Möller, and T. Nipkow, editors, *Higher-Order Algebra, Logic, and Term Rewriting (HOA '93)*, volume 816 of *Lecture Notes in Computer Science*, pages 76–95. Springer-Verlag.

van Deursen, A., Klint, P., and Tip, F. (1993). Origin tracking. *Journal of Symbolic Computation*, **15**, 523–545.

Didrich, K., Fett, A., Gerke, C., Grieskamp, W., and Pepper, P. (1994). OPAL: Design and implementation of an algebraic programming language. In J. Gutknecht, editor, *Programming Languages and System Architectures: International Conference*, volume 782 of *Lecture Notes in Computer Science*, pages 228–244. Springer-Verlag.

van Diepen, N. W. P. (1989). SMALL — Dynamic semantics of a language with GOTOs. In Bergstra *et al.* (1989), pages 133–161.

Dinesh, T. B. (1992). Object oriented programming — Inheritance to adoption. Technical Report 92–02, Department of Computer Science, University of Iowa. Ph.D. thesis.

Dinesh, T. B. (1993). Type checking revisited: Modular error handling. In D. J. Andrews, J. F. Groote, and C. A. Middelburg, editors, *Semantics of Specification Languages (SoSL)*, Workshops in Computing, pages 216–231. Springer-Verlag.

Dinesh, T. B. and Tip, F. (1992). Animators and error reporters for generated environments. Technical Report CS-R9253, Centrum voor Wiskunde en Informatica (CWI), Amsterdam.

Doh, K.-G. and Schmidt, D. A. (1992). Extraction of strong typing laws from action semantics definitions. In *Fourth European Symposium on Programming (ESOP '92)*, volume 582 of *Lecture Notes in Computer Science*, pages 151–166. Springer-Verlag.

Donzeau-Gouge, V., Huet, G., Kahn, G., and Lang, B. (1984). Programming environments based on structured editors: The Mentor experience. In D. R. Barstow, H. E. Shrobe, and E. Sandewall, editors, *Interactive Programming Environments*, pages 128–140. McGraw-Hill.

Duesterwald, E., Gupta, R., and Soffa, M. L. (1992). Rigorous data flow testing through output influences. In *Proceedings of the Second Irvine Software Symposium (ISS '92)*, pages 131–145, California.

Duke, R. (1987). Predicate rules for Pascal static semantics. Technical Report 86, Department of Computer Science, The University of Queensland.

Eker, S. M. (1992). A comparison of OBJ3 and ASF+SDF. Report CS-R9223, Centrum voor Wiskunde en Informatica (CWI), Amsterdam.

Felty, A. (1992). A logic programming approach to implementing higher-order term rewriting. In L.-H. Eriksson, L. Hallnäs, and P. Schroeder-Heister, editors, *Extensions of Logic Programming (ELP '91)*, volume 596 of *Lecture Notes in Artificial Intelligence*, pages 135–158. Springer-Verlag.

Field, J. (1992). A simple rewriting semantics for realistic imperative programs and its application to program analysis. In *Proc. ACM SIGPLAN Workshop on Partial Evaluation and Semantics-Based Program Manipulation*, pages 98–107, San Francisco. Published as Yale University Technical Report YALEU/DCS/RR–909.

Field, J. (1993). A graph reduction approach to incremental rewriting. In C. Kirchner, editor, *Rewriting Techniques and Applications (RTA '93)*, volume 690 of *Lecture Notes in Computer Science*, pages 259–273. Springer-Verlag.

Field, J. and Tip, F. (1994). Dynamic dependence in term rewriting systems and its application to program slicing. In M. Hermenegildo and J. Penjam, editors, *Programming Language Implementation and Logic Programming (PLILP '94)*, volume 844 of *Lecture Notes in Computer Science*, pages 415–431. Springer-Verlag.

Field, J., Ramalingam, G., and Tip, F. (1995). Parametric program slicing. In *Principles of Programming Languages (POPL '95)*, pages 397–392. ACM.

Fleck, A. C. (1984). A proposal for the comparison of types in Pascal and associated semantic models. *Computer Languages*, **9**, 71–87.

Futatsugi, K., Goguen, J. A., Jouannaud, J.-P., and Meseguer, J. (1985). Principles of OBJ2. In *Principles of Programming Languages (POPL '85)*, pages 52–66. ACM.

Gallagher, K. B. and Lyle, J. R. (1991). Using program slicing in software maintenance. *IEEE Transactions on Software Engineering*, **SE-17**, 751–761.

Garland, S. J. and Guttag, J. V. (1989). An overview of LP, the Larch Prover. In N. Dershowitz, editor, *Rewriting Techniques and Applications (RTA '89)*, number 355 in Lecture Notes in Computer Science, pages 137–151. Springer-Verlag.

Goguen, J. A. (1978). Abstract errors for abstract data types. In E. Neuhold, editor, *Formal descriptions of programming concepts*, pages 491–525. North-Holland.

Goguen, J. A., Thatcher, J. W., and Wagner, E. G. (1978). An initial algebra approach to the specification, correctness and implementation of abstract data types. In R. Yeh, editor, *Current Trends in Programming Methodology*, pages 80–149. Prentice-Hall.

Goguen, J. A., Kirchner, C., Kirchner, H., Mégrelis, A., Meseguer, J., and Winkler, T. (1988). An introduction to OBJ3. In S. Kaplan and J.-P. Jouannaud, editors, *Conditional Term Rewriting Systems (CTRS '88)*, volume 308 of *Lecture Notes in Computer Science*, pages 258–263. Springer-Verlag.

Goguen, J. A., Winkler, T., Meseguer, J., Futatsugi, K., and Jouannaud, J.-P. (1996). Introducing OBJ. In J. A. Goguen and G. Malcolm, editors, *Software Engineering with OBJ: Algebraic Specification in Practice*. Cambridge University Press. To appear.

Goldberg, A. and Robson, D. (1983). *SmallTalk 80: The Language and its Implementation*. Addison-Wesley.

Gordon, M. J. C. (1988). *Programming Language Theory and its Implementation: Applicative and Imperative Paradigms*. Prentice-Hall.

Gordon, M. J. C., Milner, R., Morris, L., Newey, M., and Wadsworth, C. (1978). A meta language for interactive proof in LCF. In *Principles of Programming Languages (POPL '78)*, pages 119–130. ACM.

Guttag, J. V. and Horning, J. J. (1978). The algebraic specification of abstract data types. *Acta Informatica*, **10**, 27–52.

Habermann, A. N. and Notkin, D. (1986). Gandalf: Software development environments. *IEEE Transactions on Software Engineering*, **SE-12**, 1117–1127.

Hardin, T. (1993). How to get confluence for explicit substitutions. In M. R. Sleep, M. J. Plasmeijer, and M. C. J. D. van Eekelen, editors, *Term Graph Rewriting*, pages 31–46. Wiley.

Hearn, B. M. (1995). *The Design and Implementation of Typed Languages for Algebraic Specification*. Ph.D. thesis, University of Wales, Swansea.

Hearn, B. M. and Meinke, K. (1994). ATLAS: A typed language for algebraic specification. In J. Heering, K. Meinke, B. Möller, and T. Nipkow, editors, *Higher-Order Algebra, Logic, and Term Rewriting (HOA '93)*, volume 816 of *Lecture Notes in Computer Science*, pages 146–168. Springer-Verlag.

Heering, J. (1992). Implementing higher-order algebraic specifications. In D. Miller, editor, *Proceedings of the Workshop on the λProlog Programming Language*, pages 141–157. University of Pennsylvania, Philadelphia. Published as Technical Report MS-CIS-92-86.

Heering, J. and Klint, P. (1995). The prehistory of ASF+SDF (1980–1984). In van den Brand *et al.* (1995a), pages 1–4.

Heering, J., Hendriks, P. R. H., Klint, P., and Rekers, J. (1989). The syntax definition formalism SDF — Reference manual. *SIGPLAN Notices*, **24**(11), 43–75. Most recent version available at URL: http://www.cwi.nl/~gipe/.

Heering, J., Klint, P., and Rekers, J. (1990). Incremental generation of parsers. *IEEE Transactions on Software Engineering*, **SE-16**, 1344–1351.

Heering, J., Klint, P., and Rekers, J. (1992). Incremental generation of lexical scanners. *ACM Transactions on Programming Languages and Systems*, **14**, 490–520.

Heering, J., Klint, P., and Rekers, J. (1994). Lazy and incremental program generation. *ACM Transactions on Programming Languages and Systems*, **16**, 1010–1023.

Hendriks, P. R. H. (1988). ASF system user's guide. Technical Report CS-R8823, Centrum voor Wiskunde en Informatica (CWI), Amsterdam. Extended abstract in *Computing Science in the Netherlands (CSN '88)*, Part 1, pages 83–94, SION (1988).

Hendriks, P. R. H. (1989). Typechecking Mini-ML. In Bergstra *et al.* (1989), pages 299–337.

Hendriks, P. R. H. (1991). *Implementation of Modular Algebraic Specifications*. Ph.D. thesis, University of Amsterdam.

Herndon, R. M. and Berzins, V. A. (1988). The realizable benefits of a language prototyping language. *IEEE Transactions on Software Engineering*, **SE-14**, 803–809.

Hillebrand, J. and Korver, H. (1995). A well-formedness checker for μCRL. In A. Ponse, C. Verhoef, and S. F. M. van Vlijmen, editors, *Algebra of Communicating Processes (ACP '95)*, pages 81–119. Eindhoven University of Technology, Computing Science Report 95/14.

Hindley, R. (1969). The principal type-scheme of an object in combinatory logic. *Transactions of the American Mathematical Society*, **146**, 29–60.

Hoare, C. A. R. and Wirth, N. (1973). An axiomatic definition of the programming language Pascal. *Acta Informatica*, **2**, 335–355.

Hoover, R. (1986). Dynamically bypassing copy rule chains in attribute grammars. In *Principles of Programming Languages (POPL '86)*, pages 14–25. ACM.

Hoover, R. and Teitelbaum, T. (1986). Efficient incremental evaluation of aggregate values in attribute grammars. *SIGPLAN Notices*, **21**(7), 39–50. *Proceedings of the ACM SIGPLAN '86 Symposium on Compiler Construction*.

Horwitz, S. and Teitelbaum, T. (1986). Generating editing environments based on relations and attributes. *ACM Transactions on Programming Languages and Systems*, **8**, 577–608.

Hudak, P. *et al.* (1992). Report on the programming language Haskell. A non-strict, purely functional language. Version 1.2. *SIGPLAN Notices*, **27**(5).

Hudson, S. E. (1991). Incremental attribute evaluation: A flexible algorithm for lazy update. *ACM Transactions on Programming Languages and Systems*, **13**, 315–341.

Huet, G. and Lang, B. (1978). Proving and applying program transformations expressed with second-order patterns. *Acta Informatica*, **11**, 31–55.

Huet, G. and Lévy, J.-J. (1991). Computations in orthogonal rewriting systems I and II. In J.-L. Lassez and G. Plotkin, editors, *Computational Logic: Essays in Honour of Alan Robinson*, pages 395–443. MIT Press.

Hussmann, H. (1988). The Passau RAP system: Rapid prototyping for algebraic specifications. In S. Kaplan and J.-P. Jouannaud, editors, *Conditional Term Rewriting Systems (CTRS '88)*, volume 308 of *Lecture Notes in Computer Science*, pages 264–265. Springer-Verlag.

Hussmann, H. (1993). *Nondeterminism in Algebraic Specifications and Algebraic Programs*. Birkhäuser.

ISO (1983). *International Standard ISO 7185, Programming Languages — Pascal*. International Organization for Standardization, first edition. Ref. no. 7185-1983(E).

Jensen, K. and Wirth, N. (1985). *Pascal User Manual and Report. ISO Pascal Standard*. Springer-Verlag, third edition.

Johnson, G. F. and Walz, J. A. (1986). A maximum-flow approach to anomaly isolation in unification-based incremental type inference. In *Principles of Programming Languages (POPL '86)*, pages 44–57. ACM.

Jones, M. P. (1992). A theory of qualified types. In B. Krieg-Brückner, editor, *Fourth European Symposium on Programming (ESOP '92)*, volume 582 of *LNCS*, pages 287–306. Springer-Verlag.

Jones, M. P. (1995). A system of constructor classes: Overloading and implicit higher-order polymorphism. *Journal of Functional Programming*, **5**, 1–35.

Jouannaud, J.-P. and Kirchner, C. (1991). Solving equations in abstract algebras: A rule-based survey of unification. In J.-L. Lassez and G. Plotkin, editors, *Computational Logic. Essays in Honour of Alan Robinson*, pages 257–321. MIT Press.

Jourdan, M. (1984). Strongly non-circular attribute grammars and their recursive evaluation. *SIGPLAN Notices*, **19**(6), 81–93. *Proceedings of the ACM SIGPLAN '84 Symposium on Compiler Construction*.

Jourdan, M. and Parigot, D. (1991). Internals and externals of the FNC-2 attribute grammar system. In H. Alblas and B. Melichar, editors, *Attribute Grammars, Applications and Systems*, volume 545 of *Lecture Notes in Computer Science*, pages 485–504. Springer-Verlag.

Jourdan, M., Le Bellec, C., and Parigot, D. (1990). The Olga attribute grammar description language: Design, implementation and evaluation. In P. Deransart and M. Jourdan, editors, *Attribute Grammars and Their Applications (WAGA '90)*, volume 461 of *Lecture Notes in Computer Science*, pages 222–237. Springer-Verlag.

Kahn, G. (1987). Natural Semantics. In F. J. Brandenburg, G. Vidal-Naquet, and M. Wirsing, editors, *Fourth Symposium on Theoretical Aspects of Computer Science (STACS '87)*, volume 247 of *Lecture Notes in Computer Science*, pages 22–39. Springer-Verlag.

Kahn, G., Lang, B., Mélèse, B., and Morcos, E. (1983). Metal: A formalism to specify formalisms. *Science of Computer Programming*, **3**, 151–188.

Kamkar, M. (1995). An overview and comparative classification of program slicing techniques. *Journal of Systems and Software*, **31**, 197–214.

Kamkar, M., Shahmehri, N., and Fritzson, P. (1992). Interprocedural dynamic slicing. In M. Bruynooghe and M. Wirsing, editors, *Programming Language Implementation and Logic Programming (PLILP '92)*, volume 631 of *Lecture Notes in Computer Science*, pages 370–384. Springer-Verlag.

Kamkar, M., Fritzson, P., and Shahmehri, N. (1993). Interprocedural dynamic slicing applied to interprocedural data flow testing. In D. Card, editor, *Conference on Software Maintenance (CSM '93)*, pages 386–395. IEEE Computer Society.

Kamperman, J. F. Th. (1994). GEL, a graph exchange language. Technical Report CS-R9440, Centrum voor Wiskunde en Informatica (CWI), Amsterdam.

Kamperman, J. F. Th. and Walters, H. R. (1995). Lazy rewriting and eager machinery. In J. Hsiang, editor, *Rewriting Techniques and Applications (RTA '95)*, volume 914 of *Lecture Notes in Computer Science*, pages 147–162. Springer-Verlag.

Kamperman, J. F. Th. and Walters, H. R. (1996). Minimal term rewriting systems. In *Recent Trends in Data Type Specification (WADT '95)*, volume xxx of *Lecture Notes in Computer Science*. Springer-Verlag. To appear. Earlier version: ARM — Abstract rewriting machine, in *Computing Science in the Netherlands (CSN '93)*, pages 193–204, Stichting Mathematisch Centrum, Amsterdam.

Kaplan, S. (1988). Positive/negative conditional rewriting. In S. Kaplan and J.-P. Jouannaud, editors, *Conditional Term Rewriting Systems (CTRS '88)*, volume 308 of *Lecture Notes in Computer Science*, pages 129–143. Springer-Verlag.

Kapur, D., Narendran, P., and Zhang, H. (1987). On sufficient completeness and related properties of term rewriting systems. *Acta Informatica*, **24**, 395–416.

Kastens, U. (1980). Ordered attribute grammars. *Acta Informatica*, **13**, 229–256.

Kastens, U. (1984). The GAG-System — A tool for compiler construction. In B. Lorho, editor, *Methods and Tools for Compiler Construction*, pages 165–181. Cambridge University Press.

Kastens, U. (1993). Executable specifications for language implementation. In M. Bruynooghe and J. Penjam, editors, *Pogramming Language Implementation and Logic Programming (PLILP '93)*, volume 714 of *Lecture Notes in Computer Science*, pages 1–11. Springer-Verlag.

Kastens, U., Hutt, B., and Zimmermann, E. (1982). *GAG: A Practical Compiler Generator*, volume 141 of *Lecture Notes in Computer Science*. Springer-Verlag.

Katayama, T. (1984). Translation of attribute grammars into procedures. *ACM Transactions on Programming Languages and Systems*, **6**, 345–369.

Kilov, H. (1995). Special issue on formal description techniques. *Computer Standards and Interfaces*, **17**(5–6).

Klint, P. (1980). An overview of the SUMMER programming language. In *Principles of Programming Languages (POPL '80)*, pages 47–55. ACM.

Klint, P. (1985). *A Study in String Processing Languages*, volume 205 of *Lecture Notes in Computer Science*. Springer-Verlag.

Klint, P. (1993). A meta-environment for generating programming environments. *ACM Transactions on Software Engineering and Methodology*, **2**, 176–201.

Klint, P., editor (1995a). *The ASF+SDF Meta-Environment User's Guide*. Centrum voor Wiskunde en Informatica (CWI), Amsterdam. Version June 4, 1995. URL: http://www.cwi.nl/~gipe/.

Klint, P. (1995b). The evolution of implementation techniques in the ASF+SDF meta-environment. In van den Brand *et al.* (1995a), pages 5–26.

Klint, P. (1995c). From line numbers to origins. In E. H. L. Aarts, H. M. M. ten Eikelder, C. Hemerik, and M. Rem, editors, *Simplex Sigillum Veri. Liber Amicorum Prof. dr. F. E. J. Kruseman Aretz*, pages 215–230. Eindhoven University of Technology.

Klint, P. and Visser, E. (1994). Using filtes for the disambiguation of context-free grammars. In G. Pighizzini and P. S. Pietro, editors, *Proceedings ASMICS Workshop on Parsing Theory*, pages 1–20. Published as Technical Report 126-1994, Computer Science Department, University of Milan.

Klop, J. W. (1992). Term rewriting systems. In S. Abramsky, D. Gabbay, and T. S. E. Maibaum, editors, *Handbook of Logic in Computer Science, volume 2*, pages 1–116. Oxford University Press.

Knuth, D. (1992). *Literate Programming*, volume 27 of *CSLI Lecture Notes*. Center for the Study of Language and Information.

Koorn, J. W. C. (1994). *Generating Uniform User-Interfaces for Interactive Programming Environments*. Ph.D. thesis, University of Amsterdam.

Koskimies, K. and Paakki, J. (1990). *Automating Language Implementation — A Pragmatic Approach*. Ellis Horwood.

Lang, B. (1974). Deterministic techniques for efficient non-deterministic parsers. In J. Loeckx, editor, *Automata, Languages and Programming (ICALP '74)*, volume 14 of *Lecture Notes in Computer Science*, pages 255–269.

Lee, P. and Pleban, U. (1987). A realistic compiler generator based on high-level semantics. In *Principles of Programming Languages (POPL '87)*, pages 284–295. ACM.

Lehmann, T. and Loeckx, J. (1993). OBSCURE: A specification language for abstract data types. *Acta Informatica*, **30**, 303–350.

Lévy, J.-J. (1975). An algebraic interpretation of the $\lambda\beta K$-calculus and a labelled λ-calculus. In C. Böhm, editor, *λ-Calculus and Computer Science Theory*, volume 37 of *Lecture Notes in Computer Science*, pages 147–165. Springer-Verlag.

Magnusson, B., Begtsson, M., Dahlin, L. O., Fries, G., Gustavson, A., Hedin, G., Minör, S., Oscarsson, D., and Taube, M. (1990). An overview of the Mjølner/ORM environment: Incremental language and software development. Technical Report LU-CS-TR:90-57 and LUTEDX/(TECS-3026)/1-12/(1990), Lund University and Lund Institute of Technology.

Maranget, L. (1991). Optimal derivations in weak lambda-calculi and in orthogonal term rewriting systems. In *Principles of Programming Languages (POPL '91)*, pages 225–269. ACM.

Marriott, K. (1993). Frameworks for abstract interpretation. *Acta Informatica*, **30**, 103–129.

Martelli, A. and Montanari, U. (1982). An efficient unification algorithm. *ACM Transactions on Programming Languages and Systems*, **4**, 258–282.

Martin, A. (1993). Encoding W: A logic for Z in 2OBJ. In J. C. P. Woodcock and P. G. Larsen, editors, *FME '93: Industrial Strength Formal Methods*, volume 670 of *Lecture Notes in Computer Science*, pages 462–481.

Mauw, S. and van der Meulen, E. A. (1995). Specification of tools for message sequence charts. In van den Brand *et al.* (1995a), pages 175–209.

Meinke, K. (1992a). Equational specification of abstract types and combinators. In E. Börger, G. Jäger, and H. Kleine Büning, editors, *Computer Science Logic (CSL '91)*, volume 626 of *Lecture Notes in Computer Science*, pages 257–271. Springer-Verlag.

Meinke, K. (1992b). Universal algebra in higher types. *Theoretical Computer Science*, **100**, 385–417.

Meinke, K. (1993). Algebraic semantics of rewriting terms and types. In J. L. Remy and M. Rusinowitch, editors, *Conditional Term Rewriting Systems (CTRS '93)*, volume 656 of *Lecture Notes in Computer Science*, pages 1–20. Springer-Verlag.

Meinke, K. and Tucker, J. V. (1992). Universal algebra. In S. Abramsky, D. Gabbay, and T. S. E. Maibaum, editors, *Handbook of Logic in Computer Science, volume 1*, pages 189–411. Oxford University Press.

Meseguer, J. and Goguen, J. A. (1985). Initiality, induction, and computability. In M. Nivat and J. C. Reynolds, editors, *Algebraic Methods in Semantics*, pages 459–541. Cambridge University Press.

van der Meulen, E. A. (1988). Algebraic specification of a compiler for a language with pointers. Technical Report CS-R8848, Centrum voor Wiskunde en Informatica (CWI), Amsterdam.

van der Meulen, E. A. (1994). *Incremental Rewriting*. Ph.D. thesis, University of Amsterdam.

Meyer, B. (1988). *Object-Oriented Software Construction*. Prentice-Hall.

Michaelson, G. J. (1993). *Interpreter Prototypes from Formal Language Definitions*. Ph.D. thesis, Heriot-Watt University.

Milner, R. (1978). A theory of type polymorphism in programming. *Journal of Computer and System Sciences*, **17**, 348–375.

Milner, R., Tofte, M., and Harper, R. (1990). *The Definition of Standard ML*. MIT Press.

Mitchell, J. (1990a). Towards a typed foundation for method specialization and inheritance. In *Principles of Programming Languages (POPL '90)*, pages 109–124. ACM.

Mitchell, J. (1990b). Type theories in programming languages. In J. van Leeuwen, editor, *Handbook of Theoretical Computer Science, volume B*, chapter 8. Elsevier Science Publishers.

Mohan, C. K. (1989). Priority rewriting: Semantics, confluence, and conditionals. In N. Dershowitz, editor, *Rewriting Techniques and Applications (RTA '89)*, volume 355 of *Lecture Notes in Computer Science*, pages 278–292. Springer-Verlag.

Mohan, C. K. and Srivas, M. K. (1988). Conditional specifications with inequational assumptions. In S. Kaplan and J.-P. Jouannaud, editors, *Conditional Term Rewriting Systems (CTRS '88)*, volume 308 of *Lecture Notes in Computer Science*, pages 161–178. Springer-Verlag.

Mohan, C. K. and Srivas, M. K. (1989). Negation with logical variables in conditional rewriting. In N. Dershowitz, editor, *Rewriting Techniques and Applications (RTA '89)*, volume 355 of *Lecture Notes in Computer Science*, pages 292–310. Springer-Verlag.

Möller, B. (1987). Algebraic specification with higher-order operators. In L. G. L. T. Meertens, editor, *Program Specification and Transformation*, pages 367–398. North-Holland.

Mosses, P. D. (1979). SIS — Semantics Implementation System: Reference manual and user guide. Technical Report DAIMI MD-30, Computer Science Department, Aarhus University.

Mosses, P. D. (1992). *Action Semantics*. Cambridge University Press.

Mosses, P. D. (1993). The use of sorts in algebraic specifications. In M. Bidoit and C. Choppy, editors, *Recent Trends in Data Type Specification (WADT '91)*, volume 655 of *Lecture Notes in Computer Science*, pages 66–92. Springer-Verlag.

Mosses, P. D. and Watt, D. A. (1993). Pascal Action Semantics. Technical report, Aarhus University. Draft, version 0.6. URL: ftp://ftp.daimi.aau.dk/pub/action/papers/pascal/pas-0.6.ps.Z.

Nadathur, G. and Miller, D. (1988). An overview of λProlog. In R. A. Kowalsi and K. A. Bowen, editors, *Logic Programming: Fifth International Conference*, volume 1, pages 810–827. MIT Press.

Naur, P. (1965). Checking of operand types in Algol compilers. *BIT*, 5, 151–163.

Nazareth, D. (1995). *A Polymorphic Sort System for Axiomatic Specification Languages*. Ph.D. thesis, Technische Universität München. Technical Report TUM-I9515.

Nipkow, T. (1991). Higher-order critical pairs. In *Logic in Computer Science (LICS '91)*, pages 342–349. IEEE Computer Society.

Nipkow, T. and Prehofer, C. (1995). Type reconstruction for type classes. *Journal of Functional Programming*, 5, 201–224.

van Oostrom, V. (1994). *Confluence for Abstract and Higher-Order Rewriting.* Ph.D. thesis, Vrije Universiteit, Amsterdam.

van Oostrom, V. and van Raamsdonk, F. (1994). Comparing combinatory reduction systems and higher-order rewrite systems. In J. Heering, K. Meinke, B. Möller, and T. Nipkow, editors, *Higher-Order Algebra, Logic, and Term Rewriting (HOA '93)*, volume 816 of *Lecture Notes in Computer Science*, pages 276–304. Springer-Verlag.

Paakki, J. (1995). Attribute grammar paradigms — A high-level methodology in language implementation. *ACM Computing Surveys*, **27**, 196–255.

Paulson, L. (1982). A semantics-directed compiler generator. In *Principles of Programmgin Languages (POPL '82)*, pages 224–233. ACM.

Pennings, M., Swierstra, D., and Vogt, H. (1992). Using cached functions and constructors for incremental attribute evaluation. In M. Bruynooghe and M. Wirsing, editors, *Programming Language Implementation and Logic Programming (PLILP'92)*, volume 631 of *Lecture Notes in Computer Science*, pages 130–144. Springer-Verlag.

Poigné, A. (1986). On specifications, theories, and models with higher types. *Information and Control*, **68**, 1–46.

Pugh, W. and Teitelbaum, T. (1989). Incremental computation via function caching. In *Principles of Programming Languages (POPL '89)*, pages 315–328. ACM.

Ramalingam, G. and Reps, T. (1993). A categorized bibliography on incremental computation. In *Principles of Programming Languages (POPL '93)*, pages 502–510. ACM.

Rekers, J. (1992). *Parser Generation for Interactive Environments.* Ph.D. thesis, University of Amsterdam.

Reps, T. and Teitelbaum, T. (1989a). *The Synthesizer Generator: A System for Constructing Language-Based Editors.* Springer-Verlag, third edition.

Reps, T. and Teitelbaum, T. (1989b). *The Synthesizer Generator Reference Manual.* Springer-Verlag.

Reps, T., Marceau, C., and Teitelbaum, T. (1986). Remote attribute updating for language-based editors. In *Principles of Programming Languages (POPL '86)*, pages 1–13. ACM.

Riedewald, G. (1992). The LDL — Language Development Laboratory. In U. Kastens and P. Pfahler, editors, *Compiler Construction (CC '92)*, volume 641 of *Lecture Notes in Computer Science*, pages 88–94. Springer-Verlag.

Rutten, E. P. B. M. and Thiébaux, S. (1992). Semantics of Manifold: Specification in ASF+SDF and extension. Technical Report CS-R9269, Centrum voor Wiskunde en Informatica (CWI), Amsterdam.

Slonneger, K. and Kurtz, B. L. (1995). *Formal Syntax and Semantics of Programming Languages: A Laboratory Based Approach.* Addison-Wesley.

Stallman, R. (1991). *GNU Emacs Manual.* Free Software Foundation, 675 Mass Ave., Cambridge, MA, USA, Emacs version 18 edition. For Unix users.

Teitelbaum, T. and Chapman, R. (1990). Higher-order attribute grammars and editing environment. *SIGPLAN Notices*, **25**(6), 197–208. *Proceedings of the ACM SIGPLAN '90 Conference on Programming Languages Design and Implementation.*

Tennent, R. D. (1977). A denotational definition of the programming language Pascal. Technical Report TR 47, Department of Computing and Information Science, Queen's University of Kingston.

Thiel, J.-J. (1984). Stop losing sleep over incomplete data type specifications. In *Principles of Programming Languages (POPL '84)*, pages 76–82. ACM.

Tip, F. (1993). Animators for generated programming environments. In P. Fritzson, editor, *Automated and Algorithmic Debugging (AADEBUG '93)*, volume 749 of *Lecture Notes in Computer Science*, pages 241–254. Springer-Verlag.

Tip, F. (1995a). *Generation of Program Analysis Tools.* Ph.D. thesis, University of Amsterdam.

Tip, F. (1995b). Generic techniques for source-level debugging and dynamic program slicing. In P. D. Mosses, M. Nielsen, and M. I. Schwartzback, editors, *Theory and Practice of Software Development (TAPSOFT '95)*, Lecture Notes in Computer Science, pages 516–530. Springer-Verlag.

Tip, F. (1995c). A survey of program slicing techniques. *Journal of Programming Languages*, **3**, 121–189.

Tofte, M. (1990). *Compiler Generators: What They Can Do, What They Might Do, and What They Will Probably Never Do.* Springer-Verlag.

Tomita, M. (1985). *Efficient Parsing for Natural Languages.* Kluwer.

Turner, D. A. (1985). Miranda: A non-strict functional language with polymorphic types. In J.-P. Jouannaud, editor, *Functional Programming Languages and Computer Architecture (FPCA '85)*, volume 201 of *Lecture Notes in Computer Science*, pages 1–16. Springer-Verlag.

Üsküdarlı, S. (1994). Generating visual editors for formally specified languages. In A. L. Ambler and T. D. Kimura, editors, *Proceedings of the 1994 IEEE Symposium on Visual Languages (VL '94)*, pages 278–287. IEEE Computer Society.

Vigna, S. (1995). Specifying IMP(G) using ASF+SDF: A case study. In van den Brand *et al.* (1995a), pages 65–88.

Vigna, S. (1996). *Distributive Computability*. Ph.D. thesis, Università degli Studi di Milano e di Torino.

Visser, E. (1992). Syntax and static semantics of Eiffel. A case study in algebraic specification techniques. URL: ftp://ftp.cwi.nl/pub/gipe/reports/Vis92.ps.Z.

Visser, E. (1995a). *ASF+SDF to LaTeX: The User Manual*. Programming Research Group, University of Amsterdam. URL: http://adam.fwi.uva.nl/~visser/tolatex/.

Visser, E. (1995b). A family of syntax definition formalisms. In van den Brand *et al.* (1995a), pages 89–126.

Visser, E. (1995c). Polymorphic syntax definition (extended abstract). In A. Nijholt, G. Scollo, and R. Steetskamp, editors, *Algebraic Methods in Language Processing (AMiLP '95)*, volume 10 of *Twente Workshops in Language Technology*, pages 43–54. Twente University of Technology.

Vogt, H. H. (1993). *Higher Order Attribute Grammars*. Ph.D. thesis, University of Utrecht.

Vogt, H. H., Swierstra, S. D., and Kuiper, M. F. (1989). Higher order attribute grammars. *SIGPLAN Notices*, **24**(7), 131–145. *Proceedings of the ACM SIGPLAN '89 Conference on Programming Language Design and Implementation*.

Vogt, H. H., Swierstra, S. D., and Kuiper, M. F. (1991). Efficient incremental evaluation of higher order attribute grammars. In J. Maluszyński and M. Wirsing, editors, *Programming Language Implementation and Logic Programming (PLILP '91)*, volume 528 of *Lecture Notes in Computer Science*, pages 231–242. Springer-Verlag.

Voisin, F. (1986). CIGALE: A tool for interactive grammar construction and expression parsing. *Science of Computer Programming*, **7**, 61–86.

Wadler, P. and Blott, S. (1989). How to make *ad-hoc* polymorphism less *ad hoc*. In *Principles of Programming Languages (POPL '89)*, pages 60–76. ACM.

Wadsworth, C. P. (1980). Some unusual λ-calculus numeral systems. In J. P. Seldin and J. R. Hindly, editors, *To H. B. Curry: Essays on Combinatory Logic, λ-Calculus, and Formalism*, pages 215–229. Academic Press.

Walters, H. R. (1989). The static semantics of POOL. In Bergstra *et al.* (1989), pages 163–198.

Walters, H. R. (1991). *On Equal Terms — Implementing Algebraic Specifications.* Ph.D. thesis, University of Amsterdam.

Walters, H. R. and Kamperman, J. F. Th. (1996a). Epic: An equational language — Abstract machine and supporting tools. In H. Ganzinger, editor, *Rewriting Techniques and Applications (RTA '96)*, volume xxx of *Lecture Notes in Computer Science*. Springer-Verlag. To appear. Full version of the language definition: Technical Report CS-R9604, Centrum voor Wiskunde en Informatica (CWI), Amsterdam.

Walters, H. R. and Kamperman, J. F. Th. (1996b). A model for I/O in equational languages with *don't care* non-determinism. In *Recent Trends in Data Type Specification (WADT '95)*, volume xxx of *Lecture Notes in Computer Science*. Springer-Verlag. To appear. Technical Report CS-R9572, Centrum voor Wiskunde en Informatica (CWI), Amsterdam.

Walters, H. R., Kamperman, J. F. Th., and Dinesh, T. B. (1994). An extensible language for the generation of parallel Data Manipulation and Control Packages. In P. Fritszon, editor, *Compiler Construction (CC '94) — Poster Session*, pages 163–172. Linköping University. Published as Technical Report LiTH-IDA-R-94-11.

Wand, M. (1984). A semantic prototyping system. *SIGPLAN Notices*, **19**(6), 213–221. *Proceedings of the ACM SIGPLAN '84 Symposium on Compiler Construction.*

Wand, M. (1986). Finding the source of type errors. In *Principles of Programming Languages (POPL '86)*, pages 38–43. ACM.

Watt, D. A. (1979). An extended attribute grammar for Pascal. *SIGPLAN Notices*, **14**(2), 60–74.

Watt, D. A. (1991). *Programming Language Syntax and Semantics.* Prentice-Hall.

Wechler, W. (1992). *Universal Algebra for Computer Scientists.* Springer-Verlag.

Weiser, M. (1979). *Program slices: Formal, psychological, and practical investigations of an automatic program abstraction method.* Ph.D. thesis, University of Michigan, Ann Arbor.

Wiedijk, F. (1991). *Persistence in Algebraic Specifications.* Ph.D. thesis, University of Amsterdam.

Wilhelm, R. and Maurer, D. (1995). *Compiler Design.* Addison-Wesley.

Wirsing, M. (1990). Algebraic specification. In J. van Leeuwen, editor, *Handbook of Theoretical Computer Science, volume B*, pages 675–789. Elsevier Science Publishers.

Wirsing, M. (1995). Algebraic specification languages: An overview. In E. Astesiano, G. Reggio, and A. Tarlecki, editors, *Recent Trends in Data Type Specification (WADT '94)*, volume 906 of *Lecture Notes in Computer Science*, pages 81–115. Springer-Verlag.

Wolfram, D. A. (1993). *The Clausal Theory of Types*. Cambridge University Press.

Zhang, H. (1992). Herky: High performance rewriting in RRL. In D. Kapur, editor, *Automated Deduction (CADE '92)*, volume 607 of *Lecture Notes in Artificial Intelligence*, pages 698–700. Springer-Verlag.

Index